Visual Impairment in Children and Adolescents

Visual Impairment in Children and Adolescents

JAMES E. JAN, M.D., F.R.C.P.(C)
Coordinator
Neuropediatric and Blind Program
Children's Hospital Diagnostic Centre
Vancouver, British Columbia

ROGER D. FREEMAN, M.D.
Associate Professor
Department of Psychiatry
Faculty of Medicine
University of British Columbia

EILEEN P. SCOTT, B.A., E.Ed., B.S.W., R.S.W.
National Coordinator
of Children's Services
Canadian National Institute for the Blind

GRUNE & STRATTON
A Subsidiary of Harcourt Brace Jovanovich, Publishers
New York   **San Francisco**   **London**

Library of Congress Cataloging in Publication Data

Main entry under title:

Visual impairment in children and adolescents.

    Bibliography: p.
    Includes indexes.
    1. Visually handicapped children. 2. Blindness.
3. Blind—Education. 4. Blindness—Prevention.
I. Jan, James E. II. Freeman, Roger D.
III. Scott, Eileen P. [DNLM: 1. Vision disorders
—In infancy and childhood. 2. Vision disorders—
In adolescence. WW276 J33v]
HV1593.V55   362.4'1   77-2154

Grune & Stratton, Inc.
111 Fifth Avenue
New York, New York 10003

Distributed in the United Kingdom by
Academic Press, Inc. (London) Ltd.
24/28 Oval Road, London NW1

Library of Congress Catalog Number 77-2154
International Standard Book Number 0-8089-1010-8

Printed in the United States of America

32.00

CONTENTS

FOREWORD

The problem of managing visually impaired children and adolescents has been with us since time immemorial. It is surprising, therefore, that there are no comprehensive texts on the subject. During the last 20 years, a number of changes have made the problem of greater interest to society. Among them are the therapeutic, technological, and preventive measures that have eradicated many of the acute illnesses facing us a generation ago as well as changes in moral values and means of rapid dissemination of information which have altered attitudes towards the visually impaired and blind. The affluence of Western societies has enabled us to concentrate on chronic problems, which previously were given lower priority or neglected altogether. The survival of many multihandicapped children who would otherwise have died has increased the prevalence of those who are visually impaired. The increase in the life expectancy of diabetics is creating a relatively new problem of the young visually impaired and blind.

Traditionally, the diagnostic skills of ophthalmology, neurology, and pediatrics have not lacked the ability to establish a diagnosis of visual impairment or blindness, but the facts that many visually impaired children have multiple handicaps and that one handicap may imitate others have only recently been well recognized. The management of these children has typically been poor. The many practitioners of medicine and social sciences have dealt with patients and parents in a haphazard and disjointed manner, often presenting indigestible, contradictory sources of information which have confused, and by their very tone clouded, attitudes of the parents towards these children. It is now recognized that management requires the cooperative approach of a number of disciplines, including ophthalmology, pediatrics, child psychiatry, neurology, family practice, psychology, social sciences, and others. The benefit accruing to patients from such a team approach is measurable only over the years, not days or weeks.

It is timely for a book to appear that embodies the experiences, expertise, and research of one successful multidisciplinary team. This comprehensive book will provide physicians, other professionals, and students with additional knowledge in the area. It reminds all those involved that they have more to offer the blind child and his family than just a diagnosis or treatment of the disease that caused the visual impairment; it stresses that the blind child is not only an individual with impaired vision, but one who has special needs which make him different from the sighted in many other aspects as well. It is made clear that mental retardation, autism, and brain damage are still frequently diagnosed in blind children who are really quite normal apart from their visual disability—and this mistake can lead to tragic consequences in their management.

Anyone reading the text will become convinced of the value of such a team of various professionals—each of whom contributes a particular expertise to the complicated problems facing these children and their families. Better understanding will undoubtedly lead to an improvement in the quality of life for those who are visually impaired or blind.

Stephen M. Drance, MD

Professor and Head
Department of Ophthalmology
University of British Columbia
Vancouver, Canada

ACKNOWLEDGMENTS

This book could not have been written without the generous financial help of the Hospital for Sick Children Foundation, Toronto, and the continuing support and encouragement of its vice-president, Mr. F. H. Hunnisett.

The Canadian National Institute for the Blind (British Columbia-Yukon Division) encouraged the participation of children and families in our studies and provided us with essential staff time and facilities.

Much credit goes also to Dr. G. C. Robinson, Professor of Paediatrics, University of British Columbia, who was instumental in developing the Children's Hospital Diagnostic Centre, one component of which is the team approach to the visually impaired child.

We also wish to thank Dr. R. H. Lennox, Senior Consultant, Child and Adult Health, Health Programs Branch, Canada; Dr. David H. Warren, University of California, Riverside; Dr. Sydney Israels, Professor and Head, Department of Paediatrics, University of British Columbia; Mr. George Whetstone, Superintendent, W. Ross Macdonald School, Brantford, Ontario; Zofja S. Jastrzembska, formerly with the American Foundation for the Blind; the Department of Biomedical Communications, University of British Columbia—especially Peter Thomas, for the photographs; Lily Ekelund; and Pauline Brown and Jo-Anne MacAdam, who typed the manuscript. We are especially grateful to Jo-Anne MacAdam, whose extensive experience was an invaluable help in the organization of the manuscript.

INTRODUCTION

Although there is a large amount of potentially available information about visual impairment in children, the busy practitioner confronted with an immediate problem will not find ready access to it. Furthermore, too many families have received little or no help beyond the diagnosis of the ocular disorder and when they did, it was frequently disastrously wrong. As part of the broad change in attitudes towards the delivery of health care, parents of the handicapped expect better treatment than this.

Professionals may not realize the vitally important effect their contact with parents will have on the life of the visually impaired child and his entire family, who are especially vulnerable around the time of diagnosis. However, physicians and other professionals cannot be expected to be knowledgeable about all handicaps and their implications.

Recognizing this dilemma, we have compiled in this book the material we consider to be most useful for those working with visually impaired children and their families: pediatricians, ophthalmologists, child psychiatrists, neurologists, family physicians, social workers, teachers, nurses, and many others.

We believe that the child with a visual impairment is not just an individual who does not see normally, but one who has special needs which affect other aspects of his functioning in complex ways. Unless this is understood by both professionals and parents, his entire development may be jeopardized.

While there is a tendency for professionals to focus only upon pathology, greater emphasis should be placed on utilizing intact areas of the child's functioning and taking a strong positive approach.

In the past some parents and children have "muddled through" remarkably well on their own without the benefit of adequate support from professionals; some have not. This is not good enough. Nor is an informed approach by any *one* discipline sufficient as the combined skills of many are usually necessary.

Parents usually look to professionals for practical guidance on how to raise their visually-impaired child. Since this is obviously a highly specialized area with which most professionals are unfamiliar, we have devoted a companion volume to it, namely,

Scott, E, P., Jan, J. E., and Freeman, R. D. *Can't Your Child See? A Guide for Parents and Professionals.* Baltimore: University Park Press, 1977.

The interested reader will find in the *Guide* sections which could not be included here, and which we feel will be suitable for the average parent.

In writing the present volume, we have selected material from a highly complex and developing field and from our own studies and experience. We would be interested in hearing the views of readers and any suggestions for inclusion in future editions.

CONTRIBUTORS

E. J. Chorniak, Principal, The W. Ross Macdonald School, Brantford, Ontario.

D. M. Corrigan, Principal, Jericho Hill School for the Blind; Consultant for the Visually Impaired for the Province of British Columbia, Vancouver, British Columbia.

R. D. Freeman, M.D., Associate Professor, Director of Services for Handicapped Children, Division of Child Psychiatry, University of British Columbia, Vancouver, British Columbia.

J. E. Jan, M.D., F.R.C.P.(C), Clinical Associate Professor, Division of Pediatric Neurology, Department of Paediatrics, University of British Columbia; Coordinator of Neuropediatric and Blind Program, Children's Hospital Diagnostic Centre, Vancouver, British Columbia.

S. F. Malkin, M.S.W., Social Worker, Western Institute for the Deaf, Vancouver, British Columbia.

J. M. McInnes, Assistant Superintendent—Instruction, The W. Ross Macdonald School, Brantford, Ontario.

L. O'Connor, M.A., Clinical Psychologist for the Blind, Children's Hospital Diagnostic Centre, Vancouver, British Columbia.

W. G. Pearce, M.D., F.R.C.S., F.R.C.S.(E), F.R.C.S.(C), Associate Professor, Department of Ophthalmology, University of Alberta, Edmonton, Alberta.

G. C. Robinson, M.D. F.R.C.P.(C), Professor, Department of Paediatrics, University of British Columbia, Vancouver, British Columbia.

E. P. Scott, National Coordinator of Children's Services, Canadian National Institute for the Blind; Clinical Assistant Professor, Department of Ophthalmology, University of British Columbia, Vancouver, British Columbia.

J. A. Treffry, Coordinator of Deaf-Blind Program, The W. Ross Macdonald School, Brantford, Ontario.

M. E. Wilmot, B.S.R., Physiotherapist for the Blind, formerly with the Children's Hospital Diagnostic Centre, Vancouver, British Columbia.

1

Historical Aspects

THE STAGES OF LIABILITY, PROTECTION, AND INTEGRATION

Those who work with blind people can acquire a deeper understanding of the different aspects of visual impairment when these are viewed historically.

Early societies tended to treat the blind as a liability, as they did others with major handicaps. In the days when the chief concerns were food, clothing, and shelter, any member of the group who could not make his full contribution was eliminated. The old, the sick, and the handicapped were often disposed of in various ways. Although these negative practices were common in prehistoric societies, they were not always universal. One can conclude this from the studies of present primitive tribes who may treat their handicapped, sick, or old people well.

Considerable information is available about the attitudes of the ancient Greeks and Romans toward blindness. Their laws generally encouraged the killing of blind infants since they were a burden to the state. On the other hand, there were many well-respected, renowned sightless poets, philosophers, scholars, politicians, and prophets, but most acquired their visual impairment. In general, the socioeconomic position of the blind was better in Greece than in Rome. At one time there were even special assistance programs for blind Athenians.[1]

The early Christians provided food and shelter to the handicapped, but this approach did not last long. During the Middle Ages blind people lived in great misery, relying mainly on begging, although isolated attempts were made to improve their meagre existence (Fig. 1-1). Monasteries offered shelter and occasionally "hospitals" were built for the needy.[1]

Fig 1-1. Parable of the Blind. Painted by Pieter Breughel (1528–1569). The painting pessimistically depicts the miserable condition of the blind. The leader of the group falls into a ditch and the others helplessly follow him. Blind people are far more capable than this.

During the Middle Ages

Blindness was viewed as the greatest misfortune that could befall a person—even worse than death. This helps one understand why blinding of people was such a frequently practiced form of extreme punishment. Defeated armies, criminals, heretics, and political foes were blinded by many celebrated kings.[2] Later, however, the early Christian practice of protecting the handicapped was resumed and, although blind children were trained to be beggars, singers, or clowns, they were protected and received charity.

The blind received variable treatment through the centuries in non-Western societies. Emperor Hadrian of Rome praised the welfare approach of the Egyptians since a large number of their sightless were gainfully employed and independent.[3] Egyptian priests developed a welfare program for the disabled and made charity a religious duty.[1] Blind persons in Japan, who were protected and honored, frequently achieved fame in the fields of music, literature, politics, and religion. This approach probably started in 858 AD when Prince Hitoyasu, the son of the Emperor, lost his sight. Blind men became his attendants and, in return, he divided part of his income among them. In 886, in memory of the dead prince, blind officers were appointed to look after the welfare of the visually impaired throughout the country, and a tax was even levied for their benefit. In this protected environment, the blind devoted their time to the arts, music, massage, acupuncture, and religion, distinguishing themselves in many ways. In 1870, however, the Japanese government adopted European laws and abolished pensions and the protected way of life for the blind. Competition became stronger as sighted people began invading occupations that previously were monopolized by the visually impaired. The conditions of the blind gradually worsened and became much like those in Europe.[4]

Integration of the blind is the third phase with which most industrialized nations are struggling. Although commencing in the Middle Ages, when an increasing number of sightless individuals proved their capabilities by outstanding achievements, the era of integration really started with the organized education for the blind.

All three stages—liability, protection, and integration—still exist in many societies. Even now the newly blinded among the Maori are punished by their fellow tribesmen, who steal all their belongings.[5] In several tribes in West Africa they are rejected, scorned, and excluded from the possibility of ever becoming a chief.[5] In China, until recent times, a congenitally blind child was regarded as "human waste," bad luck, and a disgrace to his family. Their misery was accepted by the sighted since they were "born to suffer."[6] The laws of many countries now protect the blind with pensions, tax exemptions, and other legislation, fostering their increasing integration into sighted society.

HISTORY OF EDUCATION

For centuries, blind children were educated with the sighted while rich parents were able to afford private tutors. As a historical curiosity, in 970 AD, the University of Al-Ashar in Egypt established the first educational program for the blind, which was a 12-year course requiring the memorization of all material.[3] But the establishment of the first school for blind students by Haüy in 1785 was the beginning of organized education for the visually impaired. Contrary to anecdotes, the idea of establishing schools for the blind did not originate with Valentin Haüy (1745-1822); this topic was "in the air," as shown by various essays and letters.[1] Furthermore, there is evidence that Johann Wilhelm Klein had no knowledge of Haüy's activities when he established his own school for the blind in 1804 in Vienna. Haüy, who is considered to be the Apostle of the Blind, lived from the age of Louis XV through the French Revolution, the First Empire, and into the Bourbon Restoration. With great difficulty—sometimes risking his own life—he influenced each succeeding regime to help his school.

Other schools were subsequently established in Liverpool (1791), Berlin (1806), Milan (1807), Amsterdam (1808), and other European cities. Almost simultaneously in the United States in 1829 and 1831, two residential schools were organized in Massachusetts and New York, and more followed in other states. In Canada, the Nazareth Institute for the Blind in Montreal was established in 1861, the Halifax School in 1867, and the Ontario School for the Blind at Brantford in 1872. The first school in Australia opened in 1863 in Melbourne. The first in China was started in Peking in 1876, in Japan in 1878, and in India in 1887 at Amritsar, Punjab. The schools mushroomed all over the world, reaching a peak during the retrolental fibroplasia era in the 1950s. Missionaries, especially during the last century, built many fine schools for the blind in developing countries while preaching the philosophy of protection.

Although there were many early gifted educators for the blind, the names of three must be singled out: Valentin Haüy, Johann Wilhelm Klein, and Samuel Gridley Howe. Howe (1801–1876) was the first director of the New England Asylum for the Blind, which was later renamed the Perkins Institution. All three men published numerous articles and books on blindness and exerted far-reaching influence in the education of visually impaired children. Great credit goes to a blind person, Louis Braille (1809–1852), who invented Braille writing in 1824 at the age of 15 while he was a student in Haüy's school. He modified the system of night writing, which had been developed a few years before by an artillery captain, Charles Barbier.

The teaching offered in schools for the blind was hampered by the fact that many different institutions began sponsoring their own embossed type of alphabet and, therefore, books for the blind were limited in number and costly in price. The idea of embossed letters was not new, since centuries ago blind persons were taught by the use of letters cut into wooden blocks. Even the dot system was mentioned during the seventeenth century in Italy as a communication system for the blind.[1]

Although Braille writing was vastly superior to the embossed alphabet, the schools at first resisted the change, arguing that its use would further isolate the blind from the sighted world. "First, the dot system had to be proven superior to the embossed letter system and, second, the Braille system had to be accepted over other dot systems"[1] (p. 176). Thus, a long struggle—referred to as the "battle of the dots"—developed between various groups. Robert Irwin describes this period in the United States vividly in his book, As I Saw It.[7] Braille writing was fully accepted by the end of the nineteenth and the beginning of the twentieth centuries. In 1932, an agreement was finally reached regarding a standardized English Braille code, now called Standard English Grade Two (also known as English Braille).

DEVELOPMENT OF PUBLIC SCHOOL EDUCATION

Both Klein and Howe recommended that blind students should be educated in regular schools. However, suggestions to place blind children with sighted students were strongly resisted. It was not until the end of the last century that the doors of public schools first opened to the visually impaired in Glasgow and later in London.[1] In North America, the first class for blind students in a public school started in 1900 in Chicago. Today, visually impaired children commonly receive their education together with the sighted.

DEVELOPMENT OF PRESCHOOL EDUCATION

Even during the last century, educators of the blind realized that the preschool years are too important in the life of the congenitally blind child to be ignored. Too often, beginners in residential schools were immature and unprepared for their formal education. There were no preschool services offered, with the exception of a few short pamphlets.

In 1918, the Royal National Institute for the Blind in England opened its first residential nursery school, which was known as the Sunshine Home for Blind Babies. The emphasis was on training of the child in everyday living skills by "experts" instead of parents. The blind infant could be admitted at a few months of age; at 5 or 6 years, he was transferred to a residential school for the blind to obtain his formal education. At one stage, the separation of the child from his family was carried to such extremes that the parents were considered to be the greatest hindrance to the child's development. These residential nursery schools also spread to North America during the early years of this century but gradually disappeared as educators and psychologists began realizing the importance of the family unit in the development of the young visually impaired child. Today, in both England and North America, few blind children are admitted to residential nursery schools, and the child now may stay at home while the family receives appropriate counseling. The preschool education of the blind child is of crucial importance and will be discussed throughout this book.

DEVELOPMENT OF SERVICES

As special schools grew in number, they provided more and more blind children with education and limited vocational training. But once these students graduated, they were often on their own and could only

turn to charitable organizations for help. In this respect, the blind were
not alone. Even today, although they have received extensive training
in their childhood, young adults with deafness, mental retardation, or
cerebral palsy are all too often dropped into society without supporting
services. All European countries have a long history of philanthropic
work (sometimes extending back to medieval times) but rehabilitative
services to blind adults were nonexistent. There were charitable organizations of which the best known is the Congregation of the Three Hundred,
founded in 1254 in France to care for the blind crusaders. Homes of
refuge for the blind had been established and pension systems were
created in several countries. It was not until the First World War, when
young newly blinded adults began to return home, that specialized service
agencies began to appear, although isolated agencies did exist before.
In his book, Sir Arthur Pearson tells how such an agency was organized
at St. Dunstan's, England.[8] Similar organizations were quickly established
in Canada, Australia, New Zealand, and South Africa. In the United
States, rehabilitation services for the blind mushroomed after World
War II. Most countries are now offering services to the blind of all
ages. In the United States alone, at recent count there were over 800
organizations spending over $470 million annually to provide education,
training, and services to the blind and their families.[5] A recent book
summarizes the history of services in that country.[9]

DEVELOPMENT OF RESEARCH

During the early part of the nineteenth century, much effort was
channeled into modification of attitudes toward the blind. This was done
primarily by educators who organized demonstrations for the sighted
community on a regular basis. Certain schools still maintain this activity.
Similarly, much work was done on the preparation and design of raised
letters. During the second half of the nineteenth century, many statistical
papers appeared and interesting case reports were presented, mostly
in anecdotal form. Many articles were also written on the prevention
of blindness.

During the last century, science mingled strangely with superstitious
beliefs. W. H. Levy's book *Blindness and the Blind*, which was published
over 100 years ago in 1872, reflects this mixture. For example, he advises
not to read in trains: "Reading while travelling by rail should be studiously
avoided, for the practice produces blindness. The cause of this appears
to be the extra strain on the sight produced by the motion of the vehicle."[2]
(p. 345) Dark colors were also thought to be harmful to the eyes while
congenital blindness was often "ascribed to the mother having seen
a blind person before the birth of a child." Snow and cold were "most

injurious to the eyes," which was purported to explain why there was a greater percentage of blind people in British North American (Canada) than in the adjacent United States. There were other false beliefs, such as smoking causing optic atrophy, while some "attributed preservation of sight to drinking nothing but water."

The literature was repetitious and emotional during the first half of the twentieth century. The church played a strong role in the welfare of the blind throughout the centuries, and it is not surprising that it has left its mark on the literature. Today, some blind people resent such emotional overtones, which not infrequently cover up attitudes that can be interpreted as charitable.

Valuable scientific research began only 20 to 30 years ago, precipitated by the epidemic appearance of retrolental fibroplasia and, also, by the arrival of newly blinded young men from the Second World War. Society's recent interest in technology is reflected in the literature on the blind, as a large proportion of the research is devoted to various visual and mobility aids.

REFERENCES

1. Lowenfeld B: The Changing Status of the Blind. From Separation to Integration. Springfield, Ill. Charles C Thomas, 1975
2. Levy WH: Blindness and the Blind. London, Chapman & Hall, 1872
3. Kirtley DD: The Psychology of Blindness. Chicago, Nelson-Hall, 1975
4. Yoshimoto T: "Your 'progress' is a subtle form of murder . . . ," in Diamond IS (ed): Blindness 1970. Washington, DC, American Association of Workers for the Blind, Inc, 1970, pp 146-149
5. Brown NA: A cross-cultural review of the causes and management of blindness, 1975 (unpublished data)
6. Ching L: Blind welfare in Hong Kong. Speech delivered to the Hong Kong Round Table No 7, September 30, 1975
7. Irwin RB: As I Saw It. New York, American Foundation for the Blind, 1955
8. Pearson Sir A: Victory Over Blindness. London, Hodder & Stoughton, 1919
9. Koestler FA: The Unseen Minority. A Social History of Blindness in the United States. New York, David McKay, 1976

2
Anatomical and Physiological Aspects of Vision

It is beyond the scope of this book to provide an extensive account of the anatomy and physiology of the visual system; therefore, only a short description is given.

The eyeball is the peripheral organ of sight and is optically comparable to a photographic camera, for it has a lens system, a variable aperture system, and a retina, which corresponds to the film. This is, of course, a vast oversimplification. The anatomy of the eye is shown in Figure 2-1. The light travels through the convex lens system and is projected on the retina in such a way that the image is inverted and reversed with respect to the object. The reason the mind perceives objects in the upright position is that the brain has trained itself to consider inverted images on the retina as being in the upright position.

The retina is the light-sensitive portion of the eye. It contains two types of light receptors that change light into nerve impulses—the cones and the rods. The cone receptors are concentrated in an oval area of the posterior part of the retina, the macula, although they are also present in smaller numbers throughout the retina. The rods, on the other hand, are not present in the macula but are scattered throughout the periphery.

The macular area has the highest visual acuity in well-illuminated situations, whereas the peripheral or extramacular retina is the most efficient in reduced illumination. Only the cone receptors can perceive colors. Thus, vision is divided into two types, central (macular) and peripheral. Central vision is needed for detecting fine detail, whereas peripheral vision is more important for traveling. There are visually impaired children whose defect is limited to one or the other type of vision.

9

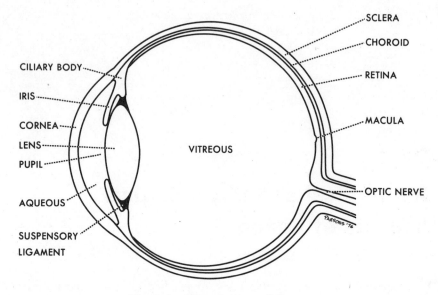

CILIARY BODY

IRIS

CORNEA

LENS

PUPIL

AQUEOUS

SUSPENSORY
LIGAMENT

VITREOUS

SCLERA

CHOROID

RETINA

MACULA

OPTIC NERVE

PARSONS '76

Fig. 2-1.   The anatomy of the eye.

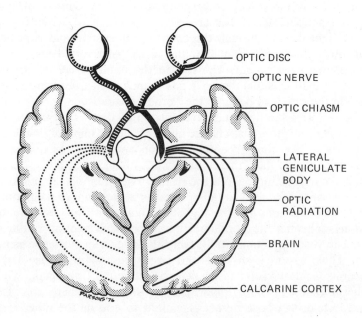

OPTIC DISC

OPTIC NERVE

OPTIC CHIASM

LATERAL
GENICULATE
BODY

OPTIC
RADIATION

BRAIN

CALCARINE CORTEX

PARSONS '76

Fig. 2-2.   The visual pathways.

The impulses leave the retina through the optic nerve. At the optic chiasm, all fibres from the nasal half of each retina cross to the opposite optic tract. The fibres of the optic tract synapse in the lateral geniculate body with the geniculocalcarine fibres. These then pass through the optic radiation, which spreads through the parietal and occipital lobes ending in the visual cortex, in and adjacent to the calcarine fissure of the occipital lobes (Fig. 2-2). Central vision—the macula—has a proportionately larger area on the corresponding visual cortex than does peripheral vision.

ACCOMMODATION

Accommodation is a process by which the image of objects is clearly focused on the retina. This is done by changing the curvature of the lens in the eye. The power of accommodation changes with age. It is strongest in early childhood and often absent by the age of 65. Because of this process, distance visual acuity is not exactly the same as near visual acuity. Children with distance visual acuity of 20/200 or even less may be able to read fine print because of their strong accommodation power, provided that this system is intact anatomically and physiologically. It is important to remember, however, that as these children grow older their near visual acuity gradually deteriorates because of the lesser effectiveness of accommodation. Children, parents, and teachers often interpret this incorrectly as "failing vision," even though it is an expected physiological phenomenon. A child with partial vision who is able to read fine print at 6 or 7 may not be able to do so in his teens without a low-vision aid.

When the lens is removed or needled and aspirated, accommodation is totally destroyed. This is an important point to consider in the treatment of congenital cataracts.

VISUAL ACUITY AND ITS MATURATION

Visual acuity is a measure of the smallest retinal formed image that can be distinguished by the human eye. It is influenced by the judgment and experience of the observer, the region of the retina stimulated, the intensity and distribution of the illumination, the spectral nature of the light, the time of exposure, the effect of the movements of the object, and whether the test is performed on each eye singly or both eyes together.[1]

Studies indicate that the visual acuity of the newborn is not the same as that of the adult.[2] Histologically, the fovea is poorly developed until the age of 6 months, although a newborn can fixate. In contrast, the occipital visual cortex is well myelinated at birth. Research indicates that adult visual acuity is generally reached by 3 years of age, but the rate often varies from child to child.[2] Others feel that the sight of infants is better than generally realized and, in fact, adult visual acuity is already seen in two-year-olds.[3] Thus, visually impaired children who in infancy appeared to have only light perception often "develop" more vision with increasing age. Parents often misinterpret this as a change in the child's ocular status when in fact it is due to better visual acuity and improved visual efficiency.

Tests for Distance Visual Acuity

In 1862, Snellen published a chart for measuring visual acuity by producing carefully graduated letters which could be read from a certain distance. This is still the most widely used test today. Snellen used the following formula:

$$V = \frac{d}{D}$$

V = visual acuity

d = distance at which test types are read

D = distance at which letters subtend an overall visual angle of 5 minutes

Testing is usually done from 20 feet (d) and if the child can see the letters at the 20 line (D), then his distance visual acuity (V) is 20/20, which is considered to be normal. If the child sees only the largest numbers, designated as 200 (D), then his distance visual acuity is 20/200. For purposes of clearer understanding, an individual who has 20/100 vision sees the same detail from 20 feet as a normal person can from a distance of 100 feet. If one tests the child's vision from a distance of 10 rather than 20 feet (d) and he can see the letters at the 40 line (D), then his distance visual acuity is 20/80 (10/40 × 2/2 = 20/80). Most charts do not include letters to test vision between 20/200 and 20/100. Therefore, some children whose vision is in this area but not as bad as 20/200 may still be classified as blind. Fonda recommends that, with these children, vision should be tested as close as 3 to 5 feet.[4] If he reads the 40 line (D) from 5 feet (d) his visual acuity is 5/40 or 20/160 (5/40 × 4/4 = 20/160). Of course, he would have been classified as blind if he had been tested from 20 feet.

Table 2-1 gives the conversion figures from feet to meters, as in certain countries the metric system is used for measuring the distance

Table 2-1
Snellen Conversion Table Used for Distance Visual Acuity

English	Metric	Decimal
20/20	6/6	1.0
20/30	6/9	0.6
20/40	6/12	0.5
20/50	6/15	0.4
20/64	6/20	0.3
20/100	6/30	0.2
20/200	6/60	0.1

visual acuity. It also includes the decimal notation, which is a commonly used scale.

Accurate early assessment of the distance visual acuity is difficult and usually cannot be carried out until 3 to 3½ years of age or even later if the visually impaired child is multihandicapped because testing requires comprehension and cooperation. Various charts have been developed to test young children, illiterate adults, or mentally retarded individuals. There are the Koehler picture cards, E-test, Beale Collins picture, Clement Clarke picture, Sjögren's hand and Stycar, among others. The interested reader can look up the details.[4] The reliability and general use of the various visual charts have been studied, and the Stycar appeared to be one of the best tests for young or multihandicapped children.[5] Visual acuity tests used for children under 3 to 3½ years of age are also based on responses elicited by an object that can just be perceived; therefore, they measure only the minimally visible. Sheridan used small white balls mounted or rolled on a black background;[3] Catford and Oliver designed a hand-held, electrically operated instrument, which operated on the phenomenon of optokinetic fixation nystagmus;[2] while some were using other methods. Most of these tests are time-consuming and not practical for the busy practitioner. Although accurate distance visual acuity testing in this age group may be important for research purposes, one could obtain a satisfactory impression of the child's visual impairment after a short "play period" and with the help of a history from the parents. This will be described in detail in chapter 6. As mentioned earlier, neurophysiologically, the visual acuity improves from birth until about 2 to 3 years of age, with variation from child to child.[2,3] Furthermore, because of cerebral maturation and increasing intelligence, a visually impaired child is able to use his remaining sight more effectively with age. For example, a 6-year-old child's visual efficiency is better than that of a 3-year-old. This is why many infants who appear to have only light perception may have more vision later. Thus, predictions of future visual acuity made when children are under 2 to 3 years of age may be incorrect if physicians forget about the process of visual maturation and visual efficiency.

Testing of Near Visual Acuity

Three major systems are used for determining the near vision of a visually limited child: Snellen, Jaeger, and Point. The Snellen employs the metric system, and it is the only test that indicates visual acuity, whereas the Jaeger and Point are type sizes used by printers. The Jaeger is an unscientific but popular system, which consists of 20 different sizes in increasing graduation. In the Point system, one point equals 1/72 of an inch. Many ophthalmologists indicate the child's near visual acuity with the above notations but do not interpret in their reports what it means from the practical point of view, forgetting that the family physicians, pediatricians, psychologists, or teachers do not understand these scales.

Table 2-2 compares the three systems in practical terms.[4]

VISUAL SCREENING

There is general agreement that the diagnosis and treatment of ocular defects in early life is of utmost importance. Since these are often not discovered by parents, mass visual screening of preschool children has been organized in many countries. Fifteen percent of unselected preschool children had previously undetected visual problems in one study.[6] Furthermore, most children with cerebral palsy, seizures, mental retardation, poor coordination, or deafness have some type of ocular abnormality and, therefore, should be routinely referred to an ophthalmologist. Mass

Table 2-2
Comparative Near Vision Notations

Jaeger Type Sizes	Snellen Meters	Point Type Sizes	Example of Print Material
1	0.5	4	Small Bible type
2	0.6	5	Want ads (newspaper)
3	0.7	6	Telephone directory
4	0.8	8	Newspaper text
6	1.0	9	Magazines
9	1.5	12	Typewriter type (pica)
13	2.0	18	Children's books (5-8 yr)

Table used with permission from Fonda, Gerald: Management of the Patient with Subnormal Vision, ed 2. St. Louis, C.V. Mosby Co., 1970, p 126.

visual screening does not need to be done by ophthalmologists, but these programs are expensive, nevertheless. The Vernon report in Britain recommends that all children should be screened for visual impairment at health clinics as part of a generalized developmental assessment, and those who are identified as possibly having a visual abnormality should be referred to an ophthalmologist.[7] Congenitally blind children are rarely discovered by routine screening since in most the diagnosis is already made in infancy.

CONCLUSIONS

1. Distance visual acuity is not the same as near visual acuity in children.
2. Neurophysiologically, visual acuity improves from birth until about 2 to 3 years of age but, in addition, children are able to use their remaining vision more as they grow older, due to their improved visual efficiency.
3. Predictions of future visual acuity for children under 2 to 3 years of age may be incorrect if physicians forget about the process of visual maturation and visual efficiency.
4. The Stycar appears to be one of the best tests for estimating visual acuity in young children.
5. Congenitally blind children are rarely discovered by routine screening since in most the diagnosis is already made in infancy.

REFERENCES

1. Duke-Elder SA: Systems of Ophthalmology. St. Louis, CV Mosby Co, 1968, vol 4
2. Catford GV, Oliver A: Development of visual acuity. Arch Dis Child 48:47–50, 1973
3. Sheridan MD: Vision screening procedures for very young or handicapped children, in Gardiner P, MacKeith R, Smith V (eds): Aspects of Developmental and Paediatric Ophthalmology. Clinics in Developmental Medicine No 32. London, Heinemann, 1969, pp 39–47
4. Fonda G: Management of the Patient with Subnormal Vision, ed 2. St. Louis, CV Mosby Co, 1970
5. Keith CG, Diamond Z, Stansfield A: Visual acuity testing in young children. Br J Ophthalmol 56:827–832, 1972
6. Kohler L, Stigmar G: Visual screening of four-year-old children. Acta Paediatr Scand 62:17–27, 1973
7. Vernon MD (chairman): The Education of the Visually Handicapped. Report of the Committee of Enquiry appointed by the Secretary of State for Education and Science in October 1968. London, Her Majesty's Stationery Office, 1972

3
Definitions and Classifications of Visual Impairment

DEFINITIONS OF VISUAL IMPAIRMENT

The visually impaired are a highly heterogeneous group whose one and perhaps only common characteristic is some degree of visual loss (Figs. 3–1 to 3–6). Some are totally blind while others are able to distinguish between light and dark or even see a couple of feet away. Individuals with tunnel vision have good sight for distance but are handicapped by very narrow visual fields. Others have such a high degree of photophobia that, even with minor visual impairment, they are restricted in certain activities. These persons all function differently in their environment. It is not surprising, therefore, that it is hard to define who is and who is not handicapped by his visual impairment. Absolute blindness, when there is not even light perception, is the only condition that is easy to define and about which there is no disagreement. A comprehensive survey of the blind conducted by the World Health Organization in 1966 lists 65 different definitions of visual impairment throughout the world.[1] There is no universally accepted definition of blindness and because of this, one cannot satisfactorily compare epidemiological studies of the visually impaired from one country to another.

There are countries that rely on functional descriptions in defining blindness and mention the individual's inability to perform certain tasks in daily living, such as harvesting, feeding livestock, tilling the soil, and so on. For example, a person may be called blind when he is "unable to perform any work for which eyesight is essential."[2] Other countries use ophthalmic measurements pertaining to visual acuity or field of vision. The latter originated out of concern for the welfare of visually impaired

17

Fig. 3-1.   Vancouver. (Courtesy of Dr. B. Huntsman.)

adults during the 1930s, when unemployment was high in the United
States. At the request of the Department of Public Welfare of the State
of Illinois, a committee of the Section of Ophthalmology of the American
Medical Association was appointed to develop a scientific definition
of blindness suitable for development of statutes. Several definitions
of blindness were thus created in 1934.[3] The following year one of
the definitions—that of "economic blindness"—was modified and was
accepted as an administrative aid in blind programs. Subsequently, its
use spread and most industrialized nations now use the following
description:

>   Blindness is defined as visual acuity, in the better eye with correction,
>   of not more than 20/200 or a defect in the visual field so that
>   the widest diameter of vision subtends an angle no greater than
>   20°.

These measurements are discussed in detail in physiological terms in
chapter 2. This legal definition was not based on conclusions drawn
from a carefully designed set of experiments but represented the best
estimates of a group of professionals. It had advantages and disadvantages
but has been subjected to increasing criticism in recent years.

The legal definition of blindness was not created for children but
for adults in view of determining eligibility for welfare. It has many

Fig. 3-2. The city as seen by a child with impaired central vision. Note that the details in the periphery are indistinct. (Courtesy of Dr. B. Huntsman.)

disadvantages. An accurate diagnosis of distance visual acuity can rarely be established until about 3 or 4 years of age and, when the child is multihandicapped, only years later or perhaps never. Many "legally blind" persons do not consider themselves blind and resent this term because they are able to function in sighted society.) Furthermore, the word *blindness* represents a set of attitudes toward the visually impaired and also toward the sighted. Therefore, it is not surprising that children, especially those with useful vision, often strongly oppose this label. Some educators in the past accepted the legal definition of blindness as a criterion for choosing the type of education for visually impaired students. Those with a distance visual acuity of 20/200 or below were sent to residential schools and taught Braille, while those with distance visual acuity up to 20/70 were taught print, often in "sight-saving classes." This is no longer the case. Now there is much more emphasis on how the child uses his remaining vision, i.e., his visual efficiency. In fact, the selection of a proper educational facility for a child depends not only on his visual efficiency but on other factors, such as the presence of additional handicaps, the location of his home, economic restraints, the presence or absence of special educational facilities in his community, etc. In the past most agencies used the legal definition of blindness as the sole criterion to determine eligibility for receiving service. This

Fig. 3-3.   The same landscape through tunnel vision. The viewing area of these children enlarges with distance. (Courtesy of Dr. B. Huntsman.)

was unwise and unfair, since children with slightly better sight also need special help from professionals. Even in resea h, one cannot lump children together whose distance visual acuity in the better eye with correction is 20/200 or below, because this group is also very heterogeneous. It includes those with total blindness (both congenital and acquired); those with light perception; as well as those with some useful vision. All these children function differently.

Is the legal definition of blindness useful at all for children? Yes. It does give us a measuring device that is helpful in describing a single aspect of functioning, but we must always look at the total visually impaired child.

The grouping of children with various degrees of visual impairment who are not totally blind is difficult and is based on distance visual acuity measurements or on function. A child is said to have *light perception* when he can only differentiate light from darkness. The distance visual acuity of a *visually impaired* child who is legally blind ranges from light perception up to 20/200 in the better eye with best correction and/or a defect in the visual field so that the widest diameter of vision subtends an angle no greater than 20°. The distance visual acuity of a visually impaired child who is not legally blind is above this level

Fig. 3-4.   Patchy vision. (Courtesy of Dr. B. Huntsman.)

but still below normal. These definitions are based on physiological measurements rather than on function and, therefore, they represent more of an ophthalmological or medical classification.

Educators tend to use functional definitions, such as partial or residual vision. The child's vision is considered to be *partial* when it interferes with efficient learning but still enables him to use print as his chief medium of learning. *Residual vision* is defined as insufficient vision to read print of any size but more vision than light perception.[4]

Attempts have been made to describe partial vision according to distance visual acuity, and thus an artificial range of 20/70 to 20/200 was created. This was an incorrect concept, because one cannot define the functional ability of a child with a simple physiological measurement. Many youngsters are considered to have partial sight because they read print, even though their distance visual acuity is below 20/200.

One can conclude that definitions based on function are superior to those based on physiological measurements, as they are more flexible and less artificial. There are other terms which are often used interchangeably in the literature, such as guiding, residual, limited, or useful vision. They should always be well defined when used, otherwise vagueness or confusion may result.

The various definitions of visual loss are not well understood by the public or even by most health professionals, who often understand blindness not in its legal sense but as total lack of vision. Sometimes

Fig. 3-5. The traffic as observed by a child with high myopia. (Courtesy of Dr. B. Huntsman.)

those who are legally blind but still have some remaining vision are regarded as fakes because of the confusion arising from the definition. Perhaps for this reason, among others, it has been suggested that the term *blind* should be applied only to those individuals who are totally blind or have light perception only, and that the *legal definition of blindness* should be changed to the *legal definition of visual impairment*. Of course, only an international agreement would clarify this issue.

Visual impairment, disability, and handicap are also used interchangeably in the literature and in the strict sense their meaning is quite different. *Visual impairment* refers to a loss of visual acuity or one or more functions of the eye and visual system. It is not necessarily a disability or a handicap for the individual. *Visual disability* is an objective limitation in a person's working capacity due to his visual impairment. It is not necessarily seen as a handicap. Finally, *visual handicap* is the total negative effect of the condition, which includes the restrictions imposed by society and the attitudes of others as well as the person's self-concept. (He may not even have a loss of visual acuity or visual fields, but he has other problems.) These terms are used so interchangeably in the literature today that it seems a hopeless task to try to ask professionals to use them correctly.

Presently, the American Academy of Ophthalmology and Oto-

Fig. 3-6. The view of a child with cataracts. (Courtesy of Dr. B. Huntsman.)

laryngology and the International Council of Ophthalmology are trying to clarify the use of terms relating to visual performance.[5] They propose to classify visually impaired individuals into three groups from the functional point of view:

1. Normal or near-normal vision indicates the ability to perform all visual tasks adequately without special aids.
2. Low vision indicates that, without special aids, a person is unable to perform tasks that normally require detailed vision.
3. Blindness means that, without increased reliance on other senses, a person is unable to perform tasks that normally require gross vision.

They suggest that the term *legal blindness* should be discontinued and *severe visual impairment* substituted.

CLASSIFICATIONS OF OCULAR PATHOLOGY AND CAUSES

As has been shown earlier, uniform definitions of visual impairment are needed in order to satisfactorily compare statistical information about blind people in various countries. Similarly, a uniform classification system must be used if we wish to understand the incidence and prevalence figures for certain ocular disorders and their causes as they occur in different parts of the world. Medical diagnostic terms vary even for the same ocular disorder. *It is important to understand that the ocular pathology is not the same as its cause or etiology.* For example, when the ophthalmologist looks into a blind child's eye and discovers optic atrophy, he reports the ocular pathology as optic atrophy. The cause or etiology of optic atrophy can vary: it might be due to a brain tumor or increased intracranial pressure, an infection, a head injury, an episode of hypoxia, and so on. A cataract again represents ocular pathology, and it could be caused by congenital rubella syndrome, other types of viral infections, or metabolic defects; it may even be familial. One still sees statistical papers in which the author confuses ocular pathology with etiology and, therefore, the results are distorted.

An efficient and useful statistical system must satisfy the following criteria:

1. The definitions used are uniformly agreed upon;
2. The classification notation system is standardized;
3. The reporting is complete;
4. All reports are subject to inspection and strict quality control at a central facility.[6]

The need for an internationally used classification system was realized and the Standard Classification of Causes of Severe Vision Impairment and Blindness was developed by the Subcommittee on Classification of the Committee on Operational Research of the National Society for the Prevention of Blindness (NSPB) in the United States.[7] This classification consists of two parts: (1) site or type of disorder and (2) etiology or underlying cause. It is the best classification system and should be used internationally. However, its use is not easy because of the vast variety of ocular disorders and their numerous etiologies and, therefore, it requires careful study. It is essential that those who report such statistical data should be familiar with the use of both parts of this classification system. The manual can be obtained from the National Society for the Prevention of Blindness, 16 East 40th Street, New York, New York 10016.

CONCLUSIONS

1. The visually impaired are a highly heterogeneous group.
2. There is no universally accepted definition of blindness.
3. The legal definition of blindness was not created for children but for adults in view of determining eligibility for welfare and thus has disadvantages.

4. Definitions of visual impairment based on function are superior to those based on physiological measurements.
5. A uniform classification system must be used if we wish to understand the incidence and prevalence figures for certain ocular disorders and their causes as they occur in different parts of the world.
6. Ocular pathology is not the same as its cause.

REFERENCES

1. Blindness: Information collected from various sources. WHO Epidem Vital Statist Rep 19: 437–511, 1966
2. The incidence and causes of blindness in England and Wales 1963–68. Reports on Public Health and Medical Subjects No 128. Dept of Health and Social Security, London, Her Majesty's Stationery Office, 1972, p 41
3. Schloss IP: Implications of altering the definition of blindness. Research Bulletin No 3. New York, American Foundation for the Blind, 1963, pp 111–116
4. Bishop VE: Teaching the Visually Limited Child. Springfield, Ill, Charles C Thomas, 1971
5. Colenbrander A: Classification of visual performance. Tentative definitions, 1976 (unpublished data)
6. Graham MD (ed): editor's comments following Demography of blindness by H. Goldstein, in Science and Blindness: Retrospective and Prospective. New York, American Foundation for the Blind, 1972, pp 14–15
7. National Society for the Prevention of Blindness: Manual on use of the NSPB Standard Classification of Causes of Severe Vision Impairment and Blindness. I. Classification by site and type of affection. II. Index of diagnostic terms pertaining to severe vision impairment and blindness. New York, National Society for the Prevention of Blindness, 1966

G. C. Robinson

4
Causes, Ocular Disorders, Associated Handicaps, and Incidence and Prevalence of Blindness in Childhood

INTRODUCTION

Epidemiological surveys of visually impaired children have been appearing in the literature for the last two centuries. Most of these studies were based on three types of populations. Students from blind schools were most commonly studied because they were relatively well known to the researcher, and they usually lived in one area. In recent years, children registered with agencies for the blind were repeatedly surveyed, and those examined in hospitals or clinics were also frequently reported. Finally, in some surveys, children from schools and agencies were combined, but total populations were rarely studied. Incorrect generalizations were frequently made by many investigators, not only because they did not study the entire blind population but also because of small samples.

It is well known that residential schools prefer to educate bright blind students without additional impairments. Since the majority of visually impaired children are multihandicapped, this school population represents only a relatively small and highly select group. Most registers of agencies for the blind are not sufficiently accurate for medical-research purposes (including epidemiological or genetic studies), or for assisting in health-service policy formulations (such as estimating service needs).[1] Agencies for the blind generally offer social and economic assistance, not medical treatment; therefore, physicians frequently do not refer visually impaired children to them, since they may not be aware of the advantages. Countries that provide liberal benefits to the blind and that have national registers of the blind are more apt to have accurate information on the number of severely visually impaired individuals.[2] The names of those who move or die must be removed, and the register must be constantly updated but, on the whole, blindness is generally under-reported. Registration is often resented and avoided by those with partial vision, who do not wish to regard themselves as blind. Ophthalmologists may delay referrals when there is uncertainty about the degree of residual vision, and children whose major impairment is not blindness are frequently referred to other agencies, especially if they are mentally retarded. Iivanainen's work shows that 12 percent of profoundly mentally retarded subjects have optic atrophy.[3] In fact, the prevalence of blind children in institutions for the retarded is much higher than in the general population. These may be some of the reasons why there are wide variations in the incidence and prevalence of blindness from region to region. Furthermore, many researchers do not distinguish between incidence and prevalence and, thus, reach incorrect conclusions. These terms will be explained later in this chapter.

But the greatest impediments to satisfactory epidemiological research on a world scale are the failure to use internationally recognized uniform definitions, and the lack of a standardized classification system of ocular pathology and its causes. For these reasons, it is often impossible to compare statistical data from one study to another. One must be careful in comparing data from various parts of the world without knowing exactly what segments of the visually impaired population are studied and what definitions are used. Thus, the proliferation of statistical research has often resulted in different conclusions, and those who try to make sense of this "numbers game" may be hopelessly lost. The National Institutes of Health have organized a Model Reporting Area for Blindness Statistics (MRA), and several reports have appeared in the literature with regard to incidence and prevalence of blindness.[2,4] In a lucid discussion, Goldstein highlights the complexity of obtaining accurate statistical data on blindness.[2] He stresses that in addition to standard definitions and classification one also requires collection of data by knowledgeable physicians who record both the cause and the site and type of ocular disorder and use a standard eye report form to ensure that accurate conclusions are drawn from the records.

Relatively little research has been carried out on the characteristics of visually impaired multihandicapped children, even though these comprise the majority of blind children. Obviously, it is much easier to study the "beautiful blind" who are without difficulties and, consequently, many problems facing the visually impaired have been ignored. As Chase so eloquently stated:

Future research rests not with the neurologist, psychologist, psychiatrist, or other specialist alone but with the combined talents of all, if we are to determine the etiology, nature, sequelae and most effective remediation of neurological damage. In the widest sense, this is also true of understanding the basis of all behaviour.[5]

Those who advocate the continuation of epidemiological research are not without opposition. It is obvious that in developing countries it is not realistic to spend large sums of money on accurate statistical data when, at the same time, there are not enough funds to prevent and treat blindness. Some point out that

there is no profound need to know for certain every single blind person. The sheer cost of maintaining this degree of perfection would be foolhardy. Furthermore, statistical data on blindness is far more complete and more readily available than for cerebral palsy or mental retardation.[6]

Well-planned, statistically sound epidemiological research is still crucial if we are to understand the problems confronting blind children, identify etiological factors, develop programs, and effect legislative changes. These notions are not the idle dreams of the purist. They represent a plea for hard data by the seasoned researcher perhaps tired of trying to analyze the unanalyzable. This is a plea that recognizes the reality that information on the incidence, prevalence, and etiology of blindness, and comparisons of rates and causes over periods of time from one country to the next, determine the expenditure of vast sums of money for rehabilitation programs. Only accurate data can reveal which preventive measures were effective and permit planning for education and vocational training of the blind.

A STUDY OF CONGENITAL AND ACQUIRED
BLINDNESS IN CHILDHOOD IN BRITISH COLUMBIA

This section describes our experience with those children and adolescents who were born in British Columbia during 1944–1973 and developed blindness before their twentieth birthday. The geography of the province is such that the great majority of handicapped persons are directed to the southwest corner for their medical care. This referral pattern aids the researcher in identification and documentation of categories of different chronic disabilities. Furthermore, a longstanding link between the British Columbia-Yukon Division of the Canadian National Institute for the Blind (CNIB.), Jericho Hill School for the Blind (the only residential school for visually impaired students in Western Canada), and the Department of Paediatrics at the University of British Columbia, has resulted in collaborative studies of the young blind population. As a result, the entire childhood blind population born since 1944 has been repeatedly analyzed, making this study unusual, if not unique.

The etiology, site and type of ocular lesion, and associated handicaps of this population, together with the incidence and prevalence of congenital blindness, are described and compared with similar studies in the literature during the same time period.

The Study Population

The study population includes anyone born in British Columbia in the years 1944–1973 who developed blindness while in the 0–19-year age group.

In the 1960s, a precoded questionnaire was developed to record etiology, site and type of lesion, and associated handicaps, and subsequently retrospective studies of congenital blindness were reported.[7-9] The main sources of identification were the CNIB and the British Columbia Health Surveillance Registry. A careful search for blind children and adolescents has also been made at schools and institutions for the mentally retarded, while standardized forms have been completed on all newly identified cases. Since 1970, most new and old cases have been evaluated by a multidisciplinary team at the Children's Hospital Diagnostic Centre.[10] Thus, the majority of the population have been examined by one of the authors, all have been seen by ophthalmologists, and all are known to one social worker, who has worked with these children and their families since 1947.

Definition and Classification

In this study, the legal definition of blindness and the Standard Classification of Causes of Severe Vision Impairment and Blindness (1966 Revision) was used.[11] This classification system has been described in detail in chapter 3. Cortical blindness was excluded because these children are usually profoundly retarded mentally and their visual function is difficult to assess.

General Characteristics of the Study Population

A total of 454 children were included in the study—382 in the congenital and 72 in the acquired subgroups. The distribution of groups by year of birth is shown in Table 4-1. In 94 percent of families, both parents were Caucasian, and in 3 percent one or both parents were Native Indian. One-third of the population had no sight or light perception

Table 4-1
Sex and Year of Birth

	Congenital		Acquired		Total	
	n	%	n	%	n	%
Total	382	100.0	72	100.0	454	100.0
Sex						
Male	196	51.3	43	59.7	239	52.6
Female	186	48.7	29	40.3	215	47.4
Year of Birth						
1943–1944	5	1.3	1	1.4	6	1.3
1945–1949	49	12.8	19	26.4	68	15.0
1950–1954	110	28.8	20	27.8	130	28.6
1955–1959	60	15.7	12	16.7	72	15.9
1960–1964	72	18.8	12	16.7	84	18.5
1965–1969	53	13.9	6	8.3	59	13.0
1970–1974	33	8.6	2	2.8	35	7.7

only, and two-thirds had some useful vision (Table 4-2). These percentages were similar in the congenital and acquired subgroups.

Age of Suspicion and Referral

The age of suspicion and referral in the congenital subgroup is shown in Figure 4-1. While parental suspicion in the first year of life was almost the rule, the percentage of early referrals to the CNIB fell after the epidemic of retrolental fibroplasia subsided but has been rising again during the last 15 years. The agency has provided a counseling program for the parents of blind infants and children for 30 years. The importance of this program has been stressed to successive classes of medical students, ophthalmologists, pediatricians and other specialists. The increasing referral rate has probably been related to this educational effort.

Table 4-2
Present Degree of Visual Impairment

	Congenital		Acquired		Total	
	n	%	n	%	n	%
Nil or Light perception	132	35.9	22	31.0	154	35.1
Useful vision	236	64.1	49	69.0	285	64.9
No information	14	—	1	—	15	—
Total	382		72		454	

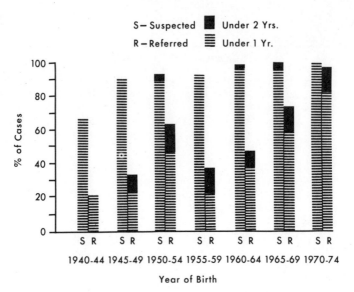

Fig. 4-1. Percent of congenitally blind children suspected and referred under 1 and 2 years of age, by year of birth.

Etiology

The causes of blindness during 1944–1973 are shown in Table 4-3.

The commonest category of congenital cause was *prenatal influence* and, of these, three-quarters were of hereditary and one-quarter of unknown origin. *Injuries, poisonings* was next (almost entirely due to excessive arterial oxygen resulting in retrolental fibroplasia), followed by *infectious diseases*, principally rubella (Fig. 4-2). The common sub-groups in the acquired cases were *prenatal influence* (entirely hereditary), *neoplasms*, and *injuries, poisonings* (Fig. 4-3). The latter group included 6 cases of battering.

The sex distribution in the congenital group was quite evenly divided but *infectious diseases* (almost entirely rubella) was more common in females (Table 4-4). In the acquired group, males predominated in the *injuries, poisonings* and *hereditary* etiologies.

Despite differences in definition, classification of visual impairment, and populations studied in childhood, the *prenatal influence* category has emerged as the leading cause of blindness in a number of other epidemiological studies from Western countries.[2,12-18]

The Site and Type of Lesion

In the total study population during 1944–1973, the common ocular lesions were retinal (36 percent), optic nerve and pathways (22 percent),

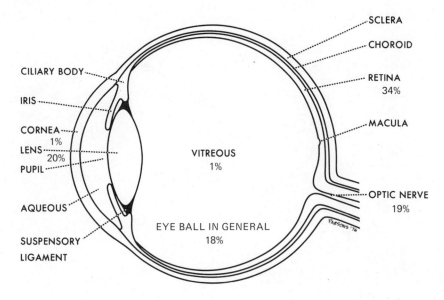

CILIARY BODY
IRIS
CORNEA
1%
LENS
20%
PUPIL
AQUEOUS
SUSPENSORY
LIGAMENT

SCLERA
CHOROID
RETINA
34%
MACULA
VITREOUS
1%
OPTIC NERVE
19%
EYE BALL IN GENERAL
18%

PARSONS '76

Fig. 4-4. Ocular lesions of children with congenital blindness.

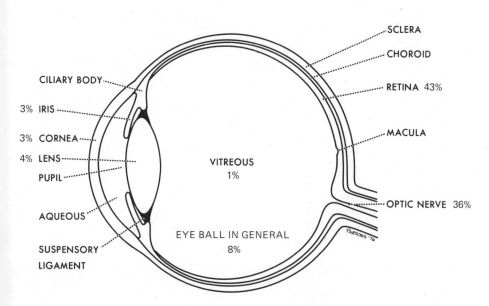

CILIARY BODY
3% IRIS
3% CORNEA
4% LENS
PUPIL
AQUEOUS
SUSPENSORY
LIGAMENT

SCLERA
CHOROID
RETINA 43%
MACULA
VITREOUS
1%
OPTIC NERVE 36%
EYE BALL IN GENERAL
8%

PARSONS '76

Fig. 4-5. Ocular lesions of children with acquired blindness.

Table 4-5
Cross-Classification by Etiology and Site and Type of Lesion

Site and Type	Infectious Diseases	Injuries, Poisoning	Prenatal Influence Not Elsewhere Clas. Hereditary	Cong. Nec	Other & Unknown	Total
Eyeball in general						
Glaucoma			15			15
Albinism			23			23
Myopia			10	1	2	13
Microphthalmos/anophthalmos			8			8
Multiple malformations			7			7
Other				1		1
Cornea, sclera	1		2	2		5
Lens: cataract	38		36	1	1	76
Uveal tract						
Chorioretinitis	3			3	2	8
Absence of iris			8			8
Other			5			5
Retina						
Retrolental fibroplasia		101				101
Macular degen.			10			10
Retinitis pigmentosa			3			3
Other			11	5	1	17
Optic nerve, etc.						
Optic neuritis						
Optic nerve atrophy			5	36	1	42
Nystagmus			20			20
Other			3	7	1	11
Vitreous				2	1	3
Indef., not reported			2	2	2	6
Total	42	101	168	60	11	382

Table 4-5
(Continued)

Site and Type	Infectious Diseases	Injuries, Poisoning	Neoplasms	Prenatal Influence Not Elsewhere Clas.		Other & Unknown	Total
				Hereditary	Cong. Nec		
Eyeball in general							
Glaucoma							
Albinism				1			1
Myopia				1		1	2
Microphthalmos / anophthalmos							
Multiple malformations							
Other		1		1		1	3
Cornea, sclera		1		1			2
Lens: cataract				2		1	3
Uveal tract							
Chorioretinitis							
Absence of iris							
Other						2	2
Retina							
Retrolental fibroplasia							
Macular degen.				9		4	13
Retinitis pigmentosa				6			6
Other		1	10	1			12
Optic nerve, etc.							
Optic neuritis	1	2	1	2			6
Optic nerve atrophy	1	3	8	2		4	18
Nystagmus							
Other		2					2
Vitreous		1					1
Indef., not reported				1			1
Total	2	11	19	27	0	13	72

39

Table 4-6
Number of Children with Associated Handicaps

	Congenital		Acquired		Total	
	n	%	n	%	n	%
None	82	25.9	38	52.8	120	30.8
Mental Retardation						
(MR)	78	24.6	15	20.8	93	23.9
Cerebral Palsy (CP)	23	7.3	1	1.4	24	6.2
Epilepsy	19	6.0	10	13.9	29	7.5
Hearing Loss	36	11.4	3	4.2	39	10.0
Congenital Heart						
Defect (CHD)	26	8.2	1	1.4	27	6.9
Other	58	18.3	20	27.8	78	20.1
Total patients	317	100.0	72	100.0	389	100.0
No information	65	—	—		—	

retrolental fibroplasia) is used to compare etiological trends and patterns of multihandicaps in children in a geographical area and it reflects the effectiveness of local preventive strategies and identifies the unsolved problem groups.

The prevalence rate of blindness is the number of cases that exist in the population *at risk* at a given point or period of time and includes all living blind residents in the population at risk, regardless of where they were born or the age of onset of blindness. The prevalence rate is used to plan programs for the existing load of children with a given handicap in a geographical area. This calculation utilizes a different numerator and denominator—for example, the number of school-age children (5 to 19 years) with a given handicap and the total number of school-age children in a given year.

The Incidence Rates of Different Etiologies Over Time

The annual incidence of congenital blindness in British Columbia has varied between 1 and 8 per 10,000 during the 30-year study period (Fig. 4-6). The profound effect of retrolental fibroplasia during the late 1940s and early 1950s is obvious. The incidence rates of the major etiological subgroups and their trends over time are shown in Figure 4-7. While retrolental fibroplasia is now much less frequent, the components of the *prenatal influence NEC* (hereditary and congenital NEC) followed by rubella, have emerged as the most common causes during the past 20 years. The congenital NEC subgroup, which includes children blinded by unknown causes, has a parallel relationship to the clusters

Table 4-7

Differences Over Time in the Number of Congenitally Blind Children with Associated Handicaps by Etiology

Year of Birth	Total No. of Children	Children with Associated Handicaps (%)						
		1 or More	MR	CP	Epilepsy	Hearing Loss	CHD	Other
Infectious Diseases								
Rubella								
1946–1959	15	100.0	73.3	13.3	—	66.7	53.3	26.7
1960–1973	18	88.9	33.3	11.1	—	55.6	77.8	11.1
Total	33	93.9	51.5	12.1	—	60.6	66.7	18.2
Significance*		ns	P<0.05	ns	—	ns	ns	ns
Injuries, poisonings								
Excessive oxygen								
1946–1954†	47	91.5	76.6	21.3	23.4	6.4	2.1	21.3
1955–1973	17	41.2	11.8	11.8	23.5	5.9	0.0	17.6
Total	64	78.1	59.4	18.8	23.4	6.2	1.6	20.3
Significance		P<0.001	P<0.001	ns	ns	ns	ns	ns
Prenatal influence NEC								
Hereditary								
1946–1959	50	56.0	42.0	4.0	2.0	10.0	2.0	22.0
1960–1973	72	48.6	23.6	5.6	9.7	8.3	4.2	26.4
Total	122	51.6	31.1	4.9	6.6	9.0	3.3	24.6
Significance		ns	ns	ns	ns	ns	ns	ns
Congenital NEC								
1946–1959	24	83.3	58.3	33.3	37.5	12.5	—	25.0
1960–1973	27	51.9	22.2	14.8	3.7	3.7	—	44.4
Total	51	66.7	39.2	23.5	19.6	7.8	—	35.3
Significance		P<0.05	P<0.05	ns	P<0.01	ns	—	ns

*χ^2 tests of the 2 × 2 tables.
†Variation in class intervals because of small numbers in later years.

Table 4-8

Differences Between Males and Females in the Number of Children with Associated Handicaps, by Etiology

	Total cases Reported	Children with Associated Handicaps (%)						
		1 or More	MR	CP	Epilepsy	Hearing Loss	CHD	Other
Congenital								
Infectious diseases								
Rubella								
Male	14	92.9	64.3	14.3	0.0	57.1	64.3	28.6
Female	19	94.7	42.1	10.5	0.0	63.2	68.4	10.5
Total	33							
Significance		ns	ns	ns	ns	ns	ns	ns
Injuries, poisonings								
Excessive oxygen								
(Retrolental Fibroplasia)								
Male	34	83.3	76.5	20.6	26.5	5.6	0.0	26.5
Female	30	70.0	40.0	16.7	20.0	6.7	3.0	13.3
Total	64							
Significance		ns	P<0.001	ns	ns	ns	ns	ns
Prenatal influence NEC								
Hereditary								
Male	66	42.4	28.8	3.0	6.1	4.5	3.0	21.2
Female	56	62.5	33.9	7.1	7.1	14.3	3.6	28.6
Total	122							
Significance		P<0.05	ns	ns	ns	ns	ns	ns
Congenital NEC								
Male	25	56.0	32.0	16.0	20.0	0.0	0.0	36.0
Female	26	76.9	46.2	30.8	19.2	15.4	0.0	34.6
Total	51							
Significance		ns	ns	ns	ns	ns	ns	ns
Acquired								
Male	43	46.5	30.2	0.0	18.6	4.7	0.0	27.9
Female	29	48.3	6.9	3.4	6.9	3.4	3.4	27.6
Total	72							
Significance		ns	P<0.05	ns	ns	ns	ns	ns

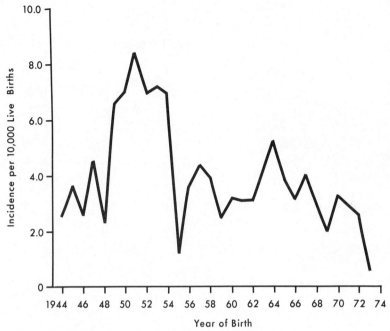

Fig. 4-6.   Total incidence of congenital blindness.

of rubella cases. This raises the possibility that some of these children may have undiagnosed maternal rubella. However, it is quite clear that the incidence of congenital blindness is not increasing in British Columbia and, in fact, the control of maternal rubella should result in its decline in the future.

Differences in definitions and classification of visual impairment make comparisons between different studies difficult and of limited value. Various studies, however, suggest that prevalence, rather than incidence, of congenital blindness is rising.[2,4,14,16] This suggests that advances in acute pediatric care are enabling more blind children to survive who formerly would have died.

PREVALENCE OF BLINDNESS IN DEVELOPING COUNTRIES

The prevalence of blindness in childhood is much higher in developing nations than in the Western world. *Infectious diseases,* which are now uncommon causes of severe visual impairment in industrialized countries, are frequent in developing countries.[19-21] Trachoma, onchocerciasis (river blindness), measles, smallpox, gonorrhea, syphilis, tuberculosis, bacterial

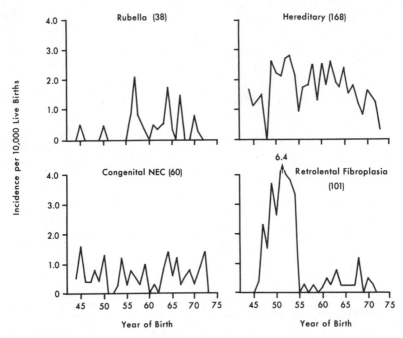

Fig. 4-7.   The incidence rates of the major congenital etiological subgroups.

meningitis, and others still affect thousands of children yearly. Malnutrition[22] and vitamin A deficiency[23] are other major causes. *Prenatal influence*, which is the major cause of blindness in childhood among industrialized nations, is in contrast only an insignificant fraction in the developing countries. Prevalence rates (which are generally only estimates) may reach 3 to 4 percent in some areas of the world.[21] Tragically, in 70 to 90 percent of these people, blindness could have been prevented.[21,24,25]

COMMENT

A review of the literature from Western countries shows that precise epidemiological methods have not been applied to the study of visually impaired children. The sustained incidence of congenital blindness since the retrolental fibroplasia era as seen in our study and the rising prevalence clearly indicate that this chronic disability is not yet on the decline. The control of maternal rubella, however, may well be followed by a decline in the incidence rate of congenital blindness, but this has not yet been shown and remains a major problem of preventive medicine. Public health authorities should continue to promote rubella immunization.

The virtual disappearance of ophthalmia neonatorum (blindness caused by gonorrheal eye infection at birth) and ocular disorders due to syphilis, and the substantial drop in retrolental fibroplasia, have reduced the number of children with known blindness. The two major causes of visual impairment in childhood are now hereditary and unknown. Clearly, research in these areas is warranted and genetic counseling programs must be established.

The rising prevalence of blindness in childhood and the high percentage of multiple handicaps dictate the need for systematic collection of accurate data and integrated planning by educational, health, and social welfare authorities.

The early onset of blindness in this study (three-quarters under 1 year) and its impact on the development of the child call for early detection and immediate referral for parent counseling and teaching of special skills. Government agencies have an important responsibility to develop appropriate early detection and assessment centers to cope with these multihandicapped children.

CONCLUSIONS

1. A review of the literature shows that precise epidemiological methods have not been applied to the study of visually impaired children.
2. Well-planned, statistically sound epidemiological research is crucial if we are to understand the problems confronting blind children, identify etiological factors, plan rational programs, and effect legislative changes.
3. The majority of blind children are visually impaired since birth and one-third of them have no useful vision.
4. The *prenatal influence* category has emerged as the leading cause of blindness in childhood.
5. Hereditary disorders of the eye are the commonest known causes of blindness in childhood.
6. Congenital blindness due to unknown causes should be carefully studied.
7. The majority of visually impaired children are multihandicapped.
8. Children who were born with rubella, hereditary, and unknown blindness prior to 1960 and with retrolental fibroplasia before 1955 have more additional handicaps than those who were born since.
9. The incidence of congenital blindness since the retrolental fibroplasia era is unchanged whereas the prevalence of blindness is increasing. The latter observation suggests that advances in acute pediatric care are enabling more children to survive who formerly would have died.

10. The control of maternal rubella should be followed by a decline in the incidence and prevalence of congenital blindness.
11. Genetic counseling services on a regional basis are important to reduce hereditary blindness.
12. Competent early diagnosis is important to determine visual acuity, etiology, ocular lesion, and associated handicaps of the child. This is best achieved by a multidisciplinary team.

REFERENCES

1. Brennan ME, Knox EG: An investigation into the purposes, accuracy and effective uses of the blind register in England. Br J Prev Soc Med 27:154–159, 1973
2. Goldstein H: Incidence, prevalence and causes of blindness in selected countries. Public Health Reviews 1:42–69, 1972
3. Iivanainen M: A Study on the Origins of Mental Retardation. Clinics in Developmental Medicine No 51. London, Heinemann, 1974
4. Kahn HA, Moorhead HB: Statistics on Blindness in the Model Reporting Area, 1969–1970. DHEW Publication No (NIH) 73-427. Washington, DC, US Government Printing Office, 1973
5. Chase JB: Retrolental fibroplasia and autistic symptomatology. Research Bulletin No 24. New York, American Foundation for the Blind, 1972, p 149
6. Kohn J: Discussant, in Graham MD (ed): Science and Blindness, Retrospective and Prospective. New York, American Foundation for the Blind, 1972, p 108
7. Robinson GC, Watt JA, Scott E: A study of congenital blindness in British Columbia: Methodology and medical findings. Can Med Assoc J 99:831–836, 1968
8. Robinson GC, Watt JA, Scott E: A study of congenital blindness in British Columbia: Epidemiological findings. Can J Ophthalmol 4:152–162, 1969
9. Robinson GC: Epidemiological studies of congenital and acquired blindness in blind children born in British Columbia—1944–1973. First National Multidisciplinary Conference on Blind Children, Vancouver, Canada, 1974, pp 1–21
10. Jan JE, Robinson GC, Scott E: A multidisciplinary approach to the problems of the multihandicapped blind child. Can Med Assoc J 109:705–707, 1973
11. National Society for the Prevention of Blindness: Manual on use of the NSPB Standard Classification of Causes of Severe Vision Impairment and Blindness. I. Classification by site and type of affection. II. Index of diagnostic terms pertaining to severe vision impairment and blindness. New York, National Society for the Prevention of Blindness, 1966
12. Hatfield EM: Causes of blindness in school children. Sight Sav Rev 33:218–233, 1963
13. Hatfield EM: Blindness in infants and young children. Sight Sav Rev 42:69–89, 1972

14. Hatfield EM: Why are they blind? Sight Sav Rev 45:3–22, 1975
15. Pearce WG: Causes of blindness in children: 1064 cases registered with the Canadian National Institute for the Blind 1970-73. First National Multidisciplinary Conference on Blind Children, Vancouver, Canada, 1974, pp 39–49
16. The incidence and causes of blindness in England and Wales 1963-68. Reports on Public Health and Medical Subjects No 128. Dept of Health and Social Security, London, Her Majesty's Stationery Office, 1972
17. Lindstedt E: Severe visual impairment in Swedish children. Doc Ophthalmol 31:173–204, 1972
18. Fraser GR, Friedmann AI: The Causes of Blindness in Childhood. Baltimore, Johns Hopkins Press, 1967
19. Rodger FC: Blindness in West Africa. London, HK Lewis, 1959
20. Olurin O: Causes of blindness in Nigeria—A study of 1,000 hospital patients. West Afr Med J 22:97–107, 1973
21. Jain IS: A report on blindness in two rural blocks in Northwestern India. Research Bulletin No 27. New York, American Foundation for the Blind, 1974, pp 45–86
22. Sood NN: Ocular manifestations in malnourished children. J Pediatr Ophthalmol 7:106–109, 1970
23. Oomen HAPC: Vitamin A deficiency, xerophthalmia and blindness. Nutr Rev 32:161–166, 1974
24. Taylor WW, Taylor IW: Services for the Handicapped in India. Bombay, Western Printers and Publishers, 1970
25. Mackenzie C, Flowers WS: Blindness in China. Report to the Government of China. Rochester, Kent, Stanhope Press, 1947

5
Prevention of Blindness

The need for preventive measures varies in different parts of the world. Many diseases that led to blindness in childhood have been eliminated in industrialized nations. One does not have to go far back in history to note how many children were blinded in North America by measles, diphtheria, tuberculosis, trachoma, syphilis, gonorrhea, and other infections. In 1906, Park Lewis of Buffalo headed a commision to study the conditions of the blind in the state of New York. His report, completed in 1907, painted a disastrous picture of infants blinded by gonorrheal ophthalmia. As a result, the National Society for the Prevention of Blindness was established in 1908.[1] Due to its efforts, all states and Canada brought in legislation for prophylaxis with silver nitrate in the neonatal period which has entirely eliminated this type of ocular pathology.

During the 1940s and 1950s, thousands of premature infants were blinded by the excessive use of oxygen, but this ocular disorder is now rare. Improvements in medical care and the introduction of antibiotics have resulted in a further reduction in the prevalence of blindness. In recent years, large-scale immunization of the susceptible population against rubella has been initiated. So far, epidemiological studies have not been able to show a reduction in the incidence of congenital rubella syndrome, mostly because registration of newly blinded infants takes time, and this health measure is too recent. No doubt, however, this cause of severe visual impairment will be eliminated in the near future.

In Western countries after the retrolental fibroplasia epidemic (see chapter 4), the incidence of congenital blindness remained unchanged. This was due to the fact that although improved maternal and neonatal care reduced the number of visually impaired newborn infants, more

49

seriously ill blind babies survived—even with marked central nervous system anomalies—who would have died in the past. Today, genetic and unknown causes are responsible for the majority of congenitally blind children (see figure 2 in chapter 4). Thus, genetic counseling has an increasingly important role to play in the prevention of blindness. Ideally, this should be the responsibility of ophthalmologists, often in cooperation with other professionals, but few of them have received such training. (The significance of hereditary ocular disease and genetic counseling is discussed in chapter 8.)

The etiology of congenital blindness is frequently obscure. The growing embryo can be affected by a wide range of disorders which are due to infections, drugs, malnutrition, and other factors. Further research in this area is clearly indicated.

Although the majority of blind children are born with their visual impairment, there are many in the acquired group whose blindness could have been prevented. Hockey, which is one of the world's fastest games, is Canada's national sport. Eye injuries in this sport are less common than other types of injury, but their results may be disastrous. The highest number of eye injuries occurs in players 11 to 15 years of age and, in 15 percent of cases, the eye becomes legally blind.[2] Two to four percent of the general population is amblyopic.[3] Depending on the degree of amblyopia, an injury to the normal eye could be tragic. Because of this study,[2] cooperation with hockey authorities has resulted in rule changes and formulation of standards for face protection.

There are still special threats to children's eyes from fireworks, sticks, and "air rifles," but the public and physicians are becoming increasingly safety minded. Approximately 900 children's eyes per year were blinded by injuries between 1960-1962 in the United States, and eye accidents accounted for approximately 3 percent of the total reportable accidents in the school system.[4] Public education and special legislation have been helpful in reducing accidental blindness. In areas where fireworks are outlawed, the fireworks-injury rate is below 0.5/100,000, whereas in areas without such laws it is 7/100,000.[4] Unbreakable plastic or case-hardened lenses have also been used for children requiring glasses, in order to prevent eye injury. Careless use of cigarettes by parents is another cause of unilateral visual impairment. In 1975, 61 infants with cigarette burns to their eye were treated at Toronto's Hospital for Sick Children.[5]

Increased intracranial pressure from malfunctioning shunts also blinds many hydrocephalic children unnecessarily. Neurosurgeons must watch for complications in these children more carefully.[6] The authors know five youngsters living in British Columbia who lost their sight in both eyes due to battering. This might have been prevented by early intervention. During this century, public health measures curtailed an outbreak in British Columbia of trachoma, which was brought in by immigrant families.[7] This disease, which was common during the last century in North America, has now been virtually eliminated. Today medical science is able to prevent the occurrence of visual impairment in many ways.

Myopia is a major cause of visual impairment. In a few children with myopia, rapid progression of the refractive error with degenerative changes of the retina and the vitreous can occur, leading to blindness. Increasing evidence suggests that in some cases this disorder may be acquired, rather than genetic as formerly believed. Over 100 years ago, Levy made the following comment:

> A curious work was published a few years ago at Breslau by Dr. Herman Cohn, giving the results of an examination of the eyes of 10,000 school children, when it appeared that the proportion of those who were shortsighted was 17.1%, or more than one-sixth of the pupils. No village children were found to be shortsighted until they had been at least half a year at school.[8]

Various authors have tried to explain the low prevalence of myopia among primitive people and the recent epidemic increase of this ocular condition among Eskimo children. Canadian studies have shown that the introduction of schooling is an associated factor.[9] Similarly, myopia was frequently observed among school children of the Yakut region in Siberia. Soviet ophthalmologists believe that the lack of sunshine and the presence of artificial light is the major factor in the development of myopia, and that children with impaired accommodation and astigmatism are especially predisposed. It is possible that preventive measures will reduce the prevalence of myopia in the future.[10] One must emphasize that "excessive" use of sight by the visually impaired is not damaging to the eyes, as it was thought at one time. The cause or causes of myopia, however, should be investigated.

It is evident from the above discussions that there are still cases of preventable blindness in childhood in the Western world, but the number of such cases is relatively small.

The situation is vastly different among developing nations. Millions of children are still being blinded in Asia, Africa, and Latin America by infections such as measles, diphtheria, smallpox, tuberculosis, trachoma, and onchocerciasis (river blindness), among others. Malnutrition coupled with nonspecific infections, vitamin A deficiency (xerophthalmia), and even "homemade remedies" are frequent causes of severe visual impairment.[11] The financial burden of these children on the economy is enormous. Widespread educational and economic programs are needed to reduce the incidence of blindness in these areas. In Brazil, hypovitaminosis A is now being prevented by fortification of certain foods, such as sugar, with this vitamin, whereas in India, Indonesia, and elsewhere, periodic injections of large doses of vitamin A for susceptible children is being tried.[12-13] Furthermore, thousands of blind people could be helped by ophthalmic surgery or the provision of glasses.[14]

Prevention goes beyond the concept of sight saving. Once a child is blind, great effort should be made to prevent problems in every area of his functioning. This is one of the main messages in this book.

CONCLUSION

The need for preventive measures varies in different parts of the world. There is still preventable blindness in childhood in the Western countries, but the number of such cases is relatively small. The situation is vastly different among developing nations.

REFERENCES

1. Newell FW: The National Society for the Prevention of Blindness celebrates its 65th year. Am J Ophthalmol 76:1022-1023, 1973
2. Pashby TJ, Pashby RC, Chisholm LDJ, et al: Eye injuries in Canadian hockey. Can Med Assoc J 113:663-674, 1975
3. Wybar K: Ocular motility and strabismus, in Duke-Elder S (ed): Systems of Ophthalmology, London, Kimpton, 1973, vol 9, p 294
4. Low MB: The significance of vision. Problems of children and youth. Eye safety in pediatric practice. J Pediatr Ophthalmol 6:223-226, 1969
5. Hennighausen SJ: Prevention of blindness. Second Canadian National Interdisciplinary Conference on Blind Children, London, Canada, 1976
6. Jan JE, Robinson GC, Kinnis C, et al: Blindness due to optic nerve atrophy and hypoplasia in children. An epidemiological study (1944-1974). Dev Med Child Neurol (in press)
7. Byers GM: Trachoma in Canada. Can Med Assoc J 27:372-376, 1932
8. Levy WH: Blindness and the Blind. London, Chapman & Hall, 1872, p 454
9. Morgan RW, Speakman JS, Grimshaw SE: Inuit myopia: An environmentally induced "epidemic"? Can Med Assoc J 112:575-577, 1975
10. Tsvetkov VL: The conference on prevention, pathogenesis and treatment of eye disease in children. J Pediatr Ophthalmol 9:121-123, 1972
11. Sorsby A: The incidence and causes of blindness: An international survey. Br J Ophthalmol (monograph suppl 14) 1950
12. Simmons WK, de Mello AV: Blindness in the nine states of Northeast Brazil. Am J Clin Nutr 28:202, 1975
13. Oomen HAPC: Vitamin A deficiency, xerophthalmia and blindness. Nutr Rev 32:161-166, 1974
14. Jain IS: A report on blindness in two rural blocks in Northwestern India. Research Bulletin No 27. New York, American Foundation for the Blind, 1974, pp 45-86

In Cooperation with
L. O'Connor

6
Evaluation and Psychological Testing

INTRODUCTION

Families of many visually impaired children have had negative encounters with the health professions for a number of reasons.[1] Physicians are traditionally trained in acute-care hospitals where most patients are admitted for relatively short periods of time. They are exposed to only a small percentage of the health problems that are seen in actual practice. Most have not had any experience with handicapped children during their undergraduate years, and therefore they are unlikely to be familiar with cerebral palsy, blindness, deafness, and other developmental disorders. There is no simple solution to the problems of blind children with optic atrophy, anophthalmia, retinal disorders, or other visual impairments, who in addition may have cerebral palsy, mental retardation, behavioral problems, deafness, or developmental delay. They need treatment for their difficulties, but the approach is more of a problem-solving one. Such treatment is time-consuming and sometimes frustrating. Success is not attained in days but in years, and this is precisely why many physicians do not like to treat chronically handicapped children. Furthermore, physicians in many countries cannot work for the long hours needed by the chronically handicapped because the existing fee structure limits their available time.

Health professionals tend to share society's current attitudes toward the visually impaired. Blindness is often conceived of as the greatest disaster—worse than death. Sometimes parents of blind infants are told by someone expressing sincere sorrow—even physicians—that their child would be better off dead than alive. Such a negative approach has a profound effect on the family, who may perceive the blindness of their infant as so overwhelming a tragedy that they will be unable to participate in any effective training program.

Health professionals who have not worked with the visually impaired tend to have pessimistic attitudes toward their habilitation. They do not realize that blind individuals can have a happy, often fruitful and productive life. Those who deal with the chronically handicapped should have a hopeful, realistic approach.

There are other difficulties with existing health care because it is not geared to serving the multihandicapped. For example, a child with congenital rubella syndrome may have cataracts, deafness, slow development, heart defects, small stature, and other problems. The child's family physician or pediatrician refers him to a variety of highly trained specialists. The process of evaluation is, thus, painfully slow and fragmented. Furthermore, since some professionals tend to express opinions that are beyond the areas of their expertise or may have differences of opinion, the parents are often exposed to conflicting advice, which leaves them hopelessly confused. Frequently, they are not told about the results of all the investigations, or they are given a short, highly technical summary which may be difficult to understand. Referrals to appropriate agencies are often delayed because physicians who come in contact with only a few blind children in their practice are frequently unaware of the services provided.

In conclusion, it is not surprising that parents of blind children have negative encounters with health professionals within the presently existing models of health care.

MULTIDISCIPLINARY APPROACH TO DIAGNOSIS AND TREATMENT

Diagnostic and treatment centers have been introduced in various countries in an attempt to resolve the present difficulties in providing health care to the multihandicapped child, including the visually impaired.[2-5] These are still few in number but are proving to be successful. Team work between professions is the basic philosophy. Under this system, it is not the child and his family who go to the specialists in various locations throughout the city, but the professionals who come to see the child at the diagnostic center.

When a visually impaired child is referred to a diagnostic center, detailed information is first obtained about his problems and appropriate appointments are then arranged within a well-organized time period. The child's difficulties determine the composition of the team, which may consist of a combination of the following professionals: pediatrician, psychiatrist, neurologist, otolaryngologist, neurosurgeon, ophthalmologist, physiotherapist, psychologist, speech pathologist, audiologist, social worker, and others. Each specialist talks to the parents, examines the child, and necessary tests are done. During these evaluations, individual professionals may have a limited preliminary conversation with the family, but the detailed, lengthy discussion occurs during a conference with the team members, parents, and invited professionals, such as the community health nurse, teachers, and representatives of involved agencies. Parents must be looked upon as members of the team and should be told the truth. During the conference, the child's diagnostic profile is clearly spelled out, and his management is planned. The team should always have a "captain" or leader who may be any one of the members but not necessarily a physician, depending on the child's major problem. Therefore, the coordinator may be a psychologist, physiotherapist, speech pathologist, or social worker. It is the team captain's responsibility to see that the evaluation is satisfactorily completed, appropriate reports are sent out, and follow-up appointments are arranged. The parents then communicate with this individual from time to time as they feel the need.

The family physician, whose role is crucial in the management of the visually impaired child, should be included in such an evaluation whenever possible. He should receive detailed reports, even if he cannot attend the conference.

It is important that during the conference the parents are encouraged to ask questions until they are satisfied. This "extra" time from the professionals will pay off in the future. Carefully written case reports are sent, with the parents' permission, to the involved agencies. These should include the history, examination, tests, diagnostic profile, impressions, and management plans. Technical medical terms should be avoided if possible because they may not be familiar to other professionals.

There are many advantages to interdisciplinary health care. The evaluation, in most cases, can be done accurately enough in a couple of days to understand the child's main problems. Hospitalization, which often adversely affects the blind child's development[6] and, in fact, may distort the results of the evaluation,[7] can frequently be avoided. The parents are not given conflicting opinions and generally do not go "shopping around" for more advice. They are less exposed to the prejudices and damaging attitudes of individual professionals. The entire child is looked at, not just his medical problems. The evaluation is likely to be more accurate since the team members are familiar with the multihandicapped blind child, and through interaction they reinforce each others' findings. It is very difficult to compare the cost of the interdisciplinary model of care with the model of private practice, but it is probably cheaper in the longrun.

DISTURBED AND PSEUDORETARDED BLIND CHILDREN

Disturbed blind children, usually with multiple handicaps and severe visual impairment, are poorly understood, even after a multidisciplinary evaluation. They may have bizarre stereotyped mannerisms, autistic behavior, and abnormal sleep patterns; they may lack language and social skills and the ability to chew and swallow solids; they may not be toilet trained. The parent-child relationship is usually also disturbed.[8] In spite of their low level of functioning, their intellectual capacity may be higher and, thus, the diagnosis of mental retardation is inappropriate. These children have often been given several diagnostic labels, such as brain damaged, mentally retarded, or autistic. Their parents may be guilt-ridden, confused, and frequently bitter against health professionals who may have too easily blamed them for all the difficulties. Schools refuse to take them, the family can no longer cope, and not infrequently, as a last resort, they are institutionalized.

These children may be called the "deviant blind,"[8,9] but perhaps the "disturbed" description is better since deviant could categorize any individual who is not entirely normal. There are many such cases in the literature.[1,8-12]

Gruber and Moor described Bobby, a 5-year-old boy who

banged his head against the floor and rocked furiously . . . when people walked by, he hit out—scratching, striking with his fists . . . was not toilet trained . . . and was parrotting. His superior intelligence was recognized by some. . . . He was removed from kindergarten after a time as he was judged a threat to other children. . . . He had no place to go.[9] (pp. 5-7)

Intensive efforts to rehabilitate him helped only to some degree.

Williams described a hydrocephalic child whose mother rejected him, with the support of medical advisors. When he was first seen at the age of 5 years by a psychiatric consultant in an institution for the retarded, the medical chart described him in the following manner:

He is an idiot. He appears blind. . . . He does not feed himself' with a spoon, nor does he convey bread and butter to his mouth. . . . He is doubly incontinent. He cannot walk, talk or even stand. He will hold an object in either hand. He has the mannerism . . . of pressing his fingers into his eyes . . . and it is not certain whether he hears. His assessment on the Vineland Social Maturity Scale was given as 9½ months.[12] (p. 166)

Subsequently, this child learned to function well through intensive rehabilitative efforts. A complete recovery is unlikely, however, when the early formative years are neglected,[13] although startling improvements can often be seen in such children after intervention.

Both children functioned at a markedly low level of development but Bobby, in addition, was also disturbed in his behavior. Bobby was a *disturbed blind child* whereas the second boy was *pseudoretarded*, due to maternal rejection and lack of opportunity for learning. The second child improved rapidly, whereas Bobby's poor development and disturbed behavior remained, even after adequate opportunities for learning and a healthier emotional environment were provided. As it appears, Bobby's low level of functioning, frustrations, and disturbed behavior were due to his own deficits, which may have been a speech and language disorder, various perceptual problems, hearing loss, and other difficulties. The parent-child relationship is occasionally disturbed in such cases as Bobby's, but it may be the result of the strain of constantly dealing with a markedly disturbed child. Visually impaired children with abnormal development should always be carefully assessed rather than immediately finding fault with the parents, as many professionals tend to do. When a multidisciplinary evaluation fails to determine whether the problems are due to an abnormal environment or to innate deficits or both, then efforts must first be made to improve the parent-child relationship and to enrich the child's environment. If counseling does not help the family, appropriate alternative placements should be sought, including therapeutic foster homes. Sometimes the various interacting factors can be understood well only when studied in such a way.

Handicaps do predispose children to developmental deviations when they live in an unsatisfactory environment. We have known normal blind children who developed quite satisfactorily in obviously disturbed homes, and we have seen multihandicapped blind children who developed poorly in such homes but subsequently did very well in a residential school for the blind where the emotional atmosphere was healthier for them.

Cohen and Alfano concluded through longitudinal studies that

> the majority of blind children who did not measure up to normal intelligence and who consequently were not making a satisfactory educational adjustment were children handicapped by generalized physiological impairments. Only in a minority of cases could we rule out physical factors and place the responsibility for poor development on an emotional basis.[14]

This statement is true only in those areas where counseling services for the families of blind children are available and satisfactorily utilized. In many countries, adequate opportunities for learning are still not provided to blind children during their early lives and, therefore, pseudo-retardation is more common.

MEDICAL DIAGNOSES OF VISUAL IMPAIRMENT

Visual information is first received by the retina and then transmitted along the optic nerves and radiation to the cerebral cortex. It is the brain, not the eye, that sees. The visual process is much more complicated, however, as information is received, analyzed, stored, and decoded continuously while the system matures in an orderly fashion paralled with the development of other motor and sensory faculties.[15]

Retinal response to light and to moving objects, as shown by reflex responses of blinking, pupillary contraction, and eye movements, is well established in the normal neonate. But this does not necessarily indicate visual awareness and, furthermore, the eye movements are not voluntary but reflexive in nature. Most normal newborn infants are able to fixate on strong light and, by 2 months of age, they must be able to follow moving objects.[16] When the infant fixates, the previously roving eyes become stationary for a few seconds and suppression of other motor activities occurs.[17] The palpebral fissure widens, other facial features relax, and respiration becomes regular.[18] Absent fixation, following, and suppression of motor activity in an infant do not necessarily indicate blindness, since the total visual process may be immature, as is commonly seen in young, severely mentally retarded children. However, if the infant has no optokinetic fixation and following responses (nystagmus), then visual impairment should be strongly suspected. Optokinetic reflex is a cerebral response, but when it is absent the pathology is not always localized in the visual cortex.

The diagnosis of severe visual impairment in suspected infants may be quite easy if the eyes show major abnormalities, such as lack of pupillary response, marked optic atrophy, cataracts, and chorioretinitis. The diagnosis is much harder, however, when ocular findings are minimal or nonexistent. If the damage to the visual process is distal to the lateral geniculate body, then even the totally blind infant may have completely normal pupillary response and normal-looking globes. In such cases, the neurological examination and investigation, such as EEGs and central nervous system contrast studies, are usually markedly abnormal. These children are "neurologically" or "cortically" blind and usually their future intellectual development is markedly limited.

There are two widely used techniques in the evaluation of visually impaired individuals: electroretinograms (ERGs) and visually evoked responses (VERs). The VER is obtained when light is directed in the eye during EEG recording, and then certain electrical changes are observed over the visual cortex.[19] The lack of cortical response to light indicates that the visual pathway is interrupted; therefore, the child is blind. On the other hand, if it is present, it does not necessarily mean that the child's vision is normal, since he may have little or no useful vision present.

The ERG, which represents the summation of electrical activity of the retina, may be abnormal in various retinal disorders. This test is especially useful when visual impairment is strongly suspected but the infant's eyes appear to be normal and when the neurological examination, including EEGs, shows no abnormalities. We have seen such children who were diagnosed as having cortical blindness, but subsequently their ERGs clearly indicated a retinal disorder.

The ERG and VER may be especially useful in a child who has a dense congenital cataract or primary persistent hyperplastic vitreous and cannot see. If these tests show that he is indeed blind, there is no need to perform surgery.

Many infants who appear to be blind may have useful vision in later years because of visual maturation and more efficient use of their remaining sight. Mentally retarded babies may show little or no evidence of being able to see, but later they readily respond to the same visual stimulus. This is why prognosis of ultimate visual function is so difficult in infancy.

Many children who gradually acquire visual impairment do not realize that they are losing their sight until they are almost blind, and even then they frequently present with the complaint of poor coordination.

Early diagnosis of congenital or acquired blindness is important for obvious reasons. Sometimes further deterioration of sight can be prevented or vision improved with appropriate corrective lenses. Early referral of visually impaired children and their families to agencies for help is just as important. Similar to deafness, cerebral palsy and other developmental handicaps, the most crucial period in the visually impaired child's life is his early formative years.

In congenitally blind infants, severe visual impairment is discovered at birth only when the ocular anomaly is obvious or when blindness is suspected for various reasons. Careful routine examination of the newborn's eyes by ophthalmologists is rarely done. Thus, even total visual loss may be missed in the nursery, but this is not entirely the physician's fault. The incidence of congenital blindness is low; therefore, it is rarely suspected. The infant's reactions are quite primitive during the first 2 weeks of life since he sleeps most of the time and wakes up only for his feedings. His eyelids are generally swollen while still in the nursery from the administration of prophylactic silver nitrate drops. A normal, full-term newborn can focus on objects but has no voluntary eye movements. Subsequently, he begins to make eye contact with his mother's face during feeding, but this does not happen with the severely visually impaired. The eyes of the blind infant may exhibit roving movements, nystagmus, and may even roll up. Almost invariably, mothers are the first to suspect that something is wrong with the infant's eyes.[20] Unfortunately, since the symptoms of visual impairment are still minimal, many physicians reassure mothers that everything is fine. Every infant deserves a careful ophthalmological examination when lack of eye contact or abnormal eye movements are noted.

When the ophthalmologist finally confirms the parents' worst suspicions that their child is blind, which is usually at 4 to 5 months of age,[20] this news hits them like lightning. The impact of the diagnosis is so great that they are usually unable to listen with any understanding to further discussions; a second office visit must therefore be arranged after a few days. How the ophthalmologist leads the parents through this critical initial period and the following next few weeks will affect the child's life much more than is generally realized.[21] He must tell the truth, since leaving false hopes for visual recovery is the greatest disservice.[22] If nothing can be done for the child's vision, he should clearly say so. This is, of course, difficult because no one likes to tell bad news, and he is admitting that medical science and he as a practitioner have failed.[21] Only when the parents fully accept the fact that the child is irreversibly blind will they be ready to listen to the advice of the parent counselor and begin the child's successful habilitation.

The ophthalmologist's own attitudes can definitely influence the parents' attitudes toward their child. If he perceives blindness as the greatest tragedy, the parents will sense this even though it may not be expressed in words. This is why it is advisable for the ophthalmologist to examine his own attitudes before counseling.[21] The parents almost invariably ask the same questions: Why did it happen? Just what is wrong? Can his eyes be fixed? Is he going to be retarded? Is he going to talk or walk? Will he be able to support himself in his adulthood? Can it happen again? Both parents should be present during these crucial discussions. The parents' reactions and the importance of proper counseling will be discussed in more detail in a subsequent chapter.

After the initial diagnosis of visual impairment, the ophthalmologist should refer the child's family to the appropriate agencies for help. He must take an interest in the child beyond the boundaries of the ocular pathology, as only then does he practice true medicine. Some ophthalmologists invite representatives of agencies for the blind to be present during their second examination of the child so as to familiarize them with the visual problems and initiate the process of long-term counseling. The ophthalmologist must remember that most visually impaired children are multihandicapped; therefore, the diagnosis of ocular disorder is only one aspect of the total evaluation.

THE APPEARANCE

Clinicans who have worked with the visually impaired are able to tell much about them just by looking. In fact, watching these children is an important part of the examination.

As the child approaches the examiner, several quick observations can be made. When he walks "out-toeing" with a wide base, he most likely was born with a marked visual impairment and his early motor development was delayed (Fig. 9-5). When the back of his skull is flattened, it is because he spent excessive time on his back in infancy (Fig. 6-1). These children are often hypotonic, flat-footed, and poorly coordinated.

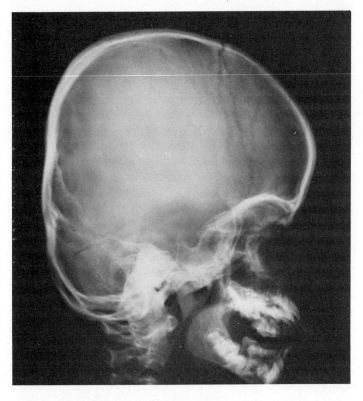

Fig. 6-1. The skull x-ray of a visually impaired child who was left on his back for long periods during his early years. Note the marked occipital flattening.

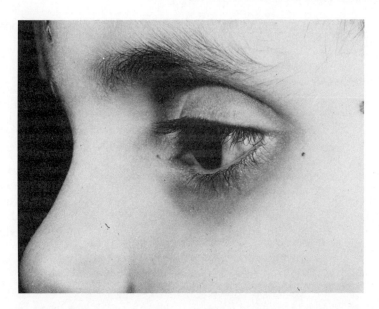

Fig. 6-2. The deep-set eyes of a congenitally blind boy who excessively "presses" his eyes. Note the dark pigmentation of the skin around the eye and the indentation in the upper medial edge of the orbit. The constant pressure on the bone has distorted its growth.

Postural and gait deviations are closely related to the degree of visual impairment, but they also signify the fact that parents or professionals have not tried to correct them.

Deep-set eyes with dark circles around them indicate that the child has been excessively pressing his eyes (Figs. 6-2, 6-3). This and other mannerisms are discussed in detail in chapter 18. The lack of voluntary eye movements, the presence of roving nystagmus, together with other obvious ocular pathology again suggests markedly poor vision.

The young child who has not been taught to use his hands often brings them up beside his head when they are touched. His hands are slender and floppy because the musculature is poorly developed. Children with normal peripheral but poor central vision have good mobility, giving the impression that their distance visual acuity is much better than it is. However, when they examine a small object many of these children use their touch rather than sight. This indicates that central vision is markedly diminished in contrast to peripheral sight.

The impression a visually impaired child makes on his sighted friends is much more important than parents and professionals generally realize. Successful integration of the blind into sighted society is often jeopardized because of socially unacceptable "blind mannerisms," his postural and

Fig. 6-3. The same boy (Fig. 6-2) presses on his eye while resting on his elbow.

gait problems, and inadequate grooming and dressing. Ophthalmologists should make sure that artificial eyes are properly fitted and, when necessary, plastic surgery should be done to improve facial appearance. The reaction of people to the appearance and behavior of a blind child determines to a large extent how he will feel about himself—about his own worth as a person.

PSYCHOLOGICAL ASSESSMENT OF BLIND CHILDREN

The major purpose of psychological assessment is to develop a picture of a person's attributes in the hope that this information will help in determining present interventions and future expectations. Tests, which can be described as structured interviews—instances of behavior in a certain context from which we attempt to generalize[23]—are the instruments ordinarily used to obtain information. They encompass measures of achievement, aptitude, interest, personality, dexterity, social maturity, and many more. But attempts to quantify what is termed *intelligence* are usually the primary concern when a psychological evaluation is sought. Defining intelligence and describing what tests measure has been disputed since Binet initiated standardized testing in 1904, but currently it is defined as the ability to profit from experience or the ease with which one can learn a new set of behaviors. Piaget's more general terms describe it as one aspect of biological adaptation, such as coping with the environment and organizing and reorganizing thought and action. Identifying and measuring these attributes in blind children presents special problems to the psychologist.

Traditionally, the only way to describe ability to learn has been to ascertain that a particular skill or piece of information has been learned by attempting to extract this knowledge from a person at a particular time; this is the testing situation. Assumption of equal opportunity to learn, implying a similarity in relationships to the outside world, is basic to standardized tests, but these assumptions do not hold for the blind child. Development and use of language, thinking, and perception differ. It is not known how a blind child develops a self-concept, how he experiences the physical world, or what clues he uses for learning. One cannot even be certain that words have the same meaning as for sighted children.[24] Burlingham has written extensively about the developmental processes of visually impaired children, and some observations related to the learning experiences of these children and their methods of relating and profiting from experience—a part of the definition of intelligence—are relevant when evaluating the abilities of these children. She noted that, in learning speech, the blind find uses for words that the sighted do not require: for orientation, differentiating between characteristics of persons, or discovering some way an object can be identified. However, many of their words are meaningless or have a different meaning, concepts may be misunderstood or only partially understood, or words may be used merely to parrot or imitate the sighted. Speech is less firmly connected with sensory experience, so at times a child may appear to acquire understanding while in reality acquiring only words. Absence of visual cues makes mental representation uncertain. The following examples demonstrate these difficulties: a blind child may understand that a circle is round, and can feel around an object, but cannot understand "go in a circle" or "go around." Some children can not identify round objects unless they can be contained completely in the hand—big balls are harder to recognize as round. Statements such as "in front" and "behind" are not accurately comprehended. Burlingham also points out that many toys, especially miniatures (dolls, houses, animals, etc.) help sighted children to experience mastery of their environment, and this path to mastery is not available to the blind child. Evidence suggests that the world is often understood in a different manner by these children and that, due to lack of visual perception of the facts, greater confusion exists between reality and make-believe. There is less basis on which to generalize, resulting in less generalization from previous experience, as well as only partial understanding of common objects due to insufficient cues.[25]

Before mentioning specific tests that may be useful in the assessment process, the importance of other information must be stressed. The psychologist should be aware of the etiology and prognosis of the visual impairment, amount and quality of remaining sight, if any, and presence of visual memories, if any. Partial vision may result in difficulties in the field of vision, figure/ground confusion, and differences in awareness of just what is seen.[26] These factors influence test performance and are relevant to interpretation of test data.

Often blindness separates children from their environment, and they remain in a nonstimulated, self-preoccupied state if not actively forced to join in the activity around them. In assessing these children, it is essential to establish whether or not they have had an opportunity to learn things expected of a child that age, and whether, after they have been adequately stimulated, they are still unable to do such tasks.[27] Delay in language acquisition is common in blind children, and sometimes speech has not developed by the age of 3. Echolalia and improper or inappropriate use of words may be found and should be analyzed within the context of the child's handicap, rather than in relation to disorders they resemble, such as autism. Observing the child-parent interaction has been found very useful for a better understanding of developmental levels; at one diagnostic center, the entire family is observed for a number of days.

Each individual child's specific handicap, general language facility, degree of mobility, quality of coordination, extent of experiential background, and level of social development must be noted. The assessment of visually impaired children must be approached first of all by rejecting many standards set by the sighted, recognizing that patterns of growth and development assumed by tests may not apply to the blind.

The first major pioneer in testing the blind, Samuel P. Hayes, adapted the Binet Scales in 1920 and then revised his test in 1942, basing it on the Stanford-Binet 1937 Revision. Named the Interim Hayes-Binet because of uncertainty about placement of some of the items which might require correction after further study, the original form has been widely used until recently. A new revision, consisting of items selected from earlier forms and called the Perkins-Binet, has been standardized on over 2000 subjects from 5 to 15 years of age from all parts of the United States. Two final forms were established, for blind subjects with and without usable vision, with a total of almost 100 items with 73 common to both forms. These materials are now becoming available.[28]

The Wechsler scales have been in general use since 1950 and were accepted as useful for blind and sighted alike without significant changes, as they provide separate verbal and performance subtests. The format was not altered in the 1974 Revision, although some items were dropped and others modified. The reliability of the measures (which means merely the extent to which results tend to be consistent over time) is similar for blind and sighted groups. Content validity, however, should be examined in terms of appropriateness for the blind. One would imagine that visually biased items could be determined by inspection—for example, the items "What is the color of rubies?" or "What should you do if you see a train approaching a broken track?" It has been found that blind children gave better answers on the train-track item and more know the number of days in a week than sighted children. "How many pennies in a nickel?" and "How many things in a dozen?" were two items on which the sighted children excelled. Visual bias may not be easily discernible.

Studies of the Wechsler Intelligence Scale for Children have shown that mean scaled scores of normal sighted children do not usually differ from subtest to subtest. If large discrepancies do occur it is considered significant, various interpretations are made, and learning disabilities, emotional problems, and various other syndromes can be identified. Analysis of protocols of visually handicapped children demonstrates the reasons that subtest scatter does not have the same significance. Responses to *information*, dependent on more formal educational experiences, show that facts retained by blind children are less integrated and tend to stand alone. *Comprehension* involves understanding and reacting to reality at two levels: common-sense type judgment and judgment based on social experience, with both factors poorly defined for the blind. *Arithmetic* skills appear to be comparable in both groups. *Similarities*, involving abstract conceptualizations, show that the blind have shifted the concrete-abstract continuum and supports the notion that early onset of blindness may result in deficiencies in the ability to abstract. *Vocabulary* for the blind appears to be simply a word-definition test, while for the sighted more verbal comprehension and word-richness are found. To summarize these findings:

1.   There appears to be a lack of integration in educational experiences, resulting in isolated bits of knowledge.
2.   Verbal abilities focus on a basic vocabulary with little elaboration.
3.   The blind approach abstract conceptualization from a concrete and functional level.
4.   Numerical ability is comparable.[29]

The same researcher has reported the following patterns of subtest variability with blind children: high mean scores on *digit span* (rote memory) and on *information* (general knowledge) with low mean scores on *comprehension* (common-sense reasoning). Combining subtests and comparing directly with sighted groups, the combination of the blind group's higher mean performance on digit span and lower mean performance on *similarities* (verbal concept formation) discriminated between the two groups when they were equated for total verbal intelligence quotient.[30]

Other tests frequently used in the assessment of blind children are the Maxfield-Fjeld Social Maturity Scale for preschool children; the Vineland Social Maturity Scale for older children; and the Bailey Infant Intelligence Scales, whose behavior scale is particularly useful (though many items of the mental scale are too dependent on vision). The Illinois Test of Psycholinguistic Abilities (ITPA) has an auditory-vocal channel which helps to determine patterns of strengths and weaknesses in language development. Adaptations of other measures, such as the Tactual Progressive Matrices, the Ohwaki-Kohs blocks, or a verbal version of the Draw-a-Person technique may also be found useful for older children. Partially sighted children can attempt the Bender Gestalt Test and the Columbia Mental Maturity Scale. The latter is suitable for children over 4 years of age who are able to respond to the large, brightly colored stimulus cards.

Attempts have been made to focus more on "learning aptitude" rather than on the results of intelligence tests; that is, on the *process* or psychological operations fundamental to learning, rather than on the *product*, which reflects knowledge already acquired. For example, activities such as selecting items that go together on the basis of some recognized relationship between them, or completing a number series by establishing logical relationships, reflect the process crucial to learning rather than merely repeating what has been learned. Tasks such as these, as well as problems involving tactile stimuli, have been incorporated into the Blind Learning Aptitude Test.[31]

The purpose of assessment, as mentioned above, is to better understand an individual's personal organization and, from that, to predict the level of performance that can be expected in the future. The time usually allotted for this difficult task is much too brief, since extensive fact-gathering, observation, and at times retesting may be necessary before statements can be made about a blind child's knowledge or lack of it, and whether problems are caused by lack of experience, lack of ability, distortion through fantasy, or whatever. An assessment is expected to provide information that will lead to the selection of procedures to maximize development, and results should be reported in such a way as to foster enriching experiences, improve the educational situation, and increase the possibilities for social relationships. The most productive information should describe specific, rather than global, abilities and answer questions about readiness for certain activities and more effective teaching methods. Discussing difficulties that may be encountered due to delays and weaknesses will provide useful and needed information to persons working with a child. Continuity of contact is essential between the evaluator and others concerned with a child's development in order that information can be correctly interpreted and meaningfully presented. Given reports that consider all aspects of a child's development and contain practical information that points to definite procedures rather than mere classification, a blind child's chances to realize his potential can be greatly enhanced.

CONCLUSIONS

1. Families of many visually impaired children have had negative encounters with professionals within the presently existing models of health care.
2. Diagnostic and treatment centers have been introduced in an attempt to resolve present difficulties in providing health care to the multihandicapped.
3. Pseudoretardation can occur in blind children if adequate opportunities are not provided for learning.
4. Visually impaired children with abnormal development should always be carefully assessed rather than immediately finding fault with the parents, as many professionals tend to do.
5. Handicaps predispose children to developmental deviations when they live in an unsatisfactory environment.
6. Early diagnosis of visual impairment is important for obvious medical reasons. Early referral of blind children and their families to agencies for help is just as crucial.
7. Almost invariably, mothers are the first to suspect that something is wrong with their infant's eyes. An ophthalmological examination, rather than simple reassurance, is needed.
8. How the ophthalmologist leads the parents through the period after diagnosis and the following next few weeks will affect the child's life much more than is generally realized.
9. The major purpose of psychological assessment is to develop a picture of a person's attributes in the hope that this information will help in determining present interventions and future expectations.
10. Great caution must be exercised in interpreting and applying information obtained from psychological testing of blind children.

REFERENCES

1. Elonen AS, Cain AC: Diagnostic evaluation and treatment of deviant blind children. Am J Orthopsychiatry 34: 625–633, 1964
2. Jan JE, Robinson GC, Scott E: A multidisciplinary approach to the problems

of the multihandicapped blind child. Can Med Assoc J 109:705–707, 1973

3. Wilson W: Experience with a multidiscipline assessment team for visually handicapped children. Proc R Soc Med 66:32–34, 1973

4. Cruickshank WM: The multiple-handicapped child and courageous action. International Journal for the Education of the Blind 13:65–75, 1964

5. Donlon ET: An evaluation center for the blind child with multiple handicaps. International Journal for the Education of the Blind 13:75–78, 1964

6. Fraiberg S: Separation crisis in two blind children. Psychoanal Study Child 26:355–371, 1971

7. Smith VH: The ophthalmological examination of the handicapped child, in Gardiner P, MacKeith R, Smith V (eds): Aspects of Developmental and Paediatric Ophthalmology. Clinics in Developmental Medicine No. 32. London, Heinemann, 1969, pp 101–102

8. Moor PM: Blind children with developmental problems. Children 8:9–13, 1961

9. Gruber KF, Moor PM (eds): No Place to Go. New York, American Foundation for the Blind, 1963, p 5

10. Burlingham D: Psychoanalytic Studies of the Sighted and the Blind. New York, International Universities Press, 1972

11. Elonen AS, Polzien M, Zwarensteyn SB: The "uncommitted" blind child: Results of intensive training of children formerly committed to institutions for the retarded. Except Child 33:301–306, 1967

12. Williams CE: A blind idiot who became a normal blind adolescent. Dev Med Child Neurol 8:166–169, 1966

13. Jan JE, Robinson GC, Scott E, et al: Hypotonia in the blind child. Dev Med Child Neurol 17:35–40, 1975

14. Cohen J, Alfano J: The effects of blindness on children's development, in Taylor BM (ed): Blind Preschool. Colorado Springs, Colorado Industrial Printers, 1974, p 25

15. Ffooks OF: Neurophysiology and assessment of visual function in children, in Gardiner P, MacKeith R, Smith V (eds): Aspects of Developmental and Paediatric Ophthalmology. Clinics in Developmental Medicine No 32. London, Heinemann, 1969, pp. 5–8

16. Wolff PH: Observations on the newborn infant. Psychosom Med 21:110–118, 1959

17. Ling BC: Genetic study of sustained visual fixation and associated behaviour in the human infant from birth to six months. J Genet Psychol 61: 227–277, 1942

18. Brazelton TB, Scholl ML, Robey JS: Visual responses in the new-born. Pediatrics 37:284–290, 1966

19. Walsh TJ, Smith JL, Shipley T: Blindness in infants. Am J Ophthalmol 62:546–556, 1966

20. Robinson GC, Watt JA, Scott E: A study of congenital blindness in British Columbia: Epidemiological findings. Can J Ophthalmol 4:152–162, 1969

21. Cholden LS: A Psychiatrist Works with Blindness. New York, American Foundation for the Blind, 1958

22. Finestone S, Gold S: The Role of the Ophthalmologist in the Rehabilitation

of Blind Patients. New York, American Foundation for the Blind, 1959

23. Mayer J: Difficulties in handling the "human element" in the psychological evaluation of blind children. International Journal for the Education of the Blind 15:97-101, 1966

24. Newland TE: Prediction and evaluation of academic learning by blind children: II. Problems and procedures in evaluation. International Journal for the Education of the Blind 14:42-51, 1964

25. Burlingham D: Some notes on the development of the blind. Psychoanal Study Child 16:121-145, 1964

26. Morse JL: Answering the questions of the psychologist assessing the visually handicapped child. New Outlook for the Blind 69:350-353, 1975

27. Elonen AS: Assessment of the nontestable blind child, in Clark LL, Jastrzembska ZS (eds): Proceedings of the Conference on New Approaches to the Evaluation of Blind Persons. New York, American Foundation for the Blind, 1970, pp 104-110

28. Davis CJ: New developments in the intelligence testing of blind children, in Clark LL, Jastrzembska ZS (eds): Proceedings of the Conference on New Approaches to the Evaluation of Blind Persons. New York, American Foundation for the Blind, 1970, pp 83-92

29. Tillman MH: The performance of blind and sighted children on the Wechsler Intelligence Scale for Children: Study II. International Journal for the Education of the Blind 16:106-112, 1967

30. Tillman MH: Intelligence scales for the blind: A review with implications for research. Journal of School Psychology 11:80-87, 1973

31. Newland TE: The Blind Learning Aptitude Test. New York, American Foundation for the Blind, 1961, pp 40-51

7
The Multihandicapped
Visually Impaired Child

The interest in the health and welfare of the chronically handicapped has increased during recent years in the Western world. Life-threatening acute infections have declined dramatically and the birth rate has fallen; thus, physicians gradually had more time to spend with the chronically ill. The emphasis in health care is slowly shifting from the acutely ill to the chronically handicapped.

Fewer handicapped infants are born today than 20 or 30 years ago because of the reduced birth rate. Maternal and neonatal care have significantly improved and many newborns are healthy who formerly would have been adversely affected by abnormal prenatal or birth events. On the other hand, medical care now prolongs and saves the lives of many severely handicapped infants who in the past would have died. Thus, a great number of prenatally affected infants with major central nervous system dysmorphogenesis, mental retardation, cerebral palsy, or optic atrophy survive. The end result, as was pointed out in chapter 4, is that the prevalence of blindness in childhood has been increasing, while the incidence of congenital blindness after the retrolental fibroplasia era has remained substantially unchanged.

STUDIES OF MULTIHANDICAPPED VISUALLY IMPAIRED CHILDREN

The increasing concern for the health, welfare, and education of multihandicapped blind children has led to many surveys, especially during the last 10 years. These studies were of great value since they identified many problems which now face professionals. Not surprisingly,

71

some of the results varied greatly, but they all revealed the same conclusion: the majority of blind children are multihandicapped.

The prevalence of other handicaps is lower in studies that surveyed residential blind schools,[1,2] or in earlier reports when the incidence of retrolental fibroplasia was higher. The results tended to be inaccurate when mail questionnaires were used,[3,4] and more reliable when a team studied certain segments of the blind population.[5] Definitions and categorization of handicaps also vary from study to study, which makes comparisons difficult. Some studies involved a certain age group;[6] others were focused on children with one type of ocular disorder.[7,8,9]

THE MULTIDISCIPLINARY TEAM APPROACH

The high proportion of other handicaps among blind children has influenced their education, medical care, and the services provided for them by agencies.

In recent years, there have been more multihandicapped visually impaired students in schools for the blind all across North America.[3,10] More blind students without additional disabilities are being educated with the sighted as a result of integration, and more of the multihandicapped stay in residential schools since they are harder, on the average, to integrate. They are also more acceptable now to most residential schools. It is obvious that these schools can provide better services for their multihandicapped students if they are located near medical centers.[10] Unfortunately, many are situated where they have difficulty attracting a multidisciplinary staff who can provide comprehensive and essential services. Residential schools require many professionally trained staff besides teachers, such as ophthalmologists, psychologists, physio-, speech and occupational therapists, pediatric neurologists, psychiatrists, otologists, and various other medical specialists. The evaluation of a multihandicapped blind child is similar to solving a puzzle when one or two pieces are missing—the picture is unclear. It is not possible to determine the individual's potential unless the full extent of his handicaps, detailed social information, and the degree and quality of stimulation to which he has been exposed are known.

There is a need, therefore, for a multidisciplinary team approach to the evaluation and treatment of blind children. To function in a team requires practice. The availability of the same personnel is important since too few ophthalmologists, neurologists, and psychologists have seen enough multihandicapped blind children to understand them. It goes without saying that the child's health and education are closely related. But sometimes conflicts do develop between educators, who view the school as strictly an educational setting, and the health team, who emphasize the importance of health. Evaluation and treatment are, of course, time-consuming and teachers may not appreciate the removal of children from their classes for prolonged periods of time. Barriers must be broken down between professions.

The increased concern for visually impaired multihandicapped children has also significantly influenced the function of agencies. The coordination of care is sometimes very difficult as it is not unusual to have a multihandicapped blind child who is served by four or five different agencies. There is increasing awareness that existing models of health care fail to bring together the professional personnel or other resources to meet the needs of children with multiple handicaps. Society has responded to this lack with the development of interdisciplinary facilities in an attempt to provide coordinated care for children and their families. Diagnostic and treatment centers have been introduced in Europe and North America. Agencies working with blind children must make increasing efforts to communicate better with educators and health professionals.

MENTAL RETARDATION

The precise definitions of mental subnormality are of importance in research as well as being essential for making practical decisions. The present vagueness makes comparisons between studies difficult because of the different intelligence ranges and criteria used in the samples. Although there are many classification systems of mental retardation, that of the American Association on Mental Deficiency (AAMD)[11] is being used more and more in research. It has five levels of intelligence. On the Stanford-Binet scale, the intelligence ranges corresponding to these levels are as follows: (5) *borderline* (1-2 standard deviations [SDs] below the mean), 83-68; (4) *Mild* (2-3 SDs below the mean), 67-52; (3) *moderate* (3-4 SDs below the mean), 51-36; (2) *severe* (4-5 SDs below the mean), 35-20; (1) *profound* (more than 5 SDs below the mean), less than 20.

Furthermore, the AAMD uses another classification system for the etiology of mental retardation: (1) infection; (2) intoxication; (3) trauma or physical agent; (4) disorders of metabolism, growth or nutrition; (5) new growths; (6) (unknown) prenatal influence; (7) unknown or uncertain cause with structural reactions manifest. The vast majority of children with mental retardation in the general population fall into the borderline or mild categories and, in most, the etiology is unknown. However, in most cases of severe or profound mental retardation, there is evidence of brain abnormality on postmortem examination. The prevalence of mental retardation in the general population varies somewhat from study to study. On the Isle of Wight, the overall prevalence for the subnormal (IQ of 70 or less) is 2.5 percent.[12] Pilling has summarized the current research on mental retardation,[13] and the interested reader should look up these references.

The prevalence of mental retardation is much higher among visually impaired children than in the general population and it ranges from 25[1] to 80 percent.[4] This discrepancy is due to the use of different definitions and to the fact that various segments of the blind population are surveyed, often with unreliable questionnaires. Visually impaired students in schools obviously have higher intelligence than blind children in institutions for the retarded. The prevalence rate of mental retardation (IQ below 80) in the total population of legally blind children is 24 percent.[14] As shown in chapter 4, the prevalence of mental retardation has been decreasing during the last 30 years, parallel to the reduction of additional handicaps in these children. The most likely reason for this is the improvement in pediatric medicine.[3,5] Mental retardation is the commonest additional impairment followed by hearing loss and seizures (Table 4-7).

The diagnosis of mental retardation in a child's life has major implications and yet many physicians reach such a conclusion after only a short office visit. The tragedy of many visually impaired children who were mistakenly diagnosed and placed in institutions for the retarded still lingers with us. Several examples of such misdiagnoses are reported in the literature.[15,16] but most teachers of the blind can vividly recall their own examples.

There are several reasons why the diagnosis of mental retardation is so difficult in blind children. The education of medical students is still centered around acute illness in hospitals and, consequently, many students are not exposed to chronic disabilities, such as visual impairment, until they are in practice. Many professionals incorrectly assume that blindness is almost invariably associated with mental retardation because the eyes develop from the brain, and with impaired eyes there must be damage to the brain. The presence of multiple congenital anomalies or other handicaps often misleads the physician into diagnosing mental subnormality, but this assumption is not always correct. Most importantly, however, professionals do not realize that, in contrast to the sighted, the blind child can appear pseudoretarded when lacking exposure to adequate opportunities to learn various skills. The totally blind must be taught even the simplest developmental skills, such as sitting, standing, jumping, and so on. If the congenitally blind child's development is delayed because of inadequate teaching and opportunities, hypotonia is also often present, which may result from lack of physical activity. Furthermore, the electroencephalograms of visually impaired children are normally different from those of the sighted. Physicians, even neurologists who have not been exposed to blindness, may easily diagnose mental retardation in such a child with delayed development, hypotonia, and "abnormal EEG." It is even worse if young blind children are hospitalized for an evaluation because they often temporarily regress in their development. If the diagnosis is incorrect, untold suffering, irreparable damage, and anxiety are brought to the child and his family. Parents will never forget such a mistake.

When the degree of subnormality is profound, the neurological examination is typically markedly abnormal and, together with various medical investigations, the diagnosis of mental retardation can be safely made at almost any age. However, if the subnormality is mild or moderate, the diagnosis should only be made after 2½ to 3 years of age, a multidisciplinary evaluation, an adequate program and satisfactory follow-up. The psychological examination of the visually impaired is difficult. Psychologists who have had little previous experience testing the blind often over- or underestimate abilities. Children with marked stereotyped mannerisms are at risk of having their intelligence underestimated and more so if, in addition, they show behavioral problems.

Certain types of ocular pathology are frequently associated with mental retardation. The majority of children with congenital optic atrophy (other than familial) are subnormal in their intelligence.[9] Glaucoma occurring in boys should suggest the diagnosis of Lowe syndrome which often includes profound mental retardation. On the other hand, children blinded by bilateral retinoblastomas almost always have superior intelligence, even when they are compared to their sibs. This is a fascinating and well-documented but unexplained phenomenon.[17,18] Children with cataracts, whether due to congenital rubella syndrome or hereditary factors, should be considered to have average intelligence until proven otherwise.

The mentally retarded blind child was educationally neglected in the past and often left in a "no man's land." He was not committed to an institution nor did he receive a satisfactory education. Those who were in institutions for the retarded sometimes received a training program, all too often one of questionable value. A change in attitudes occurred in the 1940s, when visually impaired retarded children were more and more accepted into special classes within schools for the blind. Fortunately, the hopeless attitude toward the subnormal blind is gradually disappearing.

CEREBRAL PALSY

The term *cerebral palsy* literally means "paralysis of the cerebrum." Several definitions have been formulated and most include references to an abnormal orthopedic or neurological condition due to brain damage before, during, or after birth that results in a particular sensorimotor disability.[19] The American Academy for Cerebral Palsy classifies cerebral palsy in the following groups: (1) spasticity, (2) athetosis, (3) rigidity, (4) ataxia, (5) tremor, (6) atonia, and (7) mixed.

The prevalence of cerebral palsy in the general population lies between one and two per thousand, and the majority are spastic in type. The etiology is variable and includes any disorder which can inflict brain damage before, during, and after birth. However, in more than one-third of cases, there is no known cause. It is not a progressive neurological condition. Children with cerebral palsy tend to be multi-handicapped, and the majority have ocular problems as well. There is no medical cure and the treatment includes physiotherapy, orthopedic surgery, and management of various associated problems. Each child must be handled individually. There are many fine articles and books on this subject, and the interested reader is referred to these.[19-21]

Approximately 6 to 15 percent of blind children have cerebral palsy.[3,4,14] Spastic quadriplegia, the commonest type, is frequently accompanied by optic atrophy or optic nerve hypoplasia.[9] Most of these children are profoundly retarded and also have seizures. Spastic diplegia, which is usually associated with prematurity, is occasionally seen in children with retrolental fibroplasia. The muscle tone is characteristically increased more in the legs than in the arms, but sometimes the degree of this neuromuscular disorder is so minimal that only the heelcords are tight. This is one major reason why some children with retrolental fibroplasia walk or run on tiptoes, which is sometimes mistakenly thought of as a stereotyped blind mannerism. Individuals with spastic diplegia generally have average intelligence, in contrast to those with spastic quadriplegia. Children with optic nerve hypoplasia who have cerebral palsy frequently have evidence of major central nervous system anomalies which commonly include porencephalic cysts.[9] Studies of spastic children have commonly revealed an impairment of recognizing objects by touch (stereognosis). Spasticity and blindness are a bad combination since, through touch, the "hands of the blind are his eyes."

Visually impaired cerebral palsied children in schools for the blind and public schools were surveyed,[22] but most are in institutions for the retarded. Residential schools for the blind are often unable to take these children because the schools lack trained personnel and specialized equipment and also because of the low mental ability of most such applicants.

SPECIFIC LEARNING DISABILITIES

There is an enormous volume of literature on specific learning disability, which by some estimates may occur in 5 to 10 percent of school children, depending on the definition used. There is no satisfactory or uniformly accepted definition of learning disability because of the complexity of the learning process.[20]

Blind children may also have learning disabilities, but the incidence is unknown. Psychological testing of the severely visually impaired is difficult, especially if they are multihandicapped. We have observed children who were known to have a specific learning disability prior to losing their sight, and they continued to have it while using Braille. In fact, learning Braille may be more difficult than print for blind children who have certain types of learning disability.

There is a current belief, among some practitioners, that minor refractive errors and muscle imbalance can cause reading and writing disorders. A number of workers have proposed that reading difficulties are due to defects in binocular coordination or mixed ocular dominance. We feel this belief is incorrect and, in fact, refractive errors and various squints, which are common in school age children, do not exist in any greater degree in children with reading problems than in other children.[23] Schain summarizes the major studies done in this area and concludes:

> If there is evidence of squint, heterophoria, eyestrain or headache after close work, an ophthalmologist should be consulted. It should not be expected, however, that these measures will reverse or prevent reading disorders in susceptible children.[24]

Although visual impairment does not cause a learning disability, it can interfere with the process of learning, and this will be discussed in a subsequent chapter.

EPILEPSY

The prevalence of epilepsy in the general population is between 0.5 and 1.0 percent. It is primarily a disorder of infancy and childhood since, in 50 percent of these individuals, the seizures appear prior to the age of 3 and, in 90 percent, before the age of 20 years. By definition, a seizure is a symptom of paroxysmal cerebral dysfunction, the consequence of an excessive neuronal discharge. It is beyond the scope of this book to describe the various types of seizures and their treatment. There are many excellent references in medical libraries.

Visually impaired children frequently have seizures[3,4,14] (6.6 to 14 percent), which is not surprising since brain damage is more commonly seen among the blind than the sighted.

In many respects, epilepsy is a dual handicap because of society's adverse attitudes toward it. Therefore, physicians must devote more time to the education and guidance of the family. Associated emotional disturbances are common in youngsters with seizures, and the convulsive disorder tends to increase the risk of psychiatric disorder.[12] Parents may have an intense feeling of guilt that they are responsible for the child's convulsive disorder, although, in the majority of cases, it is not caused by inherited factors. They may be ashamed and hide this information but teachers, school counselors, and others involved ought to know and be well prepared for the possible occurrence of a convulsion. Children with epilepsy may participate in almost any sport under supervision. The visually impaired do not have one specific variety of seizure but all types occur (just like the sighted) and, with appropriate medication, the majority can be controlled. Furthermore, many children "outgrow" their convulsive disorder as their brain matures.

The EEGs of normal blind children are different from those of the sighted. This subject is discussed in detail in chapter 12. However, this difference in the electrical activity of the brain does not predispose them to seizures.

PSYCHIATRIC DISORDERS

The incidence of psychiatric disorders in visually impaired children ranges from 17[4] to 49 percent[25] or more. This topic will be discussed in more detail in a later chapter.

SPEECH AND LANGUAGE DISORDERS

These are described in detail in chapter 10.

HEARING LOSS

The prevalence of hearing loss among visually impaired children is around 10 percent.[14] This high rate is due to the fact that the majority of blind children with congenital rubella have a hearing impairment (Table 4-7). It is beyond the scope of this book to discuss the diagnosis and management of deafness, but a separate chapter will deal with the deaf-blind child.

MINIMAL BRAIN DYSFUNCTION

In recent years, the diagnosis of minimal brain dysfunction (MBD) became a popular term for describing children with hyperactivity, short attention span, easy distractibility, certain behavior disorders, poor coordination, learning disabilities, minimal abnormalities of neurological examination and EEGs, or with a scatter of abilities on their psychological tests, and so on. Minimal brain dysfunction has been defined by a national task force as a state descriptive of

children of near average, average or above average general intelligence with certain learning and/or behavioural disabilities ranging from mild to severe which are associated with deviations of function of the central nervous system. These deviations may manifest themselves by various combinations of impairment in perception, conceptualization, language, memory and control of attention, impulse or motor function.[26] (p. 9-10)*

Initially, these children were often said to have "minimal brain damage." The degree of brain damage, however, has no relationship to the symptoms; certain patients with marked central nervous system pathology do not have the above-described problems[27] while others who have no central nervous system pathology may have marked similar difficulties. For this reason, the term was dropped and now these children are labeled with the diagnosis of minimal brain dysfunction.

Almost any child with minor behavioral and developmental deviations could fit into this medical diagnosis because the definition of the syndrome is so vague. Children with the diagnosis of MBD are not a homogeneous group and their management varies markedly from one individual to another. Thus it is more meaningful to specify problems such as poor coordination, hyperactivity, learning disorders, etc., than to use a medical label which is meaningless by itself. In fact, such labels could harm the child in the long run. Many teachers wrongly assume that, if children are diagnosed as having MBD or minimal brain damage, nothing can be done for them, or else there should be a specific treatment (e.g., drugs) or educational approach.

Unfortunately, attempts have been made to label blind children with the diagnosis of MBD.[28] Visually impaired children without central nervous system pathology can show minimal abnormalities on their neurological examinations, such as hypotonia, reduced muscle strength, poor coordination, and abnormal gait patterns and posture. The blind child's EEG normally differs from that of the sighted, and usually he has some scatter on the subtests of psychological tests, which is more noticeable if, in his environment, he has been exposed to uneven learning opportunities. Thus, in a blind child, the diagnosis of MBD is hazardous and usually unhelpful.

CONCLUSIONS

1. The emphasis in health care is slowly shifting from the acutely ill to the chronically handicapped.
2. The increasing concern about the multihandicapped blind is reflected in the literature.

---

*We do not wish to recommend this definition as valid or helpful, however.

3. There is a need for a multidisciplinary team approach to the evaluation and treatment of blind children.
4. The diagnosis of mental retardation in blind children is difficult and misdiagnoses are still frequent.
5. Cerebral palsy and profound visual impairment is a bad combination.
6. Visual impairment alone does not predispose to a specific learning disability.
7. The EEGs of normal blind children are different from those of the sighted, but this difference in electrical activity of the brain does not predispose them to seizures.
8. The diagnosis of minimal brain dysfunction in the visually impaired is hazardous and generally unhelpful.

REFERENCES

1. Wolf JM: The Blind Child with Concomitant Disabilities. Research Series No 16. New York, American Foundation for the Blind, 1967
2. Keet SJ: A survey of blindness and partial sight in the Atlantic provinces. First National Multidisciplinary Conference on Blind Children, Vancouver, Canada, 1974, pp. 22–38.
3. Lowenfeld B: Multihandicapped blind and deaf-blind children in California. Research Bulletin No. 19. New York, American Foundation for the Blind, 1969, pp. 1–72.
4. Graham MD: Multiply-Impaired Blind Children: A National Problem. New York, American Foundation for the Blind, 1968
5. Jan JE, Robinson GC, Scott E: A multidisciplinary approach to the problems of the multihandicapped blind child. Can Med Assoc J 109:705–707, 1973
6. Norris M, Spaulding P, Brodie F: Blindness in Children. Chicago, University of Chicago Press, 1957
7. Cohen J, Alfano JE, Boshes LD, et al: Clinical evaluation of school aged children with retrolental fibroplasia. Am J Ophthalmol 57:41–57, 1964
8. Boshes LD, Cohen J, Alfano JE, et al: Longitudinal appraisal of school-age children with retrolental fibroplasia. Dis Nerv Syst 28:221–230, 1967
9. Jan JE, Robinson GC, Kinnis C, et al: Blindness due to optic nerve atrophy and hypoplasia in children. An epidemiological study (1944–1974). Dev Med Child Neurol (in press)
10. Cruickshank WM: The multiple-handicapped child and courageous action. International Journal for the Education of the Blind 13:65–75, 1964
11. Heber R: A manual on terminology and classification in mental retardation. Am J Ment Def 64 (monograph suppl 2):1–111, 1959
12. Rutter M, Graham P, Yule W: A Neuropsychiatric Study in Childhood. Clinics in Developmental Medicine Nos 35/36. London, Heinemann, 1970
13. Pilling D: The Handicapped Child—Research Review. Studies in Child Development Series. London, Longman, 1973, Vol 3
14. Robinson GC: Epidemiological studies of congenital and acquired blindness

in blind children born in British Columbia—1944-1973. First National Multidisciplinary Conference on Blind Children, Vancouver, Canada, 1974, pp 1-21

15. Williams CE: A blind idiot who became a normal blind adolescent. Dev Med Child Neurol 8:166-169, 1966

16. Gruber KF, Moor PM (eds): No Place to Go. New York, American Foundation for the Blind, 1963

17. Levitt EA, Rosenbaum AL, Willerman L, et al: Intelligence of retinoblastoma patients and their siblings. Child Dev 43:939-948, 1972

18. Thurrell RJ, Josephson TS: Retinoblastoma and intelligence. Psychosomatics 7:368-370, 1966

19. Wolf JM, Anderson RM: The Multiply Handicapped Child: An Overview. Springfield, Ill, Charles C Thomas, 1969

20. Dinnage R: The Handicapped Child—Research Review. Studies in Child Development Series. London, Longman, 1970, Vol 1

21. Christensen E, Melchior J: Cerebral Palsy—A Clinical and Neuropathological Study. Clinics in Developmental Medicine No 25. London, Heinemann, 1967

22. Long EH: The Challenge of the Cerebral Palsied Blind Child. New York, American Foundation for the Blind, 1952

23. Park GE: Functional dyslexia (reading failures) vs. normal reading. Eye Ear Nose Throat Mon 45:74-80, 1966

24. Schain RJ: Neurology of Childhood Learning Disorders. Baltimore, Williams & Wilkins Co, 1972, pp 111-112

25. Buckman FG: Multiple-handicapped blind children. International Journal for the Education of the Blind 15:46-49, 1965

26. Clements SD: Minimal Brain Dysfunction in Children. Publications No 1415. US Public Health Services, 1966

27. Crome L, Stern J: Pathology of Mental Retardation, (ed 2). Edinburgh, Churchill Livingstone, 1972, pp 184-185

28. Arbit J: Evaluation of the minimal brain damage syndrome in blind children, in Clark LL, Jastrzembska ZS (eds): Proceedings of the Conference on New Approaches to the Evaluation of Blind Persons. New York, American Foundation for the Blind, 1970

W. G. Pearce

8
Genetic Ocular Disease in Children and Adolescents

During the past decade ophthalmologists, government agencies, various foundations, and university ophthalmology departments have gradually become aware of the sizable contribution that genetically determined ocular disorders make to childhood blindness. In England, Wales[1] and Australia[2] hereditary disease is responsible for about 50 percent of blindness in children; in Cyprus[3] and Lebanon[4] between 75 and 80 percent is due to genetic causes. Canadian studies have also indicated that genetic disorders are an important cause of profound visual impairment in children despite some regional variation between the eastern provinces, where 57 percent of blindness was genetic in origin,[5] and the western region, where it was 33 percent.[6] The importance of genetic ocular disease is also discussed in chapter 4.

Many of these studies were not truly representative of the blind population as a whole since they were carried out in schools for blind children and therefore excluded those who were ineducable or in the preschool age group. Despite this deficiency, there is no doubt about the importance of genetic eye disease as a cause of blindness in many areas of the world today. In each of the areas surveyed, the commonest genetic disturbance responsible for the disorder was an abnormal single gene either appearing as a new mutation or segregating within a family in a clearly definable pattern.

Recognition of the significant contribution that blindness of genetic origin makes to the blind population as a whole is the first step toward the establishment of procedures whereby such persons can be helped and advised by those responsible for providing all aspects of medical and social care. The above statistics reveal that children with severe visual impairment have at least a 50 percent chance of the disorder being genetic in origin. It is understandable that those ophthalmologists who have training in and knowledge of genetic eye disease are more likely to recognize disorders of a hereditary nature and are therefore better equipped to deal with the patient who presents with a possible or probable genetic ocular disorder. Satisfactory management will include consideration of the following.

SPECIFIC DIAGNOSIS

Many genetic ocular disorders pose little or no problem in diagnosis to the ophthalmologist. These include such conditions as infantile glaucoma, congenital cataract, and retinoblastoma. Others, however, are more difficult to diagnose and often require further investigation before the site of involvement and the nature of the disorder are clearly determined. These include, for example, lesions of the visual pathways, various types of congenital nystagmus, and several chorioretinal dystrophies. A list of investigations that might be indicated for this latter group of patients would include electroretinography, electro-oculography, dark adaptometry, visual field determination, visually evoked responses (VERs), color-vision testing, fluorescein fundus angiography, chromosome analysis, biochemistry of urine and blood samples, biopsy, and histochemistry.

Despite having such an impressive array of investigative techniques, a recent study of causes of blindness in Canadian children revealed that approximately 20 percent of the registered diagnoses were of the nonspecific type.[7] Without an accurate diagnosis, it was not possible to state whether the disturbance was of environmental or genetic origin. If a child is encountered in whom a specific diagnosis has not been made, no effort should be spared to answer this question, including referral to a major center with recognized expertise in solving such problems.

A correct diagnosis applied to a particular ocular disease will sometimes be sufficient evidence alone that one is dealing with a hereditary disorder. Conditions such as bilateral retinoblastoma, albinism, and lattice dystrophy of the cornea are examples of disorders that are 100 percent genetically determined. Nevertheless, the examiner should be sure that he is not dealing with a disorder that mimics retinoblastoma (pseudoglioma), that simulates a number of the features of albinism (congenital nystagmus), or that could be due to an environmentally determined corneal disease (phlyctenular keratitis).

Many other disorders lack the certainty of being wholly genetic in origin. Fraser and Friedmann showed that 90 percent of chorioretinal dystrophies, 40 percent of congenital cataracts, and only 10 percent of optic-atrophy cases were genetic in origin.[1] In this situation further clarification is necessary. Answers to questions such as, What is the functional impairment and clinical appearance of the chorioretinal dystrophy? What particular region of the lens is involved in the congenital cataract? or What are the visual field characteristics of the optic atrophy? are usually required before one can confidently conclude that the origin of the disorder is genetic. Occasionally, it may not be possible on clinical or laboratory evidence to state whether the condition is of genetic or environmental origin. In these situations, a search of the patients' relatives for similarly affected members may provide the support necessary to conclude that the disorder is genetic in nature.

FAMILY INVESTIGATION

This will require the drawing up of a pedigree and the examination of relatives which, when completed, often provides the pattern of inheritance.

A patient's word concerning which of his relatives are affected is valuable as a guide to who must be examined but cannot be accepted as accurate without confirmation. In some instances a history indicates that additional members of the family are affected with the particular disorder being investigated, but on clinical examination they are found to have entirely unrelated problems. Sometimes the problem is refractive; in other cases, it may be due to a nongenetic disorder.

Under ideal circumstances, examinations should take place in the ophthalmologist's office or in eye centers located close to the family being investigated. Attempts to detect the minimal phenotypic effects of autosomal dominant disorders or to discern the variable manifestations in carriers of X-linked genetic disease are not well served by perfunctory examinations in the family's kitchen or sitting room, where other interested family members and neighbors are often drawn to watch and comment on the examinations being carried out.

As a general rule, first-degree relatives are always examined. In addition, those more distant relations in whom there is the slightest suspicion of involvement should also be approached for an eye examination. Social workers, agency field staff, and public health nurses can be of considerable assistance in making contacts and in gaining cooperation of possibly affected relatives.

MEDICAL SUPERVISION

The responsibility for medical supervision lies with the ophthalmologist when the patient's genetic disorder is primarily ocular in nature. He or she will initiate treatment when it is required for those disorders susceptible to medical or surgical therapy. This will include such diverse conditions as retinoblastoma, congenital cataracts, dislocated lenses, corneal opacities, and congenital glaucoma. Even if the disorder is not treatable by any of the present methods available, the ophthalmologist can provide information about the progress of the disorder, the value of visual aids, what activities should be avoided or undertaken, etc. This group will include such disorders as microphthalmia, retinitis pigmentosa, hereditary optic atrophy, and albinism. Follow-up examination of these patients every year or two gives the ophthalmologist an opportunity to reassess their visual status, keep informed of their achievements, and provide them with more recent information concerning their conditions.

GENETIC COUNSELING

Genetic counseling is the provision of information on the risks of recurrence to individuals from a family in whom one or more members is affected by a genetically determined disorder.

Before proceeding, it is imperative that the disorder has been correctly diagnosed, its genetic origin recognized, and its pattern or segregation within the family determined. Failure to follow these guidelines has occurred in the past, resulting in inaccurate counseling for the individual and his or her family. The similarity of many environmentally determined ocular disorders to those of genetic origin is well recognized, such as the macular scars of toxoplasmosis (maternal infection) and hereditary macular coloboma (dominant inheritance). In addition, similarity within the genetic group of disorders (genetic heterogeneity) can also be a source of inaccurate counsel. It is not impossible to confuse achondroplasia (autosomal dominant) with Down's syndrome (chromosomal abnormality), Marfan's syndrome (autosomal dominant) with homocystinuria (autosomal recessive), or choroideremia (X-linked recessive) with degenerative myopia (polygenic inheritance). On the other hand, careful precounsel investigation and assessment will usually identify certain genetic mechanisms responsible for these disorders and thus prevent misdiagnosis.

Chromosomal Abnormalities

Major chromosomal abnormalities in number of structure of whole or partial chromosomes produce severe systemic effects which, aside from Down's syndrome, usually lead to death during infancy or early childhood. In these disorders, the generalized and neurological disturbances are of greater importance than the accompanying ocular malformations. However, some rare chromosomal abnormalities have been found in which a major eye defect has been associated with less pronounced mental and physical disturbances.[8,9] Despite this, the number of cases of chromosomal abnormalities encountered by an ophthalmologist is minute compared to those disorders arising from other genetic mechanisms.

Polygenic Inheritance

Many of an individual's features—such as height, intelligence, and blood pressure—are due to the additive effects of many genes rather than the specific action of one gene.[10] Systemic disorders due to polygenic inheritance include such diverse conditions as hypertension, congenital pyloric stenosis, cleft lip, and congenital hip dislocation.[11,12] In the eye, disorders affecting the state of refraction, such as myopia and hyperopia, some types of glaucoma, and certain forms of strabismus, have been shown to be due to the effect of many genes.[13-15] However, when pedigrees are charted and relatives examined, a pattern of inheritance often appears that simulates one or other of the patterns of single mutant gene inheritance.[16] As a result, many publications in the past relating to these disorders reported incorrect hereditary mechanisms. Since this feature is recognized today, disorders due to polygenic inheritance only present infrequently for genetic assessment, although they contribute a not insubstantial number to the total blind population in Canada.[17]

Single-Gene Inheritance

The vast majority of genetic ocular diseases are due to the effect of a single mutant gene. Figures from the studies previously referred to relate primarily to single-gene disorders. These conditions make such a large contribution to ophthalmic disease that during the past 10 or 15 years a number of ophthalmic textbooks have appeared dealing with this subject.[18-22] The mechanism of transmission of these deleterious genes are well known as autosomal dominant, autosomal recessive, and X-linked, under which headings they are categorized. McKusick, in his catalogue of single-gene disorders in man, lists 1142 certain single-gene disorders.[23] Over 150 of these show a major abnormality affecting the eye or periorbital regions. Many of these have a serious affect on visual function, while others are characterized by structural abnormalities of the eye or periorbital region. The end of this chapter includes a list of those single-gene disorders encountered in ambulant patients under 20 years of age (Table 8-1). In many instances, the clinical manifestations are present at birth or develop in early childhood; in a considerable number, the effects of the abnormal gene are first detected in late

Table 8-1
Single-Gene Disorders Affecting Vision or Ocular and Periocular Structures in Children and Adolescents*

Site	Autosomal Dominant	Autosomal Recessive	X-Linked
GLOBE	Coloboma/microphthalmos Oculodentodigital dysplasia (microphthalmos)	Anophthalmos	
EYELIDS	Blepharophimosis + ptosis + epicanthus inversus		
EXTRAOCULAR MUSCLES	Familial ophthalmoplegia		Congenital nystagmus External ophthalmoplegia + myopia
PERIORBITAL TISSUES	Crouzon's craniofacial dysostosis (exophthalmos + hypertelorism + exotropia) Collins' mandibulofacial dysostosis (antimongoloid slant + lower eyelid coloboma) Waardenburg's syndrome (lateral displacement of medial canthi and lacrimal puncta)		
CORNEA	Corneal dystrophies—many forms	Corneal dystrophies—several forms	Fabry's disease (corneal dystrophy) Megalocornea
ANGLE OF AC	Aniridia Juvenile glaucoma	Congenital glaucoma (buphthalmos)	

*Where a named syndrome is given, the major ocular feature(s) follow in parentheses.

Table 8-1
(Continued)

Site	Autosomal Dominant	Autosomal Recessive	X-Linked
LENS	Rieger's syndrome (angle dysgenesis) Congenital cataract—many forms Ectopia lentis Marfan's syndrome (ectopia lentis) Alport's syndrome (anterior lenticonus)	Congenital cataract—several forms Homocystinuria (ectopia lentis) Werner's syndrome (adolescent cataracts) Marinesco-Sjögren syndrome (congenital cataracts) Rothmund-Thomson syndrome (juvenile cataracts) Weill-Marchesani syndrome (spherophakia)	Congenital cataract—few forms Lowe's syndrome (congenital cataract)
RETINA	Progressive Arthro-ophthalmopathy (myopia + retinal detachment) Wagner's hyaloideo-retinal degeneration Vitelliform macular dystrophy Congenital night blindness Bilateral retinoblastoma Retinitis pigmentosa Spondyloepiphyseal dysplasia (myopia + retinal detachment)	Albinism type I (complete) and type II (incomplete) Leber's congenital amaurosis Stargardt's macular dystrophy Gyrate chorioretinal atrophy Favre's hyaloidoretinal tapeto-retinal degeneration Pseudoxanthoma elasticum (angioid streaks) Retinitis pigmentosa Complete achromatopsia	Ocular albinism Choroideremia Incomplete achromatopsia Partial color blindness (protan and deutan) Myopia + night blindness Norrie's disease (pseudoglioma) Retinitis pigmentosa Juvenile retinoschisis

Table 8-1
(Continued)

Site	Autosomal Dominant	Autosomal Recessive	X-Linked
OPTIC NERVE	Optic atrophy—congenital and juvenile	Optic atrophy—congenital and infantile	Leber's optic atrophy†
CNS & EYE	Neurofibromatosis (optic nerve glioma, exophthalmos, glaucoma)	Cerebral lipofuscinosis/juvenile amaurotic idiocy (maculocerebral degeneration)	
	Olivopontocerebellar atrophy with retinal degeneration (macular or peripheral)	Retinitis pigmentosa	
	Tuberous sclerosis (retinal astrocytomas)	Laurence-Moon-Bardet-Biedl syndrome (retinitis pigmentosa)	
	von Hippel-Lindau syndrome (retinal angiomatosis)	Cockayne's syndrome (retinitis pigmentosa)	
		Refsum's syndrome (retinitis pigmentosa)	
		Usher's syndrome (retinitis pigmentosa)	
		Abetalipoproteinemia (retinitis pigmentosa)	

†The inheritance of Leber's optic atrophy resembles that of X-linked disorders but does not fulfill all criteria. There is no transmission from affected males to their daughters, while most if not all sisters of affected males are carriers and transmit the trait to both sons and daughters.[25]

childhood or early adolescence; while in the remainder the clinical onset is not until the later teenage years.

AUTOSOMAL DOMINANT INHERITANCE.

Disorders transmitted by this mechanism include bilateral retinoblastoma, most forms of congenital cataracts, the coloboma/microphthalmos group, and Marfan's syndrome (Table 8-1). These are disorders in which there is an abnormal gene on one member of a chromosome pair, while the gene at that locus on the other member (allele) is normal. When two different alleles are present, the individual is said to be *heterozygous* and, in dominant autosomal inheritance, there is clinical expression of the abnormal gene. Minimal criteria for acceptance of autosomal dominant inheritance for the usual mating of one homozygous normal parent and one heterozygous affected parent are (1) The disorder is transmitted to 50 percent of the children (on the average); and (2) there are equal numbers of affected males and females (on the average).

Usually each individual who inherits the deleterious gene will express it as a relatively consistent ocular abnormality, as occurs in congenital cataracts. Problems arise when an individual from a family wherein an autosomal dominant condition is segregating shows no clinical effect but is known to possess the abnormal gene by virtue of having had affected children.

In these circumstances, the clinical expression (phenotype) is normal, yet the individual is known to possess the abnormal gene (genotype). In such an individual, the abnormal gene is said to be nonpenetrant. Numerous pedigrees have been compiled showing skipping of a generation in certain autosomal dominant conditions, such as bilateral retinoblastoma and coloboma/microphthalmos. When such pedigrees are found, the trait is said to show reduced penetrance. In this situation, counseling an affected member that there is a 50 percent chance of each offspring being affected is relatively straightforward. Providing information to an unaffected brother or sister is more complicated, as some unaffected sibs can be expected to have the abnormal genotype but not show evidence of it and so are at risk of producing affected children.

An additional problem occurs when counseling apparently normal members of a family among whom an autosomal dominant condition is segregating. Careful examination may reveal a minor degree of abnormality that was initially not considered to be a manifestation of the hereditary disorder. This variability in expression of the abnormal gene is not infrequently encountered and is considered to be due to the modifying effects of the normal allele and other genes on the chromosome. Such findings markedly alter the risk estimates of that individual bearing affected children.[24]

AUTOSOMAL RECESSIVE INHERITANCE.

Disorders transmitted by this mechanism include generalized albinism, anophthalmos, Leber's congenital amaurosis, and many cases of retinitis pigmentosa (Table 8-1). These are disorders in which the clinical picture is due to the expression of identically abnormal genes located at the same site (locus) on *both* members of a chromosome pair. The individual is said to be *homozygous* at that particular gene locus. Affected children have received one member of the abnormal gene pair from *each* of the parents who are usually carriers of the disorder (rather than being affected) and who therefore are *heterozygous* at that particular gene locus.

Minimal criteria for acceptance of autosomal recessive inheritance for the usual mating of two phenotypically normal but heterozygous parents are (1) The disorder is transmitted to 25 percent of children (on the average); and (2) there are equal numbers of affected males and females. Counseling such parents that there is a 25 percent chance of having further affected children is straightforward when the children have a condition that is readily apparent at birth or during infancy, e.g., anophthalmos or albinism. Some conditions, however, do not manifest themselves until late childhood or adolescence, such as Stargardt's macular dystrophy or retinitis pigmentosa, by which time the family is often complete. An additional concern is that the younger, presently unaffected children are still at risk to develop the disorder.

Counseling persons affected with autosomal recessive disorders is generally based on the assumption that the homozygous but affected individual will have a spouse who is homozygous but with the normal alleles at that particular locus. All children of such a mating will be like the parents of the affected mother or father—heterozygous but unaffected. If marriage is contemplated to a distant relative in whom the likelihood of being a heterozygous carrier is much greater than in the general population, there is an increased risk of having an affected child. This feature of a high incidence of consanguineous marriages between parents of a child affected with an autosomal recessive disorder is well recognized.

X-LINKED INHERITANCE.

X-linked ocular disorders are less common than autosomal conditions and include juvenile retinoschisis, choroideremia, myopia with night blindness, and the well-known red/green color blindness (Table 8-1). Unlike autosomal disorders where males and females usually show a similar amount of gene effect, in X-linked disorders the clinical manifestation of the gene differs considerably as females have two X chromosomes while males have only one. In a man the effect of the gene is fully expressed as the other male sex chromosome—the Y chromosome—codes for little other than testicular development. The male is said to be *hemizygous* at that particular gene locus. The manifestation occurring in a female who is heterozygous for an X-linked disorder, i.e., who carries the abnormal gene on one of her two X chromosomes, depends on whether the abnormal gene product does or does not take precedence over the normal gene product. In those disorders where the former occurs, the inheritance is said to be X-linked *dominant,* while in the latter the inheritance is X-linked *recessive.* In a number of disorders, such as choroideremia and ocular albinism, there is a mixture of both normal and abnormal genes in heterozygous females wherein the term *intermediate X-linked inheritance* is often used.[25,26]

Criteria for acceptance of X-linked inheritance as the consequence of the mating of an affected male with a homozygous normal female are (1) all daughters are heterozygous carriers; and (2) there is no father-to-son transmission.

Criteria for acceptance of X-linked inheritance as the consequence of the mating of a heterozygous carrier female with a normal male are (1) 50 percent of sons are affected; (2) 50 percent of daughters are heterozygous carriers.

These criteria are true for what are referred to as X-linked recessives or intermediate X-linked inheritance. In those few disorders inherited as X-linked dominants, none of which, except certain forms of congenital nystagmus, primarily affects the eye, the criteria require modification. All daughters of affected males would themselves be affected while 50 percent of daughters of affected females would similarly be affected. There would be no change in the numbers of males affected. It can be seen that, in X-linked recessive inheritance, affected females are only rarely found, while in X-linked dominant conditions there is a marked preponderance of affected females.

Occasionally, with X-linked recessive inheritance, the disorder can "turn up" in males after two or three generations of being "hidden" in the unaffected female carrier. A classic example of this occurred with hemophilia among some European royal families who were descendants of Queen Victoria, a carrier of hemophilia.[10]

COMMENTS

It seems appropriate to indicate here that, as with many different groups of handicapped, the mating pattern of blind people is far from random. Visually impaired persons meet and associate together in schools, jobs, in their social lives, and in various organizations catering to their particular disability. It is often at schools for the blind that attachments develop, which not infrequently lead to marriage. Sooner or later a marriage occurs between two individuals who have identical genetic disorders. If both parents are affected with the same autosomal recessive disorder, all children would be expected to be affected. If both were affected with the same autosomal dominant condition, 25 percent of children would be affected homozygotes—a state which may be lethal to the zygote—while a further 50 percent would be affected heterozygotes, and only 25 percent would be normal. Few females in schools for the blind have X-linked disorders, so these comments apply particularly to autosomal conditions.

Because of the tendency to assortative mating, it would be of considerable benefit for blind high school students to know if their ocular disease was genetic in origin. Counseling could then be provided, which would be particularly valuable if marriage to another blind student was being contemplated. In such situations, joint counseling could be considered and, if both are visually impaired because of identical single-gene disorders, the much greater risk of affected children could be pointed out.

When presented with an explanation of how these recurrence-risk figures of 25 percent and 50 percent are derived from the type of hereditary pattern present, few persons have difficulty in understanding what has occurred and what is likely to occur. Furthermore, affected children, their parents, and other relatives are often anxious and pleased to obtain this kind of information, which can have such an important bearing on the manner in which they organize and plan their lives. Most affected individuals seem to draw a conclusion concerning future children that is based on the extent to which their own visual handicap affects their ability to function as they desire. In addition, patients with a risk of producing a severely visually handicapped child are in general more likely to be deterred from having further children than those in whom the risk is of a less severe visual defect. Studies elsewhere on the effectiveness of genetic clinics dealing with all types of hereditary disorders have shown that where the recurrence risk was in excess of one in ten, a greater number of couples were deterred from having further children than amongst those couples where the recurrence risk was less than one in ten.[27] It appears, then, that people will use restraint when provided with accurate information upon which to base their considerations.

Despite these statements, it is recognized that people differ considerably in their attitude to stated risk estimates and that this personal subjective interpretation affects their decisions. Related factors include the preconceived ideas patients entertain concerning the likelihood of having an affected child; whether or not they have already had an affected child; and the personality of the patients themselves, i.e., optimistic or pessimistic. All these phenomena influence to a greater or lesser extent the patient's decision with regard to having children.[28]

CONCLUSION

Professionals in all disciplines involved in providing assistance to visually handicapped young people should be aware of the sizable proportion who are blind from genetic eye disease and should encourage the referral of such patients to regional eye genetics centers where the necessary investigations and genetic counseling can be provided.

REFERENCES

1. Fraser GR, Friedmann AI: The Causes of Blindness in Childhood. Baltimore, Johns Hopkins Press, 1967
2. Fraser GR: The causes of severe visual handicap among school children in South Australia. Med J Aust 1:615-620, 1968.
3. Merin S, Lapithis AG, Horovitz D, et al: Childhood blindness in Cyprus. Am J Ophthalmol 74:538-542, 1972
4. Baghdassarian SA, Tabbara KF: Childhood blindness in Lebanon. Am J Ophthalmol 79:827-830, 1975
5. Keet SJ: A survey of blindness and partial sight in the Atlantic Provinces. First National Multidisciplinary Conference on Blind Children, Vancouver, Canada, 1974, pp 22-38
6. Robinson GC, Watt JA, Scott E: A study of congenital blindness in British Columbia: Methodology and medical findings. Can Med Assoc J 99:831-836, 1968
7. Pearce WG: The causes of blindness in children: An analysis of 1046 cases registered with the Canadian National Institute for the Blind. Can J Ophthalmol 10:469-472, 1975
8. Grace E, Drennan J, Colver D, et al: The 13q-deletion syndrome. J Med Genet 8:351-357, 1971
9. Smith DW: Recognizable Patterns of Human Malformation. Toronto, WB Saunders, 1970, pp 46-54
10. McKusick VA: Human Genetics. Englewood Cliffs, Prentice Hall, 1969, p 154
11. Carter CO: The genetics of congenital malformations. Proc R Soc Med 61:991-995, 1968
12. Carter CO: Polygenic inheritance and common disease. Lancet 1:1252-1256, 1969
13. Sorsby A, Fraser GR: Statistical note on the components of ocular refraction in twins. J Med Genet 1:47-49, 1964
14. Jay B, Paterson G: The genetics of simple glaucoma. Trans Ophthalmol Soc UK 90:161-171, 1970

15. Richter S: Untersuchungen Über die Heredität des Strabismus Concomitans. Abhandlungen aus dem Gebiete der Augenheilkunde, vol 35. Leipzig, Thieme, 1967

16. Edwards JH: The simulation of Mendelism. Acta Geneticae et Statistica Medica 10:63–70, 1960

17. McDonald AE: Causes of blindness in Canada—An analysis of 24,605 cases registered with the C.N.I.B. Can Med Assoc J 92:264–279, 1965

18. Deutman AF: The Hereditary Dystrophies of the Posterior Pole of the Eye. Assen, Netherlands, Royal Van Gorcum, 1971

19. Goldberg MF (ed): Genetic and Metabolic Eye Disease. Boston, Little Brown & Co, 1974

20. Krill AE: Hereditary Retinal and Choroidal Diseases. Hagerstown, Harper & Row, 1972, vol 1

21. Sorsby A: Ophthalmic Genetics, ed 2. London, Butterworths, 1970

22. Waardenburg PJ, Franceschetti A, Klein D: Genetics and Ophthalmology. Assen, Netherlands, Royal Van Gorcum, 1961, vols 1 & 2 1963

23. McKusick VA: Mendelian Inheritance in Man, ed 4. Baltimore, Johns Hopkins, 1975

24. Thomson JS, Thomson MW: Genetics in Medicine, ed 2. Philadelphia, Saunders, 1973, p 73

25. François J: Heredity in Ophthalmology. St Louis, CV Mosby Co, 1961, p 103

26. Lyon MF: Sex chromatin and gene action in the mammalian X-chromosome. Am J Hum Genet 14:135–148, 1962

27. Carter CO, Roberts JAF, Evans KA, et al: Genetic clinic: A follow-up. Lancet 1:281–285, 1971

28. Pearn JH: Patient's subjective interpretation of risks offered in genetic counselling. J Med Genet 10:129–134, 1973

In Cooperation with
M. E. Wilmot

9

Motor Development, Posture, and Physiotherapy

MOTOR DEVELOPMENT

The motor development of blind children is often said to be delayed, and the lag is not infrequently related to inadequate opportunities for learning provided by the parents. This is only partially true. The lack of vision has the greatest influence on the early stages of development. The degree of visual impairment must always be specified when the motor development of visually impaired children is discussed, because infants who have partial sight behave quite differently from those who are totally blind, even though they are all classified as legally blind. Furthermore, blind children frequently have multiple handicaps, such as cerebral palsy, mental retardation, seizures, congenital heart disease, and others, which may interfere with the various stages of growth.

Vision plays a crucial role in the life of sighted children because they learn largely by imitation. They have something to see as long as there is light, and various objects in their environment constantly attract their curiosity, which triggers off their motor activity. Since there is no visual contact, it is more difficult for parents to establish a communicating relationship with their blind infant or to help him learn the meaning of sounds. It is not surprising that severely visually impaired infants move less and tend to be passive and quiet. Therefore, the blind child needs more quantitative and qualitative opportunities for learning motor skills. No person can truly be a substitute for informed and loving parents, who can best provide these opportunities. Parents should be aware of the major differences between the development of the sighted and visually impaired. Certain stages are prolonged while the acquisition of others is delayed, and this may greatly concern parents if they have not been given adequate explanations. In the life of a blind child, professional counseling for the parents is important, and it is especially important during the early formative years.

The behavior of an infant is mostly under the influence of the lower part of the brain, the "brain stem," which is well developed at birth compared to the higher cortical centers. Most of the activities observed in early infancy are reflex in nature, but as the child matures the higher cortical centers in his cerebrum take control by suppressing reflex behavior. For example, all infants go through a stage of looking at their hands as they hand-play. Even blind infants have been observed to do so,[1] which is, of course, a reflex activity. Satisfactory predictions of future development are risky on the basis of early motor development. Occasionally, an infant with anencephaly appears to be quite normal for a couple of months but fails to progress because the cerebral hemispheres are absent. Delayed motor development in the blind child, especially under the age of 3 years, should not be automatically related to slow mental development because they represent different functions from different parts of the brain.

Many clinicians and researchers have contributed much to the understanding of motor development in blind children.[1-14] Fraiberg followed the growth of totally blind "optimally" stimulated infants with intact central nervous system function, but unfortunately her population sample was small.[2-4] Several clinicians studied visually impaired children under suboptimal conditions[5-8] and, finally, the behavior of the sighted has also been analyzed when they were blindfolded.[1]

The acquisition of various motor skills by normal sighted children is described first in order to illustrate the differences in the development of the visually impaired.

The sighted newborn has weak neck control. In the prone position, he usually keeps his head resting on its side until about 6 weeks, when he can hold it up momentarily. At 12 weeks, he can support his head and shoulders on his arms, he looks around and observes, while his visual curiosity prolongs this position. Infants without sight, even at this early stage, behave differently. They dislike lying prone and, as a result of crying and fussing, they are often kept on their back constantly. Head and trunk control have less chance to develop in this position. Even if the parents insist on keeping them prone for periods of time, as they should, head lifting with arching is less commonly observed because vision, which is the strongest stimulus to motor movement, is absent (Fig. 9-1). Hearing will not compensate for the lack of sight until after the first year of life, when sound can also become a trigger for motor activity. This does not mean that they ignore sound, since

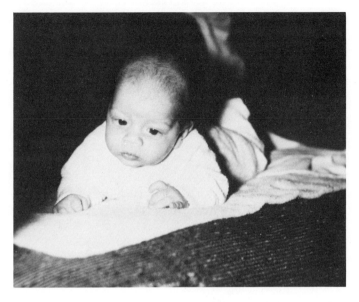

Fig. 9-1. Parents should rest their blind infants on their stomach regularly because in this position head control develops faster.

already at 4 to 5 weeks they listen to voices and inhibit their movement. Burlingham calls this "motionless attention,"[9] which may be misinterpreted by mothers whose blind infants stop moving when spoken to instead of giving a response. The mother may feel that "He does not seem to hear me," but this is far from the case. Parents should cuddle, hug, lift, and play with their visually impaired infant and, in this way, his head control will be strengthened. However, if he is left in his crib on his back because he appears to be content, the development of satisfactory head control may be delayed. As mentioned earlier, the totally blind are at greater risk because any residual vision is an advantage in the acquisition of motor skills.

Sighted infants learn to sit briefly between 4 to 8 months, while leaning forward on their hands. The blind infant can also achieve this at the same time if he has been adequately taught, his readiness for this skill is recognized, and his parents sit him up (Fig. 9-2). Those severely visually impaired infants who were left in their cribs lying on their backs do not have the necessary head and trunk control to be able to sit. The prolonged supine position by this time is often evidenced by a bald spot on the back of the head and by some occipital flattening of the skull.

The sighted and blind can roll from supine to prone at the same

Fig. 9-2.   A 5-month-old blind boy sitting with support.

age, but again the blind infant's readiness has to be recognized and this motor skill needs to be taught.

At 5 to 6 months of age, the average sighted infant grasps objects in sight, but the blind infant does not. The sighted child is able to "bridge" on his arms and knees by 10 months and then begins to crawl. Although blind children may bridge, most will not crawl as the lack of vision specifically interferes with this stage of motor development.[4] The visual curiosity, which triggers off creeping in the sighted, cannot be replaced by sound at this early age. A blind child can reach, grasp, crawl, or walk toward an object only when his conceptual development is advanced far enough for him to associate the object with the sound cue. This stage of conceptualization (audiomotor coordination) usually occurs at around 1 year of age, whether the child is blind or sighted.[1] In this respect, the blind are not different from the sighted when the latter are blindfolded.[1] Could tactile or olfactory stimulation arouse the visually impaired child's curiosity earlier than a sound and thereby initiate crawling? The answer is yes, and, at the appropriate time, parents can teach their blind infant to crawl after a noisy toy or attract him by other means, e.g., with a cookie (Fig. 9-3). The statement frequently seen in the literature that totally blind children do not creep is incorrect, since some do at the appropriate time and others learn it after a considerable delay.

Fig. 9-3. A 13-month-old child without useful vision, crawling. This motor skill can be taught to blind infants at the appropriate age.

Supported and independent standing can be achieved at 8 to 11 months by the sighted and the blind and supported walking—again by both—shortly after. The degree of remaining vision again strongly influences the timing of independent walking. Children with intact central nervous systems who are totally blind or who only have light perception on the average walk later than those with partial vision.[10] By 12 months of age, visually impaired children are ready to walk on their own; they can associate an object with a sound cue and can conceptualize the goal of their movement (Fig. 9-4). Why is there a marked delay in achieving independent walking, especially in the case of totally blind children, even though they are ready neurophysiologically? Is it insecurity—the fear of bumping and falling? It is most likely because they lack a mental map of their environment. Mobility is influenced by many factors, such as the parents' attitude and their efforts to keep the child safe, the child's personality, his neurological readiness, his motivation, the presence of other handicaps, and the environment.

Motor skills achieved during the early development of a visually impaired child are generally either static or dynamic. The static motor skills, such as sitting and standing, are usually acquired at the normal age, whereas dynamic skills, such as crawling and independent walking, are often delayed, depending on the degree of remaining vision and other influencing factors.

Fig. 9-4.   The same child (Fig. 9-3) walking
independently.

Severely visually impaired children with intact central nervous systems who have not been given adequate opportunities to learn motor skills are often markedly delayed in their development. They are frequently hypotonic, poorly coordinated, walk with a plano-valgus deformity on an insecure wide base, and their feet are externally rotated.[10] These are useful clinical signs as, by observing this type of gait in the older child, one can surmise that the early motor development was slow (Fig. 9-5). Some such deprived children never learn to walk and are not infrequently diagnosed as mentally retarded. Some of these infants are more active with their legs than with their arms and spend much time banging their feet against the bars of their cot.[9] When they are encouraged to walk, their legs are better developed than their arms. Their hands may be soft, small, and useless "claw hands."

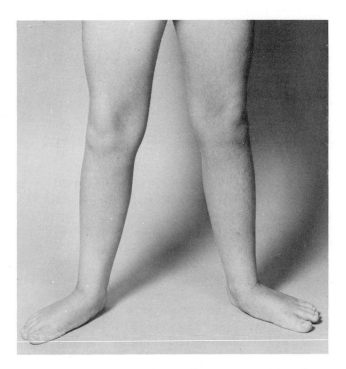

Fig. 9-5. This boy's early development was delayed because of inadequate opportunities to learn motor skills. He is now hypotonic, poorly coordinated, walks with a planovalgus deformity on an insecure wide base and his feet are externally rotated.

It is frequently said that the "hands are the eyes of the blind," but in fact many have blind hands as well.[2] Even early workers with the blind realized that neglect of hands during early childhood can later be made up only with difficulty, if at all. Indeed, blind children frequently have poor fine-hand coordination even though they have no evidence of central nervous system pathology.

During the first 4 to 5 weeks of age, the hands are closed and an active grasp reflex is present. Subsequently, this reflex weakens, disappears, and the hands open up. This state is not influenced by the lack of vision. Newborn babies, when lying supine, keep their arms flexed beside their heads but, in the understimulated blind infant, this posture may remain for a longer period of time.[11] By 4 months, the sighted child watches the movements of his own hand which is the beginning of his visuomotor coordination. Mutual fingering in the totally blind has been observed but this is not sustained. The sighted child can learn hand skills by imitation, but the visually impaired child must be taught to acquire them. At this stage, the parents must start putting objects in the child's hands and gradually encourage more and more hand games. If this is done, fine-hand coordination is likely to be normal. The early development of finger dexterity and sensitivity is important in establishing a readiness for Braille instruction at school age.

THE ROLE OF THE PHYSIOTHERAPIST

A child goes through continuous changes in his development during his early years of life. While these occur spontaneously in the growth of the sighted, the blind must be taught and helped through the different stages. Many visually impaired children have additional handicaps, such as cerebral palsy, poor coordination, orthopedic problems, and mental retardation, which may adversely influence their motor development. Thus, the physiotherapist has a very important role in counseling the parents, treating the child and advising other professionals. Once the diagnosis of blindness is confirmed, the immediate and ongoing involvement of the therapist may alleviate the severity of future problems.

Visual impairment alone does not influence the onset, duration, and disappearance of primitive infantile reflexes, such as the Moro, asymmetric tonic neck, grasp, neck-righting reflexes, or others. However, some of the reactions can be strengthened, especially when there are associated handicaps. For example, the forward-protective reaction of the arms (parachute reflex) normally appears at 6 months of age when the sitting infant begins to support his weight on his extended arms. The protective-extension response to the side develops at around 8 months and to the back at 10 to 11 months. When a visually impaired child is sitting with his hips and lower trunk supported and is pushed forward, to the side, or back, his arms will extend to the appropriate direction. This facilitates more efficient equilibrium reactions and also teaches him to explore his environment.

Most parents and professionals feel relieved when visually impaired children achieve independent walking and may neglect further motor development. Thus, many preschoolers have poor gross motor coordination and inadequate equilibrium reactions. They are often unable to balance on one foot, jump on both feet, hop from one foot to the other, somersault, step over small objects or walk on tiptoe. Without these motor skills, they will have less opportunity to move freely and enjoy active playing. It is important that motor skills are taught in consecutive stages. A partially sighted child was enrolled in a baton twirling class to improve her coordination but she could not even balance on one foot or manipulate her fingers around the baton, so this activity

Fig. 9-6. Visually impaired children should be encouraged
to do physical activities from an early age.

was most frustrating for her (Figs. 9-6 to 9-9).

Visually impaired children are frequently multihandicapped. Their management necessitates a multidisciplinary approach in which the physiotherapist may play an important coordinating role. A detailed description of a program for cerebral-palsied blind children is available from the literature.[15]

Siegel and Murphy in 1970 reviewed the existing research on postural problems of visually impaired children.[16] Those studies and their own showed that neurologically intact blind individuals, even without addi-

Fig. 9-7.   Overprotection is the greatest enemy of the blind
child. Parents should not be afraid of a few cuts and bruises.

tional handicaps, commonly have functional postural and gait problems.
Similar deviations can be observed in blindfolded dogs.[17]

When the child stands with good postural balance, the center of
gravity is maintained just over his feet, and as his body moves forward
the center of gravity is shifted ahead, thus providing a forward momentum.
Since vision plays a major role in this process, the totally blind must
rely entirely on vestibular and proprioceptive senses. Few professionals
realize that an accurate concept of verticality is lacking in congenitally
totally blind children and that functionally satisfactory posture must
be taught to them from infancy.

Visually impaired children often stand with their head hanging down,

Fig. 9-8.   Blind children are able to participate in most sports.

with round shoulders, sunken chest, protruding abdomen, and slightly flexed knees, while the spine has thoracic kyphosis and lumbar lordosis. It is not surprising, therefore, that they frequently complain of muscle fatigue and pain. Closer examination frequently reveals generalized muscle weakness with hypotonia and concurrent tightness of the hip and back extensors and hamstring muscle groups. Flat feet, due to reduced muscle tone and lax ligaments, are also commonly seen. Orthopedic shoes and arch supports are of little or no help in the majority of children.

Many totally blind children walk "toeing-out," with a wide-based gait and little arm swinging. Some suggest that this gait counteracts the lack of vision by providing more secure balance, as assumed by

Fig. 9-9.   A blind skier. The sign is necessary to warn other skiers.

boxers in a similar position in the ring. This is incorrect, however, since congenitally blind children with normal early motor development usually walk without toeing-out on a normally narrow base; they are neither hypotonic nor flat-footed and have fewer coordination difficulties. A child who acquires his visual impairment in later life does not have these problems either. It is clear, therefore, that the wide-based stand with toeing-out is not primarily due to the visual impairment itself but to poor balance.[10]

The visually impaired child should have an adequate body concept according to his age before attempts can be made to correct his postural defects. He should learn to locate and name the different parts of his body, identify basic directions, and have appropriate laterality concepts. Parents should teach these skills to their blind child during his early life.

Physiotherapists must examine carefully the causes of postural deviations. If the child has lordosis, for example, it is most likely because of weak abdominal, weak back extensor, and tight hamstring muscles. Specific exercises and purposeful activities can be introduced only when these dynamics are clearly understood. The sighted person is able to visualize his corrected posture in addition to proprioceptive feedback. The blind child must rely only on feeling the difference between the abnormal and desired posture. For example, if he has an excessive forward pelvic tilt with an associated lordosis, he must learn to be comfortable with his pelvis horizontal to the floor in which position the lordosis is eliminated. He does not understand visual-verbal commands or more abstract concepts, and the therapist cannot use mirrors for visual reinforcement. Siegel and Murphy offer specific treatment for postural and gait abnormalities, and the interested reader is referred to this work.[16] Early intervention is important because the longer abnormal postural patterns are assumed, the harder they are to correct. Furthermore, the therapist must exercise patience in dealing with these children if he or she is to succeed.

CONCLUSIONS

1. The lack of vision has a marked influence on the early stages of motor development.
2. The blind child needs more quantitative and qualitative opportunities for learning motor skills.
3. No person can truly be a substitute for informed and loving parents.
4. Parents and professionals should be aware of the differences between the development of the sighted and the visually impaired.
5. Delayed motor development in the blind child should not be automatically related to slow mental development.
6. Lying on his stomach is better for the blind infant than lying on his back.
7. Parents can teach their infant to crawl at the appropriate time.
8. The degree of vision influences the timing of independent walking.
9. Severely visually impaired children with intact central nervous systems who have not been given adequate opportunities to learn motor skills are often markedly delayed in their development. They are frequently hypotonic, poorly coordinated, walk with a plano-

valgus deformity on an insecure wide base, and their feet are externally rotated.

10. Many visually impaired children have "blind hands" as well.

11. The physiotherapist has an important role in counseling the parents, assessing and treating the blind child and advising other professionals.

12. Most parents and professionals feel relieved when visually impaired children achieve independent walking and may neglect further motor development.

13. Neurologically intact blind individuals—even without additional handicaps—commonly have functional, postural, and gait problems.

REFERENCES

1. Bower TGR: Development in Infancy. San Francisco, WH Freeman, 1974
2. Fraiberg S: Intervention in infancy: A program for blind infants. J Am Acad Child Psychiatry 10:381–405, 1971
3. Fraiberg S: Parallel and divergent patterns in blind and sighted infants. Psychoanal Study Child 23:264–299, 1968
4. Fraiberg S, Siegel B, Gibson R: The role of sound in the search behavior of a blind infant. Psychoanal Study Child 21:327–357, 1966
5. Lairy GC, Harrison-Covello A: The blind child and his parents. Congenital visual defect and the repercussion of family attitudes on the early development of the child. Research Bulletin No 25. New York, American Foundation for the Blind, 1973, pp 1–24
6. Elonen AS, Zwarensteyn SB: Appraisal of developmental lag in certain blind children. J Pediatr 65:599–610, 1964
7. Elonen AS, Cain AC: Diagnostic evaluation and treatment of deviant blind children. Am J Orthopsychiatry 34:625–633, 1964
8. Moor PM: Blind children with developmental problems. Children 8:9–13, 1961
9. Burlingham D: Psychoanalytic Studies of the Sighted and the Blind. New York, International University Press, 1972
10. Jan JE, Robinson GC, Scott E, et al: Hypotonia in the blind child. Dev Med Child Neurol 17:35–40, 1975
11. Adelson E, Fraiberg S: Gross motor development in infants blind from birth. Child Dev 45:114–126, 1974
12. Parmelee AH, Fiske CE, Wright RH: The development of ten children with blindness as a result of retrolental fibroplasia. Am J Dis Child 98:198–220, 1959
13. Wills DM: Vulnerable periods in the early development of blind children. Psychoanal Study Child 25:461–480, 1970
14. Norris M, Spaulding P, Brodie F: Blindness in Children. Chicago, University of Chicago Press, 1957
15. Frampton ME, Kerney E, Schattner R: Forgotten Children. A Program

for the Multihandicapped. Boston, Porter Sargent, 1969

16. Siegel IM, Murphy TJ: Postural determinants in the blind. Final Project Report, Grant RD-3512-SB-700C2 (from the Division of Research and Demonstration Grants, Social and Rehabilitation Service, DHEW, Washington, DC), 1970

17. Talbott RE: Modification of the postural response of the normal dog by blindfolding. J Physiol (Lond) 243:309–320, 1974

10
Communication

**SPEECH AND LANGUAGE DEVELOPMENT OF THE
VISUALLY IMPAIRED CHILD**

Speech and language development of the visually impaired child has not been studied adequately, although clinical impressions frequently appear in the literature.

Speech is not the same as language, even though many authors incorrectly use these terms interchangeably. Speech refers to the process of vocalization or articulation, therefore to spoken language and word production. On the other hand, language is a system of symbols, symbolic codes through which the thinking process of an individual is expressed so that others can understand it. The emergence of speech and language is dependent on biological maturation and, therefore, they cannot be studied in isolation from other aspects of the developmental process. It is not our purpose to describe in detail the speech and language development of normal children as those who are interested could turn to various textbooks.[1,2]

The normal blind child, just like the sighted, begins to vocalize at 8 weeks, squeals with pleasure and "talks" when spoken to at 12 weeks, says syllables "ba, ka, da" at 28 weeks, may say one word with meaning and imitates sounds at 48 weeks, and may have two to three meaningful words in his vocabulary by one year of age.[3] After this stage, the severely visually impaired child's language development usually slows down[4] while the various developmental steps tend to be prolonged.[5] For example, the normal child may frequently repeat his first words without understanding them fully; so does the blind child but for longer periods.

Burlingham feels that the delay that occurs after the first words are learned is because parents use many words with visual meaning which are difficult for the child to understand.[6] At around 16 to 18 months, when sighted children are rapidly enlarging their vocabulary, the visually impaired may even forget already learned words. They are attracted to sounds, however, and they play with them by banging, dropping, and scraping objects. While sighted children imitate gestures and expressions of other people, the blind reproduce sounds of cars, airplanes, and often imitate voices of others.

The severely visually impaired still attain normal speech and language, although maybe slightly later than the sighted child.[7] The initial stages of speech and language are developmental in nature as even the deaf child passes through vocalization, cooing similar to hearing infants, and saying "mumum" and "dada," but then he makes little further progress without appropriate training.[8]

Subsequent speech and language development will be influenced by multiple interacting factors. The blind child should not be viewed in isolation without the influence of his family and the environment.

> While there is ample evidence that a (sighted) child's language development is influenced and modified by environmental circumstances, we are only just beginning to find out which circumstances have which effects by means of which mechanism. Until these mechanisms are understood, we should be cautious in loosely ascribing "language difficulties" to "social deprivation" or to any other broad and global entity. It should also be recognized that children with biological handicaps tend to be more susceptible than normal children to adverse environmental influences. Many language disorders have more than one main determinant. When we have learned more about these complex interactions and about which specific features of the environment influence which particular aspects of language development, and in what way, we shall be in a stronger position to plan a rational and sound program of treatment.[1] (p. 64)

Clinicians frequently state that delay of speech and language of the blind child is most commonly caused by emotional and environmental factors.[9,10] The importance of the love bond between the mother and her blind child must be strongly emphasized, since rejection is a common cause of speech and language delay. One sometimes sees "blind babies who have spent much of their first year in a sensory desert—babies who have worn a groove in their crib mattress, babies who make no sound, who rarely smile and who spend most of their 24 hours a day in sleep."[11] The blind child who is not talked to may have markedly delayed speech and language, but the quality of spoken language is even more important. He becomes accustomed to a constant bombardment of sound that has no meaning, even though it may keep him happy. The constant exposure to radio and television may slow down language acquisition and should be discouraged. Some blind children learn to shut out excessive sound bombardment so successfully that they may be mistaken for deaf. The language used by parents should be associated with concrete experiences that are meaningful to the child, otherwise he tends to develop excessive verbalisms and talks for the sake of talking but with little understanding of the words.

Some parents satisfy the child so readily that he does not have to learn to talk to express his needs. Not infrequently, parents unthinkingly continue to respond to the nonverbal communication of a child who does not speak and make no demands on him to use language.

Speech problems are more common among the visually impaired than the sighted, probably because blind children tend to have more neurological disabilities. It is not entirely clear, however, whether or not there is an increased prevalence of speech and language disorders among blind children who have an intact central nervous system. Unfortunately, most research studies that deal with this topic are poorly designed and therefore inconclusive. The degree of visual impairment has not been shown to be positively correlated with speech and language difficulties, which indicates that blindness alone is not the decisive factor.[12] It is not possible to differentiate between the speech of blind and sighted children by listening to their taped voices. Sight is not needed for acquiring the skills of articulation.

Blind children often talk excessively to maintain contact with others and keep their attention. Some clinicians have noted a "broadcasting voice" in the severely visually impaired, presumably due to the fact that they may not know where the audience is located in relation to themselves.[13] Norris concluded in her large study that in no case did problems in the area of speech appear to be a direct result of blindness.[14]

The visually impaired child with a language disturbance is at a much greater disadvantage than the sighted. In fact, such children are frequently incorrectly diagnosed as mentally retarded.

ECHOLALIA

Echolalia or "parroting" (repetition of words) is commonly observed in the young sighted child but more often in the blind.[6] Although it still represents a desire on the part of the child to communicate, it gives cause for concern when excessive because it indicates disturbed language development.

The causes of echolalia have been oversimplified in the literature.

Most psychiatrically oriented observers explain excessive echolalia in terms of autistic symptomatology and view the disturbed child-parent relationship as the cause. Although there may well be such a disturbance, this may originate partly from the child's disturbed language, which parents may interpret as rejection.

Neurologically oriented authors view excessive echolalia (like autism) as a manifestation of an organic central nervous system disorder. A good deal of work suggests that this concept is correct. Excessive echolalia is commonly seen in children who have a "central language disorder" or in those who are mentally retarded.[15] Most likely excessive echolalia is due to a range of interacting neurological and psychiatric factors.

VERBALISM

Verbal learning without adequate concrete experience is considered to be a significant problem in the education of the blind. The visually impaired child frequently accepts verbal descriptions from the sighted instead of having them based on his own concrete experience. This is not surprising since he is limited in exploring the world around him and, at the same time, he is bombarded constantly with "visual terms." In gaining concrete experience he cannot touch objects that the sighted can see, such as the moon, a waterfall, a rainbow, certain animals, fire, or lightning, and he cannot conceive of colors; therefore, he must accept many visually oriented verbal descriptions from the sighted. The sense of sight permits a much greater perceptual activity than the sense of touch. Although in time he is able to describe visual concepts well verbally, he still may have a hazy, partial, and inaccurate understanding of them. This phenomenon is called *verbalism*, which is closely related to concept formation.

Harley, in his study of verbalisms, found three major factors which strongly correlate with their use: experience, chronological age, and intelligence.[16] The older, more experienced, and more intelligent a visually impaired child, the less he uses poorly conceptualized verbal expressions. He found no significant relationship between verbalisms and personal adjustment, in contrast to previous beliefs. Verbalisms and inaccurate concept formation, however, do have a negative effect on academic learning and therefore it is vital that the blind child be taught from infancy by as much first-hand experience as possible.

NONVERBAL COMMUNICATION

Communication between people includes much more than just verbal language (Fig. 10-1). We express ourselves with movements of our face, eyes, and hands; with the way we walk, the type of colors we choose

Fig. 10-1. Communication between people includes much more than just talking.

in our dress; as well as with the use of deodorants, perfumes, and so on. One can see, therefore, that the blind could be restricted in many areas of nonverbal communication.

Parents look for communication from their infants soon after birth and try to establish contact by talking to them. The infant's cry becomes meaningful to the parents, who soon learn when it is due to hunger or pain. In contrast to the blind, the sighted infant when fed focuses his eyes on his mother's face within the first few weeks of life.[17] Mothers quickly learn that there is something wrong when this eye-to-eye communication is lacking and this is how many severe visual disorders are discovered. Sighted babies choose to look at the human face in preference to anything else, and they even spend more time fixating their eyes on a diagram of a face than on other areas.[18]

Smiling is another type of communication which appears during the first few weeks of life in the full-term infant with or without sight, usually when just falling asleep. Consistent smiling in response to touch or voice is seen after the first month but, while the sighted infant begins to show prolonged smiling soon after, this process is delayed in the blind until 4 or 5 months of age, and instead they exhibit fleeting reflex-like smiling. As they grow older, the sighted are stimulated through social interaction to imitate expressions they see on the faces of others, and they build up a repertoire of learned motor patterns from their natural expressive rudiments. Totally blind children, lacking visual stimulation and feedback, tend to use their facial musculature less and less and, as a result, spontaneous expressions are underdeveloped and voluntary expressions are totally inadequate. Still, as part of an emotional outflow, facial movements may be normal when experiencing disdain, disgust, horror, amusement, or anger. There is considerable evidence now that basic, naturally occurring expressions are innate. The lack of facial movement often disturbs those who have not had much contact with the blind. They may feel that the blind child is inattentive or lacks feelings. Attempts have been made to teach facial expressions to blind subjects using biofeedback obtained by transducing the myoelectric activity of the facial muscles.[19] Although the appropriateness and adequacy of expression can be significantly improved as a result of training, this technique is still experimental.

Sighted infants generally begin to follow objects before 2 months of age and then learn how to correlate their eye movements with their facial expressions. Totally blind infants do not learn voluntary eye movements, and the child with acquired total blindness generally loses this ability. The sighted may experience discomfort when talking to a blind person or to someone with a severe squint because they cannot establish proper visual contact. The lack of voluntary eye movements in the blind is usually quite apparent since their eyes often seem to "stare." Attempts have been made to teach eye movements to the blind in order to improve their nonverbal communication,[20] but this is also experimental.

KINESICS

In order to make ourselves more clearly understood, we constantly use gestures and changes in our posture in addition to facial expressions. The systematic study of human communication through the use of gestures and body movement is called *kinesics* but it has not been studied well in the blind. Although some of our gestures and changes in our body position during human communication are innate,[21] most, like facial expressions, are learned. Imitation of gestures begins at 6 months of age when the sighted infant starts imitating gross movements with his arms and hands. He subsequently learns complex patterns of body language, which are strongly influenced by the society in which he lives. This, of course, does not happen with the blind child, even though he would find some gestures advantageous as an aid to communication and social adjustment. His body language tends to remain almost at the toddler stage; for example, even as a teenager he may jump up and down clapping his hands when excited. The blind child could be taught to effectively use positive and negative responses, such as head shakes and doubtful or indecisive shoulder shrugs; motioning signals, such as "come to, go away," or "hi"; and pointing to "over there, here, this, that, you, he, him, me," and "I." He could learn to describe with his hand, arm, and finger movements "big, large, huge, little, small, tiny, tall, short, two-three-four, round, thin," etc.[21] In some schools for the blind, these skills are actively taught.

CONCLUSIONS

1. Speech and language development of visually impaired children has not been studied adequately.
2. Blind children may attain normal speech and language, although often slightly later than the sighted.
3. Speech and language development of blind children are influenced by multiple interacting factors; therefore, they may be delayed for a number of reasons.
4. Speech problems are more common among the visually impaired than the sighted because the former tend to have more neurological disabilities.
5. The degree of visual impairment has not been shown to be positively correlated with speech and language difficulties, which indicates that blindness alone is not the decisive factor.
6. Sight is not needed for acquiring skills of articulation.
7. Excessive echolalia in the blind child indicates disturbed language development but not necessarily that any one factor is the cause.
8. Verbalism and inaccurate concept formation have a negative effect on academic learning; therefore, it is vital that the blind child be taught from infancy by as much first-hand experience as possible.
9. Communication between people includes more than just verbal language and in those areas the blind are restricted.

REFERENCES

1. Rutter M, Mittler P: Environmental influences on language development, in Rutter M, Martin JAM (eds): The Child with Delayed Speech. Clinics in Developmental Medicine No 43. London, Heinemann, 1972, pp 52-67

2. Perkins WH: Speech Pathology. An Applied Behavioral Science. St. Louis, CV Mosby Co, 1971
3. Illingworth RS: The Development of the Infant and Young Child, ed 4. Edinburgh, E & S Livingstone, 1970
4. Lairy GC, Harrison-Covello A: The blind child and his parents. Congenital visual defect and the repercussion of family attitudes on the early development of the child. Research Bulletin No 25, New York, American Foundation for the Blind, 1973, pp 1-24
5. Elonen AS, Zwarensteyn SB: Appraisal of developmental lag in certain blind children. J Pediatr 65:599-610, 1964
6. Burlingham D: Psychoanalytic Studies of the Sighted and the Blind. New York, International Univeristies Press, 1972
7. Lowenfeld B: Our Blind Children: Growing and Learning with Them. Springfield, Ill, Charles C Thomas, 1956
8. Lenneberg EH, Rebelsky FG, Nichols IA: The vocalizations of infants born deaf. Hum Dev 8:23-27, 1965
9. Gruber KF, Moor PM (eds): No Place to Go. New York, American Foundation for the Blind, 1963
10. Fraiberg S, Adelson E: Self-representation in language and play: Observations of blind children. Psychoanal Q 42:539-562, 1973
11. Fraiberg S, Adelson E, Smith M: An educational program for blind infants. Journal of Special Education 3:125, 1969
12. Rowe EM: Speech Problems of Blind Children. New York, American Foundation for the Blind, 1958
13. Cutsforth TD: The Blind in School and Society. New York, American Foundation for the Blind, 1952
14. Norris M, Spaulding P, Brodie F: Blindness in Children. Chicago, University of Chicago Press, 1957
15. Fay WH: On the echolalia of the blind and of the autistic child. J Speech and Hear Disord 38:478-489, 1973
16. Harley RK: Verbalism Among Blind Children. New York, American Foundation for the Blind, 1963
17. Freedman DG: Smiling in blind infants and the issue of innate vs. acquired. J Child Psychol Psychiatry 5:171-184, 1964
18. Abercrombie MLJ: Eye movements and perceptual development, in Gardiner P, MacKeith R, Smith V (eds): Aspects of Developmental and Paediatric Ophthalmology. Clinics in Developmental Medicine No 32. London, Heinemann, 1969, pp 15-24
19. Webb NC: The use of myoelectric feedback in teaching facial expressions to the blind. Research Bulletin No 27, New York, American Foundation for the Blind, 1974, pp 231-262
20. Toonen BL, Wilson JP: Learning eye fixation without visual feedback. Research Bulletin No 19. New York, American Foundation for the Blind, 1969, pp 123-128
21. Apple MM: Kinesic training for blind persons: A vital means of communication. New Outlook for the Blind 66:201-208, 1972

11
Effect of Blindness on the Other Senses

Since ancient times, people have believed that the congenitally blind child was born with superior nonvisual senses and that, when someone became visually impaired later in life, he magically acquired these abilities overnight. Indeed, even the literature of the Classical Age reflected this belief: "Gods after having punished a person with blindness rewarded him with an extraordinary gift in partial compensation."[1] It is easy to understand the reason for this belief when one notices the surprise of the casual observer watching a totally blind child ride a bicycle, skate, or perform many other activities. The blind often perform beyond the expectations of the sighted, and the naive observer often tends to rely on the supernatural as an explanation.

The hypothesis of "sensory compensation" has been the subject of a number of scientific investigations since the nineteenth century and has been strongly rejected. Those who work with blind children know that their abilities are not gifts from God but are the result of training. Many of the visually impaired do not use their hearing, touch, smell, and taste efficiently, simply because they did not have adequate early sensory training and experience. There is evidence that for each individual there are optimal stages for learning various skills. When opportunities to develop their remaining senses are not provided, especially during the early childhood of congenitally blind children, it will become increasingly more difficult to acquire them at a later age.[2] Such neglect must be prevented by the most strenuous efforts.

Research has not been able to prove that training can change the acuity of hearing, touch, smell, or taste of the congenitally blind, but it has shown that these senses can be used more efficiently. It is not the visual acuity but the visual efficiency of a partially blind child that improves with training.[3] Similarly, audiograms do not show a change in the threshold of receiving sound, even though the child is able to use his hearing more effectively. It is not how much sight or hearing he has but what he does with it that counts.

ECHOLOCATION

Centuries ago, it was noted that some blind people appeared to have a special ability to avoid obstacles in their path. This ability was called "obstacle sense," "blind man's sense," or a "special sixth sense" supposedly given by God as compensation for the lack of sight. It was also called "facial vision" because, in the vicinity of objects, blind or blindfolded individuals often felt "facial pressure," especially on the skin covering their forehead, temples, and cheeks. Until 1940, when this faculty of orientation was finally related to hearing, a controversy raged over the basis of this "sense," even though Truschel stated this relationship in 1909.[4]

Animals such as bats, certain types of fish, birds, dolphins, California sea lions, porpoises, and whales are known to be able to navigate by echolocation. In total darkness, bats catch tiny flying insects and avoid wires that are smaller than 1 mm in diameter. Dolphins can distinguish one fish from another by using their sonar system. For centuries, blind people have found their way tapping their canes without realizing the scientific explanation for it.

The theory of facial vision was disproven by applying anaesthetic to the skin of the face and, thus, demonstrating that the crucial cues were actually received by the acoustic rather than tactile receptors.[5] The mechanism of echolocation is based on the perception of modified sound which is produced by the reflection on near obstacles. As a person walks toward an object, various noises are produced, such as footsteps, rustling of clothes, breathing, coughing, tapping of the cane, etc., which are reflected together with the random noise coming from other sources. These are not as satisfactory in echolocation as special sounds like whistling, hissing, snapping fingers, tongue-clicking, and tapping, which are often used by blind children. Useful echo sounds are in the range of 8000 to 10,000 cycles per second.[6] Increased atmospheric pressure and humidity enhance the ability to echolocate, while wind or background noise impair it. Like the sighted who glance around, echo signals may be used by the blind as an "auditory glance" to detect where certain objects are.[7] Blindfolded sighted individuals, after considerable training, were able to perceive the displacement of as little as 4.3 inches of a 1-foot disc placed 2 feet away.[8] Some even distinguished between targets of the same size that were made of different materials, like metal, wood, or velvet, by saying that they sounded different. However, human echolocation in practice is satisfactory only for the detection of large obstacles without perceiving their exact size or shape.

Successful orientation by aural clues is not a special gift since many visually impaired children have not had an opportunity to develop this ability. Longitudinal research has not been done on the development of echolocation and orientation by aural clues. Bright and mobile blind children at 1½ to 2 years of age spontaneously begin producing their own echo sounds which may be misinterpreted by uninformed professionals as a manifestation of autism. The use of this sonar system should not only be encouraged but sometimes taught by the parents (Figs. 11-1 and 11-2).

MUSICAL ABILITY

Most people regard visually impaired children as being musically gifted, which is not surprising. Through the centuries they were taught to sing for their living, and there have been many well-known blind musicians.[9] In the absence of vision, blind children spend much time playing with sounds, imitating people, cars, trains, and various noises, and they appear to be keenly interested in music. But again, research has shown that fundamentally the visually impaired are no better at music than the sighted.[10] They are not extraordinarily gifted musically as many believe, and they have to receive just as much, perhaps even more, training.

Braille music, which is written with completely different codes, is difficult to learn and students must first be proficient in the use of regular Braille. The notes are written separately for the right and left hands. Students can learn music by Braille, ear, dictation, or any combination of these.[11]

THE TACTILE SENSE

The hands of the blind are often called their "eyes" because through touch they gain much useful information about their immediate environment. The tactile sense is more important for survival than the other sensory systems, such as sight, hearing, taste, or smell. The life span of individuals with complete sensory neuropathy may be limited but, fortunately, this disorder is extremely rare.

Learning by touch has distinct limitations since direct contact is necessary to perceive shape, size, texture, temperature, and other qualities. Thus, many objects are inaccessible to the blind because they

Fig. 11-1.   A totally blind teenager bicycling. He relies heavily on aural clues.

Fig. 11-2.   Blind children are playing floor hockey. A noisy can substitutes for the puck.

arc too far, too large, too small, or cannot even be touched. When the blind child must rely on "visual descriptions" from the sighted to gain information rather than on direct experience, knowledge may remain incomplete. For example, a congenitally totally blind child may have heard sighted people talk about the roof of his house. If he has not had a chance to explore the ceiling, the shingles, the chimney, and so on by tactile means, his conception remains partial. Exposure to small replicas of buildings does not help him that much, since he may conceptualize the replica but still not the real object. (This is why special books which are provided with raised illustrations of animals, people, and other objects are not too appealing or helpful for blind children.)

Many blind children are afraid of touching dogs and, therefore, their knowledge of them is often incomplete and incorrect. From modeling clay, they may create a dog standing on two legs with a human face and a tail which sticks out of its back.[12] They conceive space mostly through touch, and visual descriptions or echolocation are of little help. Tactile perception is slowly received, which is another major limitation. A good Braille reader under optimum conditions may reach 80-100 words per minute (wpm), whereas perception of speech may be 450-500 wpm. Sensory devices which attempt to substitute touch for sight are also at a considerable disadvantage. The Optacon is a small reading aid translating print into tactile form with which some people are able to achieve a reading speed of up to 80 wpm. When such a device gives off sound simultaneously, the same individuals may read up to 200 wpm.[13] The skin may become a much better receptor with appropriate training than is generally believed.[7] Unfortunately, there are many blind children who also have "blind hands" because they have not been given a chance to develop their touch to the optimum. From an early age, visually impaired children must be encouraged by their parents to handle various kinds of materials to gain myriads of kinesthetic experiences, such as rough, smooth, hard, soft, wet, dry, cold, hot, plastic, metal, big, small, wood, and paper. The theory of sensory compensation has been disproven here as well. Furthermore, not just the blind but the sighted can also develop a "superior sense of touch" when adequately trained.

It was once a popular belief that some totally blind individuals who had never been able to see were mysteriously able to identify colors through touch. This was proven incorrect. Color is meaningless to the congenitally blind. However, as they listen to the sighted, they are constantly exposed to visual descriptions. Consequently, they may identify their coat, for example, as red, not because they perceive it as such, but because they associate the word red with the texture of that cloth. Blind people who recovered their sight through operative procedures claim that previously they could not conceptualize colors and also that their nonvisual concept of space was totally different from the visual one. Hands cannot replace sight!

SMELL AND TASTE

Blind children frequently recognize objects by their odor and may identify people by their perfume, but they are generally restrained from doing this. Once, when a young blind man was asked why he liked a certain lady friend, his answer was, "Because her voice was pleasant and her perfume was so fragrant." One frequently sees congenitally blind children sniffing at objects. Although this may appear to be strange to the unaccustomed sighted, it should be encouraged and they should be actively taught from early childhood to enrich their experience by relying more on the senses of smell and taste. The different odors should be identified to visually impaired children and should be associated with first-hand experience. Parents soon realize that meals must be tasty since, in the absence of sight, it is the smell and taste that make them attractive to the blind.

CONCLUSIONS

1. The hypothesis of "sensory compensation" has been the subject of a number of scientific investigations since the nineteenth century and has been conclusively rejected.
2. Many of the visually impaired do not use their hearing, touch, smell, and taste efficiently simply because they did not have adequate early sensory training and experience.
3. Research has not been able to prove that training can change the acuity of hearing, touch, smell, or taste of the congenitally blind, but it has shown that these senses can be used more efficiently.
4. The mechanism of echolocation is based on the perception of modified sound which is produced by reflection on near obstacles.
5. Research has shown that, fundamentally, the visually impaired are no better at music than the sighted.
6. The tactile sense is more important for survival than the other sensory systems.
7. Books which are provided with raised illustrations of animals, people, and other objects are not too appealing or helpful for blind children.
8. With appropriate training, the skin may become a much better receptor than is generally believed.
9. Blind individuals cannot identify colors through touch.
10. Blind children should not only be encouraged but actively taught

from early childhood to enrich their experience by relying more on the senses of smell and taste.

REFERENCES

1. Twersky J: Blindness in Literature: Examples of Depictions and Attitudes. New York, American Foundation for the Blind, 1955, p 15
2. Illingworth RS: The Development of the Infant and Young Child. Normal and Abnormal, ed 4. Edinburgh, E & S Livingstone, 1970
3. Barraga N: Increased Visual Behavior in Low Vision Children. Research Series No 13. New York, American Foundation for the Blind, 1964
4. Truschel L: Das problem des sogenannten sechsten Sinnen der Blinden. Arch f d ges Psychol 14:133-178, 1909
5. Kohler I: Orientation by aural clues. Research Bulletin No 4. New York, American Foundation for the Blind, 1964, pp 14-53
6. Welsh JR: A psychoacoustic study of factors affecting human echo-localization. Research Bulletin No 4. New York, American Foundation for the Blind, 1964, pp 1-13
7. Rice CE: Early blindness, early experience and perceptual enhancement. Research Bulletin No 22. New York, American Foundation for the Blind, 1970, pp 1-22
8. Kellog WN: Sonar system of the blind. Research Bulletin No 4. New York, American Foundation for the Blind, 1964, pp 55-69
9. Mallinson GG, Mallinson JV: . . . and the blind man on the corner who sang the Beale Street blues, in: Blindness 1972 (Annual). Washington, DC, American Association of Workers for the Blind, 1972, pp 71-93
10. Pitman DJ: The musical ability of blind children. Research Bulletin No 11. New York, American Foundation for the Blind, 1965, pp 63-79
11. Mooney MK: Blind children need training, not sympathy. Music Educators Journal 58:56-59, 1972
12. Fukurai S: How Can I Make What I Cannot See? New York, Van Nostrand Reinhold, 1974
13. Bliss JC, Crane HD: Tactile perception. Research Bulletin No 19. New York, American Foundation for the Blind, 1969, pp 205-230

12
Specific Effects of Blindness on the Child

It was once a common belief that Providence compensated blind children for the loss of their vision by providing them with superior nonvisual senses. However, this theory of sensory compensation has been discarded because of a number of scientific investigations. Some who view the visually impaired from the other extreme position claim that "children with visual handicaps" are not different from the sighted and therefore should not be treated differently. It is the purpose of this section to show that lack of vision does cause specific physiological changes.

CENTRAL NERVOUS SYSTEM

Blind children often have neurological abnormalities. This is not surprising since the eye is part of the brain as it develops from the diencephalon and, therefore, brain damage is frequently associated with ocular disturbance. For example, nearly three-quarters of mentally retarded children have eye defects[1] and over one-half of patients with cerebral palsy show various types of ocular problems.[2] Similarly, blind children commonly have neurological handicaps, such as cerebral palsy, mental retardation, seizures, hearing loss, hydrocephalus, and others. Those blind children whose central nervous systems have not been "damaged" still frequently show neurological deviations on examination.

Amblyopia is a well-known complication of strabismus or cataracts. When double vision occurs in young children with strabismus, the brain may compensate by suppressing the vision in the squinting eye. Congenital cataracts, through visual deprivation, can also result in marked loss of visual acuity. Wiesel and Hubel demonstrated that visual deprivation in young kittens results in atrophic changes in the lateral geniculate body of the deprived eye.[3] This atrophy is most pronounced in animals deprived of vision from birth, less marked in kittens deprived at later ages, and absent in adult cats. This has been shown the same in man. Structural differences in the brain can be found between the sighted and blind, irrespective of the etiology of their visual handicap but strongly related to the degree of remaining vision and the age of onset.

ELECTROENCEPHALOGRAM

Electroencephalograms (EEGs) of visually impaired children commonly show abnormalities; often these findings can be explained by evidence of previously acquired brain damage. EEG research in the blind was greatly influenced by the sudden increase of retrolental fibroplasia after the Second World War when excessive oxygen was frequently given routinely to premature infants. Earlier studies of children with retrolental fibroplasia wrongly related the observed EEG abnormalities to brain damage, but now it is certain that markedly elevated oxygen content of the blood does not damage the brain, even though it can cause severe destruction in the eye.

Maturation of electrical activity follows a different pattern in the visually deprived brain than in that of the sighted. A blind child should not be labeled brain damaged or epileptic solely on the basis of his EEG, which is "abnormal" compared with the established norms for sighted subjects. Longitudinal studies clearly show that the EEGs of normal blind children may be different from those of the sighted. This area of knowledge is extensive and therefore only some of the major findings will be mentioned here, but interested readers may look up the references given.[3-13]

Severely visually impaired children without central nervous system pathology usually exhibit generous amounts of slow activity maximal in the occipital lobes, which may be generalized.

Alpha rhythm is defined as rhythmical activity of 8 to 12 cps that is blocked by eye opening and enhanced when the eyes are closed. Alpha rhythm is normally present in individuals with useful vision, but it is absent in children who have had only light perception or total blindness since birth. Those who suddenly become totally blind tend to lose their alpha rhythm but only after several years.

Approximately 30 percent of blind individuals show bilateral alpha-like rhythm in their central brain region with little spread anteriorly or posteriorly, which is referred to as the "mu" or "wicket" rhythm.[5] This EEG pattern can also be seen in the sighted population.

Small scattered spikes, predominantly in the occipital region, are often observed in the records of young totally blind and partially sighted children, especially those with retrolental fibroplasia. Occipital spikes are also common in the congenitally blind who are older than 3 years of age, regardless of the etiology of their visual impairment. Animal studies indicate that these spikes follow saccadic eye movements made either in nystagmus or attempted fixation,[11] but this has not been proven in humans. Apparently, occipital foci are more commonly seen on the left side. Left-sided occipital spikes usually occur in children with some useful vision, but in the totally blind these tend to be bilateral.[6] Many children with various ocular anomalies have EEG abnormalities, although they may not be severely visually impaired. Stillerman et al. studied the ocular disorders most often associated with occipital foci.[13] In their study they found that otherwise normal children with strabismus showed a 30 percent incidence of occipital abnormalities and that these were twice as frequent in the exotropic as in the esotropic type.

Unfortunately a large proportion of electroencephalographers still do not realize that the EEG of the blind child normally shows changes that cannot be judged by the norms of the sighted child. Physicians who are unaware of these EEG changes may incorrectly diagnose brain damage or epilepsy in normal visually impaired children. Often these records are called severely abnormal when, in fact, they are normal, or at least expected, for the blind. Seizures do not occur with these occipital foci. Anticonvulsant treatment of these children is totally unwarranted and even harmful since they are wrongly labeled as epileptics. The spike foci tend to disappear with age and are not seen in the blind adult.

Attempts have been made to correlate EEG changes seen in blind children with personality traits.[6] It has been claimed that the absence of alpha rhythm is closely associated with lack of visual imagery, whereas in the sighted it represents visual attention, mental effort, and emotional arousal. Similarly, the presence of "mu rhythm" is said by some to be related to reliance on touch, kinesis, and motor imagery since it disappears with tactile stimuli and movement. Occipital spikes have also been related to intelligence,[6] motivation, emotional disturbance, and mobility.[10] Further studies are needed to clarify all these postulated relationships.

Periodically during sleep, certain patterns are seen in the EEGs of sighted individuals, accompanied by frequent and characteristic clusters of rapid, conjugate eye movements (REM) and dreaming. REM, which is claimed to represent scanning eye movements during visual dreaming, is present during the dreams of only those blind people who still have visual imagery.[12] Those severely visually impaired who do not think in visual terms and, therefore, do not dream in visual terms either, do not have REM during their dreams. Voluntary eye movements are learned motor skills which are not acquired by the congenitally totally blind and are lost gradually in those who become completely blind in later life. Severely visually impaired children without voluntary eye movements almost invariably lack visual imagery as well. Therefore, it is not entirely clear whether the absence of REM is due to lack of voluntary eye movements, lack of visual imagery, or both. With the exception of REM, the sleep records are identical in blind and sighted children.[5,11]

Although stereotyped motor behavior of the blind, or "blind mannerisms," are discussed in detail in chapter 18, they are mentioned here because they are associated with EEG changes. Children frequently rock before going to sleep at a certain age, and it has been shown that stereotyped rhythmic movements may function as sleep-inducing stimuli. Stone classified some of the blind mannerisms into withdrawing and alerting types.[7] Rocking and swaying, which are rhythmic motor activities, are examples of withdrawal mannerisms, whereas hand clapping or hand shaking are not rhythmic and are of the alerting type. During the sustained use of withdrawal mannerisms, the child is quiet and, frequently, tired or bored. The EEG slows down and is similar to that of a drowsy, sighted child. During alerting mannerisms, the slowness of the EEG disappears. Although these findings are not surprising, they show that mannerisms can be differentiated from one another on a physiological basis.

VESTIBULAR FUNCTION

Studies of vestibular function frequently show abnormalities in children who are blind or have congenital nystagmus.[14-16] Pouring cold or warm water ("caloric testing") in the ears of normal subjects precipitates nystagmus, but this so-called vestibulo-ocular reflex is frequently absent or markedly diminished in those with visual impairment. This does not mean that blind children with abnormal caloric testing have poor balance, as there does not seem to be a relationship. Good balance is dependent not only on the function of the vestibular apparatus, but also on the integrity of the entire central and peripheral nervous system. Balance also has to be taught to the blind child and practiced like many other skills. The reason for the disturbance of vestibulo-ocular reflex in the severely visually impaired is speculative. The purpose of voluntary optical and vestibular impulses to the eye muscles is to produce visual fixation and to orientate the subject in space. With blindness, the optically elicited impulses are lost and the others become useless.

Again, the lack of the vestibulo-ocular reflex in blind children does not indicate brain damage but simply a neurophysiological change.

GROWTH

Longitudinal studies have shown that normally sighted children grow in spurts with the maximum rate occurring between January and June.[17] Blindness alone does not affect the ultimate height, weight, or head circumference, but the growth rate of blind children is evenly distributed throughout the year. The seasonal changes in the environment must act through the neuroendocrine system, but the mechanism is obscure, although there has been speculation that the amount of light is an influencing factor.[17]

Profound emotional neglect may reduce the growth rate of any child—sighted or blind—but, fortunately, this is rare. We do occasionally see visually impaired individuals with skulls markedly flattened from lying on their backs for prolonged periods during early childhood, and, rarely, we see neglected blind children with extremities underdeveloped from disuse. These problems are not directly caused by the lack of vision.

APPEARANCE

Enlargement and distortion of the bony orbit and darkening of the periorbital skin can be observed frequently in those severely visually impaired children who press and finger their eyes excessively (Fig. 6-2). This and other blind mannerisms are discussed further in chapter 18.

MENARCHE

Visual deprivation can cause earlier onset of maturation in animals.[18] Similarly, biological maturation and the onset of menarche occurs earlier in healthy severely visually impaired girls than in the sighted, depending on the degree of visual impairment. The explanation is speculative.

SUNBURNING

Easier sunburning has been reported in blind children,[18] but more research is needed to accept this as fact.

CIRCADIAN RHYTHM

Congenitally blind animals may not have circadian rhythm of certain enzymes[19] (normally there are day-night changes of enzyme levels) and blinding may result in a shift of such rhythm.[20] Similar findings in blind humans may not be surprising.

SLEEP

Visually impaired children sleep less than the sighted. This is probably best explained by the fact that the blind are less active and therefore require less rest and sleep.

VISUAL REHABILITATION AFTER LONG-LASTING BLINDNESS

A few fortunate individuals who have been blind since birth have recovered their sight through new operative techniques. Contrary to expectations, recovery of vision did not occur immediately after surgery but proved to be a long struggle. Visual rehabilitation occurred in a shorter time in those who had acquired their blindness. Initially, visual sensations were meaningless. Objects could only be recognized by touch even though they could be seen. One such case was described by Levy in 1872.

> A young woman, twenty-two years of age, born stone blind . . . was restored to perfect vision in four days by a surgical operation, and to partial vision in two minutes. . . . The effect in the young woman was most curious and something of this kind. She saw everything, but there was no idea whatever of perspective. She put her hand to the window to try to catch the trees on the other side of the street, . . . she tried to touch the ceiling of a high ward; she was utterly ignorant of common things—what such things as a bunch of keys were, of a silver watch, or a common cup and saucer; but when she shut her eyes and was allowed to touch them (the educated sense) she told them at once![21]

Many of these individuals, like those who suddenly became blind, experienced severe depression which required intensive psychiatric care. The loss or recovery of sight obviously results in major neurophysiological changes which can be very stressful.[22]

Studies of monkeys have clarified the sequence of immense physiological changes caused by blinding.[11] Enucleation in these animals alters the neurophysiology of the visual cortex suddenly and drastically, due to absence of visual input rather than to degeneration. These animals also became profoundly depressed. Such research suggests again that the severe depression following the sudden onset of total blindness in man might have physiological as well as psychological elements.[11]

CONCLUSIONS

1. Lack of vision causes specific physiological changes.
2. Structural differences in the brain can be found between the sighted and the blind, irrespective of the etiology of their visual handicap

but strongly related to the degree of remaining vision and the age of onset.
3. Longitudinal studies clearly show that the EEGs of normal blind children may be different from those of the sighted.
4. Studies of vestibular function frequently show abnormalities in children who are blind. The lack of the vestibulo-ocular reflex does not indicate brain damage but simply a neurophysiological change.
5. The growth rate of blind children is evenly distributed throughout the year in contrast to sighted children who grow in spurts.
6. The onset of menarche occurs earlier in healthy blind girls than in the sighted.
7. Blinding causes changes in the circadian rhythm of animals.
8. Research suggests that the depression that follows the onset of blindness in man might have physiological as well as psychological elements.

REFERENCES

1. Bankes KJL: Eye defects of mentally handicapped children. Br Med J 2:533–535, 1974
2. Dinnage R: The Handicapped Child—Research Review. Studies in Child Development Series. London, Longman, 1970, Vol 1
3. Wiesel TN, Hubel DH: Effects of visual deprivation on the morphology and physiology of cells in the cat's lateral geniculate body. J Neurophysiol 26:978–993, 1963
4. Kellaway P, Bloxsom A, MacGregor M: Occipital spike foci associated with retrolental fibroplasia and other forms of retinal loss in children. Electroencephalogr Clin Neurophysiol 7:469–470, 1955
5. Cohen J: Brain waves and blindness, in Clark LL, Jastrzembska ZS (eds): Proceedings of the Conference on New Approaches to the Evaluation of Blind Persons. New York, American Foundation for the Blind, 1970, pp 112–125
6. Lairy GC, Netchine S: The electroencephalogram in partially sighted children related to clinical and psychological data. Research Bulletin No 2. New York, American Foundation for the Blind, 1962, pp 38–56
7. Stone AA: Altered levels in blind retarded children. Research Bulletin No 19. New York, American Foundation for the Blind, 1969, pp 235–241
8. Novikova LA: Blindness and the Electrical Activity of the Brain. Research Series No 23. New York, American Foundation for the Blind, 1973
9. Akiyama Y, Parmelee AH, Flescher J: The electroencephalogram in visually handicapped children. J Pediatr 65:233–242, 1964
10. Jeavons PM, Harding GF, Ferries GW, et al: Alpha rhythm in totally blind children. Br J Ophthalmol 54:786–793, 1970
11. Sakakura H, Doty RW: EEG of striate cortex in blind monkeys: Effects of eye movement and sleep. 1975 (unpublished data)
12. Berger RJ, Olley P, Oswald I: The EEG, eye-movements and dreams of

the blind. Q J Exp Psychol 14:183–186, 1962

13. Stillerman M, Gibbs EL, Perlstein MA: Electroencephalographic changes in strabismus. Am J Ophthalmol 35:54–63, 1950
14. Forssman B: Vestibular reactivity in cases of congenital nystagmus and blindness. Acta Otolaryngol 57:539–555, 1964
15. Gay AJ, Newman N, Stroud MH: Vestibular studies in a case of congenital nystagmus. Lancet 2:694–695, 1969
16. Forssman B: A study of congenital nystagmus. Acta Otolaryngol 56:663–671, 1963
17. Marshall WA, Swan AV: Seasonal variation in growth rates of normal and blind children. Hum Biol 43:502–516, 1971
18. Magee K, Basinska J, Quarrington B, et al: Blindness and menarche. Life Sci 9:7–12, 1970
19. Fariss BL, Botz LD: Comparison of hydroxyindole-O-methyl-transferase levels in pineal glands of normal, blinded and congenitally anophthalmic guinea pigs. Endocrinology 96:1595–1596, 1975
20. Deguchi T: Shift of circadian rhythm of serotonin:acetyl coenzyme A N-acetyltransferase activity in pineal gland of rat in continuous darkness or in the blinded rat. J Neurochem 25:91–93, 1975
21. Levy WH: Blindness and the Blind. London, Chapman & Hall, 1872, p 504
22. Valvo A: Behavior patterns and visual rehabilitation after early and long lasting blindness. Am J Ophthalmol 65:19–24, 1968

13
Mobility and Orientation

Successful mobility of the blind is defined as an ability to "travel safely, comfortably, and independently."[1] It is one of the most important skills a visually impaired individual can acquire since it helps ensure his personal independence. Like intelligence, mobility is a combination of various abilities developed since birth. In congenitally and early-blinded children, the formative years determine to a large extent how well they will be able to travel independently in later life.[2-6] Many severely visually impaired persons cannot travel safely, comfortably, and independently, because in their early childhood they did not have adequate opportunity to acquire the various skills necessary, or else they are hindered by other handicaps. For example, cerebral palsy, muscle weakness, poor coordination, mental retardation, hearing loss, perceptual difficulties, or severe congenital heart disease may interfere with the development of adequate traveling skills, despite the provision of appropriate opportunities for learning. Children without additional handicaps and with an intact central nervous system still vary markedly in their ability to travel and, therefore, training programs must always be tailored to each individual.[3]

CHARACTERISTICS OF SUCCESSFUL MOBILITY

As discussed earlier, research disproved the theory of sensory compensation and showed that superior nonvisual senses are not special gifts to the congenitally blind but the result of training from early childhood. Tactile perception, sound localization, and smell are all used in successful orientation and mobility. A blind child should be able to detect changes of surface texture through his hands, feet, and cane; he must learn the significance of wind direction, draughts of air, and the position of the sun; he must learn to interpret varied sounds and odors; and use efficient echolocation in order to be successful in his traveling.

Residual Vision

Any residual vision—even light perception—is an advantage in mobility.[3,6,7] As described in chapter 9, the timing of independent walking in congenitally visually impaired children is determined to some degree by the amount of remaining sight. Thus, those who have partial vision begin to walk earlier, on the average, than the totally blind. This does not mean, however, that children without vision cannot walk independently at the normal time; indeed, they may do so if all appropriate opportunities are provided. On the other hand, Lord found that, although students with light perception were significantly superior to the totally blind in walking and running freely, the totally blind were better at pointing out cardinal directions and traveling routes using cardinal directions.[2]

Type of Visual Loss

A child with macular (central) vision and peripheral loss sees quite differently from one with only peripheral vision and no macular function. Those with good central but poor peripheral vision have the most difficulty in traveling. Thus, many blind children with markedly reduced distance visual acuity can ride a bike or run freeely while those with "tunnel vision," who may have normal distance visual acuity, may constantly trip or bump into objects (Figs. 13-1 to 13-4).

It has to be emphasized again and again that the kind of residual sight and how a child uses it—that is, his visual efficiency—are much more important than the simple measurement of his distance visual acuity in understanding how he functions.

Age at Onset of Blindness

Early vision provides an organizational frame of reference that serves as an integrative function for spatial information received through nonvisual senses.[3] Furthermore, newly blinded young adults are more flexible in their response to mobility training than are older adults.[8] On the other hand, congenitally blind children do not, like persons with acquired visual impairment, go through periods of depression which may interfere with their rehabilitation.

Intelligence

Although Lord and Blaha have shown that persons with lower IQ tend to have poor mobility,[9] it is much more satisfactory to relate the various intellectual abilities to traveling skills. Intelligence cannot be

Fig. 13-1. Traffic at an intersection. (Courtesy of Dr. B. Huntsman.)

Fig. 13-2. Impaired central vision. The reader should look at the center of the picture and note that the periphery is hazy. Individuals with this type of visual loss claim that the blanked out area is not completely devoid of sight. (Courtesy of Dr. B. Huntsman.)

Fig. 13-3. Tunnel vision. Individuals with marked peripheral vision loss tend to have more difficulty in traveling than those who lack central vision only. (Courtesy of Dr. B. Huntsman.)

Fig. 13-4. The traffic as observed by a person with patchy and distorted vision. (Courtesy of Dr. B. Huntsman.)

represented accurately by a number since it is made up of a complex set of variables. The extra memory load for visually impaired travelers, the importance of cognitive factors, and spatial relations have been repeatedly stressed.[3]

Posture and Balance

There is considerable evidence that good posture and balance are necessary for effective mobility.[10,11] Siegel and Murphy provided a detailed analysis of the role posture plays in orientation and mobility and showed the positive correlation between improvement in posture and improvement in mobility.[11]

Body Image

Satisfactory body image is also stressed in effective mobility.[2,4,5,11] Hapeman defines it as the child's knowledge of his various body parts,[4] Siegel and Murphy describe it as the mental image of the body in space,[11] while others use psychoanalytic terms and speak of ego formation.[12,13] No matter how body image is defined, it develops through continuous perception and interpretation of all sensory stimuli. Research clearly shows that the absence of a major sense, as in congenitally or early-blinded children, interferes with the normal development of body image.[2,4,5] It is generally agreed that any child must first know his body before he is able to learn more effectively about his environment; in other words, the development of a good body image will determine how well he will conceptualize space around him and how successfully he will travel later. In congenitally blind children, the awareness of body parts is not attained automatically but comes as the result of continuous learning through appropriate opportunities, usually provided by his parents. Cratty and Sams recommend that as soon as a blind child is able to talk, he should be taught to name the various parts of his body.[5] It seems easier for them to identify their upper than their lower body parts. By the age of 5, sighted children are generally aware of most of their fingers; on the other hand, the blind experience difficulties in naming and locating their fingers with the exception of the thumb and little finger. From 5 to 7 years of age, they should learn simple left and right discrimination on themselves; then from 6 to 9 years, more complex judgments about their bodies, such as their relationship to objects and to other persons' reference systems, should be taught. The blind are able to develop satisfactory knowledge of left and right body discrimination like the sighted but have great difficulty in projecting themselves into the left-right reference systems of others. Thus, a congenitally blind child should be able to identify his own left-right body parts by 7 years of age but usually cannot do this on the examiner at 9 years when sighted children are expected to do so.

The conceptualization of space is very different when it is constructed with vision rather than without. The sighted base their spatial concepts on information obtained visually, whereas the congenitally totally blind depend upon their other senses. The difference is so great that the sighted and the blind are simply unable to understand each other's spatial concepts. Persons who regain their vision in later life emphasize this by pointing out that they had no idea prior to the operation of "how space really looked."[14]

Several investigators have devised training programs to improve body image and spatial concepts of visually impaired children.[4,5,11,15] The interested reader is advised to look up these references.

Personality, Social, and Environmental Factors

Personality, social, and environmental factors are perhaps more important in successful mobility than the previously described characteristics. The motivation of a visually impaired child, his own and his family's attitudes toward blindness, love bonds, various personality factors such as anxiety, dependency, activity, the number and order of siblings in the family, the health of the parents, the location of the child's home, economics, and many other variables will all affect the attainment of successful mobility. No wonder that training programs must always be individually tailored as the instructor will be dealing with different factors in each person.

Mobility Aids

Professionals are often uncertain about the advantages and disadvantages of the two basic mobility aids: the long cane and the guide dog (Figs. 13-5 and 13-6). In order to use a long cane efficiently, the blind person must develop a high degree of sensory acuity and an ability to utilize the environmental information perceived. He must learn orientation, reorientation, corner detection, and a variety of cane techniques while heavily depending on his nonvisual senses. The interpretation of geography is of great importance.

The guide dog is trained to guide a blind person in safety under normal environmental conditions and is a clear-path and destination finder. The guide dog offers companionship, compensation for human error, more independence, higher speed, and less strain in traveling than the long cane, but it needs constant care and performance varies somewhat from day to day. The interpretation of geography is less important. Guide-dog training is residential whereas long-cane training is not. The interested readers who wish to know the details of these two mobility

Fig. 13-5.   An individual using long cane.

aids are advised to look up the references given.[16,17]

There are other newer mobility aids, and for the complete listing, the catalogue by Clark should be consulted.[18] The Laser Typhlocane and Binaural Sensory Aid for the Blind are the most promising.[19]

"Artificial vision," produced by electrical stimulation of the visual cortex with implanted electrodes from visual sensors, is fascinating research, but it is still in the experimental stages.[20]

Training and Testing

It has been emphasized throughout this section that mobility and orientation develop from the time of birth. In the evaluation of visually impaired children, it is helpful to be able to measure these abilities by standardized tests. Lord[2] and Cratty and Sams[5] have developed such scales, which serve this purpose well.

Fig. 13-6.   Traveling with a guide dog.

In recent years there has been a strong interest in extending mobility and orientation instruction to include school-aged blind children.[2] Although they are usually ready for formal mobility training in their teens, the timing depends largely on how well they have been prepared for this stage.

CONCLUSIONS

1. Successful mobility is one of the most important skills a visually impaired individual can acquire since it helps to ensure his personal independence.
2. Mobility is a combination of abilities developed since birth; it is not a special gift to the congenitally blind but the result of training.
3. Training programs must always be individually tailored as the instructor will be dealing with different factors in each person.
4. Any residual vision is an advantage in mobility.
5. The kind of residual sight and how the child uses it, that is, his visual efficiency, are much more important than the simple measurement of his distance visual acuity in understanding his functioning.
6. Early vision provides an organizational frame of reference that serves as an integrative function for spatial information received through nonvisual senses.
7. Good posture and balance are necessary for effective mobility.

8. In congenitally blind children, the awareness of body parts is not attained automatically but comes as the result of continuous learning through opportunities usually provided by his parents. He must know his body before he is able to learn more effectively about his environment.

9. The conceptualization of space is very different when it is constructed with vision rather than without.

10. Personality, social, and environmental factors are also important in successful mobility.

REFERENCES

1. Foulke E: The perceptual basis for mobility. Research Bulletin No 23. New York, American Foundation for the Blind, 1971, pp 1–8

2. Lord FE: Development of scales for the measurement of orientation and mobility of young blind children. Except Child 36:77–81, 1969

3. Warren DH, Kocon JA: Factors in the successful mobility of the blind: A review. Research Bulletin No 28. New York, American Foundation for the Blind, 1974, pp 191–214

4. Hapeman LB: Developmental concepts of blind children between the ages of three and six as they relate to orientation and mobility. International Journal for the Education of the Blind 17:41–48, 1967

5. Cratty BJ, Sams TA: The Body-Image of Blind Children. New York, American Foundation for the Blind, 1968

6. Jan JE, Robinson GC, Scott E, et al: Hypotonia in the blind child. Dev Med Child Neurol 17:35–40, 1975

7. Bauman MK, Yoder NM: Adjustment to Blindness Re-Viewed. Springfield, Ill, Charles C Thomas, 1966

8. Leonard JA, Newman RC: Spatial orientation in the blind. Nature 215:1413–1414, 1967

9. Lord FE, Blaha LE: Demonstration of home and community support needed to facilitate mobility instruction for blind youth. Final Report, Demonstration Project, Grant RD-1784-S (from the Division of Research and Demonstration Grants, Social and Rehabilitation Service, DHEW, Washington, DC), 1968

10. Turner M, Siegel IM: Physical therapy for the blind child. Phys Ther 49:1357–1363, 1969

11. Siegel IM, Murphy TJ: Postural determinants in the blind. Final Project Report, Grant RD-3512-SB-700C2 (from the Division of Research and Demonstration Grants, Social and Rehabilitation Service, DHEW, Washington, DC), 1970

12. Fraiberg S: Parallel and divergent patterns in blind and sighted infants. Psychoanal Study Child 23:264–299, 1968

13. Burlingham D: Psychoanalytic Studies of the Sighted and the Blind. New York, International Universities Press, 1972

14. Valvo A: Behavior patterns and visual rehabilitation after early and long-

lasting blindness. Am J Ophthalmol 65(suppl 1):19-24, 1968
15. Garry RJ, Ascarelli A: Teaching topographical orientation and spatial orientation to congenitally blind children. Journal of Education 143:1-49, 1960
16. Klee KE: The long cane and the guide dog as mobility aids. The New Beacon 59:141-147, 1975
17. Morse K, Lessard K: Mobility for the Partially Sighted. Perkins School for the Blind, Watertown, Mass., 1975
18. Clark LL (ed): International Catalog. Aids and Appliances for Blind and Visually Impaired Persons. New York, American Foundation for the Blind, 1973
19. Freiberger H: Mobility and reading aids for the blind: Recent developments in rehabilitation devices. Bull NY Acad Med 50:667-671, 1974
20. Dobelle WH, Mladejovsky MG, Girvin JP: Artificial vision for the blind: Electrical stimulation of visual cortex offers hope for functional prosthesis. Science 183:440-443, 1974

14

A Neuropsychiatric Study of Visually Impaired Children: An Introduction

A study of the psychological adjustment of visually impaired children and adolescents compared with that of the sighted was completed in 1974 and selected preliminary findings have been reported elsewhere.[1,2] Because the further analysis of this material has proven to be highly relevant to the purposes of this book and because we will refer frequently to it in other chapters, it is appropriate to provide an overview here of the method employed, characteristics of the sample studied, demographic data, medical variables, and the reasons why we claim that the index cases and controls were fairly well matched.

The number of variables investigated was so large that only a partial analysis of the data has so far been undertaken. Selected aspects will also be reported in other publications as the work proceeds, and some additional comparisons will be possible with a previous study of deaf children.[3]

OTHER COMPARATIVE STUDIES OF HANDICAPPED CHILDREN AND THEIR FAMILIES

Several other investigations of handicapped children and their families have employed a control group or population control data (see Table 14-1). But by far the most important studies—they can fairly be termed

This study was made possible by a National Health Grant (No. 609-7-372) from the Department of National Health & Welfare, Ottawa, to R. D. Freeman during 1973-74. With the collaboration of Susan F. Malkin, MSW, formerly Research Associate, Department of Psychiatry, University of British Columbia, now Social Worker, Western Institute for the Deaf, Vancouver, Canada.

Table 14-1
Other Comparative Studies
of Handicapped Children

Handicap	Reference
Cerebral palsy	Hewett,[4] Minde et al.[5]
Deaf	Freeman et al.[3]
Mental retardation	Jeffree and Cashdan[6]
Spina bifida	Hare et al.,[7] Tew et al.,[8] Martin[9]
Rubella	Chess et al.[10]
Brain damage	Shaffer et al.[11]

landmarks—have been undertaken by Professors Michael Rutter and Philip Graham and their co-workers in London.[12-20] We are indebted to their model efforts for the stimulus which led to our own, though the methodology of the present investigation was somewhat different, as will be explained below.

Their studies were performed mainly on the Isle of Wight and had the advantage of a defined population with relatively little mobility and good cooperation from the local health and social services. It has now been shown that such epidemiological techniques that eliminate or minimize selection bias have great utility both in generating new hypotheses and in providing practical guidelines for professional practice and training.

A few of the major conclusions of the Isle of Wight studies[12-14] must be mentioned here because they relate to our own study and because they have been resisted by those looking for simple answers. A strong relationship was found between "hard" signs of brain dysfunction (especially epilepsy and cerebral palsy) and psychiatric disorder (approximately 5 times the 6-percent risk in the general population). This was substantially above the rate for children with physical handicaps not involving the brain (about twice that in the general population). They also corroborated the increase in psychiatric disorder found in retarded children. However, there was *no type of behavior characteristic of children with brain dysfunction.* This conclusion has been confirmed by others before and since,[11,21,22] but seems to be unpalatable to many who invoke a stereotype of brain-damaged behavior which has been widely and uncritically accepted.[23,24] The children who did have a significant, persistent psychiatric disorder had been exposed to those factors known to be associated with such disorder in any group of children (e.g., maternal psychiatric disorder, broken home, overcrowding) but were felt to be more vulnerable to these factors because of the brain dysfunction. This view was further supported by a statistical procedure to remove the effect of factors that might otherwise account for differences (e.g., IQ, visibility of handicap, severity of handicap) and by later studies on subpopulations.[15]

What is the importance of this group of interrelated findings for visually impaired children? First, they forcefully challenge the concept that the behavioral *picture* can be accounted for by the presence or absence of brain damage or dysfunction per se. Since many visually impaired children either have signs of such damage or dysfunction, or could have it imputed to them because of developmental, neurological, motor, EEG, or behavioral peculiarities, there is a serious risk that the latter will be thereby explained away.

We make the point throughout this book that this kind of inference is invalid, counterproductive, and sometimes downright dangerous. In most situations we are clearly dealing with multiple causative and aggravating factors with unknown and variable weightings.

It will be seen that this position and the management approaches consistent with it do not merely represent a philosophy that happens to be congenial to us but are an almost inevitable consequence of the analysis of the data.

Nevertheless, the differences in our population of children may cause discrepancies when the findings are compared with those in other investigations. Perhaps the effect of visual impairment swamps or masks other trends. In our discussion of the findings, discrepancies from other studies (especially those previously mentioned) will be pointed out. It should also be realized that in the Isle of Wight studies there were only 11 children with visual impairment living at home or attending residential schools for the blind. An additional 4 were in institutions for the mentally subnormal.

LIMITATIONS OF OTHER STUDIES OF THE VISUALLY IMPAIRED

Several other studies have been published, although only a few have used the comparative method. The studies by Schindele[25] and Cowen et al.[26] failed to show significant differences between the visually impaired and sighted children. The latter study dealt with adolescents, and the question of sampling bias naturally arises. These studies also neglected family aspects, especially fathers, and excluded certain segments of the visually impaired population, e.g., the multihandicapped and the retarded. For the most part, they used a variety of sociometric and psychometric techniques rather than observation in natural (i.e., home or school) settings. There are a large number of other studies that did not use a matched control group, such as the many publications of the Fraiberg and Burlingham groups.

PURPOSES

We attempted to minimize or eliminate the previously mentioned limiting factors in order to obtain the most accurate picture possible of the lives of visually impaired children and their families. In doing this, we feel we achieved some major successes in deriving information not available elsewhere and were able to test previous speculations and opinions based on clinical lore; we also obtained some leads for further research.

LIMITATIONS OF THIS STUDY

There are also limitations of this study which should be noted: (1) absence of data on institutionalized, severely retarded individuals, of whom there were approximately eight in the provincial institution; (2) small size of certain of the subsamples, a frequent problem with the visually impaired; (3) lack of a systematic longitudinal component (possibly to be rectified by a future follow-up study)—this was a cross-sectional investigation; (4) inability to employ inter-rater reliability measures (as in Rutter et al.[13,14]), which would have substantially increased the workload but would have strengthened the validity of the conclusions.

METHOD

All the legally blind children and adolescents in British Columbia are registered with the Canadian National Institute for the Blind (CNIB), a private, multiservice agency, and most have been seen for a team evaluation by the Neuropaediatrics and Blind Services, Ambulatory Services Division, Children's Hospital Diagnostic Centre in Vancouver. (Some other studies of the larger population of the province are reported in chapters 4, 7, and 9 of this volume.) Cases were located by the CNIB, and, of 115 children in the selected region, the families of 100 agreed to participate. One dropped out and seven moved during the early stages of the project, leaving 92 who completed the study.

It should be noted that the Children's Hospital Diagnostic Centre has served as the provincial center for diagnosis and reassessment of handicapped children for the past 7 years and has had a special interest in epidemiology and case finding.

Table 14-2
Matching Adequacy

Item	Index	Control
Social class levels 1 and 2	23.4%	23.5%
Social class levels 3 to 5	54.4%	51.8%
Social class levels 6 and 7	22.2%	24.7%
Mother's age	39.80	39.85
Father's age	41.57	42.60
Years of schooling—mothers	11.34	11.46
Years of schooling—fathers	11.68	12.05
Interval before next sib born	27.6	33.2
How long at present address	83.3	85.3
Total no. of persons in home	4.8	4.8
Persons/sleeping rooms	1.53	1.55

CRITERIA FOR INCLUSION OF INDEX CASES

Criteria for inclusion were (1) age from birth to 20; and (2) legally blind and family living in the Greater Vancouver area (the largest metropolitan area of British Columbia, comprising about 1.2 million people and roughly one-half of the provincial population). There were no exclusions for the presence of other handicaps.

CONTROL GROUP

A control, nonhandicapped child was matched with the index child for sex, closest age, and closest residence. This "neighborhood control" was obtained through the public health nurse who serves the local school and has records of all children in the area. (The nurses were not told the nature of the index child's disability.)

The adequacy of matching can be seen from Table 14-2, which demonstrates that this kind of procedure results in a very close, though unintentional, matching for many variables. It should be pointed out that there was no attempt made to match for family size or tested IQ.

PROCEDURES

The 92 visually impaired children and their 92 controls each underwent the following procedures: (1) Mothers and fathers separately filled out, under supervision, a behavioral questionnaire modified slightly from that used in the Isle of Wight study[14] and, again separately, gave information on their own background, expectations of the child, relations with their relatives, feelings about the child's school situation, the child's early history, health, etc.; (2) an interview was held (usually in the home) with both parents together to discuss various aspects of child rearing, discipline, the interests parents had in common, their experience with counseling or use of psychoactive medication, etc.

Other procedures for the families of the index cases and their children (but not the controls) included the following: (3) pediatric neurological examination by a specialist in work with the visually impaired (J. Jan); (4) review of medical records; (5) school questionnaires filled out by teachers after sufficient time in the school year had passed so all children were well known to them (this covered the behavioral list, some items similar to those on the parent forms, and in addition inquired into their judgments about the child's social relationships, habits, learning capacity, speech, mobility, travel to and from school, and relations with the home); (6) psychological testing on all children not adequately assessed within the previous 2 years. (The three testing psychologists [L. Eaves, B. Huntsman, L. O'Connor] were all familiar with the assessment of blind and partially sighted children and the limitations of such tests); (7) an extensive standardized interview schedule to collect additional information pertinent to the visually impaired child's situation and family; (8) a semistructured psychiatric interview, if possible in the most natural setting.[27] (Most of the children were seen either at home [44 percent] or at school [17 percent].) Of the 92 children, 14 percent had been seen for consultation prior to the study (by RDF) either on private referral or through the school consultation program at the Jericho Hill School for the Blind, the provincial school; (9) a home observation form with special note made of the child's mobility, manner of relating, and sterotyped behavior, if any; and (10) in addition to ratings on the behavioral questionnaire for individual items and total scores, global ratings were made on the overall adjustment of child, parents, and marriage in previous 12 months and prior to that.

RESULTS

Sociodemographic Data

SOCIAL CLASS

As determined by the Blishen scale,[28] a seven-point occupational scale developed for Canada, there were no significant differences between the two groups.

RACE AND RELIGION

The overwhelming majority of families (96-99 percent) were of Caucasian origin and there were no significant differences between the

Table 14–3
Ordinal Position of Child

Position	Index Cases		Controls	
	n	*% (of 85)*	*n*	*% (of 85)*
Only child	12	14.1	8	9.4
Oldest	26	30.6	23	27.1
Second oldest	21	24.7	26	30.6
Third	11	12.9	20	23.5
Fourth and later	14	16.5	8	9.5
Half-sibs only	1	1.2	0	—

NOTE: No significant differences between groups.

two groups of parents in religion (approximately 70 percent Protestant, 15 percent Roman Catholic, and the remainder none or other).

SEX AND AGE

There were 50 males and 42 females. Three children were under the age of 2, eight were between 24 and 47 months, 27 between 48 and 119 months, and the remainder were older.

PARENTAL AGE

On the average, fathers were 2 to 3 years older than were mothers. For both groups, this difference reached significance at the 1 percent level.

FAMILY SIZE AND ORDINAL POSITION

There were no significant differences between the groups in numbers of full siblings, this being 2.2 for the index cases and 1.9 for the controls. The ordinal position of the child is shown in Table 14–3 where it will be seen that there were somewhat more visually impaired only children, although differences did not reach statistical significance.

LANGUAGES OTHER THAN ENGLISH SPOKEN IN
THE HOME

In 22 percent of the families, another language than English was spoken in the home. This was the same for index and control cases.

HOUSING*

Since birth, the visually impaired children had moved an average of 2.2 times (2.1). The average length of residence at present address was 83.5 months (84.7). With regard to the number of persons living

---

*In the following sections, the numbers in parentheses refer to the control-group findings.

in the home and the size of the home, there were an average of 4.9
persons in residence (4.8). A "crowding index" was calculated for each
child, representing the number of persons regularly living in the home
divided by the number of bedrooms. This figure was 1.53 (1.56). None
of these differences achieved statistical significance.

PARENTAL EDUCATION

Again, there were no significant differences between the groups,
nor between mothers and fathers. In a school system that has 12 years
of education through the end of secondary school, the mothers averaged
11.5 years of education and the fathers 12.

MISCELLANEOUS

The average number of automobiles owned by the families was
1.5 (1.7). The interval before the next child was born was 28 months
(33). These differences were not significant. We also looked at the average
number of brothers and sisters that each parent had. These averages
ranged from 1.4 to just under 2, but none of them were significant
with the exception that there were more brothers in the father's family
than there were in the mother's family for the index cases, and this
difference did achieve significance at the 5 percent level.

Medical Aspects

CAUSE OF VISUAL IMPAIRMENT

As can be seen from Figure 14-1, there was a much larger genetic
component in children without other handicaps. Children with injury
as a cause tended to have additional handicaps, and there was a larger
proportion of those in the "other handicaps" group where the cause
was infection or oxygen. These findings are consistent with those of
Robinson et al.[29] and Jan et al.,[30] showing that about 50 percent of
visually impaired children have additional handicaps. The type of additional handicap can be seen in Table 14-4. The mean age in months
of the group with additional handicaps was 109.8 and, for those with
no other handicaps, 138.0. Fifty-eight percent of the group with no
other handicaps were male, whereas this was true of 51 percent of
the group with other handicaps. It can be seen from Table 14-4 that
about 20 percent of the children were mentally retarded, almost the
same number have cerebral palsy, and about 20 percent have other
signs of distinct dysfunction of the central nervous system. Fifteen percent
have seizures and 13 percent have a hearing loss.

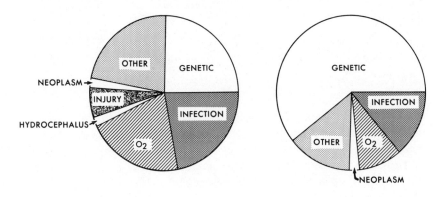

Children with Other Handicaps   Children Without Other Handicaps

Fig. 14-1. Causes of visual impairment.

SEVERITY OF VISUAL IMPAIRMENT

Fourteen of the children were totally blind, 13 had light perception, and the remaining 65 were partially sighted. Because no differences were found between the first two groups, they have been combined into a new group termed "blind" for the rest of the study.

ONSET OF VISUAL IMPAIRMENT

In 77 cases the onset was believed to be congenital. In 6 cases this occurred in the first year of life, in 2 cases in the second year, and in 5 cases over 2 years of age. (In 2 others it was insidious and difficult to date precisely.) Generally, in the analyses of this data spread throughout this book, late-onset cases have been given special consideration.

Table 14-4
Children With Other Handicaps

Handicap	n	% (of 92)*
Cerebral palsy	10	18.9
Convulsive disorder	14	15.2
Hearing impairment	12	13.0
Cardiac dysfunction	2	2.2
Other CNS dysfunction	18	19.6
Mental retardation	18	19.6
Other	12	13.0
None significant	43	46.7

*More than one choice possible.

NUMBER OF MISCARRIAGES AND STILLBIRTHS

Mothers of visually impaired children had an average of 0.43 miscarriages or stillbirths (0.47). This difference is not statistically significant.

HOSPITALIZATION

As will be discussed further in chapters 15 and 16, hospitalization was much more frequent and lengthy in the visually impaired group. There was a statistically significant difference at almost all age levels and for most of the subgroups. Very often the hospitalization was for conditions associated with the visual impairment, rather than because of the impairment itself.

HARD NEUROLOGICAL SIGNS

Using very strict criteria, it was determined that 29 percent of the visually impaired children had indications of central nervous system damage or dysfunction. This includes 24 percent of the males and 36 percent of the females. In a further 13 percent there were equivocal indications of such signs. We made no attempt to deal with the area of so-called minimal brain dysfunction, about which there is so much disagreement.

TIME IN INCUBATOR

Children with no other handicaps were in an incubator for an average of 7.9 days (SD 18.0, range 0-70); children with other handicaps spent an average of 13.5 days in an incubator (SD 22.0, range 0-75).

COMMENTS

This data is presented here to provide a background for the other chapters, into which we have incorporated some of our findings. The use of a "neighborhood control" seems to provide rather good matching on most sociodemographic variables, but one problem in this study is that the mentally retarded, visually impaired children were matched with children of probably normal intelligence. It would have been a much more cumbersome procedure to attempt to find a child with the same testable IQ who also was matched on age, sex, and social class.

Where IQ was felt to be an important variable, we have analyzed the data separately and removed the retarded group and their controls from consideration.

Another point needs emphasis: the Greater Vancouver area is a relatively advantaged area. We did not have a very large number of multiproblem families from lower social classes, and the rate of family break-up was rather low. The conclusions which we reach, therefore, must be generalized to other populations with caution, particularly those where the rate of social problems is higher.

REFERENCES

1. Freeman RD: Blind children and their families. First National Multidisciplinary Conference on Blind Children, Vancouver, Canada, 1974, pp 135–143
2. Freeman RD, Malkin SF: A comparison of the psychosocial problems of deaf, of visually impaired, and of non-handicapped children and their families. Dev Med Child Neurol (in press)
3. Freeman RD, Malkin SF, Hastings JO: Psychosocial problems of deaf children and their families: A comparative study. Am Ann Deaf 120:391–405, 1975
4. Hewett S: The Family and the Handicapped Child: A Study of Cerebral Palsied Children in Their Homes. Chicago, Aldine, 1970
5. Minde KK, Hackett JD, Killou D, et al: How they grow up: 41 physically handicapped children and their families. Am J Psychiatry 128:1554–1560, 1972
6. Jeffree DM, Cashdan A: The home background of the severely subnormal child: A second study. Br J Med Psychol 44:27–33, 1971
7. Hare EH, Laurence KM, Payne H, et al: Spina bifida cystica and family stress. Br Med J 2:757–760, 1966
8. Tew BJ, Payne H, Laurence KM: Must a family with a handicapped child be a handicapped family? Dev Med Child Neurol (suppl 32) 16:95–98, 1974
9. Martin P: Marital breakdown in families of patients with spina bifida cystica. Dev Med Child Neurol 17:757–764, 1975
10. Chess S, Korn SJ, Fernandez PB: Psychiatric Disorders of Children with Congenital Rubella. New York, Brunner/Mazel, 1971
11. Shaffer D, McNamara N, Pincus JH: Controlled observations on patterns of activity, attention, and impulsivity in brain-damaged and psychiatrically disturbed boys. Psychol Med 4:4–18, 1974
12. Graham P, Rutter M: Organic brain dysfunction and child psychiatric disorder. Br Med J 3: 695–700, 1968
13. Rutter M, Graham P, Yule W: A Neuropsychiatric Study in Childhood. Clinics in Developmental Medicine Nos 35/36. Philadelphia, Lippincott, 1970
14. Rutter M, Tizard J, Whitmore K (eds): Education, Health and Behaviour. London, Longmans, 1970
15. Seidel UP, Chadwick OFD, Rutter M: Psychological disorders in crippled children: A comparative study of children with and without brain damage. Dev Med Child Neurol 17: 563–573, 1975
16. Rutter M, Cox A, Tupling C, et al: Attainment and adjustment in two geographic areas: I. The prevalence of psychiatric disorder. Br J Psychiatry 126:493–509, 1975
17. Berger M, Yule W, Rutter M: Attainment and adjustment in two geographic

areas: II. The prevalence of specific reading retardation. Br J Psychiatry 126:510–519, 1975

18. Rutter M, Yule B, Quinton D, et al: Attainment and adjustment in two geographic areas: III. Some factors accounting for area differences. Br J Psychiatry 126:520–533, 1975

19. Cox A, Rutter M, Newman S, et al: A comparative study of infantile autism and specific developmental receptive language disorder: II. Parental characteristics. Br J Psychiatry 126:146–159, 1975

20. Bartak L, Rutter M, Cox A: A comparative study of infantile autism and specific developmental receptive language disorder: I. The children. Br J Psychiatry 126:127–145, 1975

21. Schulman JL, Kaspar JC, Throne FM: Brain Damage and Behavior: A Clinical-Experimental Study. Springfield, Ill, Charles C Thomas, 1965

22. Werry JS: Studies on the hyperactive child: IV. An empirical analysis of the minimal brain dysfunction syndrome. Arch Gen Psychiatry 19:9–16, 1968

23. Wender P: Minimal Brain Dysfunction in Children. New York, Wiley-Interscience, 1971

24. Freeman RD: Minimal brain dysfunction, hyperactivity, and learning disorders: Epidemic or episode? School Review 85:5–30, 1976

25. Schindele R: The social adjustment of visually handicapped children in different educational settings. Research Bulletin No 28. New York, American Foundation for the Blind, 1974, pp 125–144

26. Cowen EL, Underberg RP, Verrillo RT, et al: Adjustment to Visual Disability in Adolescence. New York, American Foundation for the Blind, 1961

27. Freeman RD: The home visit in child psychiatry: Its usefulness in diagnosis and training. J Am Acad Child Psychiatry 6:276–294, 1967

28. Blishen BR: The construction and use of an occupational class scale. Can J Econ Pol Sci 24:519–531, 1958

29. Robinson GC, Watt JA, Scott E: A study of congenital blindness in British Columbia: Methodology and medical findings. Can Med Assoc J 68:831–836, 1968

30. Jan JE, Robinson GC, Scott E: A multidisciplinary approach to the problems of the multihandicapped blind child. Can Med Assoc J 109:705–707, 1973

15
The Family of the Visually Impaired Child

INTRODUCTION

There have been many studies of handicapped children and their families.[1-11] Most of them do not support the stereotypes of constant emotional crisis at the brink of marital separation or divorce, at one extreme, or heroism at the other. The notion that there should be some invariant characteristics of the families of handicapped children is a rather bizarre one, and the reasons for it are not entirely clear. Perhaps it helps us to manage a complex situation with a feeling of competence that would otherwise be lacking. Another factor may be the sheer inability of most persons to imagine what it would be like to have an apparent catastrophe occur in their own families. Some of these same attitudes and expectations probably affect the judgment of a family when they are first coming to grips with the presence of a handicap.

Contrary to much widely held opinion, the presence of a visually impaired child is a relatively weak factor in determining many aspects of family life. The best description of the families can be stated in one word: variability.

In this chapter we will (1) present some findings from our own recent comparative study; (2) contrast and compare these results with those from some other studies of the families of handicapped children; and (3) present some practical implications of this findings.

WHY IS THE FAMILY IMPORTANT IN MANAGING THE HANDICAPPED CHILD?

This may seem like a nonsensical question to pose. But one needs to have some idea of the function of the family before trying to understand those aspects of the handicap and its management that may prove maladaptive for the child.

It is generally accepted that the family forms the basis for early growth and development, including the child's self-concept. There are many theories of how this comes about and its relationship to similar developmental patterns in the higher mammals. The most extensive and lucid exposition of infant development in relation to the family is probably the recent work of Bowlby.[12,13] He has attempted a synthesis of psychoanalytic developmental theory with evidence from learning theory and research on animal ethology. He postulates that the family setting gradually shapes and modifies the child's built-in behavioral plasticity. He sees the child's tie to his mother as a product of the activity of a number of behavioral systems that function to maintain proximity to the mother. Once mobility develops, fairly typical attachment behavior is usually seen. Anything frightening, such as the mother's actual or anticipated departure, will activate a system that serves to keep the child and mother close. This becomes less urgent as the child develops.

The work of Kennell and his co-workers has shown that early attachment behavior between mother and infant can have enduring effects.[14,15,15a] For example, mothers who are separated from their newborns because of a medical problem, such as prematurity, are later observed to hold the babies differently. There is some evidence that children subjected to battering had more medical problems with more disruptions of mother-infant attachment in early life. It is thus clear that there are many possibilities for impairing this essential attachment, some of which may be necessary, some avoidable.

We make the assumption that there are behavioral systems in infants and parents, which interact with each other so as to ensure bonding; generally the social system supports the effectiveness of these patterns.

But what happens with a child who is handicapped at birth? Visually impaired children are seriously at risk because of the many obstacles to bonding. These risks can include actual damage to some behavioral mechanism in the baby; the absence of eye contact between mother and infant, an important influence; physical separation of infant from mother because of medical treatment; increased anxiety on the part of the mother; and a reluctance of the mother to stimulate the baby, perhaps out of fear and uncertainty.

The birth of a handicapped child does not bring the relief that parents expect at the end of a pregnancy but, rather, a period of sustained indecision and anxiety and the need to adapt to a different child than the one anticipated.[16] The families react not only to the impairment as it actually is but to what they think it is.

We therefore need to examine some of the manifestations of positive or negative functioning of child and family and understand how it might be possible to minimize adverse influences, not only for the handicapped child but the rest of the family as well.

THE IMPACT OF SUSPICION AND DIAGNOSIS

In an excellent and concise summary of the feelings and behavior of parents of handicapped children, MacKeith has stated that when parents first learn about or suspect the handicap "until their anxieties are (to some extent) dealt with by full assessment and explanation, their child is 'not a person but a question mark'. This is a doctor's job"[17] (p. 527). He continues:

> Whatever the handicap, the reactions of parents to all varieties of handicapped children have much that is similar. Reactions will be influenced by whether the handicap is evident at birth or becomes evident later, after the parents have "fallen in love" with the child. They will be influenced by whether the handicap is obvious to other people, and by the attitudes of other people—including lay people, teachers, social workers and doctors—to handicaps and to handicapped people.[17] (p. 524)

Problems seem to be worse if the handicapped baby is the first, or has multiple difficulties. As Chess et al. observed, "When parents have already had a normal child, the grief attendant upon the birth of a defective child is still very real. But the devastation of the parents whose first baby is born with multiple handicaps is all the more dramatic"[5] (p. 151).

The Pregnancy

In our families only one-third of the pregnancies were said to be planned. This is somewhat lower than the 50 percent reported by Walker et al. for children with spina bifida.[18] This is important because, if most pregnancies are accidents, when problems occur in the child's life one should not assume that the accidental nature of the pregnancy by itself was very meaningful in affecting parental reactions later.

Seventy-one percent of the mothers felt positive throughout their pregnancy about being pregnant. Another 15 percent were initially negative but felt positive later. Five and one-half percent said they were indifferent throughout, and another 5.5 percent felt badly throughout. Seventy-eight percent of the fathers rated themselves as feeling positive during the pregnancy, but when the father was not present during the interview (because of marital break-up or other reasons), the mothers rated the fathers' reactions as positive in only 60 percent of cases. The mother's physical health was affected by major problems in one-third, only about half being in good health during pregnancy. We do not have detailed information to report how this compares with the judgment of the mother's physician. Seventy-eight percent of the mothers rated their mental state during the pregnancy as satisfactory, 6 percent persistently depressed, and 14 percent anxious. Almost 30 percent of the mothers retrospectively reported a persistent feeling that the child would be defective. (We do not have comparative data from the controls.)

The mother first saw the baby in the delivery room in three-quarters of the cases, later on the day of birth in 8 percent and not until more than 24 hours later in 15 percent.

Suspicion and Diagnosis

Table 15-1 shows the ages of suspicion and confirmation of the visual impairment, and the average delay. It can be seen that suspicion is earlier in the blind and delay is shorter, which is to be expected since children with some useful vision would be less likely to show the behavioral patterns that would alert someone to the impairment.

In twenty percent of cases, the mother alone suspected the diagnosis. In the majority of these, the father was apparently unsure as compared with the mother. In a much smaller percentage (6 percent), the father suspected and the mother disagreed or was unsure. In 28 percent, both parents suspected visual impairment. Thus, in just over 60 percent of cases, it was one or both parents who first thought there might be a problem. (This compares with 75 percent of cases in the similar study of deaf children.[3]) A relative was the first to suspect in 5 percent, a friend or neighbor in just over 2 percent, and a physician in 30 percent. The latter figure is interesting because it compares with only 5 percent in the study of the deaf. An average of 2.46 physicians were seen between suspicion and confirmation.

Diagnosis was confirmed mainly by an ophthalmologist (74 percent), although pediatricians and family doctors each provided this confirmation in 10 percent of the cases.

Most parents in our area go to their family physician for primary care, and, indeed, this is where they took their children when they suspected impairment. As compared with the study of the deaf,[3] in

Table 15-1
Suspicion, Confirmation and Delay in Diagnosis*

	Blind	Partial Vision
Number of cases	22	50
Age suspected: mean	3.18	4.16
SD	2.56	9.59
range	0-11	0-48
Age confirmed: mean	4.59	8.31
SD	3.14	15.39
range	0-12	0-72
Delay—mean	1.41	4.15

*With onset of impairment at birth; in months.

which the family physician was said to have rejected the idea of deafness in 54 percent of cases, this occurred in only 10 percent with the more obvious visual impairment. In another 10 percent, the doctor either reassured the parents or felt uncertain. In 67 percent, he felt the child was visually impaired, and, in 8 percent, he was concerned for reasons having to do with other handicaps. In the deaf study, 36 percent of family physicians were said to have refused a referral to a specialist. This was true in only one case (1.6 percent) of the visually impaired; however, an additional nine physicians (14.8 percent) felt a referral was not necessary but acceded to parental requests.

As for pediatricians, none rejected the idea but one-third were unsure. All of them referred to an ophthalmologist.

Imparting the Diagnosis

Eighty-four percent of the parents felt that the timing of the telling was correct, but 12.3 percent said it should have been earlier and 3.7 percent later. (These findings are consistent with those in other studies, which indicate the parents overwhelmingly wish to be told the truth as soon as possible.[19]) Parents were told together in 43 percent of cases and separately in 36 percent, but 16 percent of fathers were never told anything directly by the physician. (This should be a cause for some concern.) The doctor's attitude when imparting the information was said to be negative or brusque in 14 (16.9 percent) and uninterested or neutral in 18 (21.7 percent). In only 60.2 percent of cases did the parents feel that his attitude was either sympathetic or generally positive. While this may be distorted retrospectively, it goes along with the prevalent notion that a substantial minority of parents look back on the diagnostic interview as one that could have been handled better.[18]

Although the parents in almost two-thirds of the cases felt there

Table 15-2
Parents' Immediate Reaction to Diagnosis

Reactions	Mothers		Fathers	
	n	%	n	%
Shock, disbelief	29	37.2	20	36.4
Depression	7	9.0	4	7.3
Nothing felt	9	11.5	11	20.0
Relief	6	7.7	6	10.9
Guilt	2	2.6	0	—
More than one of above	5	6.4	0	—
Can't recall	3	3.8	2	3.6
Other	17	21.8	12	21.8
Totals	78	100.0	55	100.0

had been enough time to ask questions, over 35 percent felt there had not been.

Parental Reaction to the Diagnosis

As can be seen from Table 15-2, more than one-third of mothers and fathers reacted with shock or immediate disbelief when told. Some felt unable to react. A few were relieved when they could finally focus their suspicion.

From discussions with both parents, it seems that the mother's initial reaction tended to be greater than the father's in more than 40 percent (Table 15-3).

Perceived Helpfulness of Physician

About half the physicians were said to not be very helpful in providing information about the cause of the problem. (This may have been due to the cause being unknown rather than to any defect in the physician's ability to explain.) However, in giving the parents some idea about the

Table 15-3
Comparison of Parental Reactions

	n	%
Mother greater than father	35	43.2
Father greater than mother	6	7.4
About the same	39	48.1
Unsure	1	1.2
Totals	81	99.9

future, the physician was reported to be inadequate in 66.2 percent of cases (the difference between these two areas of explanation is significant at the 5 percent level—$\chi^2 = 4.10$). An equivalent level of unhelpfulness was reported regarding sources of help for the family. (We presume this has improved recently with greater awareness by ophthalmologists of the early-intervention services of the Canadian National Institute for the Blind.) Seventy-five percent of parents reported that the physician either did not discuss or adequately deal with the question of inheritance of the impairment.

We asked whether parents felt they had ever been given conflicting advice. The answer was yes with regards to the presence or absence of visual impairment for 6.8 percent, the degree of visual impairment for 11.4 percent, the prognosis for 9.1 percent, the management of the impairment for 13.6 percent, and aspects of child rearing for 2.3 percent.

Further Adaptation to the Presence of the Handicapped Child

We asked what the most difficult thing was for the parents in the first 6 months after diagnosis. As can be seen from Table 15-4, more mothers reported that their own emotions were a source of concern to them than did the fathers, who seemed to categorize this more as feelings toward the child. Relatives' reactions were not a major source of concern as compared with these others.

Almost 30 percent of the parents reported that they had had some previous contact with visually impaired persons in one way or another. In the first 6 months after the diagnosis, 31 percent made contacts with other parents of visually impaired children, and eventually two-thirds of the parents had done so. Seventy-two percent felt that these contacts were helpful, but a few found them disturbing. Most impressive was

Table 15-4
What Was Most Difficult in the First 6 Months After Diagnosis?*

| | Mothers | | Fathers | |
	n	%	n	%
Own emotions	26	35.1	4	10.0
Feelings toward child	27	36.5	24	60.0
Feelings toward spouse	1	1.4	0	—
Dealing with relatives	4	5.4	2	5.0
Other	16	21.6	10	25.0
Totals	74	100.0	40	100.0

*$\chi^2 = 9.49$; df = 2; $p < 0.01$.

the vote of confidence given by the parents to the supportive services extended by the Canadian National Institute for the Blind, since 66.7 percent reported that these were exceptionally helpful and an additional 22.3 percent that they were helpful, making a total of 90 percent.

Reading materials were found useful by just over half the parents.

Because it has often been said that religion and religious beliefs play an important part in adaptation to a handicap,[20] we asked about this area. One-third of the mothers and 28 percent of the fathers reported that religious beliefs and practices had been helpful to them (a statistically nonsignificant difference). Six percent of mothers and fathers said that their religious beliefs had undergone some change as a result of the visual impairment.

Half the parents wished to have other children after the handicap was diagnosed. The reasons given by those who did not wish other children were as follows: 31 percent feared having another visually impaired child; 28.6 percent had had enough children; 16.7 percent said their own health was a factor; and almost 12 percent feared not being able to cope with an additional child. Parental disagreement about having other children was reported in only 8.7 percent of cases. Twenty-three percent of the parents said that they had tried to avoid another pregnancy specifically because of the child's visual impairment. Eleven sets of parents sought family planning help. This was said to have been offered by the family physician in 7 cases. Eleven of the mothers (15.1 percent) had had a tubal ligation and 26 of the fathers (35.6 percent of those responding) had had a vasectomy. In half the families neither parent had undergone sterilization. (We do not have figures on the time that elapsed between the birth of the impaired child and the sterilization procedure.) We have determined, however, that in spite of the previously mentioned determination to avoid pregnancy, as many additional children were born to these families as were born to the parents of the sighted children. (The same finding emerged from the study of the deaf.[3])

HOSPITALIZATION

Early hospitalization, discussed further in chapter 16, can be a crisis for a family as well as having a lasting effect upon the child. Gibbs has presented a poignant story, largely in a mother's own words, of the effects of hospitalization and separation on a blind child and the family.[21]

Several important studies have shown that hospitalization in early life can have adverse effects, either through an increase in the parents' anxiety about the child and a view of him as vulnerable[22-25] or perhaps directly upon the child's ability to form attachments.[12]

Table 15-5
Days Hospitalized—Total Group*

Year	Index	Control	Difference	t	p (one-tailed)
1	24.65	1.14	23.51	4.96	<0.001
2	6.06	1.06	5.00	2.64	<0.01
3-4	12.19	1.02	11.17	1.90	<0.05
5-7	5.30	0.75	4.56	3.22	=0.001
8+	14.84	2.37	12.45	2.07	<0.025

*$n = 63$, df $= 62$.

Table 15-6
Days Hospitalized—Blind*

Year	Index	Control	Difference	t	p (one-tailed)
1	50.25	1.92	48.33	3.53	<0.005
2	5.83	0.17	5.67	2.07	<0.05
3-4	6.92	0.25	6.67	1.87	<0.05
5-7	3.67	0.92	2.75	1.48	trend
8+	10.25	3.50	6.75	1.34	trend

*$n = 12$, df $= 11$.

As can be seen from Tables 15-5 through 15-7, there was a great excess of days hospitalized in the first year of life for the children in our study, and this trend continued in every year, although it did not always reach statistical significance for all of the subgroups in later years. That this continues to be a problem is evident from another questionnaire we used, in which we found that in the previous 12 months five of the visually impaired children had been hospitalized for what the parents considered to be a serious illness, whereas this was true for only one of the control children. For the total visually impaired group, only 6 of 82 (7.3 percent) were never hosptialized, compared with 53.7 percent of the controls. This wide spread holds for both the

Table 15-7
Days Hospitalized—Partial Vision*

Year	Index	Control	Difference	t	p (one-tailed)
1	19.92	1.26	18.67	3.36	=0.001
2	3.44	1.31	2.13	1.30	trend
3-4	16.00	1.08	14.92	1.59	trend
5-7	6.15	0.49	5.67	2.71	=0.005
8+	16.05	2.36	13.69	1.45	trend

*$n = 39$, df $= 38$.

blind and the partially sighted subgroups. (This difference is highly significant, with $\chi^2 = 39.39$, df $= 1$; $p < 0.0001$.)

Suffice it to say here that although many of these hospitalizations probably could not have been prevented, some might have been, and some might have been shortened; it should also be possible to minimize parent-infant separation. Although the evidence previously cited seems impressive with regard to the importance of mothers having contact with premature or sick infants, many hospitals are resistant to change and require pressure before this occurs. Since half the children hospitalized in the first year will also be hospitalized in the second year and again in the third or fourth years of life, the implications for monitoring of hospital practices, visiting, and other aspects of mother-child relationships should be obvious.

There are many examples of the importance of this problem. In the book by Kvaraceus and Hayes a mother stated, "This baby needed my milk; it was the one thing I should have been able to give her—and I could not."[26] (p. 255).

Bergman and Stamm reported that the morbidity from "cardiac non-disease" was more significant than that from actual cardiac dysfunction: parents who were told that their baby or child had a heart murmur misunderstood the implications and restricted the child's activities.[27] Sigal and Gagnon reported that, when a child had been hospitalized for severe gastroenteritis between ages 2 and 5, there were more conduct problems and more dependency problems between the ages of 8 and 12.[25] They felt that parental preoccupation was important and that, because pediatricians were themselves no longer worried, they failed to act to help the parents with their worries. The parental worry was related to the perceived severity of the illness, not the actual severity.

When a baby is immediately removed, the mother may have a reaction like that described by Walker et al.:

> I only saw her through a glass door before she went away. It wasn't as if you had had a baby at all. Then she was in an incubator for ages and she seemed far away.[18] (p. 466-467)

The magnified anxieties that build up when there has not been contact were shown in the same paper:

> I saw her on the tenth day. I was terrified of that baby—scared to go and see her. I didn't know whether to expect a monster or not. I couldn't go into the room.[18] (p. 467)

We found a statistical relationship between hospitalization in the first year of life and IQ. This is probably indirect and may be an indication that the children who were hospitalized longest had additional handicaps and problems, some of them involving the central nervous system. It is also possible that one component of this correlation is psychosocial.

ADDITIONAL DIAGNOSES

We want to emphasize that many of our children had additional problems, the diagnoses of which may have occurred at any time during their lives. Our major concern is the adding of "insult to injury" until parents come to feel that the child is nothing but a collection of defects. The presence of additional handicaps may also directly impair the child's ability to learn and make sense of the world. When combined with the longer time separated from the parents in hospital, the painful or frightening experiences, the possible effects of retardation or central nervous system dysfunction on the organization of perceptions, we could expect a higher rate of serious difficulties than in the single-handicap group.

It is important to explain to parents the actual implications of additional diagnoses and sometimes the reasons why they were not apparent at a particular previous point. Physicians and nurses should model positive interactions with the baby so that the mother can see that it is possible to feed, pick up, and cuddle a baby who has several impairments. Continuing support is necessary to make sure the parents understand in what ways the visual impairment and other handicaps do and do not matter.

Although the presence of additional handicaps is associated with more difficulties, more learning problems and retardation, in the individual case it is quite possible for the child to be well adjusted and successful in spite of several impairments. (One of our teenagers who had been deaf also became blind from a hereditary condition. His mother was frequently depressed and his father did not know how to communicate with him. In spite of all these problems, this boy had an excellent personality, somehow managed to interest other teenagers in him to the point where they learned to communicate with him, and was rated as well adjusted.)

PRESCHOOL AND SCHOOL

Starting school is an important social ritual in our society. Many parents of visually impaired children will doubt the possibility of their child's success. We tend to strongly encourage them to send the child to a sighted or ordinary preschool, only introducing whatever special educational methods are necessary at a later point when the child requires them. The family also needs a respite from the child, and the visually impaired child is probably even more in need of the experience of learning how to cope with adults outside the family. Although Kershaw indicated the need for blind children as young as age 2 to go away from home to a special school,[28] we disagree. He based his ideas upon the need for physical protection and the impossibility of the parents providing this in the home. We believe it is necessary for the child to encounter awkward and even painful situations. It is absolutely imperative that children and parents take risks; otherwise the child and his family are deprived of an important growth experience.

Parents may worry whether the child has learned enough to cope with a preschool. They will worry whether other adults will accept their child, understand his quirks, and know how to discipline him. They may also be concerned about what the other children will do and whether he will be able to defend or assert himself. In addition, the visually impaired child may show separation anxiety unless there has been a gradual encouraging of such experiences. School is also the situation where the child's problems in coping may highlight, to the parents' way of thinking, deficiencies in their parenting. School may force the parents to observe, for the first time, themselves and their child in relation to a peer group or to other handicapped children.

The implications are largely straightforward: it is necessary to

Fig. 15-1.   Mother and child.

strongly encourage a normal variety of experiences building towards independence. The parents should go out, leave the child with other persons, and have the child interact with other children. Some visually impaired children, like children with other handicaps, may show temporary adverse reactions when first starting school. These should not be taken as predictive of later functioning. A physician or other professional can sometimes help the school authorities to see this. If there is severe separation anxiety, this may indicate a family problem that requires special help for resolution.

ADOLESCENCE AND DATING

Although there is no doubt that visually impaired children have more social problems, we found that in our sample the partially sighted children had had as many dating experiences as had their controls. This was true to a lesser extent for the blind. Adolescence is a time when social ineptness may become more obvious and more limiting. For the first time, deficits in knowledge of subtleties in human interaction may prove important. Also, the visually impaired teenager is becoming more aware of differences between himself and others. He may be more easily hurt by what others say. He may also start to deny some aspects of his limitations and become a dare-devil because of his sense of inadequacy in comparison with others. We saw one partially sighted student who would not date a girl more than once. He was afraid that she would find out about his impairment and would then pity him, so that he could not tell whether she was continuing to go out with him because she liked him or was afraid to hurt him. Another boy insisted on riding his bicycle on a busy highway and had several accidents, because he refused to take any precautions.

Parents may also become concerned about sexuality. (See chapter 25.) They may worry about the visually impaired teenager being "taken advantage of," expecially if a girl. There will be temptations to protect the teenager from situations of risk. Also, one must not forget the social importance of the inability to drive a car, particularly in North American secondary school and university settings. A teenager on a date does not want to be chauffeured by his parents.

The implications for this type of crisis of development is for the parents to try to provide a wide range of experiences, so as to prevent problems. Sex education in the general sense is needed—such as what people are like, how they talk together, what they dislike, and why. The need for actual supervision must be individually determined.

Sometimes there are too few conflicts between the visually impaired adolescent and the family and excessive compliance must be looked upon with some suspicion. Family therapy may have a place in such situations.

WORKING

Many problems surround the preparation for a work experience. We will shortly present our data on parental expectations. At this point we would just like to say that visually impaired persons do have more vocational problems than do others. Parents worry whether anyone will want their child for a job, whether the job market will provide sufficient variety, or whether a menial position will be all that is available. Some professionals worry that parents are pressing visually impaired adolescents to take higher education for a job that does not exist. Sometimes a major resetting of goals and expectations is necessary, and this is at times very difficult to do. Mobility is a very important component of job possibilities. Other handicaps may interfere as well. Sometimes there is also a difficulty about whether the visually impaired person obtains his own job or has this done for him through parents or relatives.

Again, attempts to prevent this kind of difficulty necessitate an exposure to real-life experiences at an earlier point. We found in our study that visually impaired children were less likely to visit the working parent or parents at their place of employment, and, therefore, knew less about what the parent did. The child needs a realistic discussion of possibilities as he grows older: what is not, what is, and what might not be realistic or possible. There is no need to impose this upon a very young child, whose fantasies in any case tend to be far from reality. But one would certainly hope to see few teenagers who seriously expect to be an airline pilot, although blind.

Part-time jobs can be very useful, as well as field trips to different kinds of work situations. Exposure to a wide variety of social experiences can help minimize the social problems that sometimes occur on the job. Attention to stereotyped behavior that may be unsightly and also to noise-making habits may be necessary.

FAMILY ATTITUDES

Parents of the visually-impaired had significantly more health concerns about the child. They were also more concerned about regularity of bowel movements, although there was no difference between the families of the visually impaired and of the controls with regard to bowel difficulty in other family members. (It is not clear whether this represents heightened concern or an actual difference, perhaps due to differences in diet and exercise.)

Parents of the visually impaired had a lower expectation for the child's achievement of a high-status position in later life than did the controls (about 25 percent expected a professional level as compared with over 40 percent of the controls). About 10 percent expected the child to continue to need a semiprotected environment. When asked whether they expected any limitations in a future job, almost 90 percent of the parents answered yes. Only 38.5 percent said they expected the child's impairment to affect his chances of marriage, and 35 percent thought that there might be some alteration in friendships.

With regard to a future living situation, about twice as many parents of the visually impaired expected the child still to be living with them, and small numbers expected the child to be in a sheltered or institutional environment. Overall, about 75 percent of the mothers and fathers of the visually impaired expected independence, whereas this was true for 95 percent of the controls. The differences in employment expectations between index cases and controls are statistically significant. This also holds true when the cases are broken down into blind and partially sighted subgroups.

MOTHER'S EMPLOYMENT

About 36 percent of the mothers were working before the child was born, and about 40 percent have worked thereafter. This does not differ significantly from the mothers of the sighted controls.

RELATIVES

Almost twice as many grandfathers are deceased as are grandmothers. Grandmothers are seen as more helpful than grandfathers, but the maternal grandparents are more involved (for both grandmother and grandfather) than are the paternal ones. Differences between maternal and paternal grandmothers in level of involvement are significant at the 5 percent level ($\chi^2 = 4.34$, df = 1). Very few grandparents refused to believe the diagnosis or continued to push for new studies.

SOCIAL LIFE OF THE FAMILY

There were no differences between the two study groups in the frequency with which parents go out and use babysitters other than relatives or siblings. Frequencies were the same for taking the children visiting and having people over to socialize. Asked whether she felt socially isolated, there was a nonsignificant trend in favor of the index mothers feeling *less* socially isolated than did mothers of control children.

This may be because of the increased social contact involved with other parents and with professionals on account of the visually impaired child. There was no difference between the groups in the number of cars owned per family and the number of mothers who had a license to drive a car.

It should be noted that half the children had had the experience of an independent holiday, either with relatives or at some organized camp, away from the family. Nevertheless, 16 of the mothers (17.6 percent) stated that they felt that constant care associated with the child was a problem for them. There was said to be a financial problem in relation to the impairment in only 6.6 percent. This is partly a feature of the Canadian medical care scheme: there would generally be no increase in cost regardless of the numbers of hospitalizations and physician visits. It might be expected that this would be quite a different situation in the United States.

Only a couple of families in both groups had any domestic assistance for the mother, either full-time or occasional.

We asked about the kinds of techniques parents used to deal with overly curious or intrusive people when they were out with the visually impaired child. Both mothers and fathers most often explain and attempt to educate others (37 percent). One-third of the parents ignore or snub the person making the comment and 20 percent of the mothers (but only 8 percent of the fathers) try to squelch the person. Only one mother and one father said that they actively try to avoid all such situations. A few mothers also said that they occasionally get very nervous or angry.

Very few families reported any difficulties with their neighbors.

PARENTAL ADJUSTMENT AND HEALTH

Mothers of the visually impaired reported more health items as bothering them than did the mothers of the controls, but this was not true for the fathers. We also asked about the use of psychoactive drugs and psychiatric or other counseling help in the past and present. These findings were of great interest. There was no difference in the numbers of parents using such medication when index cases and controls were compared; however, there was a large male-female difference. Seventeen percent of the mothers were taking such medication, whereas this was true of only 3 percent of the fathers. There were also no differences between the two groups in psychiatric counseling, but again more women had received this help than had men (21 percent versus 10 percent; $\chi^2 = 2.92$, df $= 2$; $p < 0.10$).

We also asked about alcoholism, which involved none of the mothers, but two or three fathers in each group admitted to the problem.

Table 15-8
Parent's Judgment of Effect of Child's Impairment on
Own Life

	Mothers		Fathers	
	n	%	n	%
Severe	8	9.1	2	4.4
Moderate	19	21.6	11	24.4
Neutral	29	33.0	20	44.4
Some advantages	17	19.3	8	17.8
Very good	8	9.1	2	4.4
Unsure	3	3.4	0	—
Other	4	4.5	2	4.4
Totals	88	100.0	45	99.8

PARENTAL JUDGMENT OF EFFECT OF CHILD'S
IMPAIRMENT ON THE FAMILY

Table 15-8 shows that about 30 percent of mothers and fathers felt that there has been an adverse effect upon their lives as individuals, whereas over 20 percent felt the result had been positive. The remainder were either neutral or uncertain. Table 15-9 shows the judged effects upon the marriage, with about 15 to 18 percent of both mothers and fathers negative and positive, respectively, and over 60 percent reporting neutral responses.

This certainly does not suggest that the parents generally look back on the situation negatively. This is perhaps supported by one of the most important findings of this study, shown in Table 15-10, regarding the frequency of family breakdown. While everyone seems to assume that there is increased breakdown in the families of handicapped children, such as in the study by Tew et al.,[29] we have not found this true.

Table 15-9
Parent's Judgment of Effect of Child's Impairment on
Marriage

	Mothers		Fathers	
	n	%	n	%
Severe	8	9.4	2	4.3
Moderate	8	9.4	4	8.7
Neutral	53	62.4	31	67.4
Some advantages	12	14.1	7	15.2
Very good	1	1.2	1	2.2
Unsure	3	3.5	1	2.2
Totals	85	100.0	46	100.0

Table 15-10
Family Status*

| | Index Cases | | Controls | |
	n	%	n	%
With both natural parents	58	77.3	64	85.3
Parents separated, divorced, widowed, or child adopted	11	14.7	10	13.3
With one or both foster parents	6	8.0	1	1.3
Totals	75	100.0	75	99.9

*$\chi^2 = 3.92$; df $= 2$; ns

The previously mentioned study of deaf children[3] reported no differences between index cases and controls and, as can be seen from the table, the rates of family breakdown were not significantly different. Recently another study, this time on children with spina bifida from the United States, has yielded the same results.[6]

In discussing with the parents their common interests, we obtained the findings shown in Table 15-11. Here it can be seen that the two groups were comparable in relation to the number of mutual interests. Again, this shows the importance of a control group. If one asks these questions of the average family, there is a very good chance that one will obtain silence or a surprised reaction, and then few if any named mutual interests. When the same is found for the parents of a handicapped child, one tends to place great weight on this, but our study shows that this is not valid on a purely statistical basis, without other indications.

OUR ASSESSMENT OF PARENTAL PSYCHIATRIC DISORDER AND MARITAL PROBLEMS

Our global ratings were done with all the information available and, therefore, there may be some cross-contamination from other sources

Table 15-11
Mutual Parental Interests*

| | Index Cases | | Controls | |
	n	%	n	%
Many	10	13.9	15	19.0
A few	27	37.5	37	46.8
Little or none	35	48.6	27	34.2
Totals	72	100.0	79	100.0

*$\chi^2 = 3.01$; df $= 2$; ns

of judgment. We felt that approximately one-third of the mothers showed evidence of severe or moderate psychiatric problems during the previous 12 months, and a similar number showed evidence prior to that. There were no significant differences between the parents of the blind and the parents of the partially signted. Fewer fathers were felt to have such problems, but this may be due to greater reluctance on the part of fathers to reveal information. Incidentally, these proportions are very similar to those obtained in the previous study of deaf children.[3] Unfortunately, we do not have comparable information of equivalent depth for the control group parents. The disturbances of mothers and fathers are closely related, and, in fact, the rates do not differ significantly.

With regard to the global assessment of the marriage, we rated between 22 to 30 percent of the marriages as having severe or moderate problems, depending upon the subgroup. We felt there were no problems in 48 to 58 percent.

Of those mothers rated severe or moderate, 68 percent had the same rating for their marriage; for those rated as having mild or no problems, marriage ratings were the same in 84.6 percent. Comparable figures for fathers and their marriages are 62 and 84 percent.

SIBLINGS

Siblings of handicapped children are no exception to the "rule of variety": there is no one pattern characteristic of their reactions or adjustments to their impaired brother or sister. However, there is no doubt that they frequently have feelings about it.

There does seem to be general agreement that parental attitudes and family patterns are influential. Although it is often assumed that a "healthy attitude" on the part of the parents will assure the same for the siblings, this is not always the case.

A few situations should be mentioned in which research has demonstrated some differences. Gath[30] and Farber et al.[31,32] investigated families with a severely retarded child and concluded that the sibs could be adversely affected, but that this was more likely to be true of the oldest sister, who sometimes had to assume a surrogate-mother role. Steinzor, working with the siblings of visually impaired children, reported that they were not necessarily any more understanding or free of cultural stereotypes about the handicap than other persons.[33]

In our study we found that behavioral problems were reported fairly frequently by mothers for the sibs of visually impaired children (Table 15-12). We have, however, no independent measure of the validity of this judgment. Additionally, it was thought that the sibs were affected

Table 15–12
Siblings with Behavior Problems*

	n	% (of 87)
Present	23	26.4
Absent	64	73.6
Total	87	100.0

*By maternal report.

by the presence of the visually impaired child in the proportions shown in Table 15-13. It should be clear from this that a negative effect was by no means typical, according to the parents.

The problems one may see include:

1. The sibling is not free to resent, fight with, or compete with the visually impaired child. He may have to adopt a prematurely adult type of understanding and supportive role and may even feel it incumbent upon him to enter professional work with the handicapped later on.
2. The sibling feels embarrassed in the presence of the impaired child in public and wishes to dissociate himself from the "spread of stigma" entailed; he may refuse to invite friends over, not want to accompany the family in public, and find it difficult to explain things to his friends.
3. He expresses wishes to be equally favored by his parents but in ways the parents cannot cope with, such as wanting to have the same handicap, through hypochondriasis, or other attention-getting maneuvers.
4. The sibling may be overprotected because he is "precious."
5. Excessive demands or expectations are placed upon him by the parents (and sometimes by himself), as if to compensate for what

Table 15–13
Effect of Handicap on Siblings*

	n	% (of 86)
Good	13	15.1
None	40	46.5
Bad	25	29.1
Unsure	8	9.3
Total	86	100.0

*By maternal report.

the impaired child cannot (or presumably will not) be able to accomplish.
6. The sibling presents a behavioral problem not obviously linked to the visual impairment, but the question arises as to whether the latter might have an indirect effect.
7. The parents need help in knowing what to explain to a child whose sibling has acquired (or been born with) a visual impairment.

It will be obvious that many of these reactions could occur in any family when a child's developmental needs and family stresses or coping abilities come into conflict.

A few words are necessary about the last-named problem. The sudden, unexpected onset or acquisition of a major impairment of vision can emotionally affect other children in the family. Not only the parents, but the others must undergo what Parkes has called a "psychosocial transition," a change in one's "assumptive world."[34] The sibling or a parent may feel (or occasionally actually be) responsible for the impairment or may come to feel more vulnerable to the same defect, especially if it is hereditary. The difficulty the impaired child has in gradually adjusting to a major change in himself often produces all sorts of complex stresses in other family members (see chapter 16).

Fig. 15-2.   Blind child wrestling with normal sibling.

Implications

Parents do worry about the effect of the visually impaired child upon other family members; professionals sometimes do not worry enough—enough to ask appropriate questions. The following outline suggests some approaches to these problems which may be of assistance.

1. Inquire about how the siblings are doing, what they understand about the impairment and its management, how they handle contacts between their friends and the visually impaired sib. (This is a preventative measure.)
2. Encourage the parents to see that part of "normalizing" the impaired child is to permit the sibs to express or feel negatively charged emotions toward the former, without excessive guilt or recriminations. A mixture of reactions and attitudes in the normal sib is probably healthy (some concern and protection, some annoyance, some competition).
3. Assess how much the sibs help the parents with the impaired child, but ask about this in such a way that you do not place a specific value on one or the other type of behavior. This is in an attempt to find out whether excessive pressures are being exerted, but of course there are no absolute standards to go by: one is looking more for rigidities in attitude and style that do not allow the normal child or adolescent a reasonable "out."
4. If a persistent or severe problem does develop, further inquiry and possibly a home visit or family interview may provide clues to the nature of the difficulty. (Obviously, one must not depend entirely upon one parent's information.) Group meetings for siblings may be useful in reducing feelings of uniqueness.

It is important to realize that, without any malicious or neurotic reasons, some parents impose excessive emotional or physical burdens upon normal children in the family. They may simply fall into a convenient pattern and fail to alter it unless they are helped to become aware of it. In some instances, there are deep-seated forces operating which will require very intensive and specialized assistance, but this is a rather infrequent necessity in our experience.

Professionals working with the handicapped need to constantly keep in mind the effects that may be hidden or neglected in the midst of focusing upon the impaired child's needs. Positive as well as negative outcomes are possible, so a preventative approach that recognizes the importance of the entire family structure is likely to be most beneficial.

CHILD'S RESEMBLANCE TO RELATIVES

We asked the mothers who they thought the child resembled in the family, both physically and in personality. We thought that this might be some indirect test of whether the child was really felt to be a member of the family. Interestingly, 41 percent of the mothers of the visually impaired children said that the child had not resembled either parent in personality, whereas only 25 percent of the control mothers reported the same. (This difference does not quite reach the 5 percent confidence level.) There were no differences with regard to physical resemblance.

COMMENTS

We have presented a portion of our findings from the study of visually impaired children and a comparable group. We have identified a fairly large proportion of parents with psychiatric difficulty but no increase in family breakdown. In general, there are relatively few differences between families of visually impaired children and controls. Most impressive from the home visits was the variability, as well as the difficulty of categorizing, as one spent more time and got to know the family better.

It is of great importance to see fathers, and that was one of the major thrusts of this study. This is rarely done. In a recent paper by Boyle et al. on the parents of children with cystic fibrosis, they state, "An attempt was also made to see fathers of our patients. Because of scheduling difficulties only four fathers were seen"[35] (p. 319). But later in the paper they reported, "In 18 of the 25 families studied, communication between father and mother was felt to be inadequate"[35] (p. 323). It is perfectly clear from this study that the judgment of parental communication difficulties in the majority of cases was made from maternal report alone. This is never a safe conclusion. In another recent paper, Cummings emphasizes a need to see fathers to "aid efforts to mobilize family strengths and offset effects of long-term stress"[36] (p. 247). Fathers are assuming a larger role and are experiencing their child's handicaps more immediately than was true earlier. This author also writes of the need for the worker to "allow the father to express fully his grief, frustration, and anger, rather than expecting the father to serve primarily as the controlled suppressor for the feelings of the mother and other family members"[36] (p. 254).

Fig. 15-3.   Father and child.

SUMMARY

Professionals working with the handicapped need to constantly keep in mind the risk of neglecting the family's needs while focusing upon those of the child. Although complex adaptations are necessary for every family, there may be a variety of positive as well as negative influences. In particular, divorce and separation are not more common in these families than in the general population. Social relationships and activities, insofar as they could be compared, were not found to be grossly impaired.

However, there is evidence that imparting the diagnosis and its implications could and should be improved so as to give families a better start. Attention has been drawn to the very frequent and prolonged hospitalizations these children often undergo, and their potentially adverse effects.

It seems wise to encourage the child to participate actively, from an early age, in the activities of the family, to learn more about work the parents do, and to experience being cared for and supervised by adults other than the parents.

It is possible that a study of geographical areas with a higher proportion of families with serious socioeconomic problems would demonstrate more problems than did ours. The provision of services for child and family may also be a powerful influence. Our data simply indicate that, even with a multiple handicap, families *can* function well.

Since the family members are not only the most important influences upon the growing child's personality, but also the most significant allies and co-workers of the professional, it seems essential to adopt an approach that gives due recognition to family structure and values. Effort should be devoted not only to habilitation of the visually impaired child, but also to minimizing adverse effects of the impairment upon other family members. This will usually require inquiry into many aspects of family and individual functioning.

CONCLUSIONS

1. Few stereotypes of family functioning can be sustained by available evidence.
2. The family is important for child development, but many events in the impaired child's early life may distort its influence.
3. Although most of the pregnancies were unplanned, most parents in our study felt positively about them.
4. Parents of the blind began to suspect the problem at about 3 months of age in children blind from birth and at 4 months in the congenitally partially sighted. Delay in confirmation was about 1.4 months in the former and 4.2 months in the latter.
5. Receiving the diagnosis is often a shocking experience for the parents; in too many cases, it is still not done with both parents together, and at least a substantial minority in our study felt they had had insufficient time for questions and were given little hope.
6. Contacts with other parents and the agency for the blind were generally considered helpful.
7. Although about one-quarter claimed they tried to avoid further pregnancies, there was no evidence that they succeeded.
8. Hospitalization was much more frequent and prolonged for the visually impaired than for the control group in all years.
9. The diagnosis (correct or not) of additional handicaps can be very traumatic for parents and child and should be handled with great

care and repeated clarification of the implications.
10. Risk-taking is necessary for development of the child's independence.
11. The child's early and graded exposure to the world of work, to the subtleties of human relationships, and to caretaking by other adults is advisable if optimal adjustment is to succeed.
12. Parents generally perceived relatives as helpful.
13. No major differences in family social life were discovered.
14. Although mothers of the visually impaired reported more health concerns (for themselves and the child), there was no increase in the taking of psychoactive medication or in counseling, although for both groups these were higher in mothers than fathers.
15. There was no increase in divorce or separation.
16. About one-third of marriages showed signs of significant difficulty.
17. Fathers and siblings—not just child and mother—need to be considered in any comprehensive approach to habilitation.

REFERENCES

1. Cohen PC: The impact of the handicapped child on the family. New Outlook for the Blind 58:11-15, 1964
2. Hare EH, Laurence KM, Payne H, et al: Spina bifida cystica and family stress. Br Med J 2:757-760, 1966
3. Freeman RD, Malkin SF, Hastings JO: Psychosocial problems of deaf children and their families: A comparative study. Am Ann Deaf 120:391-405, 1975
4. McMichael JK: Handicap: A Study of Physically Handicapped Children and Their Families. London, Staples, 1971
5. Chess S, Korn SJ, Fernandez PB: Psychiatric Disorders of Children with Congenital Rubella. New York, Brunner/Mazel, 1971
6. Martin P: Marital breakdown in families of patients with spina bifida cystica. Dev Med Child Neurol 17:757-764, 1975
7. Roskies E: Abnormality and Normality: The Mothering of Thalidomide Children. Ithaca, New York, Cornell University Press, 1972
8. Hewett S: The Family and the Handicapped Child: A Study of Cerebral Palsied Children in Their Homes. Chicago, Aldine and London, Allen & Unwin, 1970
9. Carr J: Young Children with Down's Syndrome: Their Development, Upbringing, and Effect on Their Families. London, Butterworths, 1975
10. Cox A, Rutter M, Newman S, et al: A comparative study of infantile autism and specific developmental receptive language disorder: II. Parental characteristics. Br J Psychiatry 126:146-159, 1975
11. Barsch R: The Parent of the Handicapped Child. The Study of Child Rearing Practices. Springfield, Ill, Charles C Thomas, 1968

12. Bowlby J: Attachment and Loss. vol 1, Attachment. New York, Basic Books, 1969

13. Bowlby J: Attachment and Loss. vol 2, Separation, Anxiety and Anger. New York, Basic Books, 1973

14. Kennell JH, Jerauld R, Wolfe H, et al: Maternal behaviour one year after early and extended post-partum contact. Dev Med Child Neurol 16:172–179, 1974

15. Ringler NM, Kennell JH, Jarvella R, et al: Mother-to-child speech at 2 years—Effects of early postnatal contact. J Pediatr 86:141–144, 1975

15a. Klaus MH, Kennell JH: Maternal-infant bonding: The impact of early separation or loss on family development. St. Louis, C. V. Mosby, 1976

16. Solnit AJ, Stark MH: Mourning and the birth of a defective child. Psychoanal Study Child 16:523–537, 1961

17. MacKeith R: The feelings and behaviour of parents of handicapped children. Dev Med Child Neurol 15:524–527, 1973

18. Walker JH, Thomas M, Russell IT: Spina bifida—and the parents. Dev Med Child Neurol 13:462–476, 1971

19. D'Arcy E: Congenital defects: Mothers' reactions to first information. Br Med J 3:796, 1968

20. Zuk GH: Cultural dilemma and spiritual crisis of the family with a handicapped child. Except Child 28:405–408, 1962

21. Gibbs N: A blind child. Dev Med Child Neurol 14:817–821, 1972

22. Green M, Solnit AJ: Reactions to the threatened loss of a child: A vulnerable child syndrome. Pediatrics 58:58–66, 1964

23. Sigal JJ, Chagoya L, Villeneuve C, et al: Later psychological consequences of near-fatal illness (nephrosis) in early childhood: Some preliminary findings. Laval Médical 42:103–108, 1971

24. Sigal JJ, Chagoya L, Villeneuve C, et al: Later psychosocial sequelae of early childhood illness (severe croup). Am J Psychiatry 130:786–789, 1973

25. Sigal JJ, Gagnon P: Effects of parents' and pediatricians' worry concerning severe gastroenteritis in early childhood on later disturbances in the child's behavior. J Pediatr 87:809–814, 1975

26. Kvaraceus WC, Hayes EN (eds): If Your Child is Handicapped. Boston, Porter Sargent, 1969

27. Bergman AB, Stamm SJ: The morbidity of cardiac nondisease in school children. N Engl J Med 276:1008–1013, 1967

28. Kershaw JD: Handicapped Children, ed 2. London, Heinemann, 1966

29. Tew BJ, Payne H, Laurence, KM: Must a family with a handicapped child be a handicapped family? Dev Med Child Neurol (suppl 32) 16:95–98, 1974

30. Gath A: Sibling reactions to mental handicap: A comparison of the brothers and sisters of mongol children. J Child Psychol Psychiatry 15:187–198, 1974

31. Farber B: Effects of a severely mentally retarded child on family integration. Monogr Soc Res Child Dev 24 (2), 1959

32. Farber B, Jenne WC, Toigo R: Family Crisis and the Decision to Institu-

tionalize the Retarded Child. Research Monograph No 1. Washington, DC, Council for Exceptional Children, 1960

33. Steinzor LV: Siblings of visually handicapped children. New Outlook for the Blind 61:48–52, 1967

34. Parkes CM: Psychosocial transitions: A field for study. Soc Sci Med 5:101–115, 1971

35. Boyle IR, di Sant'Agnese PA, Sack S, et al: Emotional adjustment of adolescents and young adults with cystic fibrosis. J Pediatr 88:318–326, 1976

36. Cummings ST: The impact of the child's deficiency on the father: A study of fathers of mentally retarded and of chronically ill children. Am J Orthopsychiatry 46:246–255, 1976

16
Behavior: Development, Pathology, and Management

INTRODUCTION

The behavior of visually impaired persons is obviously of great importance to those who live or work with them, but it is also a matter of theoretical significance in the field of child development. We have pointed out elsewhere that with the partial or complete absence of vision as an organizing sense, one would expect major changes in many areas of functioning and in personality organization. When this is not observed to be the case, one naturally wonders by what route and with what substitute mechanisms visually impaired individuals accomplish the same as the sighted.

There are in fact very marked disagreements over the prevalence of behavioral pathology or deviance among the visually impaired, both children and adults, and the interpretation that is to be placed upon these prevalence figures. One has the feeling sometimes in reading these studies that it is not only a matter of evidence but also how that evidence is collected and the viewpoints and values of the investigators.

Certain aspects of behavior will be considered in separate chapters: specifically, stereotyped behavior is covered in chapter 18 and certain aspects of sexual behavior in chapter 25. The purpose of this present section is to examine certain developmental issues as represented by the studies of other investigators and ourselves, as well as clinical experience; to briefly examine certain aspects of behavioral disorder, and to outline methods of assessment and management. Our purpose is to try to answer such questions as, Is the development of the visually impaired different? If so, in what specific areas? Is this inevitable?

What are the causes of developmental deviations? How does one approach
a child who is said to have unusual or disturbing behavior? How does
one decide whether intervention is warranted, and what techniques are
available? A few case examples will also be given.

There are many problems in the description and interpretation of
behavior, particularly when it is "maladjusted" or considered to represent
psychiatric disorder. These issues have been concisely discussed by
Rutter et al.[1,2] and will be mentioned later. Generally speaking, unusual
or difficult behavior in children does not constitute a disease as such.
The nature of the behavior requires interpretation in the light of development and the particular context. The genesis of abnormal behavior seems
to be due to a complex combination of factors: hereditary endowment,
temperamental style, the nature of early attachment to the mother and
subsequent relationships with important others, structural damage to
the central nervous system or other parts of the body, the training and
experience of the child, including opportunity to learn by imitation and
identification, reinforcement of behavior by others, and in a general
way family and cultural influences.

DEVELOPMENTAL ISSUES

Introduction

In the following section, areas are presented in which there may
be developmental differences between the blind and the sighted. There
is nothing very special about the categories, and another logical system
could well have been used. It is important in reading these sections
to remember that, generally, children with significant residual vision
will follow the more usual developmental paths and milestones.

Infant-Mother Attachment

As has been mentioned in chapter 14, both early and later hospitalization is much more common among the visually impaired. In our study,
blind children were hospitalized an average of 50 days in the first year
and children with partial vision 20 days—compared with less than 2
days for the controls. They also remained longer in incubators, again
with the blind exceeding the partially sighted. This may be a major
source of difficulty in establishing a successful mother-infant bond. It
should also be noted that *breast-feeding* is significantly less common
in the visually impaired, as can be seen in Table 16-1. As if it were
not enough for the parents to suffer the impact of diagnosis of a significant
handicap, many of the parents had, and continue to have, significant
health concerns about their children. Again, in this respect the parents

Table 16-1
Breast or Bottle Feeding*

	Index Cases		Controls	
	n	%	n	%
Breast	17	21.5	32	38.1
Bottle	62	78.5	52	61.9
Totals	79	100.0	84	100.0

*χ^2 = 4.56; df = 1; $p < 0.05$.

of the visually impaired are significantly more worried than are the parents of the controls (See Table 16-2). Although about three-quarters of the mothers reported that as a baby their child was happy and receptive of attention, almost 14 percent reported that the baby was generally unhappy and seemed to want increased attention, compared with 7 percent of the mothers of controls. An additional 5 percent reported that the baby was generally unhappy but seemed to reject attention, whereas this was true of only 2.4 percent of the controls.

Lack of eye-to-eye contact may inhibit the development of the infant-mother bond, especially if other means are not found to establish and maintain contact. The mother's depression and ignorance of the baby's needs and potential may limit her involvement with a child who requires even more stimulation than normal. The importance of attachment has been extensively discussed by Bowlby[3,4] and the effects of separation demonstrated by Klaus and Kennell.[5] The latter authors have shown that mothers of premature babies tend to handle them as if they were very fragile and vulnerable. The extensive work of Burlingham and Fraiberg (to be cited later) has shown that ways can be found to demonstrate successfully to mothers that their babies know them and take pleasure in the reciprocal relationship.

Smiling and Facial Expression

An infant's smile elicits pleasurable and protective reactions from its parents and helps to cement the mother-infant bond. Vision is not a prerequisite for spontaneous smiling since even deaf-blind children

Table 16-2
Health Concerns of Parents
About the Child*

	Index Cases	Controls
Yes	38	22
No	46	63

*χ^2 = 6.09; df = 1; $0.01 < p < 0.02$.

smile. However, vision does facilitate smiling, and prolonged smiling is delayed in blind babies.[6] In the first month of life, smiling occurs without being elicited by any outside stimuli. Shortly thereafter, infants will respond to a human voice, without discriminating one person from another, and begin to respond to the human face. This is the beginning of so-called "social smiling." Maximal smiling to a nonspecific stimulus is said to occur between 4 and 6 months of age, and around this time the infant discriminates its mother's voice. As the infant gets older, more and more detail of the face is required to elicit smiling, until only the familiar human face itself will elicit it by 8 months of age, a typical age for so called "stranger anxiety." It seems that while congenitally blind children will respond to strong inner stimuli with facial expressions typical of the human species, they cannot necessarily make their faces assume such expression on command. The subtle expressions which are so involved in everyday interaction are developed by imitation and will be muted or absent. This may lead to difficulties in interpretation of what the blind person is feeling.

Eating and Oral Behavior

Many authors have described refusal to bite or chew, even to the point of continuing baby foods for years. This may be due to remaining on the bottle beyond the usual weaning period. Frequently, solid foods were not offered until past the time when children normally have the desire to bite—that is, as their first teeth erupt. The parents tended to give up and permit the child to continue infantile patterns. When the blind child does attempt to feed himself, sighted people may be repelled by the messiness (but the sighted child is messy also). This can also increase negative feelings parents may have about their child. According to Elonen and her co-workers[7,8] most multihandicapped blind children had markedly delayed chewing patterns. As can be seen from Table 16-3, our study has corroborated these findings. More than half the blind children had a history of chewing problems, and this was also reported in almost 20 percent of the children with partial vision, whereas the frequency was only approximately 4 percent in the controls. The idea that later weaning might be associated with these peculiarities was tested with our data. The mean age for weaning of the control children was 12.7 months. Using only those cases with onset of visual impairment at birth, we found that the average age of weaning of the blind was just under 20 months ($t = 1.63$; df $= 18$; $p = 0.06$). For children with partial vision, the average age of weaning was 16.25 months ($t = 1.52$; df $= 47$; $p = 0.067$). Both these differences approach the usual 5 percent confidence level (occurring by chance 5 times in 100, or less) and give

Table 16–3
Chewing Problems*

	Blind†		Controls		Partial Vision‡		Controls	
	n	%	n	%	n	%	n	%
Yes	12	52.2	1	4.3	11	21.2	2	3.8
No	11	47.8	22	95.7	41	78.8	51	96.2
Total	23	100.0	23	100.0	52	100.0	53	100.0

*Cases with onset at birth.
†$\chi^2 = 10.72$; df = 1; $p < 0.005$.
‡$\chi^2 = 5.79$; df = 1; $p < 0.02$.

some support to the relationship between chewing and swallowing difficulties and late weaning.

Even more support for this concept is found when the age of introduction of solid food is examined. This is approximately 9 months for the controls but close to 19 months for the blind and over 12 months for those with partial vision. The difference for the blind is highly significant ($t = 2.70$; df = 21; $p = 0.007$); this is also significant with those with partial vision ($t = 1.73$; df = 48; $p = 0.045$).

There was a history of pacifier use in 45 percent of the index (visually impaired) cases and 36 percent of the controls, this difference not being statistically significant; nor was the age of ceasing the use of the pacifier different between the two groups, both being close to fifteen months.

It should be pointed out, however, that in both sighted and visually impaired groups some children were not weaned until 6 years of age, and in some cases pacifier use continued until 3 or 4 years of age. In one blind child solid food was not begun until 5 years of age, whereas the extreme was 24 months for the controls.

Since some blind children learn to feed normally, deviant patterns are not inevitable.[7,8]

The use of the mouth as a highly sensitive perceptual organ tends to be much more common in the blind and is not necessarily of pathological import.[9] The habit of mouthing things was reported in 18.5 percent of our visually impaired children and was more common than smelling things (10.9 percent).

Although early in life the visually impaired were reported to have more peculiarities in food selection—and this is also reported in the literature—in later childhood there was no increase over the frequency reported for sighted children. (New foods may be resisted because the child is unable to see the family enjoying them.)

It should be pointed out that there are obvious dental implications with many of these patterns, and the importance of early dental care is covered in chapter 26.

The Role of Sound

Much attention has been directed to this area. Elonen and her co-workers[7,8] reported that the blind baby may react to his mother's approach with stillness, rather than noisy excitement which is rewarding to the mother. She may interpret this as lack of interest in her. There is also said to be a long delay until the blind baby reaches for and locates an object on sound cue alone at 7 to 12 months of age. This involves the concept of object permanence. Fraiberg et al.[10] observed that blind babies behaved as if there were nothing there when confronted with the sounds of familiar toys. They concluded that sound alone did not confer substantiality upon an object. Vision acts to unite the sound and tactile qualities of objects, but until the first year these qualities remain separate for the blind child. In constructing a concept of objects, the blind baby is dependent upon his own mobility and acoustical tracing, which is not yet sufficiently developed. The development may be arrested or distorted at this point. This was their explanation for the observation that some children remain largely immobile for years, or twirl around in place, as if the world were a meaningless void.

Other authors have pointed out that parents have been given poor or nonspecific advice to immerse their blind children in a world of sound.[7,8] The result may be parroting, if the sounds are not made meaningful, or a "tuning out" in which sounds are ignored.

In summary, careful observations of a limited number of otherwise normal blind babies suggests that the early developmental function of hearing has substantially different behavioral effects in the blind and in the sighted. Our own observations suggest that in some cases blind babies will reach for objects on sound cue alone prior to the ages mentioned by Fraiberg.

Hand Use

Contrary to the expectations of many persons that blind children will make superefficient use of both tactile abilities and sound, the hands of some blind children seem useless and may be maintained in an infantile posture.[7,8,10] Vision is an organizer of midline engagement of the hands. Without special help, the maturational sequence leading to coordinated and differentiated hand use may be impeded.[11] Various game activities have been suggested to promote midline hand use. Crawling may also be assisted by development of hand function. Some children show a developmental arrest in which their hands continue to serve primarily their mouths, rather than more advanced functions.

According to Sandler,[12] the hands gradually assume an intermediary role between eyes and mouth in the sighted child. At a later point, the eyes and hand no longer serve the mouth but develop autonomy. In the blind child, "picking up" of objects with the eyes cannot precede picking up with the hands. As Fraiberg et al. have pointed out, "for these children the hand remains in a morbid alliance with the mouth. The hand behaves as if there were nothing 'out there' "[10] (p. 330).

There is some difference of opinion as to whether or not blind infants grasp as well as sighted ones towards the end of the first year of life. Refusal to use the hands for any effective purpose has been attributed to restrictions upon self-feeding and the touching of food.

Readers interested in more details than can be presented here will find the original writings of the Fraiberg and Burlingham groups of interest.[13-18]

Differentiation between Self and Others; Separation

The sighted child is rewarded frequently by success when it reaches for and manipulates things. A blind child rarely has such frequent success through its brief search behavior. According to Fraiberg and her colleagues,[10] the awareness of the baby that a thing continues to exist without having direct contact with it only develops as the child learns to construct a trajectory in space. Vision is thought to be of tremendous assistance in developing the differentiation of self from not-self, which usually takes place through exploratory behavior and learning the differences in feeling between the perception and touching of oneself versus someone else. This differentiation involves a gradual lessening of egocentrism. Since the blind child tends to remain more body-centered and to fall back upon his own sensations, the ultimate result may be a lack of appreciation of the needs, feelings, and differences of others, although this might result from a host of other influences as well.

According to Fraiberg,[19] there is a marked difference between blind and sighted babies in the onset and peak of separation and "stranger anxiety." In sighted children, the onset is at 7 to 8 months, with the peak at about 12 months. The child's earliest method of tolerating separation from the mother appears to be through the evocation of her image. But blind babies show at least a year's delay in this function. This means that during much of his second year, the blind child lives in a hazardous world in which his human partners mysteriously disappear at times. The sighted baby actively deals with the danger of separation by means of his own mobility and by crying at the visual anticipation of his mother's departure. The blind baby cannot track mother nor anticipate her departure so easily. Hearing is not usually as efficient as vision in obtaining reassurance. Regressive behavior, such as screaming fits and panicky clinging to the mother's body, may be observed in the second year of life. The continuation of this separation anxiety, and the tendency of many parents to spare the child its consequences, may lead to difficulties when it later becomes more necessary for the child to separate from the parent. Although the second year of life may be a risky period, prolonged difficulties are not inevitable and parent counseling may help to avoid later separation problems. (These differences observed by Fraiberg have not been confirmed in all of our cases, however.)

The blind child faces more real dangers in moving about his world and has greater difficulty testing reality.[11] One might therefore reasonably expect a prolongation of dependency and less of a drive to seek independent activity. Blind babies may also find the lack of sound frightening, because it leads to a fear of abandonment. This is so even at later points in life since the child cannot determine visually whether or not a person is still present.

For a variety of reasons—some realistic, some overprotective, and some perhaps based on unrecognized hostile impulses—parents themselves may have difficulty separating from the child. Many parents (of all kinds of children) are also concerned when their child first goes to school.

It seems, then, that problems of separation which the blind child demonstrates either at home or at school may be quite varied. These may also be aggravated by reactions to hospitalization. In our study, almost 40 percent of mothers reported that their children had shown emotional reactions to hospitalization, including clinging, change of mood, and fears. The school situation may be fraught with considerable anxiety if the child has had all his whims catered to and has not learned to adapt to the caretaking of other adults or to the socialization necessary with peers.

Activity Level

All sorts of descriptions have been given of the activity level of blind children. Often they are described as being passive and hypoactive. On the other hand, hyperactivity associated with temper tantrums has been described in blind children who received inconsistent handling.[20] Activity level is actually difficult to determine, and it depends very much upon the observer's sense of whether the activity is goal-directed or not. Instead of rushing about, blind children may engage in more stereotyped behavior.

Table 16-4
Sleeping Problems in Past 12 Months

Problem*	Index Cases		Controls	
	n	% (of 85)	n	% (of 85)
Nightmares	5	5.9	8	9.4
Night terrors	0		0	
Difficulty falling asleep	17†	20.0	5	5.9
Sleepwalking	3	3.5	2	2.4
Sleep talking	3	3.5	9	10.6
Frequent awakening	8	9.4	2	2.4
Restless sleeper	6	7.1	2	2.4
Day-night reversal	0		0	
Bedtime rituals	1	1.2	0	
Bed-wetting	5	5.9	8	9.4
Into parents' bed	6	7.1	5	5.9
Into sibling's bed	1	1.2	0	
Fear of dark	6	7.1	9	10.6
Other	7	8.2	6	7.1
None	40	47.1	46	54.1

*More than one choice possible; does not sum to 100%.
†$p < 0.05$

Sleep and Dreams

Reversals of day-night rhythm have been frequently reported; these are attributed to prolonged stays in incubators and failure of the parents to set limits and provide differential day-night stimulation.[7,8,21] Babies who were handled well are said to have normal sleeping patterns.[11]

In our study, day-night reversal had not been a problem. Problems which had occurred in the previous 12 months are shown in Table 16-4. Although some writers have suggested that nightmares are more common in the blind,[22] this was not found to be the case. The only item that reached statistical significance was that 20 percent of the blind had increased difficulty in falling asleep; this compared with 6 percent of the controls. Although frequent awakening and restless sleeping were reported more commonly, these were not statistically significant differences. Most parents of the visually impaired reported that their child needed nothing special if awakened at night. With regard to getting children to sleep, in a great majority nothing specific was needed, and the small number of parents who used threats, story reading, a bottle in bed for the baby, taking to the parents bed, and so forth, did not differ between the two groups. Also, there were no differences between the judged amount of sleep the child needed as compared with his peers. For both groups, about 16 percent were judged to need more than an average amount of sleep, and 21 to 30 percent less than average. Interestingly, visually impaired children were less likely to take something to bed with them, such as a toy, doll, or stuffed animal (24.1 percent versus 42.4 percent; $\chi^2 = 5.50$; df $= 1$; $p < 0.02$). This may be related to the ineffectiveness of models and dolls as toys for the blind.

Reports on dreaming in the blind are based largely on clinical impressions.[22] However, research is underway to do more effective content analysis of dreams, although the available information is on adults.[23] It is very difficult for the sighted to imagine what it would be like to dream without vision, although it is clear that blind people do dream in the same way that they experience things when awake (with sound, touch and smell). There are disagreements as to whether there are differences in content. Blank stated that those who become blind before age 5 gradually lose visual imagery in their dreams, but if the onset is after age 7 the child tends to retain this.[22] He also felt that blind children had more of a problem with nightmares, although our own data do not bear this out.

In our interviews with blind children, only 2.9 percent claimed they never had any dreams; 27.1 percent said that they did, but could not recall any; 10 percent said that they could recall dreams and that most of them were bad; 25.7 percent reported mixed types of dreams and 17.1 percent mostly good dreams. The remainder gave different answers not otherwise categorized. We do not have comparable data for the sighted children.

Toilet Training

The cases reported by Keeler showed both delayed and difficult training.[21] Many authors report special difficulty. It would seem reasonable that such problems would be more likely because of failure to learn by imitation the behavior of other family members. The process may remain alien and frightening to the child. Fears of sitting on the toilet seat are said to be quite common, possibly related to the sound of flushing.

It may be necessary to teach this function more explicitly than is usually done, as the child may not understand what is expected of him.

In our own study we did not find that there were more problems in toileting among the visually impaired. We also compared the age of commencing bladder and bowel training, completion, and the interval between. For bladder training, training of the controls was done between 16 and 18 months on the average, and this was not different for those with partial vision. For the blind, the mean age of commencing training was 21.3 months, but this was not statistically different from the previously mentioned ages. Completion of bladder training was between 22 and 26 months for the controls, with an interval of 7 to 8 months. There was a significant delay in the completion of bladder training for those with partial vision ($t = 2.29$; df $= 37$; $p < 0.05$). However, the difference for blind children was not statistically significant, probably because the numbers were smaller.

For bowel training, the ages the mothers gave for beginning were essentially the same as for those of bladder training and this was also true for completion. There were no significant differences between the groups, with completion occurring between 23 and 30 months with an interval ranging from 5 to 10 months. (It should be emphasized that these data were obtained only on those with onset of visual impairment at birth.) Retrospective distortion in recall is, of course, a possibility.

Speech

This area is covered in more detail in chapter 10. Visually impaired children seem to begin talking at the same time as sighted children. Any differences appear to relate to what happens thereafter. Repetition, parroting and echolalia appear to be more common among the visually impaired. They may also need help in recognizing that their favorite phrases have meaning and in finding a topic of conversation. Elonen and her co-workers[7,8] have reported that speech defects of various kinds are common.

In our sample, echolalia was present in only 6 percent. Eight and two-fifths percent showed abnormalities of volume, 4.8 percent stuttered, 26.5 percent had articulation problems, and, in 12.1 percent, no speech was heard because the children were either too young or too handicapped. (More than one choice was possible in the designation of these categories.) It thus appears to us that articulation problems are more common than in the sighted population.

Fears

In our study, 9 percent of the children were reported to have a major problem with fears in the previous 12 months, 29.2 percent to have a mild problem. Prior to that 8.2 percent had major fears, an indication that these tend to diminish with increasing age. On the other hand, 28 percent were reported to be not appropriately fearful, which worried the parents. It would seem that these figures, which are probably different from the sighted population (on which we do not have comparable data), are due to a blind child's differing experiences with his world. Twelve and one-half percent of the children were said to have a persisting fear of animals, and an additional 8 percent had had such a fear which dissipated. Indeed, it would not be surprising if blind children had many fears, since so many objects in their world come upon them by surprise or are bumped into. Under these conditions it is surprising that frequency of fears is so low. It seems from descriptions of some of the psychoanalytic writers [14,16] that young blind children probably have a much higher frequency of fears, and that a variety of coping strategies are used to reduce these in later life.

Play and Fantasy

Several writers have considered the role of play for the blind child, both for theoretical reasons and for purposes of obtaining clues to early intervention. Burlingham has described a preference by the blind infant for the use of legs and feet rather than arms and hands, attributing this to the absence of visual stimulation of reaching and grasping.[24] She emphasized that the variety of objects a blind child is given for purposes of play depend for their interest upon visual function. She suggested the addition of noise-making devices to toys and mentioned that pots and pans and other household articles may be more appropriate toys for children than the expensive ones that are specially produced. Some of the repetitive play—for example, with doors—may serve to help the blind child deal with vibration and the meaning of space. However, adults might consider this dangerous or annoying. Burlingham was one of the first to emphasize that many toys that are miniature versions of something larger are not at all appropriate for blind children because the components of touch, hearing, and smell are not similar to the real objects.[13,14] Even doll play has very limited use for the young blind child. She also emphasized that since the older blind child may not have a visual plan to help organize building activities, a reversal of this process, i.e., taking things apart and then putting them together, is more useful.

Wills has written a paper specifically about play and mastery in the blind child.[25] She felt that simple, repetitive play, if it persists too long, gives the child little or no mastery of the situation and is difficult to share with an adult. Normally, blind children tend to repeat things more often until familiarity is established. She observed a striking lack of imagination in the games that young blind children play. She also felt that the presence of anxiety tended to inhibit play and that this was complicated by delayed development of reality testing in the blind. New toys may be resisted because the blind child has more difficulty coping with a surprising novelty. The mother is put in the position of having to explain much more to help the blind child deal with these obstacles.

We feel another reason for constricted play is that blind children cannot see other children using and enjoying toys, nor are they likely to be aware of the variety of toys within their reach. Sometimes other children can teach the use of toys better than can the parents, who are likely to be more inhibited.

In a somewhat later paper, Fraiberg and her associates have described their approach to the facilitation of early play behavior.[11] Parents frequently complain that the child is not interested in toys, but education of parents demonstrated that this apparent disinterest could be reversed. Babies tended to function better in a supine position rather than a prone one. A variety of hanging toys could be introduced into the crib so that they do not fall out of reach and may be found again and again. The use of a play table with a limited surface bounded by a railing was also found useful. The toys that these authors found had the greatest appeal combined both sound and textural interest. They also emphasized the delay in doll play or domestic mimicry, even in the most precocious blind child; no examples of this were found in the second and third year in their small sample of cases. "We are impressed to see how much learning through toys is denied the blind child during the period when he needs to construct an object world"[11] (p. 132).

Another interesting point is that these authors did not find that bouncing, rocking furniture led to excessive stereotyped behavior if the children had been appropriately stimulated, although the parents were afraid of this. The use of a walker was felt to possibly delay the onset of independent walking, although there were considerable differences among the children in this regard.

A reduced range of fantasies and an unusually large number of bizarre or fearful preoccupations were described in blind children with deviant development by Elonen and her co-workers.[7,8] They felt that this might be related to very traumatic experiences which had aroused anxiety in these children, but had in many cases never been satisfactorily explained to them. In some cases playing out these experiences was found to be beneficial in reducing anxiety.

A recent excellent paper by Fraiberg has shown that the observation of baby games between infant, mother, and father may provide clues to the nature of the relationship and that these games may later become incorporated into the child's own behavior.[26]

In summary, there are a number of helpful and detailed reports on longitudinal observations of the play of blind babies and young children. One of the difficulties is that the unusual play patterns may have a different function in the blind than in the sighted and may be misinterpreted as pathology when they are useful to the baby for purposes of adaptation. Although problems remain in deciding when such patterns are helpful or harmful, at least these reports have again forcefully made the point that the standards applied to blind children must be used with caution.

Socialization

Elonen and Cain[8] describe "deviant" blind children as "lone wolves." They do relatively little interacting with other children. Their development is too primitive to respond to the casual attempt of other children to approach them, and the isolation tends to be reinforced by the parents. Those children who are somewhat older or more highly developed do wish for companionship, but because they have not developed the necessary skills, they have great difficulty in sustaining social relationships.

Burlingham observed that the initial contact of these children with strangers seemed similar to institutionalized children who tried to attach themselves to everyone.[14] However, the purpose of the blind child in this situation seems to be to gain an impression of the person in place of the visual image which they cannot obtain.

Peer relationships are difficult for blind children to develop without sufficient mobility, hand use, and speech. Nursery school helps to develop these skills during the preschool years, with or without sighted children in attendance. A number of studies have been done by Steinzor.[27] He found that there were some negative attitudes of sighted elementary school children who shared a class with blind children. He suggested that perhaps sighted children needed preparation for the presence of these children in their classes. (There appeared, however, to be no adverse effect from the presence of the blind.) He also studied the attitude of the partially sighted elementary and junior high school students toward the blind and the sighted, and he found great emphasis upon how much they could see as a determinant of self-esteem in the younger children. They felt more fortunate and less dependent than the blind, considering special classes for the blind to be for the "dumb." Their concept of blind seemed to be equivalent to not being able to do things. Being in classes with the sighted was liked because it was thought that this would help them become more competent.

Another factor that must be considered is the part that parents must play in initiating and perpetuating peer relationships. Blind children tend to be under surveillance much of the time, and it is frequently difficult for parents to leave the older children alone so that they may have some privacy. Parents may also have conflicts over how much they should attempt to facilitate a friendship; when this does seem advisable, it is frequently best when done in an indirect fashion (creating an interesting situation for sighted or other visually impaired children, rather than attempting to manipulate play opportunities directly).

Another aspect of socialization that has been raised by psychoanalytic writers has to do with increased fear of the child's own impulses, due to more difficulty in reality testing. According to this view, blind children seem to have more social difficulty because they have a limited ability to judge the seriousness of the anger or criticism of other people, just as they may overestimate their own. Caution has also been suggested in interpreting social difficulties in the same way as would be appropriate for the sighted.[25]

CASE HISTORY #1

A 15-year-old congenitally blind girl would at times become certain that there were people in the room who were looking critically at her, and she would then become anxious and upset. This was one example of how she readily attributed to others her own feelings or wishes to retaliate. However, what made this problem somewhat different than in sighted children was that it could be readily modified by supportive explanation.

CASE HISTORY #2

An 18-year-old girl who became blind at age 7, but was partially sighted previously, had an additional sensory isolation due to moderate deafness. She was diagnosed as schizophrenic because she would lean out of the window every day about the time children would ordinarily come home from school and talk to her "friends," who were in fact not there. In reality, she was an extremely isolated girl who had little contact with anyone, including her parents. In addition to this kind of behavior, she would talk to herself and smile, apparently inappropriately, as if she were responding to some inner thought or joke. Providing her with real social contact eliminated this behavior, which tended to return whenever she became totally socially isolated. It is questionable whether the diagnosis of schizophrenia was appropriate in this case.

In our study, we found that visually impaired children were much more likely than sighted children to have no friends (Table 16-5). Additionally, 28 percent of the parents reported that their child preferred to play by himself. Of school-age children, 15 percent were reported by teachers to have no friends at all, and 20.5 percent to have poor acceptance by their peers. With regard to teasing, about 30 percent of the parents reported that there had never been such experiences while 25 percent said there had been a significant problem with this in the past. The remainder described problems of intermediate degree.

There has been a considerable amount of writing about the attitudes of blind children toward their impairment; some of this has been mentioned previously. Burlingham reported that some children had the fantasy that

Table 16-5
Playmates of Visually Impaired Children and Controls*

Age Group	Index Cases n =	Index Cases % (of 84)	Controls n	Controls % (of 85)
Older	3	3.6	7	8.2
About same	26	31.0	45	52.9
Younger	11	13.1	3	3.5
Mixed ages	18	21.4	19	22.4
No friends	21	25.0	6	7.1
Siblings only	5	6.0	5	5.9
Totals	84	100.1	85	100.0

*$\chi^2 = 30.39$; df $= 5$; $p < 0.001$

blindness is a state that only occurs in childhood, and that they would grow out of it as they became adults.[14] She felt that they seemed to get a great relief from being able to talk openly about blindness, and this helped them to verbalize other loaded subjects as well. Sometimes the parent would tend to treat the subject of blindness as a secret or adult matter, so that the children persisted in being confused about it.

It is clear that attitudes among the visually impaired vary tremendously from person to person. Some talk about it openly, almost blatantly, but perhaps never really deal with its implications; others have a chip on their shoulder, are overly defensive, and feel very much a member of a discriminated against minority group; and there are those who act and talk as if blindness is not a handicap. In our own study, the use of leading questions about visual impairment led to a judgment that approximately 70 percent of the children interviewed had a realistic attitude toward the impairment, being able to admit that it did impose some limitations upon them. Five percent seemed quite preoccupied with it and mentioned many aspects spontaneously. Another 21 percent seemed to deny that there were any implications of the impairment about which they might have any feelings at all. Of those children who could describe any worries they had, 16 percent described ones related to visual impairment. Teachers were also asked about the children's awareness of visual impairment and reported that 28.6 percent of them had indicated nothing about it; 64.3 percent seemed to accept it without any question or confusion; 2.9 percent asked frequently about visual impairment but did not seem overtly upset about it; while another 2.9 percent were described as confused and upset by it.

One of the ways in which social attitudes of the blind might be judged would be whether or not they are able to associate with both blind and sighted persons without having excessively rigid ideas about this. The statement by Blank probably has some validity:

> If the blind person shows a really indiscriminating prejudice towards [the blind], we may be certain that he unconsciously shares the hostile attitudes towards himself that he attributes to those who are not blind.[20] (p. 15)

Others have frequently described blind persons' hostility toward the sighted and at times envy toward those who have more sight than they. Although this might be considered an example of typical minority-group dynamics, sighted persons should be cautious in making a judgment about this. The visually impaired do encounter incredibly stupid, frustrating, and sometimes humorous experiences with sighted persons which are difficult for those who have not gone through them to understand.

In our work with partially sighted children, we have been surprised by the apparently greater extent of teasing or hostility that they attract as compared with blind children. It is tempting to speculate that this is related to their marginal status: neither blind nor sighted. In particular, those children who are legally blind and yet demonstrate repeatedly to their classmates and friends that they can see may be accused of faking and of "trying to get away with something." These children frequently reported to us that they were tripped, harassed, and had to suffer the indignity of frequent informal visual testing by other children who were sceptical of their status. It may also be that the attitudes of pity, which are common in the sighted population and passed on to children, are not felt to apply to the partially sighted, who then suffer the consequences.

Independent Activities

Many parents of visually impaired children felt it was more difficult to teach them certain skills than was the case with their sighted children. Sixty-four percent of the parents reported this for walking, 58 percent for feeding and dressing, and 35 percent for washing. We developed a checklist for permitted activities of an independent sort which either blind or partially sighted children might be allowed to engage in by their parents. This was part of the separate parental questionnaire filled out by mothers and fathers of both visually impaired and sighted children. It was corrected for chronological age. Correlation between the scores of mothers and fathers within each group were as follows: controls of partial-vision cases, 0.58; controls of blind cases, 0.88; partial-vision cases, 0.83; blind cases, 0.74. It was found that there were highly significant differences between the groups but not between mothers and fathers. Thus, the mothers and fathers of the blind reported their children were permitted to do about one-third the number of listed items as compared with the controls ($p < 0.001$); for those with partial vision, the rough proportion was about two-thirds ($p < 0.001$ for mothers and $p < 0.005$ for fathers).

These findings simply confirm the commonsense idea that the degree of parental protectiveness is associated with the degree of visual impairment. Since we are simply interested here in group differences, rather than whether or not parents should or should not permit the child to do a particular thing, this is a description rather than a criticism of the parents of the visually impaired. The children are allowed to do less, but how much of this is overprotection is unclear. (The activities on the list should have been theoretically possible for the handicapped children as well.)

Identification

In his review of available information and research, Warren states that identification has been almost totally neglected in the literature, even though it is hypothesized to account for the child acquiring characteristics of his parents and other important people. Research is possible through a social-learning framework involving imitation, modeling, and social reinforcement, but "this is one of the most substantial and unfortunate gaps in the literature on the social development of the blind child"[28] (p. 12).

Personality

Warren has also pointed out the difficulty in considering the studies available on very small numbers of children to be representative. There is also a gap between the early ages studied and middle childhood. Personality instruments for use with blind children are not well developed.

> The fact that a given test probably cannot be administered to blind and sighted children with equivalent validity means that the goal of comparing blind with sighted children on personality characteristics or profiles is an impossible one. It may even be an inappropriate goal. Rather than comparing blind and sighted children, research should be concentrated on more intensive evaluation of blind children. To date much of the work on blind children has been simply evaluative, producing statements that blind children are more or less aggressive or introverted, etc. Such conclusions are insufficient in any meaningful sense.[28] (p. 13)

Warren suggests research in two directions: toward discovering the etiological factors that produce variation in personality dimensions, and toward the functional expression of various personality characteristics. Regarding the latter, we need to know how personality characteristics are expressed in real-life situations and what advantages or disadvantages they may confer.

Our own studies suggest to us that these recommendations are valid. We have found a wide range of variation in personality among our visually impaired children. It is certainly true that many of them have circumscribed interest patterns (51 percent according to their mothers), but this depends a great deal upon their early training and their family life and appears to be an avoidable hazard.

BEHAVIORAL DEVIANCE AND PATHOLOGY

Introduction

There are many problems, as previously stated, in determining when a difference in an individual amounts to pathology, and inevitably this must be a value judgment, even though at the extremes most people would agree. Because a child is more dependent upon others and his personality is less well established, any interpretation of behavior must not only be descriptive but give considerable attention to the context, including parents and significant others. The child who is multihandicapped will be even more difficult to assess. These problems of approach to disorder and pathology are well discussed in Rutter et al.[1,2] Like these authors, we elected a "clinical-diagnostic" approach and rejected the purely statistical method (although this has advantages), as well as one based purely upon the inference of internal conflict.

In this section, we will examine the process of assessment and some of the general principles involved, and then go on to look at some common or important types of behavioral problems. Finally, we will present some of the data from our own study.

Assessment

Psychological testing, its advantages and limitations, is a complex subject which is covered elsewhere in this book (chapter 6). It will not be discussed further here except to mention that the usefulness of its findings will be increased when it is employed as part of a comprehensive assessment and ongoing program, rather than in isolation.

When confronting a behavioral problem or complaint, emphasis must be placed upon the process of referral (with a new case) or the manner in which the problem comes to attention. This is precisely where many practitioners miss an important opportunity. They may focus upon the problem or the complaint, taking it at face value, and proceed from there. In most instances, however, it will be found extremely helpful to first try to answer the questions Why does this case or problem present at this particular time? Who says that there is a problem, who is most worried about it, and why is that person bothered by the behavior? What does the person referred or the person referring think will happen if something is not done about the behavior? What conflicts or disagreements are there within the family or between the family and professionals regarding the importance of the behavior or its referral for assessment or intervention? What is it that those doing the referring wish: taking the case off their hands, giving them additional ideas, or providing an opinion that can be used to gain points in a serious controversy? All these are possibilities and, if they are not understood at the outset or fairly soon, they may wreck the opportunity to provide useful service. Additionally, such information tells a great deal about the nature of the support system available to the child and even the nature of the conditions that may be contributing to the bothersome behavior.

Aside from the process just described, it is essential to obtain an adequate history of the complaint or complaints in detail. How do they affect the child and others? How much and in what ways do they impair the child's functioning? What is the duration of the problem and the course of its development—improving, worsening, stable, fluctuating? What has been done about it and with what results? Is there anyone else in the family (or in the class) with a similar problem that might affect the interpretation of this behavior? Are there any life events and major changes that have taken place in a significant temporal relationship with the onset or modifications of the behavior? Are there other areas of functioning which, although not complained about, might help to place the complaint in perspective? The child's strengths and those of the family must also be assessed.

Information must be obtained from several settings and persons. It is often quite unsatisfactory to depend upon the reports or descriptions of one parent or one teacher. At times, a visit to the home or school will be important, especially since the child's behavior and willingness to relate in the office setting may be vastly different from that in more natural settings.[29]

The person doing the assessment should have available sufficient information from others who have worked with the child and adequate medical information about the visual impairment.

One usually wishes to do more than merely collect the history. Baseline observations may be obtained in a variety of ways in the home or school for those who are interested in specific behavioral change.

Many will want to interview the child or adolescent, as well as the family. A few remarks are in order about this latter situation.

The interviewer will have some idea about the developmental aspects of behavior, although the person who does not remember much about his own childhood or adolescence and who does not have children in his own family may have some difficulty here. Nevertheless, one automatically starts to compare the behavior, speech and level of maturity with what one knows of other persons of the same age.

Body contact between the child or adolescent and the examiner is likely to be different from the examiner's experience of sighted children. The older child and adolescent will frequently wish to hold the examiner's arm on entering the examining room. The young child may wish to feel parts of the examiner, although this is not as common as is usually thought. Sometimes blind children will ask what might appear to be impertinent questions of a personal nature, such as how old the examiner is, but this may be because in the absence of vision the voice quality does not provide sufficient information.

The posture and physical attitude of the visually impaired person may be a problem. If the person is partially sighted, this is not likely to be the case. However, with a very substantial reduction in vision, and certainly with congenital blindness, the person may not hold his head up or turn his face toward the interviewer. This may have an entirely different meaning than it would for the sighted. Sometimes blind individuals will turn an ear, rather than the face, toward the person doing the interviewing. What would otherwise be a "downcast" demeanor possibly indicative of depression or withdrawal behavior may have quite a different significance in a blind person.

Sometimes the speech of blind persons (but not usually the partially sighted) will cause confusion. The quality of voice and modulation of tone and volume may be quite different from the sighted. This is the previously mentioned "broadcasting voice" of the blind, which seems somehow impersonal. Words with visual meanings will also be used, and if the interviewer is not accustomed to dealing with blind persons, this can seem shocking or be misinterpreted as denial of handicap.

The range of facial expression is usually reduced in congenitally blind persons and cannot be used as a clear indication of mood or mental state nor of how much rapport has been established in the interview. Bodily activities, such as nervous habits, mannerisms, or fidgetiness, may give a better indication.

Sometimes the interviewer will be momentarily distracted by an awareness that a blind person has a reduced range of general information and the fact that one has to occasionally stop and explain something that would not be necessary with most sighted persons.

It has already been pointed out that, in play, models are of relatively little value to the blind, although they may be useful with the partially sighted. Some of the latter can also produce drawings if this is something which the interviewer likes to use. It is important to remember that it is more difficult for the visually impaired to "warm up" to a new environment, and, therefore, the kind of relaxation and familiarity necessary to reduce the child's inhibitions and permit engagement in play may not occur as rapidly as it would with the sighted. For young children, the repetitiveness of play and the importance of noise and smell must be taken into account and not assumed to represent significant psychopathology.

As with other children of the same age, one can usually enquire about interests, family life, hobbies, wishes, dreams, friends, and similar matters.

It is usually thought to be a good idea to explain to children and adolescents (and for that matter adults) what the purposes are in an interview. This is perhaps even more true with a visually impaired person, who may in fact need explanation if the interviewer is taking notes, moving around the room, and so forth—activities the sighted child will perceive without explanation. Long periods of silence on the part of the interviewer may be even more disturbing to a blind child than to one who is sighted and should generally be avoided.

Finally, it is important for the interviewer to feel comfortable talking with blind children or adolescents about the meaning of blindness for them; talking with the partially sighted is somewhat different in that one has to be aware of their sensitivities to the connotations of the word *blind*. The marginality of their social status in regard to this degree of impairment may also need to be openly discussed with them.

It should not be necessary to say that the same courtesies extended to sighted children and adolescents with regard to confidentiality and relaying information to their parents should be accorded the visually impaired as well.

In drawing conclusions from the assessment of visually impaired children, one needs to give special attention to the modifiability of particular behavioral patterns, rather than merely their existence.[30] Thus, behavior which occurs in some settings but not in others may be more readily modified and of lesser importance pathologically than behavior that is always present or always absent. It is also necessary to establish how much of an opportunity the child has had to learn new, expected, and normative patterns of behavior. Chess and Hassibi have pointed out the importance of this modifiability, giving as an important example the demonstration of stereotyped behavior.[9] The question that is important in determining pathology is not whether the child does it, but whether the child can give up or reduce the rate of stereotyping in favor of other things, such as actively engaging in sports or relating to other people.

CASE HISTORY #3

A 12-year-old blind girl was sent for evaluation because she was retaining her bowel movements. This was of special concern to the parents because of the fantastic cost incurred by having a plumber unplug their toilet every weekend when it became clogged by her huge bowel movements. She was attending a residential school during the week and returning home on weekends. One could have looked into numerous complicated factors and attitudes in relation to this distressing symptom. However, an overview of the meaning of the behavior in its total life setting quickly yielded this surprising information: The girl had become very modest when she had entered adolescence, and the residential school she was attending had very few toilets for the number of pupils—and those had had the doors removed, so that she felt too embarrassed and inhibited to use them. She dealt with this by holding her bowel movements in until she could return home—the kind of thing one sometimes sees in a much younger child in whom bowel training has not yet become completely autonomous. The important point is that a change in the school situation and some minimal support enabled her to have normal bowel movements and eliminated the problem. Naturally, in such a case one would want to find out about the history of past elimination habits and the other areas of her functioning as well.

Dependency, Passivity, Lack of Initiative

We have mentioned elsewhere that visually impaired children (and handicapped children in general) are at risk for problems of dependency, passivity, and lack of initiative. It is all too easy for them to depend upon other people, who frequently become impatient when it takes more time to teach them or to explain things. The feeling of competence and mastery of the environment, which is so powerful a force in developing motivation, may be impaired, although this is not at all inevitable. Since a certain amount of realistic dependency is also necessary, the way the parents and others handle this can be crucial for the maintenance of self-esteem in such a child. It is more difficult to become angry and rebellious towards parents upon whom one must continue to depend, especially if it is difficult to judge the effects of that aggression. A common finding with complaints of lack of initiative or passivity is that, previously, this type of approach to life was actually convenient to the parents and only became a problem later on. There are no neat and easy methods for injecting a person with enthusiasm for life. Very often it is chance that does so, not the professional. It is sometimes astonishing what the presence of a girlfriend or boyfriend of the opposite sex will do for a handicapped teenager: those who seemed unable to get about and very slow in all activities miraculously want to do all the things necessary to maintain an important relationship. At times, the professional can be helpful not in treating the child or teenager for lack of initiative but in removing obstacles to more varied choices— making it possible for the visually impaired person to profit from chance occurrences and meetings.

Developmental Delays

Many writers and investigators feel that blind children have to make a devious detour to reach the same developmental point as the sighted.[14,31] But there is a real danger in assuming that all developmental delays and imbalances are due to some structural defect in the child and are undesirable.[32] Chess and Hassibi have found that some delays are adaptive and necessary for the child to develop a particular type of skill.[9] Usually, in the child who is not otherwise handicapped, there is later developmental acceleration. They feel that if general developmental acceleration is not evident by age 2 and if emotional and motor development are still significantly below expectation by age 5, intellectual deficiency is to be suspected provided adequate stimulation has been received.

Of particular importance is the presence of such delays in the multihandicapped, such as those with both hearing and visual impairment, and in rubella children. Recent studies show that the latter can have an abnormally small head circumference without being retarded;[33] they may also be small in size and be "late bloomers," so that early slowness may not be predictive of later development.

Although there is a danger in overoptimism, there is probably even more of a danger in the reverse. This is because the parent usually suspects some degree of mental retardation anyway, and a hint or misdiagnosis of this by professionals can lead to a reduction in necessary parental stimulation and therefore a selffulfilling prophecy, which is most unfortunate.

Childhood Autism

A distinction needs to be made between the unusual or even rare condition of childhood autism and so-called "autistic features." Keeler was one of the first to suggest that autistic features were very common in children with retrolental fibroplasia and even in children blind from other causes.[21] In the Chess et al. study of rubella children, autistic features were also found to be frequent,[34] although this was not a random sampling of the population of childhood rubella. An entire book was written by Chase on autistic symptomatology in children with retrolental fibroplasia.[35] This research suggested that autistic features may be more common than otherwise expected but are not necessarily of pathological import. Chess and Hassibi have pointed out that the differentiation between stereotyped behavior in the blind and autistic features is usually not made.[9] In the blind or partially sighted child without severe psychopathology, these patterns are easily abandoned in favor of human contact, whereas severely disturbed children prefer such self-stimulation to interaction with people and may resist contact, as do children with autism. We have not been impressed by the numbers of blind children with psychosis (of which autism is the earliest form). We are convinced that such initial diagnoses by the inexperienced occur at a much higher rate than if the examiner is familiar with the visually impaired and if the child is seen over time and in an adequate program.

Controlling and Manipulative Behavior

Some visually impaired children and adolescents are excessively adept at manipulating other people, and this is sometimes either a presenting complaint or becomes obvious as an assessment proceeds. This is not surprising, since it is difficult for many parents to set limits on a handicapped child and their doing so frequently arouses the criticism of others; the attitude of pity which blindness is likely to arouse may be especially effective in creating such obstacles to parental good management. Thus, ordinary limitations may be seen as cruelty. Since all children are opportunistic, it is not difficult to see how this might lead to the use of the handicap and people's feelings about it as a method of controlling others. However, the following case is certainly extreme.

CASE HISTORY #4

A 16-year-old totally blind young man was originally seen because of the complaint of depression, which seemed to be worsening in the last years of high school. He seemed to expect people to serve his needs but was realizing that this was not going to happen and was quite disappointed. The previous history was of great interest. He had originally been evaluated during his preschool years because his movements were awkward, and he showed some developmental imbalances. Mental retardation was suspected as was some brain dysfunction. An air encephalogram showed some air over the cerebral hemispheres, and it was suggested that this might be indicative of atrophy of the brain. Unfortunately, in some way that is not entirely clear, when the discharge summary was dictated, this suggestive finding was stated as a fact. Subsequently, this boy was known as significantly mentally retarded and was also said to have cerebral palsy. In fact, on one occasion when he was seen by a physician for an undescended testicle, the comment was made that an operation was not advisable because he was mentally retarded. It was interesting that these diagnoses stuck to the boy in spite of the fact that no documentation was ever available to indicate that he had cerebral palsy. In any event, he was placed in a class for retarded children, where the teacher soon recognized that he had indications of better intelligence. She was able to convince the family physician to send him, at the age of 8, for another assessment at a different center. It was found that he had a severe and apparently progressive visual impairment and his tested intelligence was at least in the dull-normal range. Unfortunately, his parents had already been quite confused by the previous misdiagnoses and had expected little from him. This, then, was a boy who had to adjust to his visual loss and had to cope with the difficulties involved in trying to change the expectations of others with respect to himself. He felt very deprived by his family and expected each individual he met to somehow make up for it to him.

When followed subsequently, it was noted that he was developing strange symptoms. He was living in a special boarding house with a very sympathetic family who catered to his every whim. He could not eat certain foods or at certain times of the day, or else he would vomit. If he was frustrated, he would start to shake, and everyone would become worried and give in to him. At times he would fall on the ground and become stiff and have to be taken to the hospital. He felt that he was too "sick" to ever work. He was able to convince one woman that he needed love to make up for his deprived childhood, and the physical contact she provided rather innocently for him caused serious difficulties in her marriage. Later on, he would threaten suicide if he did not get his way.

The management of this case involved, among many other things, persistently treating him as an ordinary human being of whom ordinary things could be expected. This was interpreted by him as cruel and unusual punishment and led to frequent threats, yet it gradually succeeded. He found it very difficult to accept that he would have to find more appropriate ways to gain satisfaction and that he could not expect other people to feel responsible for his unhappy childhood. It was most difficult to convince other persons to treat him as a person rather than a blind man to be pitied. However, he eventually began to work, persisted with his job, and developed some friendships that were satisfying to him.

All those working with the visually impaired can help prevent situations like this, not only by helping others to make fewer mistakes in diagnosis, but by encouraging parents to set reasonable limits and to confront visually impaired children with the consequences of their behavior, even if this is negative and unpleasant. It is most difficult to do this after many years of indulgence.

Adventitious Blindness

Reactions to the loss of vision depend partly upon the rate of loss (gradual or sudden), associated problems, stage of development, family reactions, and to some extent what kind of activities were important for the child's self-esteem previously. It is well known and confirmed by much clinical experience that a child's reactions to a handicap are much more severe if it occurs after the first year of life, although early onset may certainly have effects upon total personality development. We have seen cases where gradual onset of visual deterioration was considered to be of psychogenic origin or due to malingering. Unfortunately, both parents and professionals tend to be rather hostile toward children who seem in some way to be faking their symptoms. When the symptoms later turn out to have been an indication of a real physical impairment, a variety of additional problems may result.

The work of Cholden, the first psychiatrist to work with blindness, emphasized the need for newly blinded individuals to accept the fact of blindness prior to rehabilitation.[36] The holding out of false hopes by professionals who were worried about shock, depression, or even possible suicide, was seen not as helpful but as distinctly harmful. Subsequently, this point has been generally accepted and eloquently described by many recently blinded adults. To some extent the same point can be made about children who become blind and about their families. Although the intention may be good, "softening the blow" may not be a service. Denial of the reality of blindness can throw families into serious conflict, especially where guilt is involved.

CASE HISTORY #5

A teenage boy was accidentally blinded in one eye by his brother while they were involved in mock threats to each other on a hunting trip. The other eye was lost through sympathetic ophthalmia. The fact that this had occurred as a result of one brother's actions and on a hunting trip where the father's supervision had been less than adequate produced so many repercussions that the family never really dealt with it. In many respects, they treated the blind boy as if he were not blind. Some months later, this youth became increasingly disturbed and an acute psychotic breakdown followed his removing his glass eye and destroying it. He developed the "delusion" that he was sighted. A few weeks later the brother who had blinded him also became psychotic. He claimed that his blind brother had an invisible third eye in the middle of his forehead, as has been described in some science-fiction stories about Martians.

This obviously is a rather dramatic and extreme case, and there may have been some predisposition to psychosis. Nevertheless, it can be seen that these extreme breaks with reality were unlikely to be coincidental and that the content of the psychotic process related to the dynamics of the injury and how the family had handled it.

CASE HISTORY #6

A 15-year-old boy who was a very active child rode a trail bike into a car and suffered a very severe head injury. After a prolonged coma, he was left with a hemiplegia, severe visual impairment with tunnel vision, a speech defect, occasional seizures, and a reduction in general intelligence. He went back to his regular school in his local community but found it impossible to cope for many reasons. He was extremely hypersensitive to all sounds and was so easily distracted for a period of over a year that when he was trying to do his work his brother's breathing drove him into a rage. Because of this sensitivity, his emotional lability, and his inability to accept his changed status, the school passed him on to the next grade even though he did not warrant this promotion. Because the work was more difficult, he was even less able to cope. When first seen for a psychiatric evaluation, his family was at the point of complete collapse. His reaction to frustration was so severe and so frequent that the family simply could not function any more. The boy blamed everyone else for his problem and did not feel that anything had to do with his changed physical and intellectual status. He was admitted to the school for the blind but for the better part of a year would regularly accost any visitor to indicate that "I'm not like the other children here." It took almost a year before he could see anything positive in the school and, even after returning with some greater success to a regular school, he still tended to deny the significance of his disability—but fortunately his acoustic hypersensitivity had disappeared. It is anticipated that this boy will still have problems in the future, and these may be associated with what was described as his stubborn disposition prior to his accident. It may be of interest to see the improvement which occurred in this boy's concept of himself as reflected in drawings done shortly after his accident and 2 years later (Fig. 16-1).

There are no easy methods to deal with such major adjustments. It may be very difficult for children to conceptualize how they could find other satisfactions in their remaining functions. Sometimes it is helpful to have exposure to competent blind individuals and have discussions with them, so that they can actually become convinced that the cultural stereotype of helplessness does not have to apply.

Depression

Depression in children is a complex subject. It tends either to be overdiagnosed because someone looks sad or acts miserable, or at times it may be overlooked. An excellent review of this confusing subject has been provided by Graham.[37] He points out that pure depressive illness in childhood is relatively rare. There is also a lack of evidence to connect early sadness and misery with adult depressive illness. Such disorders in children are usually best viewed as a reaction rather than an illness.

We have not found depression to be a common problem in those children we have seen. What seems to be more common is both complaining behavior and lack of initiative. Sometimes the content of the complaint may suggest depression, but a controlling element is often

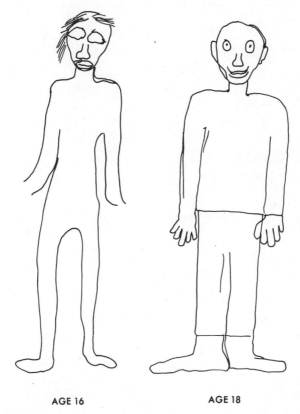

AGE 16   AGE 18

Fig. 16-1.   Change in self-representation by boy in Case History #6, shortly after injury and 2 years later.

very prominent. Suicide does not appear to be common among the visually impaired, contrary to what some sighted persons might expect.

SUMMARY OF BEHAVIORAL FINDINGS FROM OUR STUDY OF VISUALLY IMPAIRED CHILDREN

The behavior of each child was assessed in 3 ways: (1) by each parent of index cases and controls separately on the parent questionnaire; (2) by teachers on a similar questionnaire (index cases only); and (3) as a global 4-point rating from "none" to "severe" according to all the information available. In addition, psychiatric diagnoses were applied when appropriate. Additional information was obtained from the teacher questionnaires and from the semistructured interview with the parent.

Table 16-6 shows that there is a significant correlation between

Table 16-6
Questionnaire Scores (Mothers) and Global Ratings of
Behavior

Rating	Mean	SD	n
Severe	9.846	6.71	13
Moderate	10.700	5.52	20
Mild	7.091	5.38	11
None	6.414	4.76	29
Total Group	8.301	5.66	73

Analysis of Variance				
ANOVA	SS	df	MS	
Between groups	265.53	3	88.51	
Within groups	2041.84	69	29.59	$F = 2.99$; $p < 0.05$
Total	2307.37	72		$eta^2 = 0.115$
Test of Linearity				
Regression	210.36	1	210.36	$F = 0.93$; $r = -0.30$
Deviation from Linearity	55.17	2	27.59	$r^2 = 0.091$

total behavioral scores and global scores. We then looked at items of
behavior. Children with no other handicaps were described as fearful
of new situations more often than were the controls. The fathers of
the index cases saw these children as more irritable than did their mothers.
Interestingly, these children were not described as more solitary than
the controls, and it was noted that the teachers generally tended to
give the children lower ratings than did the parents, presumably indicating
either lesser degrees of awareness or a greater tendency to judge aspects
of behavior as nonsignificant. The children with other handicaps were
described as more solitary, worrisome, not much liked, fearful of new
situations, more squirmy, and less likely to tell lies than were the controls.

Looking at the differences between the blind and the partially sighted
on these behavioral items, both subgroups were described as not much
liked by their peers, but the blind were so described only by their fathers
and the partially sighted by their mothers. Both parents of the partially
sighted felt their children were bothered by new situations, but this
was only true of the fathers of the blind. The presence of mannerisms
or tics was much more frequently indicated by both mothers and fathers
of both subgroups than was true of their controls. The blind (but not
the partially sighted) were described as more solitary. The partially sighted
were described as more worried than their controls (although this was
not true of the blind).

Table 16-7
Behavior: Global Rating of Only Children and Others*

Severity of Disorder	Only Children		Children with Siblings	
	n	% (of 13)	n	% (of 78)
Severe	5	38.5	17	21.8
Moderate	3	23.1	18	23.1
Mild or transient	1	7.7	12	15.4
None, well-adjusted	4	30.8	31	39.7
Totals	13	100.1	78	100.0

*$\chi^2 = 0.66$; df = 1; ns (condensed to 2 × 2 table).

When differences between the index cases and controls are looked at with all subgroups combined, the only items that emerged as significant are as follows: not much liked by others (mothers only); irritable (fathers only); tics or mannerisms (both); fearful of new situations (highly significant for both parents); and tells fewer lies. The best discrimination between those children described as having a behavior disorder by teachers and those not so described was achieved with a parent score of 9 or above. This is very similar to the point determined by the investigators in the Isle of Wight study[1,2] from which this questionnaire was adapted. This discrimination point was best for both the blind and the partially sighted.

On global ratings, Table 16-7 shows that about 45 percent were rated as having severe or moderate disorders within the past 12 months, while the remainder had a transient disorder, or were described as well adjusted. The table also shows (although the numbers are small) that this was not significantly different for only children.

It is known that behavior disorders in children tend to be associated with broken homes and marital discord. The present study corroborates this finding. As can be seen in Table 16-8, the majority of the children from broken homes were rated as having severe or moderate disorder whereas the majority of those in intact homes were rated as having mild or no disorder. It may be of additional interest that if this is further

Table 16-8
Behavior Disorder and Broken Home*

Disorder	Broken Home		Intact Home	
	n	% (of 19)	n	% (of 51)
Severe or moderate	16	84.2	17	33.3
Mild or none	3	15.8	34	66.7

*$\chi^2 = 12.41$; df = 1; $p < 0.001$

Table 16-9

Child's Behavioral Disorder (Global Rating) and Ratings of
Parents and Marriage

Relationship with	Kendall's tau b	Significance
Mother's global rating		
Past 12 months	0.300	$p < 0.001$
Before that	0.279	$p < 0.005$
Father's global rating		
Past 12 months	0.153	ns
Before that	0.069	ns
Marriage rating		
Past 12 months	0.203	$p < 0.03$
Before that	0.211	$p < 0.02$

broken down into those children with average or above IQs and those
children with below average IQs, the same trend of increased disorder
in broken homes is found, but in intact homes the majority of children
with below-average IQs still have severe to moderate disorder, although
the trend is less marked than it is in a broken home. This is consistent
with the knowledge that behavior disorder is more common in association
with lower IQ.

The child's behavioral disorder as assessed by global rating was
also found to be highly correlated with indications of the mother's
psychiatric disorder but not with the father's; it also correlated, although
less strongly, with the rating of the marriage. This is shown in Table
16-9. It is of further interest that the association of the child's disorder
with the mother's disorder is much stronger for girls than it is for boys,
suggesting that processes of identification may be operating here.

Psychiatric diagnoses are shown in Table 16-10. Note that this
includes a category not present in the standard nomenclature, "developmental disorder," which includes peculiar and persistent deviations in
specific (usually multiple) areas that were judged as having negative
impacts on the child's total adaptation. A breakdown of these diagnoses
into blind and partially sighted cases shows the following: mental
retardation as a significant handicap was present in 27 percent of the
blind and only 10 percent of those with partial vision. Psychosis was
diagnosed in only three children, two of whom were blind and one
partially sighted. Developmental disorder was present in 41 percent of
the blind and only 8 percent of those with partial vision. A "normal"
diagnosis was applied to 32 percent of the blind and 49 percent of those
with partial vision.

When mothers were asked whether their child had an emotional
or behavioral disorder, 29.3 percent replied in the affirmative. When

Table 16-10
Psychiatric Diagnostic Categories*

Category	n	% (of 86)
Mental retardation	16	18.6
Psychosis	3	3.5
Organic brain syndrome	5	5.8
Adjustment reaction	9	10.5
Neurotic reaction	3	3.5
Behavior disorder	6	7.0
Personality disorder	7	8.1
Special symptom reaction	2	2.3
Developmental disorder	13	15.1
NORMAL	37	43.0
Missing cases (no diag.)	6	

*More than 1 choice possible, max. = 2.

teachers were asked the same question, 24.3 percent said yes, 64.3 percent no, and 11.4 percent were unsure. Thirty-six percent of the blind and 32 percent of the partially sighted in a British study were said by their teachers to be emotionally disturbed.[38]

Additionally, in describing their child's mood in the past 12 months, 10 percent of the parents described him as unhappy, 21.1 percent described temper outbursts, 7.8 percent said he was anxious and fearful, and 15.6 percent said he seemed to be in a world of his own. About one-third of both parents and teachers felt that the child's needs were not being adequately met. Twenty-eight percent of the teachers reported that they had not had enough contact with the family, but in the group the teachers felt were behaviorally disordered, lack of contact was felt to be a problem in 35 percent. The teachers described what they felt to be a problem between parent and child in only 13 percent of all the children, but in 35 percent of those they said had a behavior disorder. They also felt the needs of the children with behavior disorders were not being met in almost half the cases.

In the psychiatric interview, fewer children were assessed as having abnormalities in thinking than might be expected from the global ratings. Thinking was judged to be normal in 71 percent, 7 percent showing incoherent associations and another 7 percent judged as pathologically preoccupied or obsessed with certain topics. In 23 percent the children seemed to have no sense of humor and to be excessively serious. The range of general information was thought considerably below what would be expected of a sighted child in almost one-third of the cases interviewed.

There are several sources of possible bias in these findings: (1) Parents may have become so accustomed to deviant behavior that they do not rate it as present; (2) parents who are under stress or who are negative toward their child might do the opposite; (3) matching is of limited usefulness and a more highly heterogeneous group, like the visually impaired, is likely to demonstrate score deviations of doubtful meaning; (4) global ratings, particularly without inter-rater reliability data, may be subject to systematic bias.

Even so, it is felt that this information is of some value. It shows, on a more than usually representative sample of visually impaired children, that a large proportion of them have developmental deviations and adjustment difficulties, whether rated by teachers, parents, or a psychiatrist. We believe this is a fact that must be reckoned with, even though the validity of the absolute numbers provided may be open to dispute.

A few additional findings should be mentioned. There was no correlation between global ratings of behavioral disorder and social class nor the number of full siblings in the family. It is interesting that for this group we have confirmed the findings of the Isle of Wight study[1,2] that behavioral disorder is more common in children with additional handicaps or with hard signs of neurological dysfunction. Thus, 62.5 percent of children with other handicaps were rated as having a severe or moderate disorder, whereas this was only true for 30.2 percent of those without other handicaps. This difference was even greater for those children who showed hard signs of neurological disorder, for whom the ratings were severe or moderate in 62 percent—compared to only 22 percent in those without such signs. (Of 10 children with epilepsy, 7 were rated severe or moderate, 2 mild, and 1 normal.)

Table 16-11 shows that many more of the visually impaired children have received psychoactive medication than is true of the control cases. A further breakdown shows that the proportion receiving tranquilizers is higher for the blind than for the partially sighted; this is probably associated with a higher rate of psychiatric disorder among the blind. Table 16-12 shows that, at the time the study was performed, there was a very large difference between numbers of visually impaired children receiving tranquilizing medication and the controls, namely 21.0 percent versus 1.0 percent.

MANAGEMENT

This is not the place to detail the general principles of various types of therapy, since there are many adequate presentations of such material.[39,40,41] An adequate assessment leads one far down the road toward determining a method of intervention, or at least it should. With all handicapped children, environmental manipulation should be considered and not accorded a lower prestige status than, for example,

Table 16–11
Psychoactive Medication Received (Ever)

Kind of Medication*	Index Cases n	Index Cases % (of 85)	Control Cases n	Control Cases % (of 85)
Tranquilizer	22†	25.9	8‡	9.4
Sedative	3	3.5	0	—
Anticonvulsant	17	20.0	0	—
None, ever	49	57.6	77	90.6

*More than one choice possible
†18 on medication now
‡Only 1 on medication now.

psychotherapy. In fact, clarification of needs and misunderstandings may be all that is necessary. Sometimes providing the proper school setting which reduces excessive frustration leads to symptom reduction. Sometimes the problems posed are really ones of inadequate socialization and social learning, which may require an educational approach rather than one of a direct attack upon the symptoms. However, in the more complex cases a variety or combination of methods may be necessary, depending upon the therapists' predilections and training. The present trends are toward more flexible and eclectic approaches than was true some years ago. That is, many therapists will see a place for individual psychotherapy or play therapy, behavior-modification techniques, family therapy, parent counseling, group therapy, discussion groups, etc. Additionally, there has been more recognition of the importance of parents as cooperative therapists for their own children, and techniques for instituting behavioral change in parents have recently been developed. Unfortunately, we do not have any very conclusive evidence from carefully controlled long-term studies to suggest that one particular mode of therapy is substantially more successful than another.

Crisis intervention is another approach which, whatever the specific techniques used, rests upon the assumption that during a crisis people are more accessible to help, and that this may be important in the

Table 16–12
Children on Psychoactive Medication Now*†

	Index Cases	Controls
Yes	18	1
No	67	84

*Excludes anticonvulsants
†$\chi^2 = 15.17$; df $= 1$; $p < 0.001$

prevention of later disability.[42] Since it has already been suggested that visually impaired children are more vulnerable to stressful situations and may be able to understand them only with greater difficulty, it would seem that attention should be given to the timing of intervention, and this requires some working knowledge of available services and therapists who care enough about children to see them soon rather than placing them on a waiting list.

It is not easy to give any firm guidelines to the professional who is not a mental health worker as to when and how such cases should be referred. Sometimes it may seem that pragmatic considerations are more important than theoretical ones. Is there someone available who has some experience with the visually impaired, or who is willing to be flexible enough to learn and to consult those who do know more about it? Can such a person or service provide any meaningful help to an agency or school, given the very special assistance that may be needed? Frequently each agency or school will attempt to make its own special arrangements: if it does not have its own psychiatrist, psychologist, or social worker, it may establish informal relationships with a private practitioner or some organization that has such a person available.

It is probably not realistic to expect that generic practitioners of psychiatry, psychology, or social work will ever have much specialized knowledge about visual impairment—just as they will not have it about many other special areas. If it is not possible to seduce someone into this interesting field, on at least a part-time basis, then the other professionals who work with the visually impaired will have to be somewhat less protective of their patients or clients, or will have to develop additional skills themselves. What is particularly unfortunate, although probably diminishing, is an isolation of residential schools or agencies for the visually impaired whose personnel may never have much contact with mental health workers or may be unable to admit that some of their children or clients have behavioral or psychiatric problems.

Whatever the specific techniques that a person of a particular mental health discipline may use, it seems clear that in the majority of instances the behavioral problems and complaints that are presented can yield to a relatively straightforward approach—if only those involved will communicate well enough with each other so that helpful suggestions can be developed and tested. It is also to be hoped that, as research methodology improves, we will have better information on which to base preventive programs and sensible parent-guidance services, so that the problems discussed here will be minimized.

CONCLUSIONS

1. By whatever method of assessment, most studies agree that behavioral and developmental problems are much commoner among the visually impaired *although not inevitable.* This seems to be more true of the blind than of the partially sighted.
2. Visually impaired children are hospitalized much more frequently in early life and in later years than are sighted children, and there is a correlation between hospitalization in the first year of life and later IQ.
3. Parents have more worries about visually impaired children than do the parents of sighted children, and they permit them to engage in fewer independent activities.
4. Visually impaired children have fewer social opportunities to relate to their peers, and many more of them have no friends. They also tend to be described by their parents as solitary or socially isolated.
5. Psychiatric disorder is significantly more common in children with multiple handicaps and in children with involvement of the central nervous system.
6. Psychiatric disorder is strongly associated with maternal psychiatric disorder and with broken homes.
7. Visually impaired children are much more likely to be receiving psychiatric drugs than are sighted children.
8. Breast-feeding is less common, probably in relation to a longer time spent in an incubator and in subsequent hospitalizations.
9. Feeding problems, especially chewing, are much more common in the visually impaired and more common in the blind than in the partially sighted.
10. Weaning takes place later than in the sighted.
11. The development of manipulative behavior or passivity and lack of initiative is not uncommon.
12. These findings support the concept of an interaction effect involving psychological, developmental, attitudinal, and social factors which place the visually impaired child's functioning in considerably greater jeopardy than is the case with the sighted.
13. Evidence from other studies and longitudinal observations indicates that developmental delays and imbalances are common, especially in multihandicapped children, but in many cases there is spontaneous later acceleration or the opportunity for improvement with intervention.

14. Even very significant delays in early development suggesting major mental impairment should not discourage attempts at further stimulation and training. These may represent prolongations of developmental stages rather than permanently arrested development.
15. There are particular risks that the visually impaired child will be misdiagnosed as mentally retarded or severely emotionally disturbed when neither is the case; professionals doing such diagnosing need greater appreciation of these problems, as do parents and professionals outside the mental health field.
16. The assessment of a behavioral or developmental disorder is a complex process, which cannot be completed quickly or by any one person. It requires information from multiple persons and settings and a flexibility in interpreting behavior of the visually impaired child without the rigid application of standards that are appropriate for the sighted.
17. A very careful assessment and clarification of the situation often points the way toward fairly simple or straightforward approaches to the modification of the child's behavior; more complex and intensive treatment directed toward the child or family is only necessary in a minority of cases.
18. The professional who is not familiar with the blind may draw the wrong conclusions from the child's posture, speech, and range of facial expressions, as well as from play or descriptions of life situation and interests. It would be helpful if, in assessing such a child, a mental health professional who is inexperienced with the blind could have access to such information to avoid drawing the wrong conclusions.
19. The rate of psychiatric disorder and the risk of developmental deviation is sufficiently high according to most studies, as well as the present one, that further training in this area seems advisable for teachers, speech, physical, and occupational therapists, etc. Since behavior disorder is associated with family factors that may actually be causative, early and ongoing supportive programs for families seem to be essential. The public has frequently been found to wrongly believe that services for the visually impaired are lavishly funded and available; this is not so, and further action is needed to establish such services in many parts of the world.

REFERENCES

1. Rutter M, Tizard J, Whitmore K (eds): Education, Health and Behaviour. London, Longman, 1970
2. Rutter M, Graham P, Yule W: A Neuropsychiatric Study in Childhood.

Clinics in Developmental Medicine Nos 35/36. London, Heinemann, 1970
3. Bowlby J: Attachment and Loss, vol 1: Attachment. New York, Basic Books, 1969
4. Bowlby J: Attachment and Loss, vol 2: Separation, Anxiety and Anger. New York, Basic Books, 1973
5. Klaus MH, Kennell JH: Mothers separated from their newborn infants. Pediat Clin North Am 17:1015-1037, 1970
6. Freedman DG: Smiling in blind infants and the issue of innate vs. acquired. J Child Psychol Psychiatry 5:171-184, 1964
7. Elonen AS, Zwarensteyn SB: Appraisal of developmental lag in certain blind children. J Pediatr 65:599-610, 1964
8. Elonen AS, Cain AC: Diagnostic evaluation and treatment of deviant blind children. Am J Orthopsychiatry 34:625-633, 1964
9. Chess S, Hassibi M: Textbook of Child Psychiatry. New York, Plenum (in press)
10. Fraiberg S, Siegel B, Gibson R: The role of sound in the search behavior of a blind infant. Psychoanal Study Child 21:327-357, 1966
11. Fraiberg S, Smith M, Adelson E: An educational program for blind infants. J Spec Educ 3:121-142, 1969
12. Sandler A-M: Aspects of passivity and ego development in the blind infant. Psychoanal Study Child 18:343-361, 1963
13. Burlingham D: Hearing and its role in the development of the blind. Psychoanal Study Child 19:95-112, 1964
14. Burlingham D: Some notes on the development of the blind. Psychoanal Study Child 16:121-145, 1961
15. Fraiberg S, Freedman DA: Studies in the ego development of the congenitally blind child. Psychoanal Study Child 19:113-169, 1964
16. Wills DM: Some observations on blind nursery school children's understanding of their world. Psychoanal Study Child 20:344-363, 1965
17. Fraiberg S: Parallel and divergent patterns in blind and sighted infants. Psychoanal Study Child 23:264-300, 1968
18. Wills DM: Vulnerable periods in the early development of blind children. Psychoanal Study Child 25:461-480, 1970
19. Fraiberg S.: Separation crisis in two blind children. Psychoanal Study Child 26:355-371, 1971
20. Blank HR: Psychoanalysis and blindness. Psychoanal Q 26:4-24, 1957
21. Keeler WR: Autistic patterns and defective communication in blind children with retrolental fibroplasia, in Hoch PH, Zubin J (eds): Psychopathology of Communication. New York, Grune & Stratton, 1958, pp 64-83
22. Blank HR: Dreams of the blind. Psychoanal Q 27:158-174, 1958
23. Kirtley D, Cannistraci K: Dreams of the visually handicapped: Toward a normative approach. Research Bulletin No 27. New York, American Foundation for the Blind, 1974, pp 111-133
24. Burlingham D: Developmental considerations in the occupations of the blind. Psychoanal Study Child 22:187-198, 1967
25. Wills DM: Problems of play and mastery in the blind child. Br J Med Psychol 41:213-222, 1968

226 Visual Impairment in Children and Adolescents

26. Fraiberg S: The clinical dimension of baby games. J Am Acad Child Psychiatry 13:202-220, 1974
27. Steinzor LV: Visually handicapped children: Their attitudes toward blindness. New Outlook for the Blind 60:307-311, 1966
28. Warren DH: Blindness and early development: What is known and what needs to be studied. New Outlook for the Blind 70:5-16, 1976
29. Freeman RD: The child psychiatric home visit: Its usefulness in diagnosis and training. J Am Acad Child Psychiatry 6:276-294, 1967
30. Elonen AS: Assessment of the nontestable blind child, in Clark LL, Jastrzembska ZS (eds): Proceedings of the Conference on New Approaches to the Evaluation of Blind Persons. New York, American Foundation for the Blind, 1970, pp 104-111
31. Fraiberg S: Intervention in infancy: A program for blind infants. J Am Acad Child Psychiatry 10:381-405, 1971
32. Gillman AE: Handicap and cognition: Visual deprivation and the rate of motor development in infants. New Outlook for the Blind 67:309-314, 1973
33. Macfarlane DW, Boyd RD, Dodrill CB, et al: Intrauterine rubella, head size, and intellect. Pediatrics 55:797-801, 1975
34. Chess S, Korn SJ, Fernandez PB: Psychiatric Disorders of Children with Congenital Rubella. New York, Brunner/Mazel, 1971
35. Chase JB: Retrolental Fibroplasia and Autistic Symptomatology. New York, American Foundation for the Blind, 1972
36. Cholden LS: A Psychiatrist Works with Blindness. New York, American Foundation for the Blind, 1958
37. Graham P: Depression in pre-pubertal children. Dev Med Child Neurol 16:340-349, 1974
38. Fine SR: Blind and Partially Sighted Children. Education Survey No 4, Department of Education and Science, London, Her Majesty's Stationery Office, 1968
39. Graham P: Management in child psychiatry: Recent trends. Br J Psychiatry 129:97-108, 1976
40. Rutter M, Hersov L (eds): Child Psychiatry: Modern Approaches. Oxford, Blackwell Scientific, 1977
41. Rutter M: Helping Troubled Children. Harmondsworth and Baltimore, Penguin, 1975
42. Heard DH: Crisis intervention guided by attachment concepts—A case study. J Child Psychol Psychiatry 15:111-122, 1974

17
Perceptual and Cognitive Development

INTRODUCTION

It is a natural source of curiosity for sighted persons that blind individuals do as well as they do—since it may be impossible or difficult to imagine functioning without vision. This often surprising performance also raises important questions for the areas of mobility and compensatory skills and regarding the advisability, timing, and nature of interventions to assist the visually impaired child.

Obviously, the world will be experienced by the blind child in a different way. Sensory modalities that are normally supplementary to the organizing and efficient distal sense of vision must be viewed as primary sources of information (Figs. 17-1, 17-2). However, it is assumed (and generally supported by the evidence) that partially sighted children approximate the development of the sighted.

This chapter will consider some of the major aspects of perceptual and cognitive development. Since this is a highly specialized and confusing field, we have not attempted to duplicate several competent and comprehensive recent reviews, which the reader with a special interest will find helpful.[1-5]

Attempts to standardize the classification of the higher intellectual functions have, perhaps not surprisingly, been rather unsuccessful. Like other systems, these classes and terms have evolved. Sensation was assumed to be an entirely passive process but now is seen as influenced by central processes: feedback exists here as well. In any event, it is a function of stimulus properties, of sensory organs, and the peripheral nervous system, whereas *perception* involves interpretation of sensation and invokes memory, other senses, and obviously the central nervous system.[6,7]

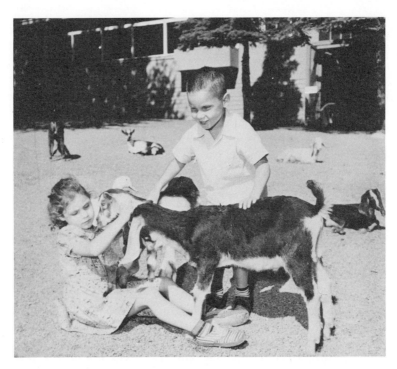

Fig. 17-1.   The blind child's hands are his eyes.

Cognition refers to the processes by which we come to know and understand relationships in the external world and between that world and ourselves.* This comprises, among other things, the association of perceptions, formulating abstract functional concepts which constantly evolve (e.g., body image), and the use of memory, judgment, and logical thinking.

It is obviously artificial to consider that these categories of higher functioning can be separated from each other, or from emotion and motivation. The separation undertaken in this book must be understood to be for purposes of exposition only. There is a danger in creating intervention programs based upon the naive idea that bits of behavior can be understood in isolation.

PROBLEMS IN RESEARCH

Although a knowledge of developmental processes in visually impaired children would have important practical consequences, there have been some very real difficulties in obtaining useful information.

---

*Some writers include perception under cognitive functions.

Fig. 17-2.   Learning can sometimes be messy.

These have been helpfully summarized in several reviews by Warren,[3,4,8] who has made the following points:

1. The visually impaired population is highly heterogeneous with respect to cause of impairment, degree of impairment, age at onset, and the presence of associated deficits.
2. It is not usually practically feasible to select a truly random sample.
3. Most investigators have been troubled by the small numbers of individuals available for study.
4. The preceding factors tend to result in the sample studied being nonrepresentative, and they explain why there are many conflicting findings reported in the literature. The use of multivariate techniques is essential.
5. Matching on all relevant variables is unusually difficult.
6. Blindfolded sighted subjects are not good for purposes of a comparison study. They may not represent a reliable and valid ability level, since they have had no chance to practice to the point of stability of the functions to be tested. (This is a variant of the "warm-up effect," which needs to be considered in testing all visually impaired persons.)

7. One of the most significant problems is that of task equivalence. The same task presented to one group may not tap the comparable characteristic of the other group. Each function tapped may play a different ecological role within the total functioning of an individual.
8. The relevance to real-life situations of many laboratory studies is often unclear.
9. If a difference or developmental lag is identified, what is its significance? Is this inherent in the visual impairment or secondary to differences in early experience?[9]
10. Are differences identified "good" or "pathological"? One cannot necessarily assume that it is appropriate to use the standards of the sighted nor that intervention is warranted.
11. There is little theoretical structure available to assist in using information that is acquired and giving direction to further research and program development.

PERCEPTION

Harmon has summarized some of the problems in obtaining useful information about perceptual processes in the blind and mentions the need to assess how the individual obtains information: actively or passively.[6] We know very little about how and when to best transform information from one modality to another and the best signal dimensions to employ in the use of artificial aids (frequency, intensity, location, temporal sequencing, and rate of delivery).

The most comprehensive summary of the literature is by Warren and the following discussion depends heavily upon his work.[3]

Audition

Despite the obvious relevance of this modality to verbal communication, learning, and mobility, auditory abilities have received much less research attention than tactile abilities. Evidence available on *sound discrimination* fails to support the popular notion that the blind have greater auditory sensitivity. Rather, superior attentive habits are postulated.[5]

Sound localization and *obstacle sense* have received attention, but the results are varied and conflicting. It is clear that so called "facial vision" depends upon auditory stimulation by high-frequency sound waves and is a skill that cannot be taught to the deaf-blind. The sighted are inferior to the blind, but may, with training and practice, reach the same levels as the blind. The early blind may be better at echo detection and echo-location, but there is some disagreement on this.

Experiential factors must be further researched, along with the effects of providing infants with a special aid, which might lead to more efficient use of this type of information in later life.

It is important to remember that reading aurally is a different perceptual task from reading visually.[7] Efficiency of information delivery may be improved through compressed speech techniques.

Touch and Proprioception

Abilities dependent upon sensations received from skin, muscles, and joints comprise *touch*. Research has attempted to explore the use of this modality for learning about the world. Again, there are conflicting results on tactile-kinesthetic abilities. Texture discrimination seems equivalent. Size discrimination (Fig. 17-3) may present some additional problems to blind children who seem to overestimate it more than do the sighted, but there are wide variations in performance strategies. Mixed evidence is available for pattern and touch perception differences in blind and sighted persons.

With regard to Braille, it is interesting that there does not seem to be any disadvantage to using the nonpreferred hand. Disabilities in reading Braille occur in about 15 percent of individuals, and the partially sighted who switch from print to Braille show the same kinds of letter and word reversals in both.

Tactile-visual substitution systems, using the skin of abdomen or back, are being researched. The Optacon converts scanned ink print to a tactile configuration read on the finger at a rate of about half that of a conventional Braille reader. Blind preadolescents were found to be consistently better than the sighted in judging similarities among vibrotactile stimulus patterns presented to the fingers.

Finally, touch functions adequately only when the person actively encounters the world, an approach our society at times frowns upon. This has implications for early counseling of parents and also for sex education.[9] It would appear that research should go beyond pure description of tactile abilities to attempt to establish causal relationships and to determine the range of "educability" of tactile functions.[3]

Space Perception

Space perception is a highly complicated subject involving body-image formation, task complexity, and, in some individuals, visualization in relation to severity and age of onset of visual loss. It has been tested by a variety of tasks, such as form perception and finger mazes. The results on *near space perception* are confusing when the blind are compared with the sighted, perhaps because the former may be superior

Fig. 17-3.   Learning about shapes and sizes.

on purely proprioceptive or kinesthetic tasks but not as the task becomes increasingly complex spatially. In the latter case, for example, the ability to use visual imagery might confer an advantage upon late-blinded or blindfolded subjects. In this area, as well as in others, Warren has emphasized the great importance of the length of visual experience prior to the onset of visual impairment and the length of life after the impairment as relevant and often neglected variables. Correlations between maze learning and IQ are consistently stronger for the blind than for the sighted; this may mean that with the advantage of vision the latter have less need for verbalization or conceptualization skills.

Body Image

Awareness of the orientation, position, and structure of the body in space is thought to be a basis for successful mobility. To the extent that vision is necessary for the perception and control of body functions, the blind should be at a disadvantage. There is some evidence that this is the case,[5] as the psychoanalytic writers have stated.[10,11] As an integrating sense, vision is a major stimulus for reaching out into the world and verifying the existence, permanence, and relationships of objects in space. These writers point out that, for a longer time than is true in sighted children, objects are not permanent; hearing does not confer permanence upon objects until the child is able to map displacements. Attempts have been made to facilitate body image development as a basis for building concepts of external space.[12]

Mobility

Cratty has studied veering in an open-field situation and found that the congenitally blind veered less than the late-blind.[13] But there are many perceptual and nonperceptual factors that are involved in this function and have been more fully reviewed elsewhere. Mobility has been shown to be highly complex, dependent upon abilities that have early formative periods. The clear implication is that attention should be paid to these factors long before the commencement of formal mobility training. Maps are useful, but there are substantial individual differences which would have to be considered.

In *geographical concepts*, the congenitally blind have been shown to lag significantly behind the sighted.

Intermodality Organization

Early vision seems to confer a permanent advantage. The question is how (and to what extent) visual influences can be replaced by others. Even a small amount of vision seems to provide a useful framework for interpreting information from other perceptual modalities. There is a relationship between the nature of the stimulus material and mode of processing: auditory or temporally presented, and visual or spatially presented information. Totally blind children would then be at a disadvantage with spatial material. Research is underway to present different dimensions of visual stimuli with the most appropriate parameter in another modality.

Visualization

The term *visualization* is usually rather loosely used to mean the ability to evoke a visual image and perform a task using that, rather than the original cues. Warren suggests that the issue of how long the period of early vision has to be to confer permanent visualization ability upon an individual has been oversimplified. There may actually be several components, each with its own sensitive developmental period. But again, research is complicated by differences in life opportunity between the blind and sighted, which are hard to analyze and specify as variables.

Summary

The advantages of the sighted or later blinded over the congenital early blind generally are positively related to task complexity. Intelligence and nonintellectual, individual differences are also relevant variables, but much further research is needed on the nature of the latter. Help might come from studies of the successfully mobile blind. However, much research has been inadequate because the approach has not been sufficiently comprehensive.

With regard to discriminative ability, the evidence runs against the popular notion of sensory compensation. It does seem true that in some areas the blind attend better and therefore make better use of information received.

Some delays in development may be to the blind child's benefit, and this point should at least be considered when one is designing intervention programs.[8]

In general, although some useful information has been gleaned, there is much to be done, even in areas of great practical importance to the blind.

COGNITIVE DEVELOPMENT

Warren has stated that this area has been "vastly understudied in comparison to perceptual development."[2] He feels that too much attention has been devoted to description and relatively little to the variables that produce differences.

Some problems of cognitive deficit may be due to information deprivation based upon the simple fact that no other input channel is available that can match the rate of visual processing. In his review, Suppes points out that many deficits attributed to the blind, whether temporary or allegedly persistent, involve tasks that are in fact influenced by visual cues.[14] For example, the validity of verbal sections of the unmodified Wechsler Intelligence Scale for Children have been questioned.

Arithmetic abilities have not been sufficiently studied. What little is known suggests again the marked effect of social and environmental variables.[14]

Children with partial vision have been found on the Illinois Test of Psycho-Linguistic Abilities (ITPA) to perform more poorly than the sighted on the Motor Encoding, Visual Decoding, and Visual-Motor

Association subtests. It was felt that the deficits on the first of these might be due to the lack of knowledge of how an object was used.

Language skills are involved in cognitive functioning.[14] Although language development has been mentioned elsewhere, a word is appropriate here about so-called "verbalisms." This refers to non-sensory-based words, the use of which has been a concern of some workers for many years. It was originally felt that blind children did this to gain social approval. Subsequent investigators disagreed on the importance of verbalisms, and Harley's research with 40 congenitally blind children showed no correlation between verbalism and personal adjustment.[15] Actually, blind children are trained both deliberately and incidentally to use such words. An example is color perception, where the blind will use the names of colors and will have associations to the words and yet cannot know what they are like.

Some research has been done to attempt to corroborate the Piagetian approach to sequential cognitive development.[2] It has been reported that the same stages are encountered by the blind child, but the rates are different. Apparently Piaget himself originally believed that differences in the early sensorimotor stage (ages 0-2) would necessarily mean a distortion of later stages. The evidence suggests that this may not in fact be the case and that different processes may be involved in compensation.

Warren has pointed out that there is relatively little work on remediation of developmental lag,[2] although some programs show promise. Remedial programs may, however, produce effects that wash out later; long-term benefits must be assessed. Also, there is a need to look at the effects of speeding up development when it is slower than in the sighted. Are the abilities acquired as stable as otherwise? The most appropriate frame of reference may not be that of the sighted, but rather whatever results in the best development of the blind child.

Finally, Warren emphasizes the need to look at aspects of the actual learning environment and at functional behaviors, not merely IQ numbers.

Tested Intelligence

Although this is not the place to emphasize the pitfalls in assessing intelligence (see chapter 6), there is one area of special interest, namely the question of higher intelligence in the retinoblastoma subgroup. Since 1966 strikingly high IQs have been reported in children blinded by retinoblastoma. Witkin et al. argued for specific rather than general intellectual superiority.[5] Levitt et al. reexamined the relationships by including unilaterally as well as bilaterally affected cases (n = 44) and siblings as sighted controls,[16] because of concern that previous studies suffered from selection bias. Those blinded from retinoblastoma tended to be superior to their sibs in verbal IQ, but those with sight had no such advantage or tended to be lower in IQ. The data thus argue against general superiority conferred by all types and visual outcomes of retinoblastoma. Interpretation of these findings is difficult, however. There may be a direct effect of a single gene in those cases of hereditary origin. Also, blindness might confer an advantage in attending and concentration. However, this group scored higher on other areas as well.

These findings are fascinating and puzzling, but must not cause us to overgeneralize group findings so as to impair individual assessment.

In our own study of visually impaired children, tested verbal intelligence was normally distributed with the exception of those children with damage to the central nervous system or those with other handicaps. Thus, there was a correlation between days hospitalized in the first year and lower IQ, probably because those were the children with the most physical and other difficulties.

IMPLICATIONS

In a useful and practical chapter, Lowenfeld has discussed special methods to deal with cognitive and perceptual differences.[9] These include the need for a wide variety of concrete experiences on common aspects of the environment, such as the store, post office, and farm. Harley emphasized the need for a unique program to learn basic concepts[15] (everyone seems to agree that blind children miss much "incidental learning" and therefore have a need for the deliberate planning of experiences).

Reality is preferable to models; the latter are often inadequate because their representation is largely visual. (Embossed pictures of three-dimensional objects are not considered a successful teaching tool.) Without information in common with the sighted, the blind child may be left out in conversation and be further handicapped socially.

In addition to concrete experiences, unifying experiences are also necessary because blind individuals seem to have more difficulty in integrating parts into wholes.[9] Additionally, self-activity opportunities are important and often less available to the blind child, partly because of time and patience factors and because it is easier to "do" for them. If the child becomes confident in doing for himself, his own self-concepts will be more positive.

CONCLUSIONS

1. In spite of theoretical predictions, relatively few enduring differences have been found in perceptual and cognitive functioning between the blind and the sighted.
2. The significance and relative importance of tasks in the blind may be quite different from the same task in the sighted.
3. We have great difficulties in assessing these functions: heterogeneity, problems of random selection of subjects, task equivalence, relevance to real-life situations, and the use of blindfolded subjects for comparison.
4. The weight of evidence suggests some differences between the blind and the sighted in the organization of mental functioning in the early years, but for the most part they appear able to compensate by the use of other modalities and other mental processes.
5. There seems to be an increased range of variation in the individual differences of the blind group as compared with the sighted.
6. Practical implications to facilitate the best possible development include fostering of early active exploration, exposure to a wide variety of concrete common experiences, and the deliberate planning of unifying experiences to substitute for the integrating power of vision.

REFERENCES

1. Warren DH: Early vs. late vision: The role of early vision in spatial reference systems. New Outlook for the Blind 68:157–162, 1974
2. Warren DH: Blindness and early development: What is known and what needs to be studied. New Outlook for the Blind 70:5–16, 1976
3. Warren DH: Perception by the blind, in Carterette EC, Friedman MP (eds): Handbook of Perception. New York and London, Academic Press, 1976, vol 10
4. Warren DH: Blindness and Early Childhood Development. New York, American Foundation for the Blind, 1977
5. Witkin HA, Oltman PK, Chase JB, et al: Cognitive patterning in the blind, in Hellmuth J (ed): Cognitive Studies. New York, Brunner/Mazel, 1971, vol 2, p 16–45
6. Harmon LD: Sensory supplementation: Non-visual information processing, in Graham MD (ed): Science and Blindness: Retrospective and Prospective. New York, American Foundation for the Blind, 1972, p 148–158
7. Barraga NC: Utilization of sensory-perceptual abilities, in Lowenfeld B (ed): The Visually Handicapped Child in School. New York, John Day, 1973, p 117–154

8. Warren DH: Blindness and early development: Issues in research methodology. New Outlook for the Blind 70:53-60, 1976
9. Lowenfeld B: Psychological considerations, in Lowenfeld B (ed): The Visually Handicapped Child in School. New York, John Day, 1973, p 27-60
10. Burlingham D: Hearing and its role in the development of the blind. Psychoanal Study Child 19:95-112, 1964
11. Fraiberg S, Siegel BL, Gibson R: The role of sound in the search behavior of a blind infant. Psychoanal Study Child 21:327-357, 1966
12. Cratty BJ, Sams TA: The Body-Image of Blind Children. New York, American Foundation for the Blind, 1968
13. Cratty BJ: Movement and Spatial Awareness in Blind Children and Youth. Springfield, Ill, Charles C Thomas, 1971
14. Suppes P: A survey of cognition in handicapped children, in Chess S, Thomas A (eds): Annual Progress in Child Psychiatry and Child Development 1975. New York, Brunner/Mazel, 1975, p 95-129
15. Harley RK: Verbalism Among Blind Children: An Investigation and Analysis. New York, American Foundation for the Blind, 1963
16. Levitt EA, Rosenbaum AL, Willerman L, et al: Intelligence of retinoblastoma patients and their siblings. Child Dev 43:939-948, 1972

18
Stereotyped Behavior

INTRODUCTION

Among those who work with the visually impaired, few subjects arouse as much concern and confusion as the cause and management of stereotyped behavior. These are the so-called blindisms or blind mannerisms and certain other patterns. There is no question that these manifestations are much more common in the visually impaired than in the sighted.

In this chapter we will examine the frequency and types of such patterns, evolutionary aspects, theories of causation, associated factors such as age of onset and severity of visual loss, and, finally, some criteria for intervention efforts.

THE PROBLEM

Before considering a more detailed description of stereotyped behavior, it is important to understand why it is considered by many to be a problem. First, these behaviors are unsightly. They disturb parents and others and may lead to a suspicion of mental retardation or severe emotional disturbance. Furthermore, they may lead to teasing by other children, with consequent social segregation. This may further handicap the child. Second, stereotyped behavior emitted at a high rate may preclude or interfere with the development of other more adaptive behaviors. Third, a multiplicity of theories of causation has led to a wide variety of types of advice and intervention. These range from noninterference (because the behavior might be adaptive) at one extreme, to complex behavior-modification programs or individual or family therapy (because of presumed adverse influences on the child) at the other extreme.

For these reasons it seems worthwhile to try to bring some order out of the present chaos.

DESCRIPTION

Kravitz and Boehm pointed out that body rocking and hand sucking are common in normal infants in our culture.[1] Normal children may show rocking, head banging, thumb sucking, handflapping, etc. Usually these are transient patterns without many different types being combined in the same individual. Potentially, then, these patterns appear to be in the behavioral repertoire of all individuals. There are also some similarities among the patterns shown in animals and in autistic, retarded, deprived, or visually impaired children. There is no completely satisfactory definition, but they are usually repetitive motor acts (simple or complex), transitory and unusual postures, or self-manipulations. By their very nature, these patterns are socially inappropriate—if not qualitatively, then by virtue of their frequency or intensity or both.

Keeler was one of the first to describe "autistic" patterns in children with retrolental fibroplasia, but seems to have confused repetitive activities, such as rocking to music, with emotional disturbance.[2]

Visually impaired children may show much of the same odd and persistent behavior seen in the retarded or autistic child, but aside from unimpaired intelligence, relationships, and language, there is one special aspect: visually impaired children much more frequently show stereotyped behavior directed to the eyes or the region around the eyes.

Many have commented that blindism is a poor term for these behaviors, because they are seen in other children. Although it may well be true that mannerisms involving the eye are almost completely limited to the visually impaired, it still seems unwise to employ the term blindism because of the fact that it embraces so many different patterns that are seen in other types of children.

There is an overlap with other habits, such as smelling or sniffing things, and staring at lights. The commonest types seen in visually impaired children are rocking, eye manipulation, handflapping, and head movements. According to Fine, they are most frequent in children whose visual impairment stems from retrolental fibroplasia (93 percent of younger children and 71 percent of the older children).[3]

The still pictures shown in this chapter (Figs. 18-1 to 18-7) can only give a very rough visual impression of the nature of mannerisms. This is especially true for the patterns that consist of complex movements of the hands, sometimes in association with peculiar postures of the head and trunk.

Fig. 18-1.   Eye pressing at 13 months.

EVOLUTIONARY ASPECTS

Williams has stated that stereotypy is species-specific and Pohl has summarized some of these specificities.[4,5] In brief, the "more evolved species tend to produce a greater variety of stereotyped behaviours."[5] He also points out the tendency to greater overall frequency and intensity as the evolutionary ladder is ascended, this being especially true of body rocking.

FREQUENCY

Everyone agrees that these patterns are common in the visually impaired.[6,7] Chess et al. reported that they occurred in 66.2 percent of children with congenital rubella, many of whom had visual impairment, but not all of whom were blind.[8] Fine did a study of 817 children in 20 special schools for the blind and 1374 children in schools and classes for the partially sighted in England and Wales during 1962-1965.[3] She found that 45 percent of children had mannerisms, many having more than one type. Ten percent of partially sighted children had mannerisms. The commonest involved the eye; others were body rocking, handflapping, headnodding, and twirling. These patterns occurred throughout the IQ range, but were commoner in those with lower IQ.

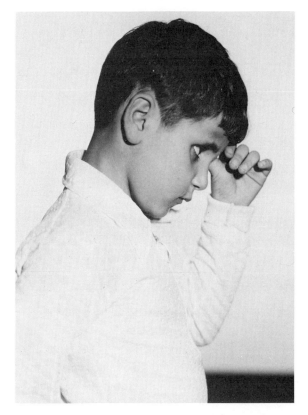

Fig. 18-2.   Sunken orbits from eye pressing (Age 8 years, total blindness).

In an extensive study of autistic symptomatology in children with retrolental fibroplasia, Chase found that only 1.3 percent of her 263 cases showed no mannerisms, while another 16.5 percent showed them only rarely.[9] This is generally in accord with the previously mentioned results from Fine's report.

In our own study, these patterns were much more common among the blind than the partially sighted, and, as will be shown later, frequency increased with the presence of other handicaps and certain other variables.

THEORIES OF CAUSATION

As previously mentioned, there is much confusion about the cause of stereotypy. Many investigators have tried to find a parsimonious explanation, and, since it has generally been observed that these patterns are more frequent under conditions loosely described as "excitation"

Fig. 18-3.   Other positions for eye pressing.

Fig. 18-4.   Other positions for eye pressing.

Fig. 18-5.   Two-handed eye pressing in a 5-year-old totally blind child; sighted sibling sucks thumb.

and "boredom," a special role has been given to the level of stimulus input or "arousal." Williams has spoken of a "homeostatic" role involving both tension and boredom, especially in individuals who are lacking in the ability to imitate.[10] The strikingly similar pattern between some animals and humans has suggested an intrinsic mechanism to Davis et al.[11] Berkson engaged in both clinical observations of the mentally retarded and research on monkeys.[12] He felt that these patterns were the consequence of disordered relationships between the individual and his physical and social environment during the early developmental period. He hypothesized that, since normal activity reduces rocking, a visual impairment might prevent an activity that would normally compete with rocking. However, he felt that blind persons do not have a reduced interaction with their environment, a conclusion that others would question. In any event, his research suggested that the deprivation of specific experiences during an early developmental period was a necessary *though not sufficient* condition for the emergence of these sustained patterns. He noted individual differences in animals, even under laboratory conditions. In summary, Berkson felt that these patterns are the outgrowth of intrinsic properties of growth of the central nervous system (CNS) combined with a specific deficit in maternal care (probably in lack of movement stimulation), and he felt that the behavior might rarely develop

Fig. 18–6.   Light gazing. (Six-year-old partially sighted girl with congenital rubella syndrome).

if the infant were carried and allowed to suckle early at a time when these patterns first emerge.[12] He also proposed the interesting idea that the greater frequency in the mentally retarded might be because of slower development, that is, treating the baby at his chronological rather than mental age level, and carrying him around less. He, like other authors, has emphasized the possible difference between the factors involved in initiating these behaviors and those that either sustain it or modify the moment-to-moment behavior.

In addition, Berkson stated that in his animals the presence of visual impairment alone was insufficient to produce these behavior patterns without concurrent lack of stimulation.[12]

Smith et al. reported their observations from longitudinal studies of a small number of blind infants.[13] They felt that blindness does impose a primary deprivation upon the developing child and that the nature of the patterns is then determined by the environment. They also emphasized the failure of imitation in these children and their tendency to focus on their own body for pleasure. These patterns seemed to emerge at times of developmental stress, under conditions of disruption of the mother-infant bond, and at times of high excitation.

Guess and Rutherford studied stereotyped behavior in 13 blind retardates ranging in age from 8 to 16.[14] The introduction of sound

Fig. 18-7.   Eye pressing while on swing (in background).

and the provision of interesting objects to manipulate were found to reduce rates of stereotypy.

There are a number of formulations involved. Some authors have seen these patterns as primarily the consequence of "high arousal" or "tension" which requires discharge, in an organism that does not have age-appropriate methods of release; others have seen it more as a consequence of boredom, or an attempt to entertain the self in the absence of adequate stimulation. Thus, stereotypy could be either the consequence of increased arousal or the means of increasing arousal when it is suboptimal.

The most useful and comprehensive study and review yet done is in an unpublished thesis by Williams.[4] Although his patients were deaf-blind children with congenital rubella syndrome, he has shown the usefulness of very detailed experimental work with a small number of children. He has reviewed the work of Schultz,[15] among others, suggesting a role for the brain-stem reticular formation in modulating arousal. It was felt that abnormal behavior might develop from disorders of peripheral input, central mediation, or both. The crucial factor may not be only the absolute *level* of arousal, but also stimulus change or *variety*. Put in another way, there may be a combination of types, levels, and sequences of external stimulation interacting with the level of central arousal. Too much or too little stimulation may disrupt learned responses and prevent new learning. In one sense, the behavior observed may be interpreted as adaptive, no matter how odd, in that its goal is the maintenance of an optimal range of functioning. Stimulation also has a discriminative or "cue" function, as well as one of arousal. Simply observing the manifest motor activity level will not necessarily indicate whether there is too much or too little stimulation or stimulus variation.

Williams points out that these children may be doubly handicapped: crucial experiences are missing in early life and the ability to learn from experiences that are available may also be reduced.[4] It also seems reasonable that the more restricted the input and stimulus variation, the more restricted will be the resulting behavioral repertoire.

Citing the earlier work of Forehand and Baumeister[16] Williams discussed the reduction in stereotyped behavior consequent upon certain types of visual stimulation.[4] His own experiment showed that retarded children with some vision will move toward a novel light stimulus. He feels that the lack of early mobility in the blind may be important in the perpetuation of these stereotyped behavior patterns. As mobility develops, depending upon the nature of the combined handicaps, stereotypy usually decreases. Early mobility thus can act as an inhibitor, and may be physically incompatible with stereotyped behavior for some individuals. Without early mobility, children may encounter little and explore little. Normally, there is a shift toward social reinforcers (such as mother) from infantile patterns. In the blind child this shift may be impaired, thus retaining a primary or intrinsic reinforcing role for the motor act. Another formulation is that a high rate of stereotypy may be reinforced because it permits escape from an aversive state, i.e., inadequate stimulation. Eyepoking presumably provides a visual stimulus similar to waving the fingers in front of lights.

Williams has conclusively shown that there is a U shaped relationship between stereotypy and level of arousal or "stimulus setting factors."[4] That is, the frequency of stereotypy will be high at either the low or high end of the "level of arousal" spectrum and will be lowest at some intermediate, optimal point. This would most parsimoniously explain the clinical observations previously mentioned and the concepts relating stereotyped behavior to boredom and excitation.

Williams' work is too complex to easily summarize here. However, it has clear implications for intervention strategies. He emphasizes that for blind children, and especially for children with multiple handicaps, it is difficult to find efficient reinforcing stimuli that compete with the development of these behaviors. This may be one of the reasons why they become so rigid and persistent. In summary, then, stereotyped behavior is seen as a learned phenomenon that emerges on a biologically determined base in relation to the need for an optimal level of functioning

Table 18-1
Frequency of Mannerisms and Chronological Age

Group	n	Relationship	Significance*
TOTAL	88	Inverse	$p < 0.0001$
No other handicaps	42	Inverse	$p < 0.0001$
Other handicaps	46	Inverse	$p < 0.01$
Blind	26	None	ns
Partial vision	62	Inverse	$p < 0.0001$
Neuroepileptic	31	Inverse	$p < 0.05$
Not neuroepileptic	57	Inverse	$p < 0.0001$

*Significance of Kendall's tau *b*.

within the CNS. This optimal level requires certain types of external and internal input, without which maladaptive behaviors will emerge. Normally, more or less optimal levels are achieved and the environment can be expected to reinforce behaviors incompatible with the ones we are discussing.

CORRELATES OF STEREOTYPED BEHAVIOR

From our own study and the studies of others, the following conclusions can be reached.

Age correlates inversely with frequency and presence of stereotyped behavior. This is statistically significant for all subgroups except the blind (Table 18-1). We interpret this to mean that there is a much stronger tendency for stereotyped behavior to persist in the blind than in the partially sighted.* As can be seen from Table 18-2, our study produced descriptions similar to those by others: rocking, eyepressing or other eye mannerisms, and hand and head mannerisms were the most common. The presence of additional handicaps, with or without involvement of the CNS, increased the frequency of stereotypy (presumably they would have less opportunity to learn incompatible behaviors). There was a positive correlation with days hospitalized in the first year of life, but this is probably confounded with the presence of additional handicaps, although the latter is only weakly related to stereotypy. Retrolental fibroplasia and optic atrophy were overrepresented among the forms of pathology present in those with stereotyped behavior; this is probably related to the high proportion of totally blind children in these subgroups.

---

*The term *neuroepileptic* in Table 18-1 refers to children with definite signs of CNS involvement, such as epilepsy and cerebral palsy, and was coined by Rutter et al.[17]

Table 18-2
Stereotyped Behavior

Description of Type	Frequency	% (of 92)*
Rocking: forward and back	16	17.4
Rocking: side to side	1	1.1
Rocking: on hands and knees	1	1.1
Eye pressing, rubbing, poking	15	16.3
Tongue clicking	1	1.1
Other repetitive noises	12	13.0
Hand flapping	10	10.9
Other hand mannerism	9	9.8
Head turning	8	8.7
Head nodding	1	1.1
Mouthing objects	4	4.3
Smelling/sniffing	4	4.3
Touching to nose/mouth area	3	3.3
Hyperventilation	2	2.2
Thumb or finger sucking	2	2.2
Nail biting	2	2.2
Others not categorized above	14	15.2
(More than 6 types in the same child)	2	2.2
None observed	49	53.3

*More than one choice possible.

We also replicated the finding that I.Q. is inversely related to the frequency of stereotypy (see Tables 18-3 and 18-4). This was previously reported by Berkson and Davenport.[7] It should also be pointed out that activity level in general is inversely related to chronological age, mental age, and I.Q.

Eye mannerisms were more likely to be present in the youngest children (mean age 5 years, 3 months); noises and headturning were intermediate in average age, and rocking and handflapping tended to persist or be present in older children. Rocking and headturning were more common in blind than in partially sighted children, even considering group differences in frequency.

With regard to ocular pathology and type of mannerism, the numbers were too small for adequate analysis. Observations suggest, however, that in children with anophthalmia (complete absence of ocular structures), there are no eye mannerisms. We conclude that the most parsimonious explanation of eye mannerisms is that they serve to produce visual tract stimulation, even in the presence of blindness.

With regard to emotional disturbance, this is a complex variable. Tizard showed that stereotyped behavior and signs of emotional distur-

Table 18-3
IQ and Mannerisms

IQ Range	Total	Those with No Mannerisms n	(% of Total)
Superior (120+)	8	7	87.5
High Average (110-119)	9	6	66.7
Average (90-109)	31	18	58.1
Dull Normal (80-89)	8	5	62.5
Borderline (70-79)	5	3	60.0
Mild Retardation (50-69)	6	1	16.7
Mod. or greater ret. (<50)	5	0	0.0
Indeterminate	15	4	26.7
Totals	87	44	(50.6)

bance in the mentally retarded were markedly reduced by a shift from an institutional to a more homelike atmosphere.[18] Chess and Hassibi demonstrated that in the mentally retarded, stereotyped behavior is not closely related to emotional disturbance.[19] Our own study showed a general correlation with emotional disturbance (Table 18-5), but this was not the case for children with no other handicaps or the children with partial vision.

Severity of visual impairment is clearly related to the frequency of mannerisms. As can be seen in Table 18-6, they are much more common in the blind than in the partially sighted, being absent in only 15 percent whereas this is true of 68 percent of those with partial vision.

The effect of age of onset of the impairment is not conclusively demonstrated in this study, as only 10 cases had late onset (over 12 months). However, since there were only two children with mannerisms in this group (both partially sighted: one with onset in the second year, one thereafter), the findings are at least consistent with the observations of others and the theories propounded by Berkson[12] and Williams.[4]

Forty-three percent of the parents thought the stereotyped behavior

Table 18-4
IQ and Frequency of Mannerisms

Frequency of Mannerisms	n	Mean IQ*
Continual/frequent	16	84.4
Occasional/rare	13	84.5
None observed	35	102.9
Total	64	

*Cases with onset of impairment at birth.

Table 18-5
Frequency of Mannerisms and Emotional Disturbance of
Child

Group	n	Significance*
Total	90	$p < 0.001$
No Other Handicaps	42	ns
Other Handicaps	48	$p < 0.01$
Blind	27	$p < 0.01$
Partial Vision	63	ns
Neuroepileptic	33	ns
Not Neuroepileptic	57	$p < 0.005$

*Significance of direct relationship, with Kendall's tau c.

was improving, 6 percent that it was worsening, and the rest noted
no change.

It is our impression that the form of hand mannerisms may change
with age to become more socially acceptable, although we have no data
to support this.

A discriminant analysis showed that 83 percent of the cases could
be correctly classified as "mannerisms" or "no mannerisms" by employing the three variables age, IQ, and days hospitalized in the first year,
with age being the most discriminating.

In summary, we have shown from a study of blind and partially
sighted children that there are the following relationships: severity of
visual impairment (direct); age (inverse); IQ (inverse); days hospitalized
in the first year (direct); and, to a less convincing degree, age of onset
of the impairment (inverse). All of these are consistent with the hypotheses
of Williams.[4] Severity of psychiatric disturbance is more complex, as
it appears to be confounded with other variables such as IQ: the subgroups
"neuroepileptic" and "no other handicaps," which show no correlation
with psychiatric disorder, do not include retarded cases.

Table 18-6
Frequency of Mannerisms and Severity of Visual Loss*

| | Blind | | Partial Vision | |
Frequency	n	% (of 26)	n	% (of 62)
Continual/frequent	14	53.9	10	16.1
Occasional/rare	8	30.8	10	16.1
None observed	4	15.4	42	67.7
Totals	26		62	

*$\chi^2 = 24.59$; df = 2; $p < 0.0001$.

CRITERIA FOR INTERVENTION

We must first determine how serious the behavior is; this involves assessment of frequency and type. Certainly, an important consideration is whether it is self-injurious. Also, who is bothered by the behavior? (Some parents and persons are more sensitive to these patterns than others.) What does the behavior mean to the persons bothered? Their theories may influence their concern: if the parent thinks it is a sign that the child is mentally retarded or crazy, his anxiety level may increase. It is also necessary to decide whether these patterns truly interfere with other adaptive behaviors. What price might be paid for stopping them? This will obviously depend upon the method and intensity of intervention.

Warren has made the excellent point that we must be careful in applying sighted standards to the visually impaired.[20] Simply stamping out such patterns by means of a behavior-modification approach, without understanding their possibly adaptive nature, might be unfortunate. (This requires further research.) One must also consider whether the child's understanding is important. Since the factors that maintain the behavior may be different from those that initiated it, one cannot assume that simply "stimulating" the child will be sufficient. At a later age, the child may be aware of the effect his behavior has on other persons and may be able to modify it on a voluntary basis.

In summary, there are no absolute criteria for intervention because of the large social component.

METHODS OF INTERVENTION

Obviously, the best method is prevention. Williams has made perhaps the most important point of all: that simply increasing generalized stimulation is unlikely to be sufficient.[4] We know too little about how the patterns of normal development modify these behavior patterns in normal children. It seems that more research is needed, but in the meantime early mobility, carrying the child around, and a host of other interventions recommended elsewhere in this book will be likely to minimize the appearance and persistence of stereotypy. One presumably should not become too excited if some do appear, as they are likely to decrease with time. Later in a child's development, intervention will involve the encouragement of interest in the child's surroundings. If it is necessary to be more specific, one may also have to devise a program though which the child will acquire behavior patterns that are incompatible with stereotyped behavior. In other words, the child will have to learn to work for the reward of a different and specific form of stimulation, rather than just having it provided. Most of these methods necessitate detailed behavioral analysis and tailoring to individual needs.

Self-injurious behavior may require rather extreme measures, such as aversive conditioning. This problem has been reported elsewhere,[21] and fortunately is not common. In our own study, it occurred in only two cases and in none severely. (Some of these children are said to seek restraint.)

DRUG EFFECTS

Davis et al. used amphetamines and thioridazine to attempt to modify stereotypy in the mentally retarded.[11] The latter drug did reduce stereotypy without affecting "normal" behavior patterns, but did not eliminate them. There was no increase under the stimulant-drug medication. Generally speaking, drugs do not appear to be very useful in these conditions.

SUMMARY

We have attempted to outline some of the knowledge and experience in this difficult area. It is to be hoped that further research will clarify the importance of methods for both the prevention and eradication of these behavior patterns, when they become sufficiently disturbing to be significant.

CONCLUSIONS

1. Stereotyped behavior occurs in animals and children, and more frequently in deprived, retarded, psychotic, and sensorially impaired children.
2. In visually impaired children, the most common types are body rocking, eye mannerisms, hand mannerisms, and head mannerisms.
3. Deprivation of certain experiences during early development—such as mobility and exploration, stimulus variety, and manipulation of objects with the hands—is thought to be important. High rates occur at both ends of the arousal continuum.
4. Statistical correlations: 1) direct (positive) with degree of visual impairment; days hospitalized in first year of life; 2) Inverse (negative) with age, IQ, and age at onset of impairment.
5. There is no simple relationship with psychiatric disorder, and none should be assumed.
6. Prevention is better than later intervention and should involve early carrying about of the child, bringing him into contact with a wide variety of experiences, and the encouragement of mobility, curiosity, and active mastery.

7. Later intervention requires detailed behavioral analysis and an assessment of the importance of stereotypy in the total functioning of the individual. Drugs generally are not useful.

8. Occasional mannerisms, especially in early life, do not require intervention. In late childhood and adolescence, voluntary efforts may be of some value, at least in replacing unusual patterns with more acceptable ones.

REFERENCES

1. Kravitz H, Boehm J J: Rhythmic habit patterns in infancy: Their sequence, age of onset, and frequency. Child Dev 42:399–413, 1971
2. Keeler W R: Autistic patterns and defective communication in blind children with retrolental fibroplasia, in Hoch PH, Zubin J (eds): Psychopathology of Communication. New York, Grune & Stratton, 1958, pp 64–83
3. Fine SR: Blind and Partially Sighted Children. Education Survey No 4. Department of Education and Science. London, Her Majesty's Stationery Office, 1968
4. Williams C: An observational study of mannerisms in the deaf-blind retarded child. Ph.D. thesis. University of Birmingham, U.K., 1975.
5. Pohl P: Phylogenetic aspects of stereotyped behaviour. Ninth International Study Group on Child Neurology and Cerebral Palsy, Oxford, England, 1974
6. Guess D: The influence of visual and ambulation restrictions on stereotyped behavior. Am J Ment Defic 70:542–547, 1966
7. Berkson G, Davenport RK Jr: Stereotyped movements of mental defectives. I. Initial survey. Am J Ment Defic 66:849–852, 1962
8. Chess S, Korn SJ, Fernandez PB: Psychiatric Disorders of Children with Congenital Rubella. New York, Brunner/Mazel, 1971.
9. Chase JB: Retrolental Fibroplasia and Autistic Symptomatology. Research Series No 24. New York, American Foundation for the Blind, 1972
10. Williams CE: Psychiatric implications of severe visual defect for the child and for the parents, in Gardiner P, MacKeith R, Smith V (eds): Aspects of Developmental and Paediatric Ophthalmology. Clinics in Developmental Medicine No 32. London, Heinemann, 1969, pp 110–119.
11. Davis KV, Sprague RL, Werry JS: Stereotyped behavior and activity level in severe retardates: The effect of drugs. Am J Ment Defic 73:721–727, 1969
12. Berkson G: Visual defect does not produce stereotyped movement. Am J Ment Defic 78:89–94, 1973
13. Smith MA, Chethik M, Adelson E: Differential assessments of "blindisms." Am J Orthopsychiatry 39:807–817, 1969
14. Guess D, Rutherford G: Experimental attempts to reduce stereotyping among blind retardates. Am J Ment Defic 71:984–986, 1967

15. Schultz DP: Sensory Restriction: Effects on Behavior. New York, Academic Press, 1965
16. Forehand R, Baumeister AA: Effect of frustration on stereotyped body rocking: A follow-up. Percept Mot Skills 31:894, 1970
17. Rutter M, Graham P, Yule W: A Neuropsychiatric Study in Childhood. Clinics in Developmental Medicine Nos 35/36. London, Heinemann, 1970
18. Tizard J: The Brooklands residential unit, in Tizard J (ed): Community Services for the Mentally Handicapped. London, Oxford University Press, 1964, pp 85-137
19. Chess S, Hassibi M: Behavior deviations in mentally retarded children. J Am Acad Child Psychiatry 9:282-297, 1970
20. Warren DH: Blindness and early development: Issues in research methodology. New Outlook for the Blind 70:53-60,1976
21. Tate B, Baroff G: Aversive control of self-injurious behaviour in a psychotic boy. Behav Res Ther 4:281-287, 1966

19
Counseling

INTRODUCTION

Counseling is a much-abused subject, for there is a vast and confusing literature on the one hand and, on the other, an assumption that every professional can do it adequately. If we see it as an attempt to influence behavior by verbal, noncoercive means, we all do it every day. To distinguish counseling from this ordinary activity it might be best to define the process of counseling as one that is planned and has specific goals. The activities that could be included under this general definition could range from imparting a diagnosis, discussing with parents how to cope with a child, advising about visual aids, interviewing a child about unacceptable behavior or school work, to prolonged psychotherapeutic intervention.

This discussion will focus on areas that are often neglected in work with the handicapped or their families and will emphasize those areas that are specifically related to visual impairment. A detailed consideration of family reactions to handicaps will be covered in a separate chapter.

There are a number of useful general references at the end of this chapter.[1-6] There is also a collection of articles dealing with various aspects of handicap, compiled by Noland.[7] Articles of specific interest to those working with the visually impaired include Froyd,[8] Langdon,[9] Warnick,[10] Telson,[11] and Kozier.[12]

THE PROBLEM OF ASSUMPTIONS AND ATTITUDES

An assumption often made, rarely examined, sometimes wrong, and frequently annoying to clients or patients is that the counselor is "in the know" or is proceeding from a firm basis of fact or theory. A little reflection will show that this attitude, so often quite natural in professionals, is authoritarian and likely to subvert or destroy the possibility of reaching the desired goal.

Put simply, the counselor is in the position of counselor by virtue of special knowledge and training (a professional representing a particular discipline) or because of power (a director, supervisor, or gatekeeper to a service). Often the client/patient has not asked for counseling of any sort or from this particular person—it may have been suggested or imposed by others, with or without a comprehensible explanation.

The unfairness of this situation may be even greater for visually impaired persons, for they are so often left out of any participation in decision making and are "talked around." The general lack of age-appropriate life experience may make them shy or naive and reluctant to ask for explanations. Parents of a handicapped child may also have a problem in dealing with the initial counseling situation, specifically because differing and confusing information received from professionals in the past may increase anxiety about the next step and its implications.

Thus, the counselor often starts from a position of no trust and little understanding of roles and goals but may not be sufficiently aware of this fact.

The importance of this phenomenon cannot be overemphasized. But if it is taken into account, the counselor's approach will necessarily change for the better and the likelihood of success will be increased. The person doing the counseling should (1) not assume he knows in advance what is most important for a person; (2) not assume that advice will be or should be accepted because it is sensible and well-intentioned; (3) be able to listen with interest to the views and feelings of the person he is counseling; and (4) be willing to revise any plan or hypothesis in light of further information.

Unfortunately, these requisites are not often fulfilled. One reason is the professional's failure to see his role as an adjunct to the patient or client: at best a partnership, but almost never a one-sided relationship.

A few words are necessary about the problem of certainty. There is a vast difference between the counselor who knows what is right and is just collecting the facts and details to corroborate this (or to get the counselee to do something in accordance with his conclusion), and the counselor who has a body of more or less useful information and principles at his disposal but is truly interested in how this other person sees the situation (even though this may require a revision or rejection of the counselor's original premise). It is also important to recognize the difference between disease- or defect-oriented approaches and person-oriented ones.[13] One hopes that both of these will coincide, but at times they may diverge, be in conflict, or only one may be appropriate. The first approach is based upon the scientific method of

inquiry—the growth of knowledge, and the awareness of norms, probabilities, exceptions, and variations in applying these to individuals. It
is often this type of information that people assume we as professionals
have and can provide, when—more often than they realize—we cannot.
The person-oriented approach considers what is meaningful to individuals
and families, how they see things, their values, and their methods of
problem solving. It seeks to minimize the influence of the counselor's
personal values and preferences and to assist others in utilizing their
own strengths to find their own best answers within their own value
system—irrespective of norms.

Unfortunately, the skills necessary to perform these functions may
be very different and often do not reside in the same professional.
Sometimes a team will be fortunate in having both these sets of skills—but
complexities of authority and contact between family and team may
even complicate this potentiality.

THE NEEDS OF PARENTS

There are many ways of conceptualizing the needs of parents, but
it seems to be important to appreciate these needs as one is engaging
in the counseling process. First, it is clear that *information* is basic.
In spite of the counselor's understandable wish to be kind and protective,
an overwhelming majority of parents have been shown to desire the
truth, conveyed with compassion. Second, parents need to know that
others in positions of authority have *faith in their ability to cope;*[14]
it is especially important during periods of crisis, when the parent may
temporarily feel overwhelmed. It is also important to know one has
someone to turn to, someone who will care, will comfort, and will in
part share the burden. (Sharing the burden, it must be noted, does not
indicate a reduction in parental responsibility.) Parents also need *practical
advice*, individually tailored to their situation. If the advice given is
too general, it may lead to failure of compliance and subsequent mistrust
and feelings of inadequacy.

Since parents are usually the ones who carry through on both
professional advice and their own child-rearing requirements, it is
important for them to receive appropriate recognition for the good and
successful things they have been able to do in spite of all difficulties.

Parents also need an approach that assists them in treating their
child in as natural a manner as possible and does not overemphasize
defects to the exclusion of assets.[15]

Finally, there is a need to monitor the course of all grief reactions.[2]
Anticipatory guidance about the grief process may also assist the family,
since it is not unusual for different family members to be out of phase

with each other during its resolution or to see its manifestations as pathological or permanent.

VICIOUS CIRCLES

It is important to understand how it is possible for certain situations to develop and worsen in spite of everyone's good intentions. Otherwise, one can easily adopt a "conspiracy theory," which assumes the special personal malice of professionals, doctors, parents, the government, or even God himself/herself.

Also, there may be specific ways to interrupt these self-perpetuating processes if they are understood, without attributing blame where it does not belong.

Example 1

A common example is the baby who is not developing well and may be floppy (hypotonic). Often there is a failure to recognize that this can occur in blind children without other handicaps such as mental retardation or brain damage. A complex set of events may ensue, which includes wrong and pessimistic diagnoses of additional handicaps, more uncertainty and consequent adverse parental emotional reactions, decreasing pleasure in the child, less stimulation of the child, continued or increasing apathy on the part of the child, and a self-fulfilling prophecy of retarded development.

COMMENT

Given the frequent misdiagnoses of additional handicaps in the visually impaired and a tendency for parents to feel incompetent, the optimistic approach which has been used in our programs seems justified, even though errors will occasionally be made.

Example 2

Lack of responsiveness of the child can also have adverse effects upon the parents and indirectly upon the child. This may occur when a blind child fails to visually engage his mother, when a child is kept in hospital in early life and mother and child fail to establish a bond, when the baby's temperament does not match parental expectations, or where there is an autistic problem.

COMMENT

It may not be possible to force the child to be more responsive; however, one may be able to assist the parents by finding an explanation for the child's failure to respond that is more reassuring than what they may be telling themselves. Sometimes the child is in fact responsive, but it is more the *manner* of response rather than the *degree* that bothers the parents. In such a case, reinterpretation of the reasons for this will probably assist in permitting the bond to develop. Similarly, the study of temperament suggests that sometimes parents and children may both be normal but simply mismatched.[16] Again, parental understanding of this as a reaction to normal variation may be quite different from an interpretation based upon assumed severe pathology.

Example 3

The organization of most services for the handicapped influences the relative proportions of time and interest that the mother and father may respectively bring to bear upon the child's problem and may indirectly affect family management. Since most fathers work during the day and most professionals and centers keep similar hours, it is not surprising that fathers find it impossible or difficult to participate in the process. The common pattern is that the mother brings the child, encounters the advisors, struggles to incorporate the information given, and then tries to pass it on to her husband, usually in a way that cannot be very satisfactory. This may widen differences between the parents, which have already been enforced by role differentiation. The end result too often is that mother learns, worries, observes, her life becomes involved not only with the child but also with other mothers with similar problems; she talks a lot about problems; whereas father goes to work, he has other things on his mind, he comes home and wants to feel that there is more to life than "problems"; he may find he cannot easily exclude the handicap from his conversations with his wife. He may then be seen by his wife as nonsupportive, perhaps envied because he can "escape," and she may describe him to professionals as uninterested. Given these forces and the organization of time previously mentioned, mothers' characterizations of fathers may be too uncritically accepted.

COMMENT

More will be made of this major problem elsewhere in the chapter; it seems that simple logic would dictate an intervention strategy to ameliorate this vicious circle—but it rarely does, for there are powerful opposing forces.

The preceding examples are merely imperfect descriptions of interacting and sequential effects, which are naturally involved in any situation. Since finite observations can always be accounted for in an infinite number of ways,[17] it is not possible to find a final or complete answer—merely a parsimonious one having the greatest practical implications. It is simpler to start with the obvious, but that does not mean that this approach will always be sufficient. A parent *may* have much more complex reasons for behavior (and these may need to be explored), but this is not the best way to begin. We are proposing that in many situations an understanding of the possible sequence of events may be helpful without invoking motivational conflicts or unconscious factors. However, the reader needs to be assured that we are not adopting simplistic notions, which necessarily exclude a role for guilt, neurotic conflict, or conflicts over values.

ACCEPTANCE

Much has been written about the need for acceptance of the child's handicap or the child's limitations, but this term is almost never adequately defined. Such vagueness permits one to arrive at very different conclusions about the same parent in relation to this variable. It seems painfully clear, in reviewing the literature on clinical practice, that a practical measure of parent functioning is preferable to this global concept. Furthermore, Wright has challenged what is often implicit in this concept of acceptance, namely, being realistic. Most parents and persons are not realistic, but when one is the parent of a handicapped child, one is suddenly expected to be. In her conclusion to this important paper, Wright states:

> The essential argument of this paper is that the great weight and idolization of the value of being realistic predisposes us 1) to ignore conditions when being *un*realistic can yield much that is of value, 2) to emphasize realistic limitations and to neglect realistic assets and opportunities, 3) to believe that reality can be adequately predicted even when it cannot, and 4) to accept that perceived reality even when it ought to and can be changed. Man not only submits to reality; he also shapes it. Being unrealistic can be a source of hope, achievement and redefinition of the boundaries of new realities.[18] (p. 296)

Roskies has also pointed out that parental "nonacceptance" may be a positive force which permits the parent to develop and sustain an emotional bond to the child and also to maintain motivation in the rehabilitation process.[19]

Olshansky suggested that parents of the retarded never fully resolve their sense of loss and termed this continuing feeling *chronic sorrow*.[4] It may be, then, that there is no such thing as complete acceptance.

Others have stressed the importance of what the situation, and the terms we professionals use to describe it, may mean to the parents.

In summary, it is important to assess what the parent currently expects of the child, the pleasure they can have together, how the parent sees the child, what qualities or activities the parent fosters in the child—and not merely agreement with the professional on the correctness of a particular diagnostic term and its implications.

GUILT

Guilt is another overused term. Because after the diagnosis is made, parents frequently express the idea that they may have done something wrong or have doubts as to whether their child rearing is adequate, many professionals have assumed that conscious or unconscious guilt is a very important element in parental behavior and must be central in the counseling process. First, it is necessary to realize that there are situations in which the parent truly is guilty of some act of omission or commission, and finding this out may not be easy once one has globally absolved the parent of guilt, as recommended in many textbooks. Secondly, expressions of concern in a professional's office may not represent parental preoccupation outside the office. Severe guilt reactions are rather uncommon and require very specialized and detailed consideration.

Gardner has done some research supporting his thesis that guilt can be an attempt to focus and control the uncontrollable.[20] Some people may, for this reason, not be at all happy with well-intentioned efforts to exonerate them and invoke an impersonal probability theory and the laws of chance. Different mechanisms may operate in different persons.

Another possibility is that guilt, if present, may derive from unacceptable feelings of hostility and frustration directed at the child—even death wishes—which the parent does not realize may be natural and not evil. Exploration of this possibility, and appropriate reassurance, may be very useful.

SOME USEFUL TECHNIQUES

These vary with the situation, person, and age, and each counselor will develop his own repertoire of techniques with which he is comfortable. The following refer primarily to situations in which an ongoing process is contemplated or emotionally loaded issues are involved.

Courtesy and Relaxation

It helps if a quiet comfortable place without unnecessary interruption can be used. A cup of coffee with an adult may be very useful, although one must be aware of the problems of setting a precedent with children

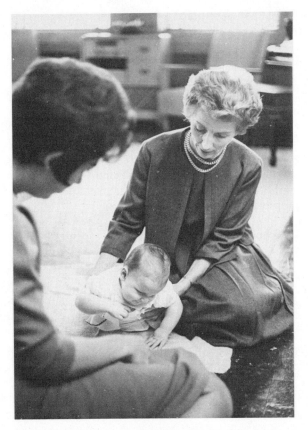

Fig. 19-1.   Counseling does not have to take place across a desk.

in providing them with soda pop, candy bars, etc. "Stress" interviews with deliberate use of prolonged silence have no place in a counseling relationship.

Eliciting Major Concerns

Korsch[21] and Raimbault et al.[22] have demonstrated the difficulties professionals have in communicating adequately with parents. Much of this difficulty stems from a failure to determine what it is the parent needs or is really concerned about, rather than what is "obvious" within the professional's frame of reference. Rather than making any assumptions, therefore, it is important to find out: Why has this person come? What would she most like me to do for her? Of course, answers to these questions may need to be modified as further comfort and trust is engendered.

Review of Previous Records

At times it is helpful to check over previous records, particularly those sent by other professionals, for clarification and corroboration. Records are fairly often wrong, or the person may never have been told something of importance; these may be easy ways of fostering relaxation and at the same time learning about the person's attitudes towards previous or current efforts to help with the problem. Caution is needed, of course, not to overdo this, to fill time with it, to give the impression that one has not read anything, or to criticize or praise other professionals who have been involved.

Clarifying the Meaning of Words

It is clear from both research and practice that parents and professionals usually agree on descriptions of behavior; disagreements more often arise because of the meaning each attributes to a particular term. For example, there may be no disagreement about the functioning level of a particular child, yet the term *mental retardation* may mean a specific degree of limitation to the professional, but to the parent may signify a vegetable like existence with no further progress. It is not surprising, then, that under those conditions the parent will reject such a professional term.

Reflecting

A useful technique is to mirror or clarify a feeling expressed, such as, "I guess you felt pretty angry," or "That seems to have been very frustrating." This also involves listening with empathy, which Pinkerton describes as the need to "project ourselves into the patient's problem and feel its character as he does."[15] It is important to recognize that the technique of reflecting and empathic listening, although it can help to elicit strong feelings and to get a relationship going, must be sincere to be effective and should not be overdone and turned into a pose or mannerism.

Taking Time

The time between sessions is not wasted. Things are happening; the parent is usually thinking and remembering. Working over some of the same issues or areas again may be surprisingly useful, important new information may emerge or previously indigestible suggestions may become acceptable.

Exploring Options

People often say they *can't* do something when they don't *want* to do it. Sometimes these supposedly closed options and the reasons for the "impossibility" must be fully explored.

Bringing in Other Areas or Problems of Living

As long as more urgent issues have been dealt with, it can be very helpful to ask about what the spouse, parent, relatives, neighbors, friends, and others think about the medical or behavioral problem, how the important persons in the child's or parent's life feel about the evaluation or counseling; whether the person has any source of emotional support, fun, or any problems with finances, with health, or is caring for anyone else, such as an elderly or infirm relative. Such questions are useful not only because they may reveal sources of help or hindrance, but also because it tells the person that the counselor has a comprehensive rather than narrow interest. In a continuing relationship this is more likely to produce important but reluctantly revealed information, or data that were simply ignored out of the belief that the counselor would not be interested.

Parents of a handicapped child often feel that they are treated as if they were an appendage to their child's disability. They need to realize that they have lives apart—and are being treated as persons in their own right.

We have often found it useful to involve a grandparent or other person in the management of the case and have sometimes been surprised at the results. Caution is needed in introducing such a person to the counseling situation, because one must guard against placing the parent in a position of being a child in relation to his own parent; this implies a clarification to all concerned as to the role this other person will play in contacts with the counselor.

Certainly one of the most overlooked aspects of counseling is the failure to bring in the father. This was discussed elsewhere, but it should suffice to say here that one must not accept a mother's judgment of her spouse's lack of interest or other characterization of him without direct contact.

Group Meetings

Group counseling can be very useful for both parents and professionals. Parents often have practical ideas, which professionals could not have acquired alone. Also, their experiences and feelings may be much more impressive and supportive to each other than the abstractions the nonparent, no matter how skilled, can employ. Linder has well described one of these groups and the group process.[23]

There are many other techniques that may be helpful, and some will be found in the suggested readings. The preceding ideas have been presented because it is felt they are essential to the proper use of the skills that may be acquired through further reading, experience, or training.

SPECIAL SITUATIONS

Imparting the Diagnosis

Much has been written about this subject, and we only wish to point out certain aspects that are frequently neglected. It is important to have both parents present, or to inform the absent parent directly as soon as possible, rather than having one parent responsible for imparting information to the other.[2] Initial reactions to the diagnosis vary widely, and it is best not to try predicting how healthy a long-term response will be from the initial reaction. It is the process over time which is important. The response of the parents will depend upon whether they suspected the diagnosis previously, the way in which the information is provided, the hope that is offered, and the presence of additional handicaps. It is particularly important to emphasize at such a time the range of positive possibilities for the child later, and not to give the parents the feeling that they will be abandoned without ongoing information and support.

It is to be expected that one session will rarely be sufficient for the parents to absorb necessary information; anxiety interferes with learning, and many parents will be in a state of emotional shock. Again, such a state is not predictive of later coping, nor correlated with intelligence.

The imparting of an additional diagnosis later on may be a more complex matter, in that it raises questions as to why it took so long to arrive at the conclusion. Explanations may be necessary, as well as placing in perspective what such an additional handicap actually means. Again, the label may mean different things to different persons.

Previous Wrong Diagnosis

It is understandable that parents feel angry about a wrong diagnosis. Sometimes we can help them understand how this not-infrequent occurrence can happen. At other times we must simply tolerate their anger and comprehend how this may make them distrust us as well. A "de-briefing" session to help the parents and others deal with the changes required in their point of view and management, consequent upon the new diagnosis, is often a good idea. Usually one can deal with these situations and their anger without having to take sides and directly criticize another professional person. (This is not to suggest that some professionals are above criticism, but usually this is neither called for nor constructive.)

With visually impaired children, the wrong diagnosis is usually mental retardation or cerebral palsy. If patterns have already been established whereby the parents see the child as more handicapped than he is, then more guidance to help them change their expectations and persistent monitoring of their behavior and its effects may be necessary.

Marital Problems

As we point out in the chapter on family aspects, the presence of a handicap and its management may stress the family, but it is never safe to assume that this is the sole cause of the problem. It is not uncommon for families to report that all the fighting and arguing centers on the handicap, but often one must look deeper to realize that it merely provides a focal point for preexisting problems.

When are Parents' Reactions Abnormal?

We have emphasized the need to keep preconceived notions and judgments to a minimum in understanding parental reactions. But when can we say a reaction is "too much" as a matter of degree, or deviant in itself? Immutable lines cannot generally be drawn, but some guidelines are possible and may be useful in considering further sources of help. These are some examples:

- Suicide attempts
- Persistent suicidal rumination
- Inability to find anything good to say about the child (if asked)
- Impending breakup of marriage, apparently related to the child
- Difficulty controlling impulses to do physical harm to the child
- Depression persisting more than a few weeks, of a severity sufficient to grossly impair functioning in everyday activities
- Inability to ever get angry with the child
- Inability to set limits on the child's behavior
- Unwillingness (after a time) to take the child out in public
- Inability to see the child as an individual
- Absence of any reaction to the diagnosis, persisting over a period of weeks
- Psychiatric symptoms showing no change over many months, especially if new (anxiety, obsessive-compulsive reaction, etc.)

- Persistent sexual dysfunction, not present before the appearance of the child's handicap

In all these examples, the guiding principle is *process*. Although almost any reaction may be within normal range for a short time of a few days or weeks (especially if the diagnosis was totally unforeseen), one expects indications of change in these reactions, at least a phasic quality with overall improvement between periods of distress.

If this does not occur, or other signs of difficulty emerge, one should cease reassuring a parent that this is probably all normal and start (if not done already) tactfully assessing the reaction and its implications in more detail, including the nature and course of similar reactions in the past or in the parents' relatives.

In some situations, such as suicidal risk or fear of harm (physical or through neglect) to the child, specialized help should be consulted without delay. Fortunately, these situations are relatively uncommon. Many will be found to represent the reappearance of an earlier pattern of reaction to other types of stress significant for that person.

It might be helpful to describe an example of a normal versus a pathological reaction.

CASE HISTORY #1—NORMAL REACTION

A mother seemed very shocked at the diagnosis, but then felt detached and emotionally cold—as if it had happened to someone else—while the child remained in hospital. She avoided intimacy with her husband for a few weeks. When the baby came home she developed some depression and feared she could not cope. At times she felt she would be better off dead. Relatives were avoided. After about 2 months she began feeling better (at times) and started taking the baby out. A babysitter was obtained for the couple to go to a company dance, but she did not enjoy herself much. She and her husband found it difficult to talk about the handicap and to have fun together, but the feeling that it had spoiled everything and would do so in the future was lifting. When seen 3 months later, both parents were starting to have positive things to say about the baby's development and were planning a summer trip to see some relatives.

CASE HISTORY #2—PATHOLOGICAL REACTION

Another set of parents had a similar beginning but were unable to resume any positive relationship. Mother remained depressed at times, aloof or remotely angry at others. Father stayed away from home as much as he could, while the mother became devoted to the child's problem. They rarely talked about it. As the child developed, the mother seemed perplexed at each new milestone, seemingly not happy at what she felt was unnecessary delay. Although preoccupied with the child's problems, she had nothing positive to say and when observed with the child at age 3, showed no obvious affection or pleasure as the child occupied himself with repetitive activities.

Notice that it is not so much *what* the parent does or does not do at a particular time (especially early) but the evolution and direction of the process. In assessing this, one must be careful to include some consideration of cultural patterns, availability and use of support systems (family, friends, others), and preexisting problems. In particular, one should not use the criterion of agreeing with professionals as a sign of health. (It is quite possible to succeed in spite of professionals.) Also, the foregoing statement about process should not lead the professional who is counseling a family to pass off all severe initial reactions as typical, unworthy of special consideration, or "a phase you have to go through." Many parents will resent this and sometimes with justification. It is much better to listen to a description of the current status of the reaction, ask why they are concerned about it, what they think is happening, or what they fear *might* happen, than to pass it off lightly. In the latter case parents might withhold significant information because of the attitude they perceive in the professional.

Subsequent Crises

One essential point to remember is that a family that has coped adequately with the initial problem may not seem to maintain such equanimity as later crises develop. They may need at least as much assistance and support as they did previously. These crises may include the birth of another child and the need to reallocate time and affection; starting school; the shift to a different kind of school; the onset of peer problems, such as the possibility and desirability of dating; and vocational problems, such as planning for future work or higher education (or the impossibility of achieving this). There are of course many others, depending upon the particular case. In all these instances, it is necessary for the counselor to find out what, specifically, is producing the crisis, rather than employing generalizations. Impatience with the parent or parents because they are "having trouble again" is to be avoided.

Questions Asked by the Child

Some parents find it very difficult to answer their child's questions about the impairment. Kvaraceus and Hayes stated: "The one occasion that parents of all blind children dread is that awful day when a youngster realizes what blindness means and demands to know why he is different from other people"[24] (p. 224). It is generally felt that the parents' comfort in dealing with these questions is directly related to their own comfort in discussing it between themselves and in coming to terms with the implications of the impairment. All of these factors are interrelated, and the need for a good start from the time of the diagnosis is obvious. The other children in the family also need, at various points, to be able to ask questions and to express annoyance and resentment toward the child with an impairment.[2] There are, of course, no perfect or easy answers to the question of why one person has an impairment and another person does not, and parents need to realize, as professionals do, that an answer that is unsatisfactory at one stage of development in a child's thinking may later prove to be much more so.

Referral for Specialized Assistance

It is not always easy to make a referral to a psychiatrist, social worker, or psychologist for ongoing counseling. Sometimes the counselor may feel possessive of the family, but a more frequently given reason for this difficulty is the presumed lack of interest or knowledge of the outside specialist in this area of impairment. This may or may not be an important factor in reality. Sometimes a cooperative relationship can be established that does not require that the outside specialist have much knowledge of visual impairment. At other times the problem is one of the attitude of the parent. It is one thing to be counseled by a professional of whatever discipline within a setting in which one's child is receiving service. It is quite another to be referred to some outside person, with all the stigma and feelings attached to the need for specialized counseling help. There are several alternatives here, including the attachment of the person with such specialized skills to a unit for the visually impaired, or the seeking of an outside specialist who is sufficiently flexible to meet the parents at the center so as to effect a smooth transition.

Another point often overlooked is the need to spell out quite specifically the reason why such specialist help is necessary, both to the parents and to the specialist. Outside counselors do not appreciate receiving a parent or set of parents who are hostile and feel that the referral is simply a dismissal, rejection, or evidence of blame for the child's problem. Parents can usually tell if the referring person is uncomfortable about the referral and this had better be worked out before it is accomplished.

Psychotherapy

Although there are many different schools of psychotherapy and "casework," there are certain features that are probably common to them. These have been very well described by Frank as follows:[25,26]

Common to all psychotherapies are an emotionally charged, confiding relationship; a therapeutic rationale accepted by patient and therapist; provision of new information by precept, example, and self-discovery; strengthening of the patient's expectation of help; providing him with success experiences; and facilitation of emotional arousal.[25] (p. 360)

We wish only to point out here that parents of handicapped children already have enough problems without being considered automatic patients in their own right. Some parents do have serious problems which require individual or other kinds of attention. In such instances it is only proper to inform them of this fact, have it well understood, and to discuss any differences of opinion. The parent thus enters a psychotherapeutic relationship willingly, with a kind of "contract" between parent and counselor. All too often this does not happen, and parents find that they have insidiously entered an undeclared patient role.

Counseling a Visually Impaired Person

A few words are necessary about working with a visually impaired person, either child or adult. As the counselor engages in this process, he will probably (if a sighted person) be monitoring what is going on in a largely visual mode. That is, the blind person's appearance, movements, posture, facial expression, habits, and mannerisms will provide constant stimulation and feedback to which the sighted person reacts automatically, based upon his own previous experiences. A problem may arise because the counselor reacts to the visually impaired person's atypical responses. This may result in erroneous conclusions by the sighted counselor who has not had extensive experience with visually impaired persons, with far-reaching consequences. Habits involving noisemaking or unusual speech patterns may compound this problem.

In trying to comprehend this phenomenon we need to recall how much of our own socialization depends on being like other people and relinquishing annoying habits, most of which are visually experienced by others. Examples are thumbsucking, scratching or rubbing certain parts of the body, picking the nose, blinking the eyes too fast, crossing or opening the legs in an "immodest" manner, and so forth. Children are told that to do things like this, at least at certain ages, is not nice. People try to change such behavior if it occurs in others, or if they become aware of it in themselves and of the negative reactions of others. Imitation of an approved model is an important part of this behavior-shaping process, but is much more difficult for the young visually impaired and almost impossible for the blind. It should not be surprising, then, if the counselor's reaction to the habit-deviance of a blind person is disgust, discomfort, or the drawing of erroneous conclusions about intelligence, motivation, socialization, or emotional disturbance. (This is not to say that such deviant patterns are solely due to defective vision and imitation.)

The seemingly aberrant behavior of the visually impaired person may not only be misinterpreted but may also be distracting to the professional. Eye contact, which the sighted depend on to monitor how the relationship or conversation is progressing, is lacking. In addition, some blind or partially sighted people have visually unsightly eyes, orbits, or facial configurations. There are thus a number of reasons why many professionals find it uncomfortable to sit with just the kind of person they may, in the past, have tried to avoid and whose "affliction" they cannot cure.

It is essential for the professional who is not very familiar with the visually impaired to recognize these natural reactions and use them constructively. It is quite proper to tactfully ask the person what visually impaired people can or cannot do and how much help they require, as well as to indicate one's lack of familiarity with the situation. As familiarity is established, it is also feasible to ask directly about certain habits and the ways in which people react to them.

Enucleation

Some visually impaired children require enucleation of an eye. This kind of situation sometimes points up the difference in feeling and understanding between the sighted professional and the child or parent. Sometimes the child has been complaining of pain and discomfort in the eye for some time. It would therefore seem logical that the child would be happy to be rid of a sightless, painful eye. Very often the reaction is just the opposite. The child fears losing the eye and may express considerable fear of mutilation. The parents may feel similarly. In trying to comprehend this, the counselor should appreciate that even a sightless eye is a part of the child's body image and that both child and parents may have hopes that vision could somehow be restored by a medical miracle at some later point. Openness to such ideas will enable the persons concerned to express their fears and desires, rather than having them shut off by the message that they must agree with the professional's feelings.

Progressive Disease

Progressive disease is a complex issue, which has been dealt with in the vast literature on terminal illnesses. Sometimes the illness itself is not terminal, but the eye disease is progressive. Whatever the situation, the person concerned (if sufficiently aware) and certainly the parents and perhaps the siblings may be engaging in some anticipatory grief over the loss. They will need more support and understanding than usual and are likely to be even more frustrated with professionals who cannot stem the onward march of the impairment than would be the case in a stationary situation. This will test the ability of the professional to see the possibilities of helping in the midst of profound frustration.

Genetic Counseling

Many forms of visual impairment have a genetic origin. Parents often need compassionate genetic counseling in order to decide on further childbearing. However, they may misunderstand the risk figures given, so the process may have to be reviewed. As the visually impaired child grows older, he or she can also profit from an understanding of causes and probabilities, because misinformation is common.

Some conditions are unusual enough that the hereditary mechanisms may be confused with another similar condition. The physician should carefully consider the limitations of his own knowledge in this rapidly changing field, as well as the availability of genetic counselors. Checking with parents after an evaluation by a special center, to see what they have understood and what their reactions are, is an excellent course to follow.

The Dissatisfied Parent

Contrary to much popular opinion, most parents do not "shop around" without very practical reasons for doing so. One is often led to believe that the parents are merely looking for a comfortable answer from some irresponsible professional. More often, the parents are seeking practical help and compassionate support. Attributing the shopping around to nonacceptance of the impairment would be unfortunate, since, as has already been pointed out in a previous section, serene acceptance of a major loss is usually not to be anticipated and is often unhelpful. Here again it is most useful to assume at the start that there is some very good reason for the parents to be dissatisfied, and to seek to understand this through their own point of view before attributing it wholly to some deeper and unconscious mental mechanisms. Agencies and professionals who are really concerned about this will seek to have frequent feedback from parents in a way that is nonthreatening and likely to lead to frank answers.

We do occasionally see parents with a persistent intolerance to having a child who is different. It is as if this is the crowning blow or the child is literally a defective extension of themselves. Specialist help is then called for and may be useful, but it must be recognized that there are situations where we are limited in the amount that we can do; not everyone can adjust.

SENSE AND NONSENSE IN UNDERSTANDING EMOTIONAL REACTIONS

It would be a disservice if this book were merely to increase the feeling of some professionals and some parents that everything, including the child himself and his family, is special and in need of very sophisticated lifelong attention—and if therefore some straightforward ideas had to be abandoned.

But it is sometimes difficult to know whether one is erring on the side of "overspecializing" or "overnormalizing." While floppy muscles and peculiar EEGs may well require specialist interpretation, very often the emotional reactions of the child or other family members are quite straightforward—only they do not seem so. We should inquire why this is. Why should the experts repeatedly have to tell parents or other professionals, "That is not surprising under the circumstances?"

It seems that the presence of an "exceptional" child may make people mistrust their usual reactions and judgments. We can perhaps understand it if a mother, when taking a handicapped newborn home from the hospital, feels she does not know how to hold it, feed it, bathe it, love it, touch it, or let it cry. She is not sure how much it really is a *child*—the usual rules seem suspended because the child's conventional identity is still in some doubt.

But similar factors are operating in other situations having to do with behavior and feelings. Parents have been told so often that they feel guilty (in some neurotic way) that they may become anxious if they cannot identify such feelings in themselves which satisfy their counselors. Or they may be "unrealistic" in expecting or hoping for great success for their visually impaired child—and people want to counsel them to get their hopes in line with the reality of statistical probability or professional prediction. Or they feel they should not be resentful of the burden that the child's care may represent, should not be bored sometimes with all the talk about handicaps, or should not ever be depressed. They may ask for a prediction or assurance of success for their visually impaired child in the future.

These phenomena are common. But how often do we point out to parents that there are no predictors of future success for unimpaired children (nor do most parents expect such predictions)? Why must parents be realistic? Parents are not realistic about normal children, and perhaps few of us are realistic most of the time.[18] Being a parent to the handicapped child or being a handicapped person may not only lead to "spread of stigma" to other areas of functioning or other individuals, but also to excessive and sometimes intrusive surveillance and outright meddling by professionals and others. There are still all too many examples of parents who do perfectly ordinary things or who feel quite conventional ways, but have these reinterpreted and treated as special problems in need of specialist intervention. Such nonsense is not only potentially harmful, wasteful, and uneconomic, but it can also bring the useful role that professionals can play into unfortunate disrepute.

For the most part, families have feelings and reactions to life events, including the impaired child, which are fairly easy to comprehend and are not rigidly neurotic, provided one is reasonably sensitive and aware of both individual differences and one's own tendency to overidentify.

To treat most situations as different from the ordinary is to rob families of competence and increase their dependency upon experts who, in fact, have relatively little factual data or norms to prescribe.

Parents often feel greatly relieved when they are told that they can do a simple thing they might intuitively do with another child.

There is, it must be emphasized, a place for intensive and extensive counseling work with mental health or other interested and trained professionals. But it is simply not necessary for most. It should be available but utilized with discretion and clear delineation of the indications, not on the basis of vague terms, such as overprotection, denial, nonacceptance, rejection, and lack of motivation.

In summary, parents may be helped by the professional person supporting them in developing their critical judgment—so that they may be better enabled to inquire, think, change their minds, experiment a bit, take risks, learn from mistakes, and eventually realize that coping with the visually impaired child and with the visual impairment itself is part of their lives, not outside of it in a special compartment to which only experts have the key.

SUMMARY

We have tried to present some of the problems that the professional may encounter in the situation loosely described as counseling. Sometimes special skills are needed, and there are various programs through which they can be developed and improved. Since it is now well recognized that all professionals have to do this, we should start preparing people to do so competently, rather than by default.

There are, however, ways in which professionals who do not have the opportunity for further training may attempt to train themselves. In addition to reading about the subject, it is very useful to undergo the following process: Write down what you think is the problem from the referral material you receive before seeing the child or family. After seeing them, do the same and note any discrepancies. Try to understand how these discrepancies might have arisen. Do the same on subsequent occasions and if information is obtained from other settings and sources. Again, revise the formulation of the problem and the impressions of the persons concerned. It is very likely that if this is done, there will be major changes between descriptions. By doing this several times, you should be able to learn how the quality and quantity of information and the nature of the relationship and its stage of development affect your conclusions. It might also be useful with some parents, and with some visually impaired persons (once a very good relationship has been established) to ask them how the relationship seemed to them at the beginning and whether you did anything that caused negative feelings in them or whether anything constructive stands out as helpful. This can be done in such a way that the persons concerned feel that you are seeking improvement in counseling skills, not simply accolades.

We have all heard, and probably accepted, that travel broadens the perspective. But surely this is true only if the traveler is open to experience. Similarly, emotional and social "traveling" to the land of the impaired can force the recasting of our ideas and feelings into new molds. If, like the tourist who stays only in first-class hotels and fails to come into contact with "the locals," we only sightsee with our colleagues or meet unrepresentative samples of impaired persons, we may not only remain grossly ignorant but, what is worse, be convinced we are not.

Who knows what other persons may suffer? Each situation is different, each in some ways the same. Statistics and categories are only a start at comprehension. If we are at all wise, we listen and attempt to see things through their eyes. The need to temper our professional thinking and judgment with such experience can never be taken for granted, or considered a frill. It is the very essence of continuing growth, without which counseling must forever remain a mass of intellectually glossed platitudes.

CONCLUSIONS

1. Most professionals doing counseling have had no training in the specific skills required; it is possible, however, to improve them by organized study of one's own counseling experiences.
2. It is best to start with the obvious and work toward the less obvious or inferential, if necessary.
3. It is essential to find out the major concerns, which may not be

obvious or readily volunteered; confusing terms need clarification of personal meanings.

4. Parents need information, practical advice, faith in their ability to cope, recognition for their efforts, and guidance to help them treat the child in as natural a manner as possible. Grief reactions require monitoring.

5. "Acceptance," "guilt," and "being realistic" are examples of terms or concepts too vague to be useful.

6. Helpful techniques include reflecting, exploring supposedly closed options, and involving other family members; group meetings may also be useful.

7. Parents "shop around" less than usually thought—most often not because they are neurotic but rather because they want certain basic assistance.

8. Caution is needed in predicting future attitudes from reactions to a crisis.

9. Help is often needed with later crises, even if the first is successfully mastered.

10. Negative child and parent reactions to enucleation of a supposedly useless eye are not really paradoxical.

11. Professionals often misinterpret the behavior of visually impaired persons.

12. Guidelines are provided for referral to specialists, based upon assessment of processes as well as specific events or attitudes.

REFERENCES

1. Cull JG, Hardy RE: Counseling Strategies with Special Populations. Springfield, Ill, Charles C Thomas, 1975

2. Freeman RD: The crisis of diagnosis: Need for intervention. J Spec Educ 5:389–414, 1971

3. Wolfensberger W: Counseling parents of the retarded, in Baumeister AA (ed): Mental Retardation: Appraisal, Education, and Rehabilitation. Chicago, Aldine, 1967, pp 329–400

4. Olshansky S: Chronic sorrow: A response to having a mentally defective child. Social Casework 43:191–194, 1962

5. Zuk GH: Cultural dilemma and spiritual crisis of the family with a handicapped child. Except Child 28:405–408, 1962

6. Mandelbaum A, Wheeler ME: The meaning of a defective child to parents. Social Casework 41:360–367, 1960

7. Noland RL (ed): Counseling Parents of the Ill and the Handicapped. Springfield, Ill, Charles C Thomas, 1971

8. Froyd HE: Counseling families of severely visually handicapped children. New Outlook for the Blind 67:251–257, 1973

9. Langdon JN: Parents talking. New Beacon 54:282-288, 1970
10. Warnick L: The effect upon a family of a child with a handicap. New Outlook for the Blind 63:299-304, 1969
11. Telson S: Parent counseling. New Outlook for the Blind 59:127-129, 1965
12. Kozier A: Casework with parents of blind children. Social Casework 43:15-22, 1962
13. Duff RS, Campbell AGM: On deciding the care of severely handicapped or dying persons: With particular reference to infants. Pediatrics 57:487-493, 1976
14. Carr J: Handicapped children—counselling the parents. Dev Med Child Neurol 12:230-231, 1970
15. Pinkerton P: Parental acceptance of the handicapped child. Dev Med Child Neurol 12:207-212, 1970
16. Thomas A, Chess S, Birch HG: Temperament and Behavior Disorders in Children. New York, New York University Press, 1968
17. Popper KR: Objective Knowledge: An Evolutionary Approach. London, Oxford University Press, 1972
18. Wright BA: The question stands: Should a person be realistic? Rehab Counseling Bull 11:291-296, 1968
19. Roskies E: Abnormality and Normality: The Mothering of Thalidomide Children. Ithaca, New York, Cornell University Press, 1972
20. Gardner RA: The guilt reaction of parents of children with severe physical disease. Am J Psychiatry 126:636-644, 1969
21. Korsch B, Gozzi EK, Francis V: Gaps in doctor-patient communication: I. Doctor-patient interaction and patient satisfaction. Pediatrics 42:855-871, 1968
22. Raimbault G, Cachin O, Limel J-M, et al: Aspects of communication between patients and doctors: An analysis of the discourse in medical interviews. Pediatrics 55:401-405, 1975
23. Linder R: Mothers of disabled children—The value of weekly group meetings. Dev Med Child Neurol 12:202-206, 1970
24. Kvaraceus WC, Hayes EN (eds): If Your Child is Handicapped. Boston, Porter Sargent, 1969
25. Frank JD: Therapeutic factors in psychotherapy. Am J Psychother 25:350-361, 1971
26. Frank JD: Psychotherapy: The restoration of morale. Am J Psychiatry 131:271-274, 1974

20
Attitudes

THE EVOLUTION OF ATTITUDES TOWARD THE VISUALLY IMPAIRED

The visually impaired have never been regarded by society as individuals without sight but as a different class of people with definite, stereotyped characteristics. In 1955, Jacob Twersky reviewed how the blind and blindness have been depicted in classical, medieval, and modern literature.[1] This valuable publication shows the evolution of attitudes toward the visually impaired in Western civilization from ancient times. Many stereotyped characteristics were contradictory to each other, but these prejudices endure.

In the classical literature, the Greeks saw blindness as the greatest punishment by their gods—a living death or worse. Most blind persons were portrayed as utterly helpless, unfortunate, and miserable human beings, although occasionally the gods rewarded them with extraordinary gifts in partial compensation. The latter belief helped to maintain social stereotypes, since some blind people were able to perform beyond the expectations of the sighted. In medieval literature these attitudes persisted, but in addition, humour directed toward the blind began to creep in. They were often depicted as comical fools or inferior, gullible people or, at the same time, described as evil, cruel, greedy and cynical. After the first school for the blind was established in Paris by Haüy in 1785, occasional blind characters were portrayed as competent and no longer helpless. The other major change was the introduction of the belief that blindness led to purity and sweetness of the soul. Blind characters would be depicted as angelic, while others were shown as evil. More contemporary literature no longer views the visually impaired as good or evil, gifted or inferior, beautiful or ugly, but in more realistic terms as people who do not see.

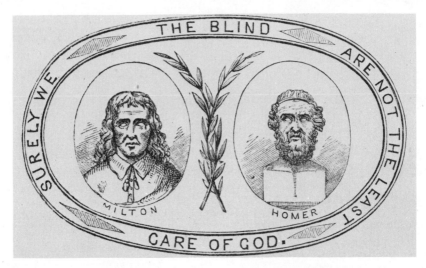

Fig. 20-1.   This picture appeared in a book written over 100 years ago (Levy WH: Blindness and the Blind. London, Chapman and Hall, 1872). It is an appeal for equality of the blind.

Unfortunately, these ancient misconceptions still exist. Parents of blind newborn infants often get the impression from physicians and nurses that the child would be better off dead since "death is better than blindness." The loss of vision is still looked upon as punishment by many, including the parents, and this may make them feel guilty. Professionals often view blind children as helpless and hopeless. This is a great disservice because, without appropriate expectations, they do not succeed in life. Pity and sorrow are still expressed toward an individual with loss of sight, which is resented by the visually impaired more than anything else. The public and even many professions still believe that blind children are born with superior hearing, touch or musical talents. Kirtley, who analyzed 155 citations relating to the word *blind*, concluded that "In language and everyday behaviour, the idea of blindness is symbolically employed in a wide variety of ways, many of which suggest or clearly indicate negative prejudicial attitudes toward blind people as a class"[2] (p. 44). Many of our common expressions reinforce these negative attitudes. A person may be called blind when he lacks common sense and *stolen blind* when someone foolishly allows himself to be cheated. Other terms, such as *blind alley, blind fury, intellectually blind,* or *morally blind* all have negative connotations. Bad pirates still wear eye patches in storybooks, while physical beauty is constantly advertised over the media. The strangest assumption commonly held is that as soon as a person becomes blind he immediately takes on all the stereotyped characteristics.

Not only Western cultures are infiltrated with negative attitudes toward the blind. In Buddhist and Hindu cultures, the blind person is rejected because he is believed to be suffering now from the sins he has committed in his previous lives. Thus, efforts to establish training programs for the blind in India have met with great resistance.[3]

In recent years in China, blind children were considered to be no more than human waste. Personal communication with Miss Ching, a blind social worker who now lives in Hong Kong, illustrates this point well as she talks about a blind child:

> During the time she lived with us, I pieced together her story—of parents who ill-treated her and considered killing her because she was blind and who eventually abandoned her in the city.[4]

Another visually impaired girl

> told us her story. She became blind from measles when she was six or seven, about six years before we met her. Her parents thought keeping a blind girl would bring bad luck to the family so when they heard of a blind woman who made a living out of training and exploiting blind girls as singing beggars, they gladly got rid of her.[4]

In China the white cane is still regarded as a symbol of a blind beggar or prostitute and, as a result, long-cane training for mobility is rather difficult.

ATTITUDES OF THE SIGHTED TOWARD BLINDNESS

Helen Keller once said that, "not blindness, but the attitude of the seeing to the blind is the hardest burden to bear." This issue of unfavorable attitudes is of such great importance that the American Foundation for the Blind "celebrated" their 50th anniversary by a symposium on this subject.

Research in this field is difficult because attitudes toward blindness are determined not by one or two simple factors but by complex interacting variables. Consequently, the results of many studies are inconclusive or even contradictory. Most of the research is adult oriented. Generally, studies tend to deal with negative attitudes, ignoring positive ones altogether. Furthermore, they are discussed in relation to the totally blind without including people with partial sight, in spite of the fact that the former are only a small segment of the visually impaired population.

Certain conclusions can be reached, however. The severely visually impaired are treated by the sighted just like people with other major handicaps. Society is geared to accommodate the majority, and thus the needs of these minorities are often forgotten. However, there is a significant difference in how people feel about blind persons and the way they view ethnic minorities. For example, the blind are not hated or blamed for the ills of society[5] but certain ethnic groups are. The socioeconomic status of the sighted determines to a degree the development of unfavorable preconceptions as, for example, middle-class individuals demonstrate a greater acceptance of the blind than the lower class.[6] While age and sex are not related to positive attitudes, the educational level of the sighted is.[7] Factual knowledge about blindness is also important. Even the early educators, such as Haüy, Klein, and Howe knew this and spent much of their time convincing the sceptical public about the abilities of blind individuals. But messages that are factual are more effective than those that only appeal to the emotions.[8] Those who come in contact with blind people are less prejudiced,[9] although the quality of the interaction is even more important.[7] This is logical since a highly educated blind person will influence the sighted more positively than a retarded blind individual. Furthermore, the personality makeup of the sighted must also be considered.

Researchers have studied the attitude of parents,[10] teachers,[11] and other professionals.[12] The attitudes of agencies (the arms of society) toward their visually impaired clients has also received considerable attention in recent years. According to Chevigny, society views the blind as weak and helpless and, therefore, assists them with service systems that make it unnecessary for the blind to have to struggle for their survival.[13] He was especially critical of sheltered workshops which, by removing competition, promote dependency. The fact that blind individuals are dependent makes them inferior to the sighted. Jacobus ten Broek even suggested that agencies tend to support segregation of the blind by the very nature of their services.[14] Scott, whose main thesis was that "blindness is a learned social role," also leveled strong criticism.[15] Scott felt that the "blindness service system," which tends to keep the blind dependent, denies service to those who do not conform to the "picture of the good client." He claimed that, although charity, pity, generosity, and sympathy were helpful to the blind in the past, today they have a negative effect on their rehabilitation. Some of this criticism is indeed deserved. Agencies must change with the times in fulfilling the needs of blind individuals. It is also clear that they are frequently made scapegoats for problems troubling the blind for which they are not responsible. The agencies, the arms of society, are viewed by many in an ambiguous manner. On the one hand, they do not give enough help—on the other, they do too much. Similarly, tax benefits, pensions, and special protective legislation are welcomed by some; others see these as promoting dependency. The fact is, of course, that some blind people can survive in our competitive society on their own, but many cannot without some support. There is a major difference between individuals who lose their sight in later life and those who are born blind or become visually impaired in early life. This difference in relation to attitudes and receiving services from agencies has not been studied adequately. Blind children without additional handicaps have a good chance of being integrated into the sighted world with assistance from the sighted, whereas multihandicapped children, who are now the majority, will need considerable help and "protection."

CHANGING THE ATTITUDES OF SOCIETY

Until recent years, it was firmly believed by educators, laymen, and many blind persons that good training and education of the visually impaired, in addition to informing the public about blindness, would allow the sightless to be integrated. Although this philosophy certainly helped, total integration did not occur. Many blind people, as well as workers for the blind, became disillusioned with the outcome of programs that tried to educate the sighted. In view of this, Lukoff recommends that it is not the "hard-to-reach" public that has to be educated if we want some impact on the integration of the blind, but the blind person's family, friends, and associates.[16] In addition, the blind themselves have to learn through training how to effectively manage negative encounters. Because of the slow change in the forces of integration (not as slow when we see it from a historical point of view), some recommend militancy for the blind in order to achieve legislative changes.[5] Through its systematic lobbying campaigns, the National Federation of the Blind in the United States has been successful in bringing about needed civil rights legislation.

More research should be done into the areas of attitudes and planned legislative changes. The medical and allied health professionals can play an important positive role in changing the attitudes of both the sighted and the blind.

ATTITUDES OF THE BLIND TOWARD THE SIGHTED

Blind persons also have some preconceived ideas about the sighted.[17] This is, of course, not surprising. However, an individual who lost his sight in later life has vastly different attitudes toward the public and his own visual impairment than a congenitally blind person. Unfortunately, studies in this area are lacking. Furthermore, blind leaders who are blinded in later life may not be acceptable as spokesmen for all the visually impaired, especially the congenitally blind.

SEGREGATION VERSUS INTEGRATION IN THE EDUCATION OF THE VISUALLY IMPAIRED

The controversy over segregated or integrated schooling for the severely visually impaired has been troubling educators for many years. This topic will be discussed with historical aspects in mind. Prior to the establishment of the first school for the blind in Paris in 1785, visually impaired students were educated either in schools for the sighted— therefore, in an integrated setting—or privately. As a result, only a few bright or well-to-do children received an education. These blind students were taught together with the sighted because there were no other alternatives. Subsequently, residential schools mushroomed throughout the world and with this the "mass education" of the blind began. As time went on, severely visually impaired children were taught almost exclusively in residential schools but children with partial vision, who were a neglected group, were left with the sighted. Generally, there was little opportunity for blind students to be educated in regular classes, because specialized help was only available for them in schools for the blind. The sceptical public had to be convinced first that the blind could, indeed, be educated and work in our sighted society. Thus, during the early days, teachers and students from the schools for the blind spent much time demonstrating newly learned skills in public. More recently, integrated education of all the handicapped has been increasingly promoted, and this is possible only because of the increasingly available special educational services in regular schools.

The controversy over segregated or integrated education for the blind continues because both systems have advantages and disadvantages. Some educators are convinced that the visually impaired should be taught together with the sighted if they hope to live and compete in sighted society, while others feel this may cause harm. Magleby and Farley in 1968 concluded on the basis of their study that

> at the time of the research interviews more of those who attended residential schools for the blind were better educated, were more interested in social activities outside their homes, voted in the last presidential election, had received vocational counselling or training, owned their own homes, made more use of libraries for the blind, were not receiving financial aid from a public or private agency, were interested in finding employment, and in some respects seemed to have a more positive outlook upon life.[18] (p. 72)

The type of relationship blind children develop with others will influence enormously how they will view themselves and their environment. Those who are educated in a school for the blind are more likely to have blind friends later than those who are educated in regular schools.[19] If they are isolated and rejected by their peers, they are more likely to develop feelings of inferiority. The available research on those exceptional children who have mental retardation,[20] cerebral palsy,[21] deafness,[22] or blindness[23] indicates that they are not accepted as normal by their peers in integrated schools. Visually impaired students cannot be integrated just by placing them with the sighted, because social segregation may even be intensified. Studies have shown that visually impaired children often have a low social status in regular classrooms, an observation that seriously questions the social and personality benefits claimed by those educators advocating integration. Havill's research indicates that in integrated classes the level of academic achievement and the type of supportive service received influence the sociometric status of visually impaired students the most, and not the degree of their visual impairment, the socioeconomic level of their families, grade level, or sex.[23] Academic achievement and the quality of remedial services are related, however. It is quite likely that, in the survey of Magleby and Farley,[18] *if satisfactory supportive services had been available, blind individuals who attended regular schools would have done equally well or even better in life than those who were educated in residential schools.* Clearly, good supportive services must be developed if we are to integrate blind students with the sighted.

The education of visually impaired children in a public school setting can be even more difficult if they have other handicaps, such as cerebral palsy, seizures, and mental retardation. Those who advocate integration often fail to mention the multihandicapped blind, in spite of the fact that they are in the majority. Most public schools cannot handle the multiply impaired, because they cannot afford to have expensive rehabilitative services to the same degree as provided by schools for the blind. Consequently, in many areas, blind students without additional handicaps can afford regular schools, whereas the multihandicapped must stay in residential schools for the blind where specialized rehabilitation services are more accessible.

In reality the educational placement of a visually handicapped child will be determined by several factors, such as the availability of a segregated school or other specialized services, age, severity of visual impairment, intelligence, health and additional disabilities, location of the home, parental and professional attitudes, socioeconomic problems, and so forth. All these factors have to be evaluated and weighed in order to arrange the best possible educational placement for that particular child. Blind children should be taught together with the sighted whenever possible, since in this way they will probably be better prepared for life, but they must achieve academically in relation to their peers and have the use of special services—otherwise, this educational placement is unsatisfactory.

CONCLUSIONS

1. The visually impaired have never been regarded by society as individuals without sight but as a different class of people with definite stereotyped characteristics.
2. Ancient misconceptions about the blind still exist.
3. "Not blindness but the attitude of the seeing to the blind is the hardest burden to bear" (Helen Keller).
4. Research in this field is difficult because attitudes toward blindness are determined not by one or two single factors but by complex interacting variables.
5. The attitudes of agencies toward their visually impaired clients have also received considerable attention in recent years.
6. There are ways to change the unfavorable attitudes of society.
7. The controversy over segregated or integrated education for the blind continues because both systems have advantages and disadvantages.
8. Blind children should be taught together with the sighted whenever possible, since possibly they will be better prepared for life, but they must achieve academically in relation to their peers and have the use of adequate special services.

REFERENCES

1. Twersky J: Blindness in Literature: Examples of Depictions and Attitudes. New York, American Foundation for the Blind, 1955
2. Kirtley DD: The Psychology of Blindness. Chicago, Nelson-Hall, 1975
3. Brown NA: A cross-cultural review of the causes and management of blindness, 1975 (unpublished data)
4. Ching L: Blind welfare in Hong Kong. Speech delivered to the Hong Kong Round Table No 7, September 30, 1975
5. Cohen O: Prejudice and the blind, in Lukoff IF (ed): Attitudes Toward Blind Persons. New York, American Foundation for the Blind, 1972, pp 16-34
6. Gowman AG: The War Blind in American Social Structure. New York, American Foundation for the Blind, 1957
7. Siller J, Chipman A, Ferguson LT, et al: Attitudes of the Nondisabled

Toward the Physically Disabled. Studies in Reaction to Disability No 9. New York, New York University, School of Education, 1967

8. Lowenfeld B: The Changing Status of the Blind. From Separation to Integration. Springfield, Ill, Charles C Thomas, 1975

9. Bateman B: Sighted children's perception of blind children's abilities. Except Child 29:42–46, 1962

10. Sommers VS: The Influence of Parental Attitudes and Social Environment on the Personality Development of the Adolescent Blind. New York, American Foundation for the Blind, 1944

11. Murphy A: Attitudes of educators toward the visually handicapped. Sight Sav Rev 30:157–161, 1960

12. Janicki M: Attitudes of health professionals toward twelve disabilities. Percept Mot Skills 30:77–78, 1970

13. Chevigny H: My Eyes Have a Cold Nose. New Haven, Yale University Press, 1946

14. ten Broek J: Within the grace of God. New Outlook for the Blind 50:328–335, 1956

15. Scott RA: The Making of a Blind Man. New York, Russell Sage Foundation, 1969

16. Lukoff IF: Attitudes toward the blind, in Lukoff IF (ed): Attitudes Toward Blind Persons. New York, American Foundation for the Blind, 1972, pp 1–15

17. Lukoff IF, Whiteman M: The Social Sources of Adjustment to Blindness. New York, American Foundation for the Blind, 1970

18. Magleby FL, Farley OW: Education for blind children. Research Bulletin No 16. New York, American Foundation for the Blind, 1968, pp 69–72

19. Lukoff IF, Whiteman M: Socialization and segregated education. Research Bulletin No 20. New York, American Foundation for the Blind, 1970, pp 91–107

20. Johnson GO, Kirk SA: Are mentally handicapped children segregated in regular grades? Except Child 17:65–68, 1950

21. Soldwedel B, Terill I: Sociometric aspects of physically handicapped and non-handicapped children in the same elementary school. Except Child 23:371–372, 1956

22. Elser RP: The social position of hearing handicapped children in the regular grades. Except Child 25:305–309, 1958

23. Havill SJ: The sociometric status of visually handicapped students in public school classes. Research Bulletin No 20. New York, 1970, pp 57–90

21
Education of Visually Impaired Children

Part I: Objectives in the Education of Visually Impaired Children
by Evelyn J. Chorniak

INTRODUCTION

The subject of education for visually impaired students is comprehensive. Those who are concerned with more details than printed in this book are advised to seek other available texts.[1-3]

Schools and programs for the blind cannot be indifferent to the social conditions of the times. Several developments in the field of education are having an impact on the visually impaired student:

1. Residential schools for the blind have taken on a more contemporary function as an integral part of the total education scheme.
2. There has been a growth in integrated public school programs for visually impaired students.
3. The emphasis on maximum use of residual vision has changed the objectives of school programs for partially sighted children.
4. More attention has been given to special education theory and practice for teacher trainees.
5. Technological advances in aids, tools, and equipment have made learning more efficient for totally blind and partially sighted students.
6. Greater diversity of employment possibilities has been made available for qualified blind applicants.
7. The number of multihandicapped visually impaired students in the school system has been increasing.

Objectives for educating visually impaired children have been stated, revised, and restated over the years as understanding of the educational implications of the impairment became more universal. There is one statement by Lowenfeld, however, that seems to be resilient enough to withstand the tides of change in philosophy and program design:

> Education must aim at giving the blind child a knowledge of the realities around him, the confidence to cope with these realities and the feeling that he is accepted as an individual in his own right.[4] (p. 158)

This statement embraces the educational, psychological, and social aspects of the visually impaired child's development. However, the writing of aims and objectives can be little more than a philosophical exercise if educational authorities, teachers, and curriculum planners fail to develop and implement programs for individual students to grow as whole persons to the fullest extent of their ability.

In the actual school setting, individual functioning levels should be established, needs identified, objectives set, plans devised and implemented, achievement evaluated, and further objectives set in terms of the evaluation.

An overall consideration for visually impaired youngsters is that they have the fullest possible contact with sighted children. Such contact has the dual purpose of helping them to relate well to the sighted world in which they must function, and of enabling the sighted to appreciate blind children as children with limitations and capabilities. This is not to say that conscious efforts should be made to keep blind youngsters away from other blind persons, since this contact also has advantages. Blind children together gain a feeling of camaraderie and equality of competition that is good for their self-concept. It is motivating for them to realize that if others with the same handicap can achieve, so can they.

Educators should have an obligation, stringently met, to have regular contact with adult visually impaired persons. They should not assume that the experiences and the feelings of these older graduates are irrelevant now. Without this continual contact, an "ivory-tower" approach is almost inevitable.

PLANNING THE LEARNING EXPERIENCE

It is not possible to offer strict rules for learning and teaching, especially for children who have never seen. However, there are certain theories that should be practiced when arranging for the learning experience. Basic teaching methods were first identified by Lowenfeld.[4] These methods are pedagogically sound and are discussed here along with other general teaching principles that we feel should be carefully regarded by educators of blind children.

Individual Differences

Lack of vision does not mean that all blind children are similar in their characteristics. They differ from each other in areas such as sex, culture, mental ability, physical growth, and social maturity, and there are added differences peculiar to the visual impairment itself. Other variations might include parental attitudes; cause, onset, and degree of blindness; preschool handling; medical involvement and additional handicaps; and hospitalization away from the family. In discovering the blind child as a complete person, thought should be given to all qualities that contribute to his individuality.

Teaching one blind child does not necessarily equip the teacher for teaching another. There are some general effects of visual impairment, but once these generalities are considered, educators must program for the needs of the individual child and his family.

Physical Encounter

Blind children must meet their environment in a direct way. They must touch and handle objects, models, and materials of every description. Teachers should provide experience-centered programs with provision for direct contact and involvement on the part of the student. Well-planned excursions where all the senses are used are valuable curriculum features. Sensory experiences with a great variety of manipulative materials are essential to perceptual and conceptual development.

Stimulation

Limitations imposed by the lack of vision restrict the variety of experiences that would stimulate a child's thinking and curiosity. Appropriate opportunities provided for learning create the desire in blind children to experience and to abstract information. A child who cannot see finds it easy to become passive and disinterested in his surroundings. Lack of external interests may cause him to turn to self-stimulation and he may acquire habits of rocking, eye poking, or turning his head from side to side. As his curiosity increases, he will be more eager to approach new experiences and exchange ideas with his peers and adults. He will become more effective in methods of gathering information and confident in his own ability to decipher it. This confidence and self-esteem will be influenced by the accumulation of knowledge that he is assimilating through his experiences.

Teachers must become "other-sense" oriented so they can replace visual stimulation with tactile, auditory, gustatory, and olfactory motivation. The teacher as a professional should know where and how to direct the child's interests from common objects to more global ideas and how to present the right amount of stimulation for the particular student under instruction.

Structure

Wholeness is a nebulous quality for a blind child. Unrelated impressions that regularly impinge upon him make structuring of the whole a difficult task.

Teachers are charged with assisting the blind child to put his world together. Thematic approaches where subjects are related to one particular topic are effective techniques. Time should be spent in explaining and showing the relationship of one impression to another. In their early education, blind children relate best to structured programs for at least part of the day.

Reinforcement

Once the blind child is exposed to an experience, he does not have an opportunity to formulate his ideas about it until he is offered more concrete exposure. The sighted child learns the word *stop* in school, then sees it on the stop sign on the way home. The blind child has little or no chance for this incidental reinforcement. Teachers will soon realize that a lesson once taught will not be retained or transferred easily for the blind student. The obvious compensation for this limitation is to present the experience over and over again in a variety of situations, showing how the same thing can appear in different surroundings. The *principle of reinforcement* applies to concept formation as well as to the teaching of skills in every subject.

Independence

Effort should be applied to teaching and allowing these youngsters to function on their own in every way possible.

TEACHER TRAINING

No blind child should be entrusted to an unqualified teacher. Special preparation courses are offered in various places for teachers who work with visually impaired youngsters. Courses can be university based, as separate studies, or they can be given in residential school settings as an integral part of the program. Teacher training courses offered by residential schools for the blind are specific and provide regular practicum over a period of 1 or 2 years. Teachers are usually already qualified to teach sighted students before they are engaged in specific studies at a residential school.

Training should enable educators to identify needs, plan objectives and curriculum, adapt methods and materials, and gain insight into the learning process. Teaching the visually impaired calls for professionalism and a personality suited to establishing compatible relationships with the handicapped. Education of teachers is not confined to course situations but is a continuing process of professional development through practice, literature, workshops, and conferences. Teachers should build a sound philosophical base from the study of educational and psychological theories and keep up to date with current educational tools and trends.

Part II: The Challenge of the Resource Center
by Doris M. Corrigan

In the last 20 years, there has been a marked worldwide increase in the number of visually impaired students enrolling in regular schools. Traditionally, most educators believed that separate schools which employed special methods were essential. Today, most countries have at least begun the integration of children with severe visual impairment (including the totally blind) into the public educational system.

Obviously, the visually impaired pupil must be provided with those materials and services that will enable him to become a fully participating member of his class. Because of the limited demand, many of the materials must be ordered from a national or an overseas supplier. Also, some must be specially prepared locally for particular units of study.

The resource center for the visually impaired exists to provide the above requirements. The challenge lies in finding ways of making such services available, with the greatest possible speed and efficiency, and of developing a quick and reliable method of distribution of materials and equipment.

Different demands will be made upon the resource center according to the method of integration in effect and the geography of the district to be served.

In one case, a residential school for the blind cautiously allows a few selected pupils to join a neighboring school for literature classes. In another, a "Braille resource room" is established in a regular school under the supervision of a specially trained teacher. The blind students, and the partially sighted with special needs, spend part of their day in this room and the rest of it in specific classes on an individual basis. The totally integrated pupil lives at home, attends the local school with his brothers and sisters, and follows the regular curriculum with a few reasonable modifications.

The totally integrated student is the one who must rely most heavily upon the services of the resource center. In addition to materials, certain supportive services and specialized personal assistance will be essential for him from time to time.[5]

The age at which children enter the regular school system varies from country to country and in some cases from district to district. Special schools will still be needed for those children who live in isolated areas and those multihandicapped who are unable to be integrated.[6]

In this chapter, it is proposed first to consider the needs of the integrated student and then to discuss organization of a resource center to meet those needs. The term *blind* refers to a Braille-using student, while *partially sighted* indicates a print user. *Visually impaired* is an inclusive term.

Certain items of equipment will be essential throughout the pupil's school career and beyond; others will be required for only a short time while a particular subject is being studied. An important point to be remembered is that print users can often benefit from the use of tactile equipment, such as a Braille ruler with raised markings. Their needs in this respect should not be overlooked.

READING MATERIALS

Many blind scholars believe that, despite technological advances making the printed word more easily accessible, Braille will continue to be of great importance for years to come (Fig. 21-1). Blind students need to have the bulk of their school texts in Braille, but the provision of some texts, particularly those not in demand by other schools, presents various problems. A professionally produced book may cost ten or twelve times as much as the print copy, and many texts simply are not available, in which case they are often transcribed by hand, often by volunteers. This process is slow, and the student may be kept waiting for his book for some time after his classmates have started using theirs. Transcription into Braille by computer is possible but the cost is very high. At present, the most practical solution for most centers is to appoint paid transcribers, if possible with some flexibility of working hours to accommodate periods of peak demand.*

---

*Usually there is no difficulty with regard to copyright. An undertaking is given that books will be lent—never sold—to the students and that a stated limit, e.g., one dozen copies, will be observed.

Fig. 21-1.   Reading Braille.

Large-print copies of specific books are often difficult to obtain. It is costly to have enlarged copies of regular texts made, some texts do not enlarge well, and often there are long delays before delivery. The problems become greater with books needed for advanced study, so it is likely that a student who has relied upon large print will find difficulty in procuring texts at the university level. Many professionals involved with the education of the visually impaired feel that the pupil who cannot read regular print, even with an aid, should develop skill in the use of Braille or an electronic reading device. They advise that large print be limited to reference material, dictionaries, mathematics, and maps.

Tape recordings, even though they are difficult for many people to use as tools of learning, are much in demand both for school work and for leisure reading.[7] Most pupils prefer cassette recorders to the reel-to-reel type because of their convenience of operation. There is a useful new device that enables a student to speed up or slow down the tape recorder. Constant vigilance is essential to maintain high quality in original production, duplication, and the checking of tapes as they become worn. The contents of books and salient features of charts and diagrams can all be made known by means of the tape recorder. Students need to become versatile in its use.

The supply of books and tape recordings, whether professionally produced or individually prepared, should be large enough to provide material for pleasure reading and the pursuit of special interests in addition to school work.

READING DEVICES

Electronic reading devices are now becoming available. With these, some blind people are able to read from an ordinary printed book as the letters are produced in tactile or audible form (Fig. 22-2). A further development, not yet being offered to the public, is the machine that actually "speaks' the words. These devices hold great promise. Students should be kept supplied with up-to-date information on them and be given the opportunity to become proficient in the use of the one of their choice.

Some partially sighted pupils can benefit from using a closed-circuit television reader (Fig. 23-5). A camera with a zoom lens photographs part of a page of print and projects a magnified image on to the television screen. The pupil moves the book so that the required portion of the page is photographed. He can control the size of the image and with some models can choose to have a black image on a white ground or vice versa. This equipment can be set up on a stand and moved around.

Both print- and Braille-using pupils will need a cassette tape recorder, which will be used for a variety of purposes. It will enable one pupil to "read" a novel; to another it will give welcome relief from the fatigue of holding his head at an awkward angle while studying a text. Notes from the blackboard may be read on to it by a sighted student for his blind friend: a teacher may read questions on to tape for an upcoming test, leaving ample space for the pupil to record his answers. Part of a music score may be recorded to be practiced at home.

It is important for all visually impaired students to become proficient in the use of media connected with the printed word. Both Braille and print users will need to develop good listening habits so that they may benefit from tape recordings and from the services of a sighted reader.[8]

Partially sighted pupils should of course be fitted with suitable aids to vision and have good lighting. An adjustable book rest may be helpful to some (Fig. 23-3).

WRITING EQUIPMENT

Braille writing equipment is obviously of great importance. Two kinds are in general use. One is a machine that produces dots that the operator can feel immediately and so read what he has written.

Fig. 21-2.   Mechanical Braille writer.

In early years, this may be the pupil's only means of writing. Probably it will always be his choice when planning essays or working problems in mathematics. The Perkins Braille writer (Fig. 21-2) is the machine most frequently used today.

As the pupil masters Braille, he will learn to use the slate and stylus, also known as the hand frame and style (Fig. 22-3). This is smaller than the Perkins writer, is much quieter in operation, and is used for note taking.

When the student is intellectually ready and his hands are sufficiently developed, he should start learning to use an ordinary typewriter. This will enable him to hand in assignments for the classroom teacher to mark and will give him a means of personal communication.[7]

Fig. 21-3.   The Cranmer abacus.

MATHEMATICS

As mentioned, the Perkins writer will probably be used quite extensively in the mathematics class. For speeding up procedures in the working out of problems, two other pieces of equipment have become popular.

The first is the Cranmer abacus (Fig. 21-3). This has raised markings and a backing that holds the beads in position. Some students, once having mastered the appropriate procedures, use this abacus very successfully. These students should have one for regular use plus a second, with connecting bracket, to use when their work becomes more complicated.

The second is the "talking calculator" (Fig. 22-5). Many regular schools are now allowing their pupils to use electronic calculators, once the basic mathematical processes have been understood. Just recently, talking calculators, having a similar range of functions to the usual ones, have been introduced. They are complete with earplug and so can be used without disturbing anyone.

Other items, such as graph materials, Braille ruler and protractor, and a special compass, will be needed. All the mathematics aids mentioned could be helpful to all visually impaired students.

Many of the items provided to the regular schools for use in other branches of the curriculum are suitable for the visually impaired students.

Examples are the plastic models of plants and animals used in biology and the landforms used in geography lessons. Many of the tools and implements used by sighted pupils in industrial arts and domestic science classes can be used well by blind pupils.

In addition, a wide variety of special aids is shown in catalogues prepared by suppliers of equipment for the visually impaired. These range from tactile maps to Braille micrometers. Selection can be made according to the needs of a particular student.

In spite of the availability of professionally produced materials, it is often necessary for items to be specially made to demonstrate a particular fact of local geography or a point in an individual lesson. The production of such materials can be very time-consuming. For example, Braille is bulky and therefore several maps, each with a page or two of legend, may be needed to convey selected parts of the information contained on one print copy.

CONSULTANT SERVICES

For any system of integration to be a complete success, it is essential for a fully trained itinerant teacher or consultant to be readily available both to the student and to the staff of the regular school.[5] With the "resource-room" type of integration, this is automatic. When the student integrates as an individual, care must be taken to ensure that the need for regular contact is not overlooked. If it is, there is a very real danger that cumulative pressures may become too great, causing the student to withdraw into himself or even leave the school altogether.

MAKING SERVICES AVAILABLE

Somehow the equipment, materials, and services outlined above must be made available to all who need them. No student will need every piece of equipment described, and several items, such as a specially adapted sewing machine, may be in only occasional demand. All students should know what is available and be given the opportunity to select, with the aid of teachers, the items most likely to help them.

Each pupil must have a certain amount of basic equipment for regular use, plus the assurance that he will be able to obtain other items as required. It follows that each must have access to a facility or resource center in which all items of equipment and all types of material can be examined and tested.

The most suitable organizational plan for making equipment and services readily available will depend upon the geography and population of the area to be served, the method or methods of integration in effect, and the services already existing in that area.

A location that is central in terms of accessibility must be chosen; the building must be of adequate size and suitable for the conduct of a variety of operations from the displaying of equipment to the duplicating of Braille texts.

OPERATIONAL PROCEDURES

Operational procedures have to be defined. For instance, will tape recordings and Braille books be produced at the resource center, or will it function solely as a distributor of these items, with production being limited to tactile aids such as maps? Will items be loaned to students or rented by the regular school authorities? Will some be offered for sale?

Parents will normally expect to provide some equipment, just as they do for their sighted children. However, unless the cost of articles for the blind is heavily subsidized, as it is in Great Britain, prices will be much higher than for equivalent articles for sighted children. Also, since blindness entails extra expenses in everyday life, the parents' resources may soon be overtaxed.

If parents are to supply expendable items, such as paper, or batteries for use in a tape recorder when a power supply is not close, they should be allowed to buy them at cost from the resource center.

Some parents will also supply one of the larger pieces of equipment, such as a typewriter, for use at home. The pupil is quite likely to acquire a cassette recorder or a writer as a gift and quite often a local service club will take an interest in a child and provide a necessary item. Some authorities may make selected aids available through their health scheme. The resource center should be the agent through which goods can be obtained.

Whatever the mechanism for acquiring equipment and materials, the resource center should be the showroom and demonstration center. It should contain samples of all items described in the earlier part of this chapter, plus adequate stocks to meet demands at short notice. A Braille and print catalogue of articles available would be an aid to efficiency of operation.

In order to function with maximum usefulness the center should offer a repair service. The work should be done on the premises as much as possible, subject of course to the restrictions imposed by guarantees.

SUPPORTIVE SERVICES

In addition to tangible resources, the student must have certain supportive services to give him access to reference material, to prepare his examination questions in a suitable medium, to provide appropriate maps and diagrams.

Also, specialized personal help outside the classroom will be essential from time to time. The staff of the regular school may request a psychological test to assist in placement. The student may need to work with a mobility instructor when he changes schools, or he may require vocational counseling. Each of these needs calls for involvement of a specialist with understanding of blindness and its effects. The coordinator of the resource center should be able to call upon these specialists as needed, and to make sure that the student received the necessary services.[5,7]

If the pupil runs into difficulty with school work, he should be able to get help with specific problems through the center, but in general he should expect to work with the class and find all possible solutions there.[9]

In its inception, the services of the resource center are often confined to the school-age population. As it fulfills its obligations to students, an expansion of interest to include all visually impaired persons in its area of responsibility could very well occur. It could eventually develop communication and cooperation with other resource centers throughout the world.

CONCLUSIONS

1. Objectives for visually impaired children must be set for the child as a unique person, while simultaneously embracing the implications of the visual deficit. Individual educational programs must be prescribed, but certain general guidelines can apply to the prescription. These guidelines should include programming for

   - The effect of the visual loss for that child
   - Use of remaining senses in relating to the environment
   - Meaningful experiences
   - Holistic experiences
   - Concept reinforcement
   - Independent activity

2. School programs and teacher training for the visually impaired should keep pace with current educational theories, practices and technology.

3. The function of the resource center is to provide materials, equipment, and services necessary for the visually impaired student to be a fully participating member of his class in the regular school.
4. The challenge lies in making services available with the greatest possible speed and efficiency and in developing a reliable method of distribution of materials and equipment.
5. The organization plan depends upon

- The type of integration—resource room with a full-time specialist teacher or total integration with a visiting consultant
- The assignment of financial responsibility for provision of equipment

6. The resource center should be the showroom and demonstration center. It should also offer a repair service.
7. Braille books, tape recordings, and electronic devices are used for reading. Special equipment is needed for writing, mathematics, and practical subjects. Some must be made by resource personnel.
8. Consultant and supportice services are needed both by the student and by the staff of the regular school. These should cover social, academic, and physical development.

REFERENCES

1. Lowenfeld B (ed): The Visually Handicapped Child in School. New York, John Day, 1973
2. Lowenfeld B, Abel GL, Hatlan PH: Blind Children Learn to Read. Springfield, Ill, Charles C Thomas, 1969
3. Bishop VE: Teaching the Visually Limited Child. Springfield, Ill, Charles C Thomas, 1971
4. Lowenfeld B: Our Blind Children: Growing and Learning With Them, ed 3. Springfield, Ill, Charles C Thomas, 1971
5. Misbach DL, Sweeney J: Education of the Visually Handicapped in California Public Schools. Sacramento, Bureau of Publications, California State Dept of Education, 1970
6. Lowenfeld B: The blind child as an integral part of the family and community. New Outlook for the Blind 59:117-121, 1965
7. Vernon MD (chairman): The Education of the Visually Handicapped. Report of the Committee of Enquiry appointed by the Secretary of State for Education and Science in October 1968. London, Her Majesty's Stationery Office, 1972.
8. Kapela EL: Junior high readiness and the blind child. New Outlook for the Blind 65:12-17, 1971
9. O'Brien R: The integrated resource room for visually impaired children. New Outlook for the Blind 67:363-368, 1973

Evelyn J. Chorniak

22
The Student with Little or No Useful Vision

The specialized techniques and equipment necessary to teach students with little or no useful vision present a particular challenge to educators. Teachers must understand how lack of sight affects learning. Statements such as "Treat the blind child as a normal child" may be misleading. Thinking of blind students first of all as children is an excellent starting point, but if educators stop there and fail to plan for the differences, these children are apt to be educationally deprived.

THE SIGNIFICANCE OF PRESCHOOL DEVELOPMENT

The instructional program for blind children will depend upon their functioning levels at the time of admission to school. The age at which milestones were met, the amount of exposure to different experiences, and how they were handled within the family should all be considered. Most blind children should have a year at nursery school and one in kindergarten before they begin a first-level program in school.

THE PARENTS

Teachers are advised to listen and learn from the parents whose children's education will be their shared responsibility. Establishing a working relationship with parents is important in any child's education, but it is vital for the handicapped. Most parents are fearful and uncertain of the abilities their blind child will evidence in school. Teachers and parents together can establish positive relationships that will strengthen educational programs. Schools that serve blind students must practice an open-door policy with their parents.

MEDICAL INFORMATION

Teachers cannot plan good courses for blind students without knowing the cause and onset of their visual impairment. For example, if sight was lost at 5 years of age or later, the child may have retained some visual imagery, which teachers can use in lessons or explanations. Many disorders are confined to the eye itself, while others are a result of systemic diseases. There are eye conditions that require ongoing treatment and observation. The student's health should always be considered in making plans for his education.

CURRICULUM CONSIDERATIONS

When blind children enter schools, the educational responsibility goes beyond the teaching of regularly outlined subjects. If adequate provision is to be made to serve the children's special needs, educators must know how to translate objectives, adapt programs, and provide experiences for total development.

Adjustments must be made in the presentation of subjects like mathematics, social sciences, and environmental studies, although the content of these subjects is essentially the same as for any other student. In addition to the regular subjects, the curriculum should include some special areas, such as orientation and mobility, concept development, daily living skills, and nonvisual communication.

Orientation and Mobility

Specific mobility skills must be taught to blind children by trained instructors, providing for both indoor and outdoor travel. The classroom teacher should know basic mobility techniques in order to encourage the child to practice them in a variety of situations. Before the cane is taught as a mobility aid, there are certain pre-cane skills that should be introduced and used both at home and at school. These include obstacle detection, mental maps, use of remaining senses, proper posture and gait, and techniques (such as trailing a wall) for safe and natural movement. Cane technique is taught when the student is ready and shows need for a wider range of independent movement. Instruction should be given by a fully qualified teacher who can provide a firm and sequential program with supervised practice. The length of the cane is important and will depend on the stride of the user.

Guide dogs are used by many blind people but school-age children usually do not need this service until they reach college or university.

While aids to independent movement are valuable, the sighted guide is the most reliable and often the most convenient. Blind children should learn how to gracefully accept the right amount of assistance and should know how to request help when necessary.

Concept Development

The blind acquire concepts with more difficulty than the sighted because information is collected in fragments by using the remaining senses. This process is slow and generalizations take longer. "Perception is the knowledge we have of objects or of their movements by direct and immediate contact."[1] (p. 53) Many things may be impossible for blind people to touch, such as bubbles, fire, apartment buildings or other objects too large to envelop with the hands. Another problem occurs because of the child's inability to notice change. Some 6-year-olds may not recognize a raw carrot as they have been exposed only to cooked vegetables. Often their information is incomplete. For example, a little boy who was asked to describe the difference between a bird and a dog said, "A dog has four legs and a mouth. A bird has a beak but it doens't need any legs because it flies around all the time." Since he had never touched a bird, he assumed it was always in flight. Blind children's limited explorations can contribute to delayed or poorly formed concepts. There is also the problem of reinforcement. When a sighted child sees a cow for the first time, that image is reinforced by pictures, television or other incidental means until it becomes a true concept. This, of course, is not so for the blind; they must rely on their teachers to provide them with enough multisensory experiences to enable them to make generalizations.

The blind child's educational program should be filled with realistic and meaningful activities. Concrete material in the form of real objects or good models should be included in every lesson. Field trips, manipulative materials, tactile displays, and audio programs will aid in the formation of good concepts.

Effort should be made to allow the child to use his own descriptions. Asking him to describe things in visual terms leads only to confusion. The congenitally blind child has no conception of colors; however, he likes to talk about them and will often attach emotional meanings to them. A child who thinks of red as blood may associate it with pain and thus dislikes that color. It is advised that teachers should teach their blind students about certain things whose colors usually do not change—for example, elephants are commonly gray and grass is usually green. The blind must use colors in their language to converse with sighted people. When they are curious about them, teachers should do their best to offer good explanations. Later these students should be taught basic color schemes and what colors go well together so that they can choose their clothes and accessories tastefully.

The transfer of knowledge from one experience to another is a basic objective in school. Learned concepts can contribute to the development of new concepts and together they lead to integration and reinforcement of ideas. This process is gradual. Meaningful concept formation for the nonvisual learner does not just happen; there must be appropriate intervention on the part of instructors.

Daily Living Skills

The skills that sighted children acquire spontaneously during their day-to-day functioning must be taught to the blind from their earliest years and should be part of their school curriculum. Step-by-step procedures to follow in dressing, arranging clothes in closets, labeling cans and boxes of food for tactile identification, eating, gesturing, brushing teeth, combing hair, bathing, using acceptable manners, managing money, communicating by telephone, and other numerous daily practices, must be taught in order to make the blind person efficient, comfortable, and independent. There are numerous manuals available to assist instructors in presenting lessons in daily living.

Nonvisual Communication

READING BY BRAILLE

Nonvisual communication skills in the area of the language-arts program alone could compose one major study in itself. Although new devices to enable the blind to read the printed word are constantly being researched, Braille remains the main medium for written communication (Fig. 21-1).

Braille is classified according to the number of contractions it contains. This graded system has no relationship to school grades. Grade One Braille has each word spelled out letter by letter, Grade One and One-Half has a few contracted forms, Grade Two has numerous contractions and Grade Three is highly contracted. Grade Two Braille, known as Standard English Braille Grade Two, is the accepted and most widely used form. It consists of the alphabet, numbers, punctuation, composition signs, and 189 contractions and short-form words. School texts and other publications are printed in Standard English Braille Grade Two. Some university students use Grade Three Braille for rapid notation.

Louis Braille applied what he called "the principle of logical sequence" to the formation of his alphabet. The last letters of the alphabet are formed the same way as the upper-cell letters *a* to *j* with the addition of certain dots in the lower cell. Since Braille was created for the French language, the letter *w* was added later and does not follow the original pattern.

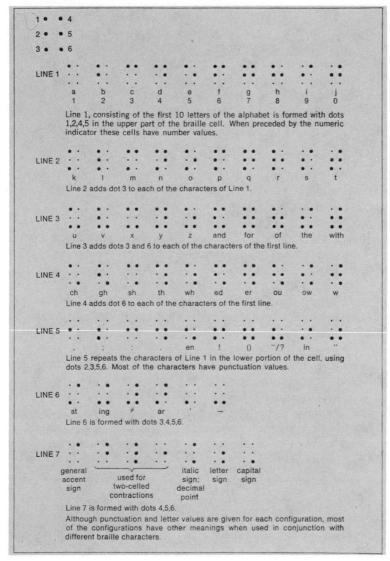

Fig. 22-1. The Braille alphabet. (Courtesy of American Foundation for the Blind. From Understanding Braille. New York, American Foundation for the Blind, 1969.)

The basic Braille characters and their meanings are illustrated in Figure 22-1. The dark dots show the position of the raised character within its six-dot cell.

The difference between teaching Braille to children and to adults is significant. Newly blinded adults must learn a new medium, but their previous reading skills can be applied. School children, on the other hand, must be taught reading skills by means of Braille.

Nearly all the objectives for print readers apply to Braille readers. Reading for information, relaxation, interpretation, viewpoint, and character development is the same for all students despite the medium. Skills of dictionary usage, context clues, fluency, word-recognition strategies, and inferred meanings are the same in Braille as in print.

During the first years of school, it is more important to emphasize the development of all experiences than it is to teach reading. Imaginative and constructive play is excellent preparation for reading. A truck whose wheels are whirled beside the ear is stimulating to a blind boy, and he will enjoy using it this way since he has not seen a real truck in operation. Someone should show him that the truck can drive to a destination and transport something. Then his play with the truck will be realistic, and he will begin to add his own creative ideas.

The teaching of Braille reading can be facilitated by proper methodology. The whole-word method with emphasis on the word's meaning is favored by most teachers. The child attaches Braille forms to concrete items or actions and recognizes the word by its shape. A functional reading vocabulary is soon acquired. This rather rapid acquisition of words is a motivating factor in learning to read. Nolan and Kederis showed that the time necessary to recognize whole words was greater than the time required to recognize characters in words.[2] This evidence suggested that the perceptual unit in Braille word recognition is the individual character rather than the whole word shape. In spite of these findings, teachers continue to prefer the whole-word method as a satisfactory approach to beginning Braille reading. However, it seems sensible to advocate the recognition of characters in Braille as well as whole words.

Children learn to read better if the reading vocabulary is taken from their own experiences. A well-planned phonics program is conducive to achieving independence in Braille reading. In fact, Braille and phonics are compatible, since single Braille characters represent phonetic combinations like "sh" and "ch."

If nonvisual communication were to depend solely on the Braille system, students would suffer substantially in their education. Braille reading is three to four times as slow as print reading. The increased time required creates a problem when the student progresses to higher education, where a greater volume and variety of reading is demanded. Braille reading can be supplemented with recorded materials, i.e., tapes and records.

Although Braille remains the most popular method of reading in

Fig. 22-2.   The Optacon.

school, technology is enabling blind readers to move beyond Braille. The "talking book" has been in use for a number of years. One of the most promising new reading devices is the Optacon—a portable machine that converts print into a form that can be felt with the fingers. A small camera is moved along the print line and letters are reproduced on a tiny screen of vibrating pins over which the reader places his finger (Fig. 22-2). The reading speed is limited because the machine displays only one letter of the word at a time.

BRAILLE WRITING, TYPING, AND HANDWRITING

Braille writing is used so that children can read what they have written. Later, students should acquire typing skills so that others can read what they have written. A skilled typist is more independent in integrated programs where teachers do not use Braille, since assignments and examinations can be typed. The disadvantage, of course, is that the blind student cannot read his own typing.

The use of Grade Two Braille poses particular spelling problems to the writer. A blind student never reads certain words spelled out because of their contracted Braille forms. For example, the word *knowledge* in Braille is just the letter *k*. Teachers must remember to teach the spelled-out version of these words so that students will spell and type correctly. Spelling lessons have a dual presentation—the Braille form and the spelled-out form of the word.

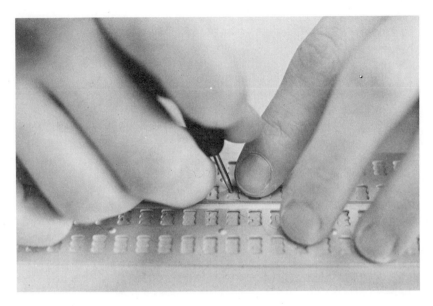

Fig. 22-3.   Slate and stylus.

The mechanics of Braille writing must be taught by specialists. The tools consist of the Braille writer and the slate and stylus (Fig. 22-3). Young students generally begin on the writer and learn the slate later, as it requires more highly developed fine motor control. When the child improves his skills with the tools and Braille system, he can be as independent in his school work as a child who uses pencil and paper.

There has been considerable discussion regarding both the need for blind persons to write with pen or pencil and the methods used for teaching this skill.[3] Hand writing of the letters of the alphabet in print or script is a difficult task for the congenitally blind. The motions of writing are learned by repetition and retention depends on memorizing the movement. Since Braille is more meaningful to the blind, and since typing skills are likely to be achieved for communication with the sighted public, there is no urgency for congenitally blind students to learn to write the entire alphabet in its various forms. They may learn this gradually when they use the Optacon. However, a serious attempt should be made to teach them how to produce their own signatures. Signature writing is essential to independence in later life, when documents and checks have to be signed. Since there is no visual concept of the completed signature, retention of the skill is often poor and constant practice is necessary. Once the student learns to write his name, he should sign each piece of work he produces.

Fig. 22-4. A blind child practicing handwriting.

Teachers will struggle with the dilemma of a foolproof method for teaching signatures. One rather helpful practice is to engrave the student's signature on heavy foil and have him follow the grooves with a pen from beginning to end. There is a variety of special materials available with which teachers can experiment, such as screen pads, raised-line paper, and writing frames (Fig. 22-4).

LISTENING

Listening is more than hearing. Teachers should remember that listening skills are essential for blind children. They must be aware of sounds and be able to interpret and respond appropriately to them. Early environmental conditions may encourage a child to ignore meaningless sounds, and indeed most sounds will be meaningless to him unless he knows their source. Long hours of television, records, or radio may make him a passive listener to voices that apparently are not coming from real people and are not associated with any concrete experience. A child who habitually ignores sound may later tune out his teacher in school.

Selecting one sound from a group is a difficult but necessary skill for the blind, not only to attend to the task, but also to clue in to the surroundings. Selective listening is vital to his mobility as it enables him to locate sounds, use them as references, and take direction from them.

Reading aloud to the blind child should be a daily event. The teacher's presentation of stories and poems is more effective than tapes or records, although these are also valuable. Audiotapes that are made by the teacher for the student's particular needs are especially useful.

SPEECH AND LANGUAGE

The educator is sometimes tricked into thinking that a blind child who verbalizes well knows more than he actually does. Children with a severe visual loss may have had so little exposure to experiences that they have not developed meaningful language. Verbalism, discussed in chapter 10, may become a problem when children have acquired language skills without meanings.

The teacher who is trying to develop the blind child's language should consider the following suggestions:

1. Provide realistic experiences and concrete materials.
2. Avoid long periods of passive listening to records, tapes, and radio. Instead, provide for active listening.
3. Teach students to face you when you are speaking to them and when they are speaking to you.
4. Relate environment by verbal explanation.
5. Blind children "read" you by your voice and imitate your style. Set a good model for them.
6. Provide a relaxed atmosphere for discussion and conversation.
7. Teach how to suit the voice to the situation.
8. Teach facial expressions, gestures, animation, and good lip movement.
9. Emphasize vocal quality and tone as well as clear enunciation.
10. Seek the help of therapists if the student has speech or language problems.

Mathematics

Blind children frequently have difficulty understanding number concepts. One obvious reason is the lack of opportunity to see things in groups, to note sets, and acquire mathematical linguistics by seeing quantity, magnitude, and number symbols. These terms are directly related to how the world is perceived, and the lack of real experiences may make mathematical words too separate from their physical content. They need a longer time in the manipulative stage of number counting, and grouping of concrete items.

There are special devices that are helpful. The abacus is a popular mathematical tool for blind students. The Cranmer abacus is lightweight and facile (Fig. 21-3), but teachers must be specifically trained in its

Fig. 22-5.   Portable talking calculator.

use.[4] The notation can be done in Braille, using a special mathematical and scientific code called the Nemeth code, which is based on the six-dot cell and, therefore, can be written on slate or braillewriter. Portable electronic calculators adapted with Braille or audible output are now also available (Fig. 22-5).[5]

Mental arithmetic is a useful skill for a blind student, and teachers should set aside time each day to practice it. Sometimes it is wise to teach rote processes if, after painstaking effort, the meaning escapes the learner. In other words, holding a blind child in mathematical limbo, because he cannot reason and seemingly cannot understand numbers, may find him doing the same activities year after year—with the same poor results. If this is happening, as it sometimes does with lower-functioning blind youngsters, it would seem better to teach memorization of facts, so that he will have some verbal facility. This sounds contradictory to good pedagogy, and it is, but blind children who are not academically inclined quite often have excellent memories. Experience has shown that understanding may come later; therefore, educators should not deny children verbal facts that can be committed to memory.

Although mathematics is difficult, a few blind people have even gone on to teach this subject in universities.

The Significance of Tactile Learning

Quite often, teachers confine tactile learning to the child's hand. Tactile exploration for a blind child must include the entire body. He must lean, press, lie, and stand against things. He must learn how to apply the pressure of fingers, hands, feet, and his whole body in order to get messages back from objects.

In schools, teachers should be careful to present materials properly for examinations. Models that can be enveloped with both hands at once are more valuable than large models that require piece by piece examination. Teachers must be careful in their verbal explanations to avoid excessive use of their own visual imagery. A happy combination is achieved when the sighted instructors can give the right amount of information to help blind students use all remaining senses to form their own clear and complete ideas. It is beneficial for both visual and tactile learners to examine and discuss concrete items together. The blind child will need more time to make tactile examinations; therefore, the items should be left in the classroom in an accessible place so they can be reexamined and become part of the conceptual memory.

If the object is moving, it is difficult for the blind child to imagine the rapid changes in position. Verbal explanations can help.

The ability to discriminate by touch is a learned skill. The role of the educator in providing a sequence of manipulative materials from simple textures and shapes to more advanced and abstract tactile activities is clearly indicated.

Representation Through Maps and
Raised-Line Diagrams

The blind student should also learn about maps and diagrams.[6] Although the abstraction of these symbolic displays may have little meaning at first to the tactile learner, if this skill is developed from very simple to complex it can be useful. Excellent relief maps are available, but some teachers prefer to make their own maps to serve a specific need. Criteria for a tactile map should include accuracy, simplicity, distinctness, durability, and a size suitable to the span of one or two hands. The amount of description on a tactile map should be limited to the necessary information. If more information is required, it should be shown by a series of maps.

Fig. 22-6.   Thermoform maps.

Outline maps and diagrams can be constructed with string or wool stuck to a plain background. These outlines can be used as master copies, and from them more copies can be made by thermoform procedure (Fig. 22-6). The American Printing House provides a heavy foil on which one can make well-defined raised lines by placing the foil on a soft surface and tracing the outline with a ballpoint pen. Copies can be thermoformed from these maps to accommodate entire classes. Braille labels and legends can easily be applied. Charts and graphs can be tactilely represented by using commercial aids, such as the Sewell raised-line drawing board, embossed paper, Braille writers, and even common dressmaker wheels.

The idea of producing raised pictures for the blind is controversial. There is usually too much detail to allow for sensible tactile interpretation. Pictures that show geometric shapes, such as coins, are easily recognized

Fig. 22-7.   Bowling. This blind teenager also has an artificial arm.

by touch, but the writer questions the value of an embossed picture containing trees, flowers, people, buildings, etc. Educators should avoid trying to make over images that look nice into objects that feel nice.

Physical Education

Many blind children come to school without having had much opportunity for vigorous physical activity. They should have a full program of physical education. The wide range of activities should include swimming, skating, games, relays, wrestling, horseback riding, dancing, calisthenics, gymnastics, and others (Figs. 22-7 to 22-9). Teachers should not be afraid of a few bumps and bruises, which are a small risk for allowing the child freedom of movement.

Sex Education

Sex differences that become gradually apparent to the sighted require special explanation for the blind child. The healthy atmosphere, both at home and school, that allows children to ask questions and have discussions concerning the body is as beneficial to the blind as it is to the sighted. However, in sex education for blind children, the presentations will have to be longer and more explicit, and materials for tactile learning should be provided.

Fig. 22-8.   Tandem bicycling. The first girl has partial sight whereas the second is totally blind.

Fig. 22-9.   Anything with wheels is fun.

Sex education embraces more than reproduction. Family life, values, and citizenship should also be taught. Blind children should be taught correct vocabulary in describing human anatomy and body functioning. Through family-life courses, they will understand their own physical, mental, and social development. The primary student should learn about reproduction by raising animals or hatching chicks in the classroom. The prenatal development may be observed by touching the abdomen of the pregnant animal, or they may be able to tactilely follow advanced stages of a human pregnancy. Father, mother, and child roles are often used in play, which leads to the understanding of different sexes. Boy and girl dolls are also useful. The teacher should be prepared to answer questions precisely.

In adolescence, when sexual curiosity becomes more acute, blind students have greater difficulty, since they cannot obtain information from television, films, a variety of magazines, and seeing others. Their most satisfying method of collecting information is touch, which is not sanctioned socially. However, there are realistic teaching models and Braille texts available to supplement this study.

The Arts

MUSIC

Blind individuals find music a common subject for communication with sighted people. The appreciation of music enriches their lives and benefits them socially. Participating in church choirs, choral or instrumental groups, or providing the sing-along accompaniment are good ways to become socially popular.

The blind student has certain problems in his study of music. The reading of Braille music line by line, then playing what has been read, slows down the learning process. Since playing and reading both require hands, they cannot be accomplished simultaneously. Tape recorders can be used to compensate for some of the difficulties in learning new music and also for evaluating the student's own performance.

The teaching of music has various objectives besides vocal or instrumental performance. Music is a vehicle for teaching almost any other subject. Dancing helps to develop body concept, coordination, listening skills, and creative expression. Music instructors should know about special techniques of teaching and the effects of visual impairment, and they should modify their lessons to the needs of each student.

DRAMA

Drama offers a fine opportunity to understand the complexities of the world. The chance to become someone else, to see another's viewpoint, and to feel and move as characters on stage is of special benefit. Role playing has helped many children come to terms with their own visual impairment and the social pressures imposed upon them by society. Spontaneous play with toys and dress-up clothes should be a part of every blind child's development. During performance, they can learn facial expressions, gestures, and understand how actions and reactions precipitate certain emotions in themselves and others. Besides strengthening the process of communication, drama builds confidence and develops mobility skills. Working behind the scenes helps understanding of how lighting, properties, and staging are involved in an entire production. Creative students will develop their own ideas and write their own scripts or plays.

Teachers must have physical contact with the blind student in order to show him positions and movement. Explanations of scenery and property placements must also be given, and ways to help locate items on stage can be invented.

A school curriculum providing for personal and creative expression should include opportunity for the blind child to participate actively in dramatic presentations on stage, in the classroom, and in free-play situations.

ART

Blind children live in an aesthetic environment very different from that of their sighted peers. Because beauty is thought to be in the eye of the beholder, school programs may pay little attention to the aesthetic growth of their blind students. However, it is recommended that these students be allowed to participate in every phase of the art program. Some media will be more meaningful than others. If teachers practice the theory that the process is more important than the finished product, they will make provision for painting, coloring, and craft work of every kind.

Motor and language development, tool manipulation, and socialization are extra benefits provided by art programs. Box sculpture, clay modeling, ceramics, woodwork, and texture collage are a few appropriate activities. Sculpting is particularly good and can begin with tactile examination of the real item, followed by reproduction and then the child's own imaginative creation. Crafts like sewing, weaving, and knitting are performable tasks for blind students.

Blind students can appreciate the design of the artist and the meaning that is attached as much as the sighted. They may learn to understand the workmanship, the skill of the artist, the portrayed story, or the historical background attached to the artistic piece. Blind youngsters easily relate to Eskimo carvings. The symmetry of the smooth, distinct outlines and the variety of textures make them tactilely attractive. Trips to displays and museums are useful if the exhibited objects can be touched.

CONCLUSIONS

1. Informed parents and counselors can assist school readiness by early intervention in the blind child's development.
2. School entry is more easily accomplished if teachers have good parent contact and thorough knowledge of the cause and onset of blindness, as well as general preschool history.
3. Curriculum planning should include, in addition to the usual subjects with necessary adaptations for the nonvisual learner, areas specifically related to implications of blindness. These areas include such subjects as orientation and mobility, concept formation and development, daily-living techniques, nonvisual communication in reading, writing, speaking and listening, use of aids to tactile learning, and recently developed devices like the Optacon.
4. Special curriculum adjustments should be made in subjects like physical education, sex education, and the arts. However, these subjects should be designed for the student's fullest participation in them.

REFERENCES

1. Piaget J: Psychology of Intelligence. Totowa, New Jersey, Littlefield & Adams, 1966
2. Nolan CY, Kederis CJ: Perceptual Factors in Braille Word Recognition. New York, American Foundation for the Blind, 1969
3. Freund ED: Longhand Writing for the Blind. Philadelphia, Overbrook School for the Blind, 1968
4. Davidow ME: The Abacus Made Easy: A Simplified Manual for Teaching the Cranmer Abacus. Philadelphia, Overbrook School for the Blind, 1966
5. Clark LL (ed): International Catalog. Aids and Appliances for Blind and Visually Impaired Persons. New York, American Foundation for the Blind, 1973
6. Groves PA, Wiedel JW: Tactual mapping: Problems of design and interpretation. International Journal for the Education of the Blind 18:10-16, 1968

23
The Dilemma of the Partially Sighted

THE PARTIALLY SIGHTED SPEAK ABOUT THEIR PROBLEMS

The difficulties that partially sighted children and adolescents experience in everyday life are best described in their own words. The following passages were written by a teenager who has a congenital retinal disorder:

Explaining My Visual Problem

I am called legally blind, although I have plenty of sight. To be legally blind, one has 20/200 vision or less. I have 20/300, which means that I can only see something at 20 feet that others can see at 300. I am also far-sighted.

I can read normal print with magnification. I have a device to help me see the board in school but I cannot use it well because I have to hold it right up against my eye to see through it. To do that, I have to take my glasses off but then my eyes blink too much and my lashes get in my way. Then I have to put my glasses back on to write and it just takes up too much time. I usually get on by listening.

If I use my eyes too much they begin to itch and hurt, and if I strain them too much things start to go blurry. Everything I look at is clear but sometimes my eyes play tricks on me. I may think that I see something else until I touch it. When somebody wants me to look at a picture or something, I have to take it in my own hands.

Neither Blind Nor Fully Sighted

It is very hard when you are not really blind or sighted because you are just hanging in the middle.

Travel

Getting from one place to another is easy as long as I am familiar with my surroundings. When I am not exactly sure where a place is but know what street it is on, I usually ask the bus driver to let me off at that corner. If I know the number of the building, I will ask someone where it is because I cannot read it.

To cross the street, I either copy other people or watch the cars. I was in Grade 9 when I was hit by a car the first time. I started to cross the street when there were no cars or people around and the light had not yet turned green for me to cross. Then a vehicle hit me while turning the corner. Another time, I started crossing the street and when I was about in the middle of the intersection, the light turned red. I had my cane out, but a bus went over my toe and grazed my arm.

Peers

When I was in elementary school, I was a perfect scholar but I had no friends. I was teased at home by my older sisters and I was also teased at school. All this made me shy and it has had a lasting effect on me. Since I have been going to high school I get along better with the other kids but I still have only a few friends. For the most part I think the kids just tolerate me and they leave me alone when there is nothing that forces them to deal with me. The teachers have helped to build up my confidence. I am grateful to them for that and they are my friends, but I want kids of my own age for friends, too. I can't seem to get it that way no matter what I try. I get mad at myself because I act differently than the other kids and don't like it. I want to be just like the others but I am not succeeding very well and they can't seem to understand. Some kids at school bug me just to see how much I can take. I try to ignore them as much as possible, but sometimes they do something I cannot ignore.

I don't want to sound like a goody-goody but I do not see why some people have to take advantage of others who are different in some ways. Why do they make life miserable for others less fortunate? I hope people think there is something good in me.

School

One teacher I had for cooking in Grade 9 was not very helpful so I had to withdraw from her class. I was not able to follow the demonstrations and she did not help me. The kids were also mean to me. I had a sewing class the same year. Here, the teacher

and the kids were all really helpful and I learned a lot. In my
English class when we are given a test, I usually do mine orally.
On another test, I didn't do too well because we were given a
lot of reading and we were not allowed to take the books out of
the room. I forgot to tell the teacher that I would have to take
the books out to be able to get the reading done. Also, he had
written the pages we had to read on the board but I could not
see them. I was tired, too and when I am tired I cannot understand
things as well.

I have only three courses right now. I do some of my homework
in two spare hours at school but if it is too bright I cannot study.
I have to do my math in the music room because the light in the
math room is too bright for me to see the lines on the paper. I
do the rest of my work on the typewriter. I usually take my music
lessons home because I cannot read fast enough with the others
in class. I do most of my homework in the evening when the sun
has gone down. I generally finish by ten o'clock so I go to bed
and get up at six in the morning. Sometimes I have to stay up
till midnight or later and I am very tired. Sometimes I fall asleep
in class because I am so tired.

To solve the problem of taking notes from the board I asked
my friend to make a carbon copy but she is away a lot and nobody
else will do it. They all say that their writing is too messy, so
I have to get by with just listening. It works okay, but I think
I could do better if I could take notes. Also, when the teacher
makes copies of notes I may not be able to read them if they
are faded or pale. If the copy is not dark enough I think that there
is nothing on the paper.

Next year I won't have any spare hours so I will probably be
tired all the time because I will have a lot of homework and will
have to stay up late. I don't mind people helping me, but I want
them to ask me first if I want help. If I need help I will ask for
it. I am going to live my own life.

The following section is part of a letter that was written by a young
and bitter partially sighted woman when she was asked to comment
on the problems of partially sighted children in schools.

As a person with partial vision, I feel I can speak for partially
sighted children. A student with a visual handicap is often ignored
since his teacher may not care, may feel he is just slow or lazy.
When I started Kindergarten, my teacher said I didn't follow
directions and disturbed the whole class. Could I help it if I couldn't
see the blackboard and the pictures above? In Grades 1 and 2,

I was considered to be a slow student. The teacher felt I didn't care and placed me at the back of the room for weeks. In Grade 3 I began to wear glasses. I had a front seat, and what a change from sitting in the back. My grades improved and I became an honour student. In Grade 4, children kept making fun of me because I wasn't good playing basketball as I always missed the ball. But I received ribbons on sports day for running. Once the principal told my parents that I would never make it to Grade 12 with my vision.

In high school, it became harder for me to keep up. I studied for hours and sometimes when my parents were asleep, I returned to my studies until 2:00–3:00 A.M. I became a complete bookworm and no longer went out regularly with my friends. My parents said I changed completely. I didn't attend graduation because I didn't have a boyfriend and the final exams were the following week. I had to do well and I did.

I feel every partially sighted child should be given an extra chance, they are not stupid. Please, don't forget about them!

DEFINITIONS OF PARTIAL SIGHT

Children with partial sight are often misdiagnosed, misunderstood, undereducated, and socially ostracised. They are neither blind nor sighted and frequently have difficulty fitting into society, which does not acknowledge their existence. It is next to impossible to overlook a child who has little or no useful vision, but it is very easy for a partially sighted person to be lost in the crowd. Because he sees some things, it is frequently assumed by parents, physicians and teachers that he sees everything and, therefore, the problems he may have are attributed to inattention, lack of ability, sheer perversity, or poor coordination.

Partial sight cannot be defined satisfactorily by distance-visual-acuity measurements alone, although it is often stated that these individuals' vision in the better eye is in the range of 20/70 to 20/200. There are several problems with the above definition. It is difficult to measure distance visual acuity in young children since their cooperation for testing may be lacking. Furthermore, this group is not homogeneous. The type of ocular disorder and its cause, as well as the degree of distance and near visual acuity, vary from person to person. A child with poor macular (central) vision but satisfactory peripheral fields may not be able to see the blackboard or read signs on the street but can travel, run, skate and even bicycle with ease. These apparent contradictions often make him seem deceptive to the public, who may accuse him of faking. There are a few children with partial sight who have such restricted visual

Fig. 23-1.   A child with tunnel vision may be able to read only one word or part of it at a time. (Courtesy of Dr. B. Huntsman.)

fields ("tunnel" or "gun barrel" vision) that in reading they can only see one word or a part of it at a time (Fig. 23-1). Glasses or various visual aids help some but not others. Some need strong illumination in the classroom while a few such as albinos, are abnormally sensitive to light. A statement of the visual acuity will give little indication of reading ability, as one child may be able to read print while another with the same vision cannot.

In the past, many children with a visual acuity of 20/200 were classified as blind and therefore taught Braille, although they could have been using print. Most agencies and schools that provided services for visually impaired youngsters concentrated their efforts on serving those who had little or no useful vision, in spite of the fact that such children constituted only about 25 percent of the legally blind. During the early part of the twentieth century, so-called sight-saving classes were started for students (mainly those with myopia) whose visual impairments classified them as partially sighted (distance visual acuity between 20/70 to 20/200 in the better eye). The concept of sight saving was based on the incorrect assumption that excessive use or eye strain would further damage the eyes and cause the remaining vision to deteriorate. Thus, many partially sighted students with different types of ocular disorders were taught in special classes. Indeed, vision does occasionally deteriorate in myopic children but for unknown medical reasons. The sight-saving concept was not only incorrect, but it was clearly shown that by using partial sight the visual efficiency can actually improve. The segregation of such students in special classes has been discontinued in most areas, although the misconception about sight saving still lingers on.

The above discussion illustrates the difficulties of defining partial sight by using distance-visual-acuity measurements alone. Since good schooling is crucially important for these children, perhaps the educational definition of low vision is the most satisfactory; namely, "the child whose visual condition is such that it interferes with efficient learning, but who is still able to use print as his chief medium of learning."[1]

PREVALENCE

The prevalence of children with low vision is unknown, not only because satisfactory definitions are lacking, but because many of the children remain undiagnosed. As expected, there are more who could be classified as partially sighted than legally blind.

THE PROBLEMS OF DIAGNOSIS

When an obvious eye defect is discovered after birth, the parents may be told that the child will be blind. The ophthalmologist makes this diagnosis by observing the immature visual functioning of the infant, but the parents may not be able to understand what he is telling them. Blindness to the layman usually means complete lack of sight. As the child grows older, his visual efficiency matures and, if he has partial sight, he gradually notices objects around him; thus the parents may begin to doubt the judgment of the ophthalmologist. Such parents may remain confused for several years because their child is not blind, but neither can he see well.

Visual impairment may not be obvious to the doctor or the parents at birth because the eyes look normal. It is only when the child's development seems slow that his parents first suspect something is wrong and may fear that he is mentally retarded. He does notice some close images, but he is different and they do not know why. His motor development may be slow, he may appear unresponsive because of impaired visual communication, he may be uneasy in strange places and cling to his mother—because if she walks five to ten feet away, he cannot find her. Then the child finally gets to an ophthalmologist, who may not be able to measure the extent of the visual impairment because of insufficient cooperation.

Young congenitally blind children do not as a rule realize that their sight is impaired, because they do not know what normal vision is. When a child has slowly deteriorating vision, parents, relatives, and teachers seldom notice it until there is marked impairment. Visual-screening programs in schools can be successful in discovering students with poor eyesight, but observant teachers could also identify many. A student may be suspected of having visual difficulties if he rubs his eyes frequently, is excessively slow copying from the blackboard, or if, while reading, he holds the book too close to his eyes and frequently changes the distance. Recurrent frontal headaches, squinting, light sensitivity, red eyes, seemingly unexplained stumbling or tripping over objects, the presence of other handicaps, and slow development should all suggest the possibility of visual impairment, and such children should be referred for an ophthalmological examination. Early recognition of visual impairment in the classroom may help prevent academic failure, behavioral problems, the development of inferiority feelings in the student, and much inconvenience to both the parents and teachers.

In conclusion, the identification of children with partial sight is often difficult and an accurate diagnosis of visual impairment may not be made until formal school years.

THE EFFECT OF PARTIAL SIGHT ON DEVELOPMENT

As it was discussed in chapter 9, the degree of remaining vision does influence motor development. Many partially sighted children walk late and hesitantly and their coordination may be impaired. They are frequently unfamiliar with the use of a pencil and do not like to color or draw. They may have little experience in looking at books. Their knowledge and awareness of the environment may be limited. Social development may also be delayed, because they cannot keep up with their peers. When they are enrolled in a preschool they may be considered slow, immature, uncooperative, inattentive and clumsy. Most of these difficulties can be prevented with early intervention.

HELPFUL SUGGESTIONS

It is useful for health professionals to know the following facts about students with low vision.

Seating

Many partially sighted children may not be able to see the blackboard unless they sit close enough. It is not practical for them to walk to the board each time they cannot see, as this is disturbing for the class, takes too long, and on the way back they may forget what they saw.

The teacher should seat them where they can function best, which may be as close as 5 or 6 feet. However, a child with tunnel vision should stay in the back of the class, since his viewing area widens with distance. Students with photophobia (e.g., albinos) should not be close to windows where the illumination is too intense. In contrast, higher illumination may be helpful for some children (e.g., those with macular disease or retinitis pigmentosa). Glare should be avoided by all children with low vision.

Fatigue

Most partially sighted children read more slowly and with greater effort than their sighted peers. They may only be able to see the words by holding the book right up to their faces, which is very fatiguing. If they have glasses, the reading material must be parallel to them. It is not surprising that in this crouching position (Fig. 23-2) they experience neck and back strain. A proper easel or book rest is helpful (Fig. 23-3). If a student assumes a particular head tilt during reading, this position should not be discouraged, since he may have learned that it enables him to see better. They are usually tired at the end of the school day and yet have to do hours of homework to keep up with the class. Teachers and parents must agree on the optimum amount of time a visually impaired student is permitted to spend on his homework.

Writing

For better contrast, a child with low vision should use black pencil or fibre-tipped marker pens, and the teacher should write with large, clear letters with a white chalk on the board. If the student still cannot see the blackboard, he should be given a copy of what the teacher is going to write, so he can copy it correctly.

Sports

Certain sports are not suitable for visually impaired children but physical activity should be encouraged. This is discussed in chapter 25.

Medical Information

A teacher must understand the partially sighted student's visual functioning. Unfortunately, few ophthalmologists take the trouble to phone or write to the school, even though it may have been the teacher who initiated the child's eye examination. Medical reports are often kept from nonmedical professionals, because it is felt "they would not

Fig. 23-2. A partially sighted student frequently experiences neck and back strain in this position.

understand them anyway'' (which may be true due to the medical terminology used). Teachers could turn to the school nurse for medical information, but it would be simpler if the ophthalmologist could speak to them over the phone or send a note.

Notation of Low Vision in School Records

It is important that a child known to have partial sight have a notation on his school record, which is drawn to his teacher's attention at the beginning of each school year. This should point out that the student has visual impairment and requires special management, which is then outlined. Any new suggestions developed during the year should be added. Such a procedure is a tremendous help to the teachers when the child changes classes or is transferred to another school.

LARGE PRINT

Many more students with impaired vision can read print than Braille. Despite a lack of research, it was traditionally believed that large print was easier to read and better for most partially sighted students than standard print. The production and distribution of large-print books was

Fig. 23-3. A proper book rest makes it much easier to read.
Note the narrow reading distance, which is not damaging
to the eyes.

originally handled by a few nonprofit organizations and volunteer groups.
These groups concentrated mainly on the children's market, particularly
elementary- and high-school textbooks. Editions were generally over-
sized, heavy, and cumbersome, the drawings were in black and white
and were uninteresting to children, there was little selection, they were
expensive, and students generally rejected them as "different."

Many students with partial sight make good progress in the regular
classes because they have the help of an interested teacher. Teachers
have been aware for years that most children with partial vision can
read standard print as fast and effectively as large print. It is apparent
that special aids and devices are not as important as the quality of
teaching.

Partially sighted students in elementary grades can usually manage to use the regular textbooks. They obtain the necessary magnification simply by holding the book closer to their eyes. For example, when a child brings a book from a 16-inch distance from his eyes to 8 inches, the size of the print is doubled. Some children are reading effectively at a distance of only 2 or 3 inches from their eyes. Holding the reading matter this close for prolonged periods will not damage the eyes or cause deterioration of eyesight. In fact it will improve visual efficiency.[2] As the child grows older, his accommodation will weaken and thereby this built-in magnification will become less effective. Therefore, low-vision aids may become necessary during the teens.

Sykes' research shows that visually impaired students, under optimum reading conditions and when corrective lenses for near vision have been prescribed, perform as well in standard print as in large print in both comprehension and reading speed.[3,4] While large print was less fatiguing, it offered little advantage insofar as reading distance was concerned and no advantage for those students who used strong corrective lenses for reading. Sykes concluded that, although the vast majority of visually impaired students should read standard print, large print may have value for some. Graham felt that, "In most cases the large print is a crutch and an excuse rather than an aid."[5]

LOW-VISION SERVICES

In 1953, the New York Association for the Blind started a research study to determine how low vision aids could be prescribed and used by a selected number of cases. From this came the study by Fonda[6]. . . . The need for aids was established immediately and the Lighthouse Low Vision Service was set up.[7] (p.241)

Twenty years later, there were at least 114 facilities providing low-vision aid in the United States alone. Fifty-four percent were located in medical settings, 18 percent were associated with agencies for the blind, and 11 percent with colleges of optometry.[8]

Low-vision clinics should not only offer a visual aid but a complex interaction of different services, depending upon individual need.[7] Most clinicians in low-vision clinics emphasize the need for a multidisciplinary approach and good follow-up services.[7,9,10] It is suggested that the best location for a low-vision clinic that uses the multidisciplinary approach to rehabilitation is within an agency serving the blind.[7] In the academic setting, the primary goal is teaching students, and the clinic tends to be a small part of the ophthalmology department with limited service and poor access to rehabilitation services.[7] Private practitioners usually have limited time, equipment, and services to offer.

There are many types of low-vision aids; some can be obtained

Fig. 23-4.   A telescope.

for a few dollars while others are very expensive. Clark's International Catalog[11] offers a complete listing, which the interested reader should consult. Those who work with low vision could use two major reference books.[6,12]

There are basically three types of aids:

1. *Nonoptical,* which includes large-print material and such miscellaneous items as reading stands, lamps, visors, side shields, and reading and writing guides.
2. *Optical,* which are lens systems, such as spectacles, contact lenses, telescopes, handheld magnifiers, stand magnifiers, and clip-on lenses (Fig. 23-4).
3. *Electronic,* such as illuminated and projection magnifiers and closed-circuit television (Fig. 23-5).

Fig. 23–5.   Closed-circuit television.

It is not advisable to offer an aid to a child without proper follow-up. The observations of other people, such as his parents, teachers, and even his friends, are valuable for making satisfactory adjustments in the use of that aid. This is why low-vision clinics are successful when the low-vision nurse is able to make repeated visits to schools, homes, or other areas.[5]

A child using a low-vision aid in a classroom does not have all his problems solved. The stronger the lens and the higher the magnification, the more critical it becomes for him to hold the lens at a fixed distance from the material in order to be able to see it clearly. Also the lens may have to be removed when his gaze is shifted from the printed material to a nearby object on the desk. The higher the magnification, the smaller the area seen and the fewer the number of letters that can be included in one eye span. Consequently, the reading speed may be painfully slow. The teacher must be patient, understanding, and give encouragement for the child's every success.

CONCLUSIONS

1. Children with partial sight are often misdiagnosed, misunderstood, undereducated and socially ostracized.
2. Partial sight can not be defined satisfactorily by distance-visual-acuity measurements alone.

3. The prevalence of children with low vision is unknown.
4. Early diagnosis of visual impairment may be difficult in children with low vision.
5. Partially sighted students can be helped in various ways to function in their class.
6. For most persons with partial sight the value of large print is limited.
7. Low-vision clinics should offer more than just a visual aid.

REFERENCES

1. Bishop VE: Teaching the Visually Limited Child. Springfield, Ill, Charles C Thomas, 1971, p 7
2. Barraga N: Increased Visual Behavior in Low Vision Children. Research Series No 13. New York, American Foundation for the Blind, 1964.
3. Sykes KC: Print reading for visually handicapped children. Education of the Visually Handicapped 4:71–75, 1972
4. Sykes KC: A comparison of the effectiveness of standard print and large print in facilitating the reading skills of visually impaired students. Education of the Visually Handicapped 3:97–105, 1971
5. Graham JE: The low vision clinic at the Hospital for Sick Children, Toronto. First National Multidisciplinary Conference on Blind Children, Vancouver, Canada, 1974, p 89
6. Fonda G: Report of 500 patients examined for low vision. Arch Ophthalmol 56:171–175, 1956
7. Faye EE, Hood CM: Low vision services in an agency: Structure and philosophy. New Outlook for the Blind 69:241–248, 1975
8. Low vision services in the United States. Sight Sav Rev 43:223–226, 1973–4
9. Jose RT, Cummings J, McAdams L: The model low vision clinical service: An interdisciplinary vision rehabilitation program. New Outlook for the Blind 69:249–254, 1975
10. Carter KD, Carter CA: Itinerant low vision services. New Outlook for the Blind 69:255–260, 1975
11. Clark LL (ed): International Catalog. Aids and Appliances for Blind and Visually Impaired Persons. New York, American Foundation for the Blind, 1973
12. Faye EE: The Low Vision Patient. Clinical Experience with Adults and Children. New York, Grune & Stratton, 1970

J. M. McInnes
and J. A. Treffry

24
The Deaf-Blind Child

The deaf-blind child has at once one of the most frightening, most glamorous, and least understood of the handicaps. Without the intervention of knowledgeable professionals, the deaf-blind child seems destined to fall into one of two categories. On the one hand, we have the aura of Helen Keller, based on all of the wonderful accomplishments of this gifted individual and her dedicated teacher and companion, Anne Sullivan, and the sense of awe that they have created in the population at large. On the other hand, we have the general diagnosis that automatically relegates the deaf-blind child to the profoundly retarded category with those who are unable to learn.

IDENTIFICATION

In reality, most deaf-blind children do not fall into either of these categories when adequate intervention is available. Intervention must be based on the understanding that the deaf-blind child is not a deaf child who cannot see, a blind child who cannot hear, nor a retarded child with visual and auditory problems. He is a child with a multiplicity of problems. It may be of use to the medical profession to identify major handicaps and, in fact, to list the handicaps in descending order of importance. However useful this information is in terms of medical treatment, it can be misleading—even damaging—in terms of programming for the deaf-blind child. If the deaf-blind child must be identified as having a major handicap, then that major handicap should be identified as *multi-sensory deprivation* (MSD).

The implications of MSD are much broader and much more profound than that of a major handicap with additional complications. Edward

J. Waterhouse, chairman of the Deaf-Blind Committee of the International Council of Educators of Blind Youth and cochairman of the Deaf-Blind Committee of the World Council for the Welfare of the Blind, explains that

> the group of people who can best be served by considering them as "the deaf-blind" is not easy to define. Yet they have special characteristics more specific than people who are deaf or blind but with other additional handicaps. . . .
>
> Consequently, those we think of as deaf-blind are not only those who are completely devoid of sight and hearing, like Helen Keller for example, but also the blind with partial hearing, the deaf with a visual defect, and even partially seeing-partially hearing children and adults.[1]

The National Committee on the Education of the Deaf-Blind have identified the deaf-blind child as

> one who has both auditory and visual handicaps, the combination of which causes such severe educational problems that he cannot be adequately accommodated in educational programs for either the hearing or visually handicapped.[2]

After careful consideration of the problems presented by the deaf-blind child, we propose the following definition:

> The deaf-blind child is one whose combination of visual and auditory impairment results in multi-sensory deprivation, which renders inadequate the traditional approaches to child rearing used to alleviate the handicaps of blindness, deafness or retardation.

RUBELLA

The terms *deaf-blind* and *rubella syndrome* are often used interchangeably. While it is true that rubella virus accounts for many of the children identified as deaf-blind, it is by no means the only cause of multisensory deprivation (Fig. 24-1). Other causes are prematurity, infections, and a wide variety of syndromes and diseases.

> Congenital rubella may result in disease of almost any organ, but a particular triad of anatomic abnormalities is characteristic—cataracts, deafness and congenital heart disease.[3] (p. 3)

Chess et al. have made a study of the problems of the rubella-syndrome child. They have found that when

> external circumstances and environmental handling are inappropriate for a particular child, stress may develop. The child's inherent

Fig. 24-1.   A child with congenital rubella syndrome.

functioning as a result of this stress may be diagnosed as "reactive behaviour disorder." The term "reactive" implies that with a beneficial change in the circumstances producing the disorder there will be a corresponding improvement in the child's behaviour.[4]

It is strongly recommended that anyone working in the field of multisensory deprivation should make himself thoroughly familiar with the studies of Chess, Korn, and Fernandez as presented in their book, *Psychiatric Disorders of Children with Congenital Rubella.* The identification of the characteristics of the difficult-child syndrome, as well as the observations on the problems of the rubella child in general, are valuable to anyone dealing with such children. The implications of the above findings and their application to programming for the MSD child will be discussed in more detail when we look at programming. Chess and other researchers in the field have found that the MSD child has problems in the areas of sleeping, eating, feeding, dressing, elimination, mood, discipline, motor activity, habit and rituals, speech, social relations, and learning.

THE MSD INFANT

The MSD infant with a combination of auditory, visual, and other problems, presents many difficulties and frustrations for parents. Medical problems often necessitate prolonged confinement in hospital. These periods in themselves may cause a disruption of some normal developmental sequences. Lack of professionals knowledgeable in the areas of MSD further complicate these problems. In addition to the physical impairments with which these parents must learn to cope, they are often misinformed that their child is also profoundly retarded.

Some Characteristics of the MSD Child

Parents of the MSD child are faced with a possibly mislabeled child who may evidence unusual sleep patterns; feeding, chewing and swallowing difficulties; adverse reactions to clothing (either because of hyperactivity or a low threshold to tactile stimulation); irregularity and delay in toilet training; lack of ability to communicate leading to frustration and resulting in discipline problems; as well as lags in social, emotional, and cognitive development. A low-functioning MSD child may be prone to head banging and other forms of self-stimulation, such as poking the eyes, waving the fingers before the eyes, rocking, or staring at lights.

The MSD infant often exhibits physical, developmental, and social handicaps, the combination of which seems to bring all interaction with his environment to a halt. Thus, for the parent, the MSD infant is often nonsatisfying. He has been effectively deprived of many of the basic extrinsic motivational forces necessary for normal development. The lack of visual and auditory input deprives the infant of the ability to anticipate events from environmental cues. Van Dijk explains that the child does not direct himself to the world. He "does not anticipate, is not prepared to respond, and . . . is unable to integrate fragments of experience into a whole"[5] (p. 17). The inability to anticipate changes before they occur makes each experience of outside intervention new and frightening. Mother's entry into the room does not signify comfort, food, or cuddling. To be picked up—snatched away from the solid physical support; to be fed—without mother's reassuring smile and comforting voice; to have diapers changed—suddenly pulled, hoisted, and rolled about; all become terrifying, stress-producing experiences. The lack of ability to perceive and thus accurately anticipate the results of actions often interferes with or prevents the child from developing acceptable behavior patterns.

Curiosity is another essential motivational factor. Curiosity about the infant's surroundings is necessary for motivating the movement that leads to normal motor development. The blind child's parents are encouraged to motivate him by sound, the deaf child's parents by visual stimuli. The MSD child is deprived of extrinsic stimulation that appeals to his curiosity. His whole world exists within the area of his random reach, but primarily within himself. The child who is functionally blind and deaf at birth, regardless of the cause of the MSD, becomes an in-turned, egocentric human being, having little or no meaningful contact with his environment. While curiosity is not a classic extrinsic motivational force, the environment which normally excites it in a developing child is such a force. Lack of an accurate perception of the environment may lead to a developmental lag in the growth of the child's curiosity. As the child grows older, this lack can inhibit his cognitive development. There can be no substitute for a program that stimulates a child and rewards him for exploratory efforts.

Acceptance, love, and affection are further extrinsic motivating factors that are often denied the MSD child. Due to his physical problems, tactile oversensitivity, and reaction to parental tension, the child is often unable to form an emotional bond with his parents. The absence of other effective extrinsic motivational forces makes the establishment of such a bond essential if successful intervention is to take place. Parental tensions often stand in the way of the formation of this bond. The parents are fearful about doing the right thing and overwhelmed by thoughts of the future facing them and their child. They receive little or no immediate return for their emotional investment. They, as well as their child, need all of the resources of the community to provide both immediate and long-range support. To offer anything less is to offer nothing.

Chambers states that

> the well-known triad of cataracts, sensory-neural hearing loss and congenital heart disease has now been supplemented by innumerable other abnormalities that statistically have been recorded as more and more of these children are seen with our present knowledge.[6] (p. 3)

Practically every system in the body has been reported involved at some time or other. In fact, the entire developmental process of the infant may have been affected. The damage of the vision and hearing of the MSD child may be apparent at birth or within the first few months. In many cases, the hearing loss may be unsuspected until a much later age. This is often the case if, for example, the child is labeled retarded.

INTERVENTION

Basis

At one time it was stated that the approach to be taken with a child who had a visual and hearing loss was to compensate by using his remaining senses. However, Chambers noted that "there is truly no such thing as a pure deaf-blind child"[6] (p. 7). As we have previously noted, recent research has disclosed that it is probable some damage has also occurred in the remaining sensory-input systems. The "compensation" approach is no longer considered adequate to meet the needs of the MSD child.

These children must be taught to tolerate, recognize, receive, discriminate, and integrate sensory input. Without an adequate program of planned intervention, they exhibit many of the developmental characteristics associated with the diagnosis of profoundly retarded. We say "many" because some astute observers who work with these children in institutional settings find disquieting incongruities in their developmental patterns. Some may exhibit the ability to feed and dress themselves and may make continued attempts at communication or exploring their surroundings. There is no doubt that these children, particularly in their early formative years, need massive doses of planned intervention if they are to develop to their full potential.

A philosophical truism is that what we perceive to be true is true for us. When we consider the double handicap of visual and auditory impairment, as well as the probable impairment of other sensory input channels, we can understand that the perception of reality by the MSD child is such that without intervention he will be denied much of the essential information necessary for growth and development, or he will perceive this information in such a distorted form that he will not be able to integrate it into a meaningful whole. Because he is unable to discern the look of displeasure on his parent's face, or hear the tone of reprimand in his parent's voice, he will continue to perform actions that the normal child would quickly realize are unacceptable. Many of us, at one time or another, have been in a position of trying to view a particular program on television when the reception of picture and sound were completely inadequate. Regardless of how badly we wanted to watch the program, if the reception was sufficiently poor, we eventually turned from the set in disgust and occupied ourselves in other ways. The MSD child's contact with the world is often so distorted that he, in self-defense, turns inward to occupy himself and functionally shuts off those disturbing, annoying, and frustrating sensory impulses, which cannot be integrated to give a meaningful picture of the world around him.

The Objective of Intervention

Intervention must be aimed at aiding the child to integrate and interpret sensory input. Some developmental theorists point out that much of the essential groundwork for a child's language development and cognitive functioning has been laid before a child is 2 years of age. In the field of the deaf, it has been long established that intervention must take place at an early age. Special programming and special help must commence long before the deaf child has reached the age of school entry. For the MSD child, it is even more vital that intervention be introduced at a very early age. The parents need specialized training and support almost from the moment of the child's birth. There is no magic age or golden rule by which we may be guided as to when or in what amounts this support should be given. Each child and family must be offered the support at the time, at the level, and for the duration that is indicated by their particular problem and their own resources.

For the parents of the severely multi-sensory deprived child, this support will have to come from all areas of the community. Medical, social, educational, and for some, religious expertise will have to be brought to bear on the problem, from the moment of birth or the identification of the problem (which in some cases, such as rubella, may be before birth). For example, in the case of a child with Usher's syndrome, it is too late if one waits until the degeneration has reached the point where he no longer is able to function as a visual child. Much of the damage caused by the trauma of the vision loss will have already occurred. Parents' anxieties and concerns for the future will have built to a breaking point. The child himself will have suffered almost irreparable emotional damage. In all cases of MSD, regardless of cause, a simple medical explanation of the cause and extent of the deprivation is not sufficient—rather, a broad range of continuing support is necessary. The patient and the family must have access to community resources in the form of knowledgeable professionals. It will be impossible to completely alleviate all the fears and apprehensions that the parents, the family, and the child will have. The fact of MSD will be hard enough for the parents to accept. This acceptance is made more difficult because it is often overlaid with feelings of guilt, frustration, remorse, and even self-pity. Some parents will seek miracles, either religious or medical, and the support must be there to aid them through the difficult times if the miraculous interventions fail to live up to expectations. Parents will hear what they want to hear and believe what they want to believe. In spite of the best and most careful medical explanations, an otherwise intelligent and logical parent may cling to the hope that an operation for cataracts somehow will miraculously cure a hearing, neurological, or other physical disability. They feel if this one operation could take place, all the child's problems will be solved.

One of best nonmedical sources of support that can be found for some parents is parents of other MSD children. There is no way that any professional can "walk a mile in their shoes." Other parents do have empathy and understanding of the problems. They are often able to offer the kind of support that is not available from professionals. The feeling that "I am not alone, there are positive things which can be done, and there is some hope for my child at some future time," will help. There are times when, without this kind of support and reassurance, no professional—no matter how dedicated and knowledgeable—can offer help. In Canada, the family doctor can turn to The Canadian Deaf-Blind and Rubella Association, c/o The W. Ross Macdonald School, Brantford, Ontario N3T 3J9, or to the local field office of the Canadian National Institute for the Blind to obtain the names of suitable parental contacts in their area.

In summary, it is impossible to adequately deal with all of the physical, social, and psychological problems of MSD as simply a medical problem requiring long- or short-term treatment. The problem is a completely engulfing one, which saps the physical, intellectual, and emotional resources of the entire family unless adequate support is received. The problem is one of expectation, of crushed hopes, and of the quality of life itself.

Professional Intervention

Parrin points out that parental support in counseling is a crucial and ongoing concern. Professionals must be aware of crisis periods for the parents of the handicapped child:

1) When the handicap is first suspected or apparent;
2) When the child is ready to go to school;
3) When a child reaches adolescence;
4) When the young handicapped adult finishes school; and
5) When the parents are no longer able to take care of the handicapped offspring.

In general there are three stages of parental adjustment and the paediatrician and social worker must recognize which stage a parent is in and support the parents in their progress to Stage III. Stage I denial: that of shock and disorganization; Stage II beginning adjustment: chronic sorrow and resulting overprotection or rejection of the handicapped child; Stage III integration: mature and realistic functioning with the child assigned a place in the family and the mothering and fathering distributed appropriately to the normal and the handicapped child.[7]

The MSD child will be identified by the doctor, the parents, or, in rare cases, by educational authorities operating programs for the blind, deaf, or retarded. It has been our experience—based on a study of the case histories of the children in the Deaf-Blind Program at The W. Ross Macdonald School and of those children evaluated by our staff—that in many cases once the initial handicap of blindness, deafness, or retardation was identified and immediate treatment for this one area initiated, little further evaluation took place. Often a significant period of time—measured in years—elapsed before further handicaps were identified. A second group identified by our study are those children who were diagnosed as having a major handicap (e.g., blindness) with an additional handicap. This approach led to the medical treatment of the major handicap but failed to uncover and treat the problems of sensory integration, which are so common in MSD children.

During routine checkups, the physician may identify major handicaps, such as blindness or deafness. However, the parents will often begin to realize that blindness or deafness is not the sole problem. Even in this case, many difficulties may arise if parents assume that the blind or deaf child normally behaves as their child does. When the parents and the physicians, working toegher, have any reason (no matter how slight) to suspect that MSD exists, steps should be taken immediately to refer the child to a competent center for complete diagnosis and evaluation. At the same time, the child's program should be modified. There should be no thought of waiting to see if he will grow out of it. Where the mother has been exposed to rubella during her pregnancy, the physician should routinely make arrangements for a full diagnosis and evaluation by a team of specialists.

The unfortunate truth is that at this critical stage it is all too easy to set up a self-fulfilling prophecy. If you treat the MSD child as blind, he will probably become a functionally retarded blind child with gradually developing severe behavior disorders. If he is treated as deaf with a visual impairment, he will probably become a functionally retarded deaf child with gradually developing severe behavior problems. It is not the severity of the impairment of blindness and deafness alone that causes a child to be multisensory deprived. It is in fact the combination of damage to various sensory-input channels, which leads to difficulty with integrating environmental information into a meaningful whole.

To repeat, in all probability the combination of the parents and the doctor will be the first to identify the possibility of MSD. Secondly, once this possibility is suspected, the child should immediately be referred to an expert team for a full diagnosis and evaluation. Thirdly, the child's program should be modified immediately to provide adequate intervention. This change in programming should not wait until all reports are completed.

The Evaluation Team

The initial in-depth evaluation of the MSD child should take place by an interdisciplinary team of specialists, including an ophthalmologist, paediatrician, geneticist, neurologist, audiologist, ear specialist, and clinical psychologist. This interdisciplinary team must be headed by a specialist from one of the above fields capable of pulling together all the reports from the different team members and placing them in perspective to give an overall picture of the child. Care must be taken that the parents do not feel they are being bounced from one specialist to another but rather see this as a total team approach, providing necessary medical and psychological background about their child. The people working on this team must not only have knowledge of the medical implications of the various degrees of handicap that lie within their specialties, but also of the interrelatedness of the various handicaps. When the diagnosis has been completed, the team should meet with the parents and explain their findings fully and carefully.

The Program Team

At this point, the parents should be introduced to a new team who will assume the ongoing responsibility of aiding and advising them in providing an adequate level of intervention for their child. The family doctor, social worker, specially trained teacher, physiotherapist, and where possible a representative of the diagnostic team, together with the parents, should form this ongoing programming and evaluation team. This team will be responsible for the planning, programming, and periodic evaluations of the intervention for the child. Where possible, the interdisciplinary team should be based in an evaluation and treatment center to which the parent can bring the child periodically.

PROBLEMS CONNECTED WITH DIAGNOSIS AND EVALUATION

Labeling

Even under ideal conditions, where the parent and the child would stay at the center for three or more days for evaluation, there are still many problems that will have to be overcome. The first and biggest is probably *labeling*. Unfortunately, there is nothing so final, so frightening and so discouraging as a label. The words *blind, deaf,* and *retarded* have an emotional and social impact that far outreaches any medical usefulness. The most final and most dread label of all for every parent is that of *deaf-blind*. A child with a degree of MSD can be helped to overcome his handicap. A child who is deaf-blind is deaf-blind. As one parent said, *"When I heard the words deaf-blind I heard nothing else. Although I know I was in the office for two hours and the doctor tried to explain to me as best he could, I heard Nothing!"*

Functionalism

In addition to the impact of labeling, there are other problems that present themselves. The ophthalmologist will have a great deal of difficulty measuring the child's ability to see when the child has no speech and is functionally deaf. The audiologist will have the same problem with the child who has no speech and is functionally blind. In fact, the whole problem of functionalism is one for which there is no quick and apparent answer.

Many MSD children by the age of 2 have effectively shut out the world. They are functionally deaf, blind, and retarded. While medical authorities may assure us that there are very few, if any, totally deaf-blind children, there are many children who function in this manner until appropriate intervention has taken place.

Myklebust[8] hypothesizes that the inconsistent responses of so-called aphasic children may be due to fluctuations in attention, not to differences in sensitivity to auditory stimuli of different frequencies. The fact that the child is not functioning attentively at all times is not peculiar to the deaf alone. Such observations may also be found from time to time in literature on blindness. Functionalism has many dimensions. The child may be functioning as a totally deaf, totally blind or totally deaf-blind child for one of several reasons. His level of functioning may fluctuate according to his ability to handle environmental stimuli, his feeling of security, or his general physical well being. Because of this problem, any evaluation by any individual or team of professionals must be conducted over a period of time and in several settings if valid, useful results are to be obtained. For many MSD children the smell of a doctor's office, hospital, or clinic is enough to completely disorient them. The parent (or parental substitute) can provide the professional with many useful clues as to the child's ability to function, auditorily and visually, in varying environments.

In attempting to assess a child on a developmental scale, the clinical psychologist must remember that many of the items on the scale are based on common action, such as matching objects and stacking cubes, which are performed by normal children at certain stages in their development. These actions are really overt examples of certain stages of physical or cognitive development. The MSD child may be functionally retarded in his development due to lack of motivation and inappropriate or insufficient intervention rather than because he is retarded in the general sense. Evaluations of this type done over an extended period of time are excellent in providing the programmer with a point at which to begin intervention, but in no way should they be looked upon as useful predictors of future accomplishment.

Another problem is that of environmental behavior. All of us behave in ways we deem appropriate to the particular time and place. For the MSD child, certain cues of touch, taste, and smell may trigger specific reactions. In the absence of these environmental cues, such reactions may not take place. Thus, we have found it necessary to view the child in his home setting as part of the evaluation process. Often he will behave at a much higher developmental level in a familiar environment than during a formal evaluation.

After the initial diagnosis, the ophthalmologist, audiologist, and psychologist should work with the program team and especially with the parent, who is a member of the team. For example, in one case the ophthalmologist, after consultation with the parents about the child's behavior at home, attempted to have him locate various small items that were dropped on the floor or placed on the desk. He did not react. Before the next evaluation was scheduled the parents and the preschool worker designed a program that developed a communication cue and introduced it to the child as "the game" of picking up objects. At the next evaluation session, when the ophthalmologist dropped a dime on the floor, the child was touched on the right elbow, and he immediately retrieved the object. This type of cooperative approach to evaluation is necessary if valid results are to be achieved.

In every case where evaluation requires a response from the child, certain key questions must be asked and answered by the evaluator:

1. "Have I communicated with the child?"
2. "Has the child understood me?"
3. "Is he motivated to respond?"
4. "Does he have a response within his repertoire that I anticipate?"

If there is any answer but an unequivocal yes to any of the above questions, then the results of the evaluation must be suspect.

We have found that an indication of curiosity combined with an attempt to communicate are the best indicators of the need for a long-term program of intervention and evaluation. Curiosity may be expressed in many ways—feeling, touching, licking, smelling, or any attempt to investigate or respond to sensory input from the environment. Communication encompasses any attempt to communicate by touch, body motion, muscular tenseness or trying to manage sensory overload with squinting, placing the hands over the eyes or ears, and other responses. Any combination of the above should be viewed as sufficient reason for initial intervention, designed with the objective of preparing the child for a more complete evaluation as his level of functioning improves.

Developmental Lag

Just as medical treatment will be an ongoing process, so must be the evaluation of the child's developmental status. Even though the developmental lag caused by MSD may never be completely overcome, the gap may be narrowed and the child can become a useful, contributing member of society.

There is no such thing as the "average" deaf-blind child. It is impossible for the medical team or the programming team to develop a single program or set of criteria that will suit the needs of such handicapped children. The onset of the impairment may vary:

1. A visual and hearing loss may have been present since birth.
2. The child may have been congenitally deaf first only to lose his vision later.
3. The child may be congenitally blind and will lose his hearing later.
4. Both impairments may be acquired, either simultaneously or independently of each other.

In addition to the differences of onset there will also be varying degrees of the impairments. One or both may remain partial or be progressive. The time of onset, degree of severity, and stability all combine with numerous other medical and sociological problems to make programming for the deaf-blind child a highly individualized exercise. The challenge to the programmer is to provide adequate intervention thoughout the child's waking hours, which will enable him to identify, interpret, and integrate the sensory input he receives. Both the deaf and the blind child have one alternative *distance sense,* which they may use as a baseline from which to verify the input of the damaged sensory channel. The MSD child has no such distance-sense baseline. It would appear that the integration of this partially distorted sensory input becomes an almost impossible task unless adequate intervention to aid in control and interpretation of environmental stimuli is present. The level of intervention will be determined by the child's ability to integrate sensory input and relate it to past experience.

PROGRAMMING FOR THE MSD CHILD

In practical terms, the problem for the programmer is to develop

1. Communication
2. The use of any existing residual vision and hearing
3. Stable social and emotional growth based on a positive self-image

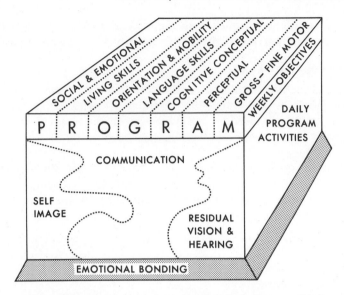

Fig. 24-2.   A schematic view of deaf-blind programming.

These three building blocks form the foundation upon which any program must be built (Fig. 24-2). Each requires equal emphasis and yet all are interdependent. People working with an MSD child must be constantly aware of these three underlying needs and of their interrelatedness. This awareness should influence every approach, technique, and activity, regardless of the program area.

Communication

When we are using the word *communication* in this sense, we would include oral, manual, and body language, gestures, and in fact every attempt by the child to communicate in any way with people or things in his environment. When the MSD child bumps into a chair, communication takes place. He may recognize the object as a chair on which he can sit if he is tired or progress around it on his way. With distorted but usable communication, he may recognize it as a barrier around which he may proceed. With unusuable sensory input, he may simply hit the chair and stop completely because he is unable to connect this with any previous experience. The more obvious levels of communication between an MSD child and another person may take place in the form of body contact, with personalized gestures, signs, finger spelling, oral communication, or any combination of these, according to the child's ability. Communication at this level is an active exchange between individuals and may range in complexity from a signal by the child to begin or end an activity to a complicated dialogue on the state of the world's economy.

Intervention is the key in the early stages of development. The intervenor must be there to receive, acknowledge, and respond to the child's attempt at communication. He must do it in such a way that the child begins to make the connection between the attempt and the resulting action by the intervenor. This beginning intervention is a time-consuming, emotionally demanding, physically exhausting, and never-ending task.

One way to initiate simple communication with the MSD child who has been functioning as totally deaf and blind is to develop a muscular pattern, such as raising and lowering his arm while he is lying on the floor in a prone position and the intervenor is on the floor beside him. Once the pattern has been established, break it and encourage him to give you a signal to start it again. Another technique is to develop the two-or-three-step pattern, such as touch the knee, then the shoulder, then the stomach. Establish it firmly with the child and repeat until he has perceived it and begins to guide your hand through the pattern rather than your moving his hand. Then change one item—for example, touch knee, shoulder, stomach versus touch knee, stomach, shoulder. When the child alerts to the change, you have less than 1 second to establish contact. To this point, the child has completely shut out the world. He has mastered the problem of integrating environmental stimuli by completely ignoring them. When he alerts to the pattern change, the world has intruded for a brief instant. When he makes visual, tactile, or auditory contact, you have begun to lay the foundation for a program to develop communication and any residual vision or hearing that may exist. Some workers in the MSD field have successfully used such self-stimulating activities as rocking as a point of intervention. They place the child in a cling position, rock with him, and then interrupt this stimulation. This approach has been criticized as reinforcing undesirable behavior. It appears to us, however, that provided this type of intervention is not carried out for too long a period of time (in a properly designed program it will not be), it may be a valuable tool which can be used in some cases.

We have found no one means of communication that may be generalized to all MSD children. The degree of useful vision, usable hearing, and other physical handicaps will all have a bearing on the eventual form that will best suit the individual child. The constraints imposed by the length of this chapter do not permit us to go into detail on various communication methods and their adaptability to the deaf-blind. There is a great deal of literature available in the area of deafness, outlining various methods and techniques. Those working with the MSD child will not have the luxury of choosing a particular approach, method or technique, however, and applying it to all comers. Oral, aural, oral-aural, visible English, signing, finger spelling, etc., all have their place in the program for MSD children.

A few generalizations might be made, which may prove of some assistance to both parents and professionals who are working with MSD children. The parents should establish a suitable communication cue. If the baby is functioning as either totally or nearly totally deaf and blind, this cue will probably consist of a particular touch, stroke on the arm, a pat on the stomach, or even a shaking of the crib. Once the cue has been given, the baby should have sufficient time to alert and anticipate the coming action. If the child is to successfully anticipate the coming action, basic routines must be set up and followed rigorously. When the mother enters the room and approaches the crib, the baby may receive no auditory or visual stimuli to alert him to coming events. Mother, therefore, should introduce her communication and give the baby a chance to alert and anticipate the coming events. If she is going to change his diaper, she then should introduce a second cue, which will always precede this action. Such cues should be natural outcomes of the normal contact between mother and baby. At the end of any given activity, the mother should give a finish cue; an example might be just touching the baby's two hands together at the midline. Wait a brief instant before beginning a new activity. Mother at all stages should talk to the baby, describing what she is doing and should encourage the responses from the child. More and not less effort should be expended to engage this child in finger-play games and movement activities. Every effort should be made from the first day to begin to get the child to function, using his residual vision and hearing as soon as and as well as possible.

Secondly, it is essential that people working with the baby or the young child should be ever alert for any attempts at communication. They should be there not to direct, push, pull, or shove the child, but to respond to the child's attempts at initiating or terminating activities. They should communicate with the child to *indicate* the activity, both during and following it.

A third generalization that might be made is to use the problem approach as much as possible. At every stage there are problems to be solved by the child as opposed to directions to be followed. It is easy to say this cannot be done; it is difficult, but in fact it can be done. A normal child's world provides him with challenges at any age. To reach the mobile dangling in the crib, to put the block in the can, to find a shoe, to open a door, to choose a hair style or an outfit to wear—all are problems that are solved by children as they grow up. It is too easy to "do for" the MSD child because of misinformed sympathy, constraints of time, or a feeling of pity for the poor unfortunate. Intervention must be designed not only to help him identify the problem but also to encourage him to find his own solutions. Do not provide solutions. Help him identify the dimensions of the problem. The problem approach provides one of the surest roads to success. It is one of the best means to develop dialogue and increase communication.

A fourth generalization, if there is any residual hearing at all, is to simply talk and keep talking.

Self-Image

Dr. Van Dijk, in his article, "Educational Approaches to Abnormal Development," states:

> as to be expected, the deaf-blind child is a child that touches. However, the child does not touch things to get to know them, but only for the sake of touching itself. It is not real perception, it has no intentionality, the child undergoes his own touching as in a dream. There is no conscious relationship to things and persons. *The personal relationship is lacking.*[5] (p. 16)

If the child is going to be an emotionally stable, social human being, it is essential not only that he communicates with the world around him, but also that he develops a positive self-image. He must see himself as a worthwhile, successful human being who is able to make a contribution to and accept contributions from the world around him. The development of this positive self-image must start at birth. For the normal child, this results from his interaction with parents, other people, and the rest of his environment. He will derive satisfaction, begin to view himself as successful, and perceive others as viewing him as a successful and worthwhile human being. For the deaf-blind child, the first stage will be the establishment of an emotional bond. This will not happen naturally, or incidentally; it is necessary to work at it. It is very closely interrelated with the development of communication and beginnings of the use of any residual vision or hearing. The parent establishes the specific cue by which he will become identified (the tactile equivalent of "Mommy" or "Daddy"). Activities are introduced to stimulate the child's movement, to give care and foster an enjoyment of physical contact between parent and child. It is often best to start these contacts with the child on the floor or a large bed. A *prone position* offers him the greatest security. The intervenor working with the child gradually moves into complete physical contact, working toward the child resting not on the floor alone but on the floor and the intervenor's body and, ultimately, on the intervenor's body alone.

The next stage will be a *cling position*, which will provide security for the child. He should be allowed to retreat to this when threatened with new or frightening interactions with his environment. The *lap position* (the child facing outward but with the physical security of the intervenor's chest, legs, and arms) will be a further physical step toward independence. Care must be taken to proceed slowly and not rush into a less physically secure position until the child is ready.

We have found that, until the child gains confidence through experience, we can anticipate a sequence of steps occurring as each new interaction with an individual or the environment takes place. The child

1. Resists the interaction
2. Tolerates the interaction
3. Cooperates passively
4. Enjoys the interaction
5. Responds cooperatively
6. Will lead in response to a signal
7. Will imitate the action
8. Will initiate the action

Without going into detail about each step listed above, we want to point out that such factors as faulty perception, the inability to anticipate results, and the lack of communication leading to understanding often cause the MSD child to *resist* new experiences. This resistance must be overcome gradually. There is absolutely no place for a sink-or-swim philosophy when working with the MSD child. As the resistance lessens, he will begin to *tolerate* new experiences because of the relationship he has with the intervenor, not because of the experience itself. The mother (or mother substitute) must bear in mind that until communication cues have been established and the child begins to recognize routines and anticipate outcomes, each experience can be a new and frightening one. She must always be prepared to stop, change to a more pleasurable activity, and try again later. The child will begin to *cooperate passively* with the intervenor, relaxing and allowing manipulation of his limbs and movement of his body to take place, until he gradually begins to *enjoy* the experience. He may even indicate that he wishes it to commence again when it is stopped. At this stage, the child is now beginning to anticipate and be aware in a general way. The child must be given time to anticipate and respond. He is reaching a stage where he can respond *cooperatively* in the activity. We are gradually working toward the child *leading* the adult through the activity. The security that is offered by the adult touch is still required. The child will reach the stage where the security of this touch is no longer necessary. Upon reception of the appropriate language cue, the child will follow the pattern without direct adult intervention. The final stage will be reached when the child demonstrates that he has integrated the responses by seeking to *initiate* the activity independently for his own enjoyment.

It will require a great deal of time and effort on the part of the parents, or the parent substitute, to aid the MSD child in developing his body image. The appropriate versions of all infant activities, such as "peek-a-boo," "clap," "I'm going to get you," etc., will have to be introduced with appropriate signals. Mother must not expect that at first the child will enjoy or show preference for any of the usual games or activities as a normal course of interaction with her. She must move slowly from the security of the known to the unknown in guiding him to begin to enjoy the interaction with herself and gradually other members of the family. Mother must understand that there is nothing wrong with her because her child does not immediately respond to her with the same kind of interaction she has experienced with other babies. If she becomes tense and apprehensive as she approaches him, she will communicate this to him and little or no positive interaction will take place. Even when the child is older, it is the cardinal rule that if you are annoyed or angry it is best to take a "cooling-off" period before physically handling him. If you do not, you will often destroy months, and even years, of work just as surely as you would if you used ridicule or sarcasm and excessive physical force with a normal child.

Residual Vision and Hearing

One of the difficulties in working with the MSD child is the identification of the amount of residual vision and hearing he has. From birth, every effort must be made to stimulate his responses to sound and visual input. There is no denying, of course, that there are children who have total lack of input of one or more sensory channels. It is strongly recommended that from the beginning the parents talk to, cuddle, and stimulate their child in every way possible. The overall result of this approach is probably as beneficial to the parents as it is to him. As he begins to be alert occasionally, either visually or auditorily, do not expect that he will be a hearing or seeing child at all times. As one of the fathers said, "At that particular moment, I know he saw me," and there is no way that we would question his words. Day in and day out, the boy functions primarily as a totally blind and deaf child who relies solely on tactile input for his knowledge of the world about him. There is no doubt, however, that, at the time the parent described, the boy did respond to visual stimuli.

We cannot judge failure or success in dealing with these children in terms of their ability to see, hear, or speak. Yet, underlying all the daily activities described, we must constantly be aware of the need to help them develop the ability to use any residual vision or hearing they may possess, in whatever way they are able to use it.

Educational Programming

Educational programming for an MSD child can be organized into seven areas. This is not to say that he proceeds from period 1 (Social and Emotional Growth) to period 2 (Living Skills) to period 3 (Orientation and Mobility), and so on. For convenience in programming and for the identification of specific developmental objectives, we have organized our formal program into

1. Social and Emotional Development
2. Living Skills
3. Orientation and Mobility
4. Language Development
5. Cognitive (conceptual) Development
6. Perceptual Development
7. Gross and Fine Motor Development

This is not a hierarchical arrangement. It does indicate that little of the MSD child's learning can be left to chance or incidental development, especially at the early stages.

The program must be based on a sound knowledge of normal developmental milestones. Activities must be designed to present him with the opportunity at each stage to acquire the skills necessary for future learning.

The Living Skills program is designed to teach the child all the skills necessary to independent or semi-independent living as an adult. The list will start with simple skills, such as putting on stockings, and move to more complicated skills, such as care of clothing and care of self (including washing, brushing teeth, and taking care of hair) to cooking, care of house, and eventually to entertaining and other of the more advanced social skills.

The Orientation and Mobility program is designed to teach the child to move about, first in a familiar and later in a less-familiar environment. Each orientation and mobility program must be designed individually, taking into account the degree of impairment and the level of functioning.

Each child must be aided to develop basic receptive and expressive language, which he can use to function in his interactions with others in his environment. It has been stated previously that we cannot afford the luxury, in programming for the MSD child, of entering into a particular philosophy of communication. His language must fit his needs, rather than the child to a system. Once a means of communication has been established with him, and he has developed an emotional bond that makes him wish to communicate, then and only then will language formation begin.

Piaget identified stages through which the child moves in his cognitive development. We recognize that Piaget's work is criticized by some experts, mainly on the basis of his attaching chronological ages to each developmental phase. We have found the stages he identified useful in forming a baseline to aid in the selection of activities for various children. Once again, it must be stressed, however, before cognitive development can satisfactorily take place the child must have intervention that will allow him to integrate information he receives from the environment into a meaningful whole.

Program Implementation

One approach we have found successful in programming for MSD children is to clearly identify developmental objectives that we hope to reach with each child in each of the areas mentioned. These objectives are usually of two types: (1) long-range and (2) short-range, or those that we identify for a specific short period of time of from 1 to 3 weeks' duration. We think these operational objectives are the key to successful programming. The intervenors working with the child must be constantly aware of the overall goals of the development of communication, positive self-image and the use of any residual vision or hearing. They also should have in mind the specific operational objectives they have for the individual. The child's program is designed around activities, such as swimming, play periods, and trips. During a swimming activity, a child will be working on language development, body image, living skills, appropriate dress, orientation and mobility, gross motor development, as well as perceptual and conceptual development. Mother (or in the case of the formal program, a mother substitute) will be aware of the specific objectives that are to be accomplished in each of the areas. For example, in language she might be stressing "sit," "wait," and "up." To develop body image, she could play a game while undressing and dressing of "my foot, your foot," "your hand, my hand," working with the child co-actively to put on his socks and to put his arms in his shirt and at the same time encouraging him to look at what he is doing. She will also be working on several areas of motor development while walking to the activity, dressing and undressing, and in the water. At this stage, part of his cognitive development will be working on the labeling of body parts. Thus, one of the daily activities in which the child takes part will provide opportunities to work toward the attainment of the operational objectives in all seven areas.

It must be stressed that the division of the child's program into seven areas is a purely artificial one, which we see as beneficial to the identification of developmental goals. As far as the child is concerned, he is taking part in a series of activities where he is being given the opportunity to anticipate coming events, to control his environment to the extent that a normal child does, and to learn by interacting with it through appropriate intervention and mediation, allowing him to perceive with a minimum of distortion the interaction that is taking place.

As the child develops to a higher level, the areas of cognitive and language development will broaden into the normal school curriculum, living skills will grow to those areas normally covered by home economics, industrial arts, and vocational training, but will always be broader in concept and greater in depth than those required by the normal child. Motor development will move into the more formal area of physical education and recreation. Even at this level, the programmer must continually focus on the use of communication skills, residual vision and hearing, the development of social and emotional stability, and the specialized skills of orientation and mobility according to the needs of the particular child involved.

Further programming help for the MSD child may be obtained from several sources. The John Tracy Clinic in Los Angeles publishes an excellent parental guide for younger deaf-blind children. The Perkins School for the Blind in Watertown, Massachusetts, has one of the oldest programs for deaf-blind children in North America and its staff are very willing to share their knowledge and expertise. Dr. Waterhouse, who was quoted earlier, was the Superintendent of the Perkins School for the Blind for many years. The authors of this chapter are preparing *A Developmental Guide for the Multi-Sensory Deprived Child*, which will contain suggestions as to the techniques and programming sequences that may be useful at various stages. Further information is forthcoming.

Outcomes

There can be no one program for all MSD children. Each child's unique set of impairments must be taken into account. The medical profession, the teacher, and the parents must be continually involved in the design, implementation, and ongoing evaluation of the program

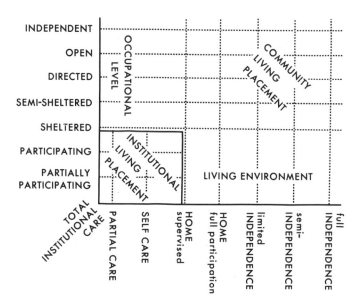

Fig. 24–3.   A goal model for sociological placement of multi-sensory-deprived children.

for each child. Similarly, there can be no one goal suitable for all. No one in either the medical or teaching profession would look at all the youngsters in a given city and say that the appropriate goal for them is to become lawyers, bricklayers, or accountants. It is equally absurd to identify one long-range plan for all the deaf-blind. The goals for each individual must be worked out according to their abilities. After all the advice has been collected from both the medical and the educational authorities, it will be the parent and, as he gets older, the child who will begin to identify the specific goal at which the program should be aimed. Figure 24–3 illustrates a two-factor model for sociological placement (living environment and occupational level). The model is simplistic and is intended only to indicate the complexity of the resulting matrix. Such factors as community resources, agency support, family expectations, and continuing development have not been indicated. They also must be taken into consideration when the goal for any MSD individual is being established or evaluated.

THE ADVENTITIOUSLY DEAF-BLIND

The adventitiously deaf-blind individual has distinct and identifiable needs. Depending on the age of onset, extent of the handicap, and prognosis, new occupational skills may have to be learned. Existing living, mobility, and recreational skills will have to be modified and new ones learned. However, before much of this new learning can take place, the individual must have the moral, spiritual, and psychological support necessary to enable him to come to grips with and cope with his handicap. Secondly, he must have the ability to communicate. Communication is the key, but it does not have to be a complicated one. The adult who knows the print alphabet can usually learn to read block print in the palm of his hand. Signing and finger spelling or the manual alphabet may be added, where appropriate. Braille and, in many cases, the Optacon will provide access to the printed word and keep open the door to recreational reading.

There are many systems to communicate with a deaf-blind person. Some require special education and some do not:[9]

Special Knowledge Not Required

1. *Block Letters in Hand*
   Using your index finger, print capital block letters in the palm of the deaf-blind person. Tap his fingertips once at the end of a word and twice at the end of the message. To make a correction wipe your palm across his.

2. *Tellatouch*
   A portable typewriter consisting of both an ink-print standard typewriter keyboard and a braillewriter keyboard. The typewritten message is simultaneously transcribed in Braille.

3. *Alphabet Glove*
   Has letters of the alphabet, numbers and two words: "and" and "the" painted on a white glove. The communicator touches the desired letters.

4. *Alphabet Plate*
   Contains embossed letters of the alphabet and numbers on a pocket-sized card. Placing the tip of the deaf-blind person's index finger on the desired letter or number allows you to spell out the message.

5. *Braille Alphabet Card*
   Contains both ink-print and Braille embossed letters and numbers. It is used as above.

6. *Tadoma*
   The deaf-blind person places his hand on the face of the communicator. He reads the message by feeling the vibrations of the vocal cords, nasal cavity, and the formation of the lips.

7. *Cut-out Letters*
   Lay out the message on a flat surface and allow the deaf-blind person to explore it with his hands.

8. *Gesture*

Place your hands over the deaf-blind person's hands and use natural gestures.
9. *Codes (e.g., Morse Code)*
Can be tapped in the deaf-blind person's hands. They may be simple—such as one tap "yes"; two taps "no"; three taps "I don't know"—or formal, such as the Morse code.

Special Knowledge Required

10. *Braille*
11. *Sign Language*
12. *Cross Method*
A system of taps and strokes. The signals can be written on any part of the body.
13. *Telephone Code-Com*
A small box containing a vibrating plate, ascending key, light, and volume control; communication is by code using vibrations.
14. *Manual Alphabet*
15. *Finger Spelling*

It is not enough that the individual master these communication skills himself. If they are to be useful, skills such as signing and finger spelling will have to be acquired as well by family members and friends. The speed and dexterity necessary to make communication meaningful will only come with constant practice by all concerned.

For efficient communication with the deaf-blind person, it is recommended that one should

1. Make him aware of your presence.
2. Never force him.
3. Make sure he understands you and you understand him.
4. Never leave him alone in a strange environment. If he is standing, let him touch a nonmobile object.
5. Leave nothing to his imagination. Explain everything and *be honest*.
6. Encourage him to communicate.

It is essential that support be available from the moment of diagnosis. To wait until the individual must function as a deaf-blind adult is to allow much irreparable damage to be done and valuable time to be lost.

COMMENT

There is no excuse for neglecting deaf-blind children or adults, identifying them as profoundly retarded, relegating them to the back wards of custodial institutions, or to a nonproductive homebound existence. Even most of the MSD individuals who will best be served by institutional placement can be taught to become functioning, contributing members of that institutional environment. Many individuals now relegated to institutional care could, or could have, become functioning members of their own family and contributing members to society, had appropriate intervention taken place.

Early identification, full and complete diagnosis by an expert medical team, and appropriate programming is essential if this needless waste of both human resources and tax dollars is to be avoided.

CONCLUSIONS

1. The deaf-blind child is a multi-sensory deprived child whose needs cannot be adequately served by approaches used to alleviate the handicaps of blindness, deafness or retardation.
2. Common causes of multisensory deprivation are rubella, Usher's syndrome, prematurity, meningitis and encephalitis.
3. The MSD child will often be low functioning, lack normal developmental drives, and because of these and other factors be mislabeled as retarded.
4. A program aimed at increasing the MSD child's ability to utilize residual vision and hearing and to integrate all sensory input into a meaningful gestalt is essential. Even when he has developed the ability to integrate all sensory input into a meanful gestalt is essential. Even when he has developed the ability to integrate sensory input, he will probably require some degree of mechanical or human intervention to supplement this input for the rest of his life.
5. Identification of the MSD child is difficult due to the problems posed by functionalism.
6. Parents are often faced with a series of shattering diagnoses— blindness, heart defect, and deafness. Retardation is often inappropriately added to the diagnosis. Unsuitable intervention may lead to the setting up of self-fulfilling prophecy and to severe emotional problems in later years.
7. Evaluation should be done by a team of specialists. Findings from this evaluation should be conveyed to the parents in such a way that the focus remains on the importance of the whole patient.
8. After the initial diagnosis has taken place, a programming team should be formed and intervention should start immediately.
9. Every evaluator, regardless of his field of specialization, must answer yes to the following questions if the evaluation is to be considered valid:

1. Have I communicated with the child?
2. Has the child clearly understood the communication?
3. Is he motivated to respond?
4. Does he have the response that I anticipate within his repertoire of responses?

10. Intervention must begin with the establishment of an emotional bond between the intervenor and the child. The focus of the intervention should be the development of residual vision and hearing, communication, and the provision of a series of successful experiences utilizing the problem-solving approach.

11. The lower functioning M.S.D. child can be expected to move through a series of eight steps each time a new interaction with the environment takes place.

12. In every situation, intervention must be provided at a level that insures that the MSD individual has a good perception of his immediate environment, an understanding of exactly what is required of him, and a clear perception of the results of his interaction.

13. The adventitiously deaf-blind individual has many problems that differ from those of the congenital deaf-blind. Adjustment and communication are a focal point for effective intervention.

14. It is inadvisable to attempt to generalize any one approach to meet the needs of the deaf-blind. The degree of loss, the stability of eye conditions, the age of onset, and many other personal and social factors make each case unique. The very nature of the handicap makes the bureaucratic approach dangerous.

15. Early identification, competent diagnosis, and appropriate intervention are essential if the needless waste of human resources and tax dollars is to be avoided.

REFERENCES

1. Waterhouse EJ: Paper presented at The Second Symposium on Planning for Public Relations and Rehabilitation, Athens, Greece, Sept 1972
2. Committee on Standards: Report. North American Committee for Services to Deaf-Blind Children and Youth. Pittsburgh, University of Pittsburgh, p 1 (unpublished material)
3. Furesz J: Laboratory diagnosis of rubella infection. Can J Public Health (monograph suppl 1) 62:1-12, 1971
4. Chess S, Korn S, Fernandez P: Psychiatric Disorders of Children with Congenital Rubella. New York, Brunner/Mazel, 1971, p 30
5. Van Dijk J: Educational approaches to abnormal development, in: Deaf-Blind Children and Their Education. Proceedings of the International Conference

on the Education of Deaf-Blind Children. Rotterdam, Rotterdam University Press, 1971

6. Chambers DC: The Role of the Pediatrician in Diagnosis and Evaluation of the Deaf-Blind Child. Denver, Colorado, Department of Education, 1973
7. Parrin CS: Pediatrics and the deaf-blind child, in Collins MT (ed): A Multi-Disciplinary Handbook for Paraprofessionals. Lansing, Michigan, Midwest Regional Center for Services to Deaf-Blind Children, 1974, p 29
8. Myklebust HR: Auditory Disorders in Children: A Manual for Differential Diagnosis, New York, Grune & Stratton, 1954
9. Pamphlet in preparation by the Canadian National Institute for the Blind, 1976

25
Special Aspects of Education

SEXUAL BEHAVIOR AND EDUCATION

There has been increasing interest in frank discussion of human sexual behavior in recent years, and the handicapped are no exception. A general and useful recent reference is the book by Johnson.[1]

This section will briefly consider some of our findings relating to masturbation and menstruation, guidelines on the management of sexual incidents, and some comments on sex education.

Masturbation

Interest in one's own body and the sensations it can produce is part of normal development. Stimulation of the sex organs at all ages is common as well. Although attitudes toward masturbation have gradually changed, it is still probably regarded with some discomfort by both parents and professionals.

In our study, parents of the visually impaired described masturbation much more often than did the parents of the sighted (Table 25-1). It is interesting that this was true of both the blind and partially sighted children (Table 25-2). Masturbation was found to be more common in those with below-average IQ. (66.7 percent versus 30 percent [$p < 0.05$] for males; 36.4 percent versus 15.4 percent [$p < 0.10$] for females). For males, those with stereotyped behavior were more likely to masturbate than those without mannerisms (70 percent versus 36.4 percent; $p < 0.01$). For females, this relationship was reversed, with 75 percent of those without mannerisms reported to masturbate as compared with 18.2 percent of those with stereotyped behavior ($p < 0.10$). (The reasons for these male-female differences are unclear.)

It was also found that no parents of the sighted children regarded the masturbation as a problem, whereas this was true of 20 percent

Table 25-1
Masturbation in Visually Impaired and Sighted Children

	Index Cases		Controls	
	n	% (of 54)	n	% (of 61)
Yes	20	37.0	6	9.8
No	34	63.0	55	90.2
Totals	54	100.0	61	100.0

$\chi^2 = 10.61$; df $= 1$; $p < 0.005$

of the parents of visually impaired children who were reported to masturbate. Additionally (although the numbers are very small), concern was more likely to be expressed over female masturbation than over male.

COMMENT

The highly significant increase in reported masturbation in the index cases as compared with the controls may mean either an actual or an apparent increase. In the latter case, one factor might be the tendency of the visually impaired to be less secretive, unaware of being observed, and less aware of what is socially acceptable; in the former case, the visually impaired child might be less directed toward the outside world and more dependent upon his own body for satisfaction.

In any event, the greater concern expressed over masturbation in the visually impaired is probably a reflection of the phenomenon that parents of an unusual child do not know how to anticipate the future: they may fear that this behavior, along with others, such as mannerisms, will continue and will stigmatize the child as he grows up. Some visually impaired children may openly engage in this behavior, which is usually considered highly private (if not taboo), and this may disgust a parent. It is important to recognize that while open masturbation in an older sighted child would be considered highly pathological, it may have quite

Table 25-2
Masturbation in Blind and Partially Sighted Children

	Blind		Partial Vision	
	n	% (of 18)	n	% (of 41)
Yes	7	38.9	15	36.6
No	11	61.1	26	63.4
Totals	18	100.0	41	100.0

$\chi^2 = 0.015$; df $= 1$; n.s.

a different significance in the blind, depending upon the child's experience and training.

Menstruation

Although we do not have corroboration from the youngsters themselves, parents reported that almost half the girls whose menses had begun had difficulty with cramps or mood changes, as compared with 20 percent of the controls. The reasons for this are unclear. Possibilities include parental overfocusing on the problem, less exercise, and poorer knowledge to counteract worry.

Sexual Incidents

Not infrequently, a sexual incident is reported by a child or about a child or children. It is of great importance to assess and manage these situations well, but it is difficult to follow this principle when there are many people involved. Elonen and Zwarensteyn have pointed out the impact that sexual abuse may have upon a blind child and have emphasized the need to tactfully enquire into the possibility of sexual misuse of a child when unexplained, peculiar behavior develops.[2]

In a residential school, there may be actual or alleged sexual interaction between pupils or between a pupil and a staff member. As is the case with any incident, such as aggression or stealing, one must be very careful to check out the evidence and not make assumptions. In a good proportion of instances, the evidence will become increasingly tenuous as the inquiry proceeds, and the child may not need to be involved at all. Hearsay, prejudice, and idiosyncratic or old-fashioned attitudes may play a large part in pseudocrises.

Other actual activities may represent harmless exploration or curiosity of a heterosexual or homosexual nature. The adults in charge must often be helped to realize that this is no different from the common behavior of young persons from time immemorial, although probably more obvious because they are under greater surveillance. Homosexual play need not indicate future homosexual orientation; the same is true of heterosexual play. Of course, proper education in the family and school should emphasize the development of socially appropriate behavior, such as the meaning of privacy in certain acts.

Our society has now moved to the point where coeducational activities and dormitories are common, and sexual curiosity and impulses will find some outlet. This concerns many parents, including some who wish to forget entirely their own similar activity years before. But greater access of the sexes to each other means that there is a responsibility of staff to include in the sex-education curriculum matters of social responsibility and also contraception and abortion in the case of teenagers. Even with the best education, children and adolescents cannot be expected to always use good judgment, and problems will occur (they always did).

Returning again to the question of sexual abuse of the visually impaired, it seems that this may be more common than is usually thought. Many factors may enter into this, including the naïveté of the blind, inability to identify the perpetrator, ideas that the blind are "fair game," and the possible curiosity aroused in the sighted and the temptation to do things the blind cannot see (but still in the presence of another person—like exhibitionism).

When abuse occurs, it is essential not to add to the problem by becoming overzealous. It is well known from work with sighted children that the adults (parents, police, teachers, and others) may create a major problem out of a minor one. Sexual incidents need not have serious consequences in later life. Calm counseling may be invaluable and might include

1. The sequence of actual events (how the person got into and out of the situation);
2. Details of sexual aspects and misunderstandings and worries, if any, about this (pregnancy, etc.);
3. Actual feelings during and after the incident;
4. Any guilt feelings about having caused or contributed to the activity;
5. Fears of parental reactions (outrage, punishment, etc.);
6. Threats from the perpetrator;
7. What such an experience means about people and relationships.

Talking with the family may be equally important, and sometimes medical examination is necessary.

Sex Education

Children who are born blind, who become blind in early life, or who have very significant visual impairment are likely to have highly distorted or limited concepts about sexuality. (In our study, many more visually impaired children were reported by their parents to be unaware of sexual differences than the sighted [15.4 percent versus 2.5 percent]. This was more true of the blind [20 percent] than the partially sighted [12 percent]). This ignorance derives partly from the taboos on touching in our society and the importance of vision as the way we learn about sexual differences and sexual behavior. A recent issue of the New Outlook for the Blind (May 1974) was entirely given over to a series of articles on this subject. Foulke and Uhde reported on a survey of sex education.[3]

Although the results were preliminary, it showed that the majority of the teenagers had never discussed sex with either parent, and, of those who did, a fair number received misinformation. Advice, when needed, was solicited from friends and not from parents. Many adults will not talk candidly to children about sex. Blind children are not as likely as the sighted to be exposed to sexual pictures and literature, nor the everyday bombardment of sexually toned advertising. Parents are often embarrassed to read material to blind children that sighted children may read for themselves. Foulke and Uhde[3] recount the story of a girl who asked her parents where she came from and was given so many different answers by different relatives (all lies) that, although she sensed it must be a lie, she felt the reason for the misinformation was that she was blind. The possible outcome, namely feeling that blindness is the result of something too shameful to discuss, is obvious.

In another paper, Scholl emphasized the difficulty in sex education and family life programs imposed by the need to provide the blind with experience with real objects. Even models are not as adequate for the blind as for the sighted, yet it is specifically in this area in which taboos on touching are so prevalent that significant difficulties may arise. This author also points out that in adolescence the normal concern over a rapidly growing and changing body may be amplified because it is more difficult for the visually impaired child to receive feedback from family and peers. The importance of independence at that developmental stage is also a problem for the blind. Scholl suggests a role for teaching the behavior of the peer group, including flirting and current fads, so that the blind person can gain a sense of belonging. "Similarly, young adults should be taught cocktail party behaviour and social interaction skills with members of the opposite sex"[4] (p. 206).

In another paper in the same issue, Torbett suggests that, because the blind child's tactile exploration is limited to his own body, this may enhance self-preoccupation.[5] He suggests that sound sex education programs should include exposure of blind individuals to the same kind of sexual culture experienced by the sighted. It is not only facts but also feelings which have to be dealt with by both the children and those who are trying to help them, and special attention should be devoted to finding and training competent workers in the field of sex education for the visually impaired.

Other useful references[6,7] and a study guide are also available.[8]

PHYSICAL EDUCATION

The value of physical education for visually impaired children is well recognized. This topic has been discussed ever since Haüy established the first school for the blind in 1785, and papers have been presented

Fig. 25-1.   Blind children being taught canoeing.

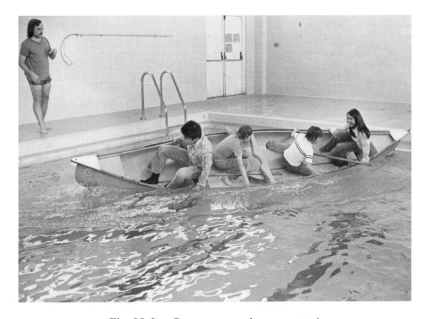

Fig. 25-2.   Canoe purposely overturned.

Fig. 25-3. The "rescue operation."

even during the last century.[9] As described earlier, children with severe visual impairment tend to be passive and avoid exercise. Appropriate physical education may be therapeutic for them, however, as it improves their muscle tone, coordination, balance, posture, gait, orientation, reduces stereotyped mannerisms, and helps to develop better self-image, among many other benefits.[10]

In his books and articles, Buell describes in detail various sports that are suitable for blind students.[11-13] Kratz also offers much practical advice.[14] (The reader who is interested in this field should obtain Buell's and Kratz's valuable work for reference.) In residential schools, the importance of physical exercise is well recognized and students are generally encouraged to swim, bowl, skate, ski, wrestle, run, tumble, do gymnastics, and many other activities (Figs. 25-1 to 25-5). Those who have not seen totally blind children ski, bowl, or play hockey are

Fig. 25-4.   A young blind child playing with his kite.

always amazed. Certain modifications may be necessary. For example, in hockey a noisy can, which the players are able to hear, substitutes for the puck. Sometimes a sound device within the ball itself is used in games. In racing, children often run beside a cable to guide them. In regular schools, unfortunately, the provision of physical education to visually impaired students may be only marginal because teachers are not acquainted with the special techniques required, and such sports as baseball, basketball, or football (which are the core of most physical education programs) are unsuitable. Even children with partial vision cannot play these games because they are unable to react to the rapidly approaching ball, and they may lose their remaining vision through injury.

Many visually impaired children have other types of handicaps, and therefore certain sports may not be suitable for them. Parents or

Fig. 25-5. Frisbee. A game for the sighted?

teachers should discuss sports with the child's ophthalmologist because body-contact sports are not recommended when certain types of ocular disorders are present.

Myopic (shortsighted) children are often said to be poorly coordinated. Bishop feels that this is because myopics avoid sports, as good distance vision is normally required for participation.[15] On the other hand, one may argue that children with poor coordination tend to read more, and there is some evidence now suggesting that excessive reading under artificial light during early childhood may cause myopia.[16,17] Thus, there may be an interaction effect.

One cannot overemphasize the harm that can be done to visually handicapped children if well-meaning parents or teachers are overprotective and, as a result, physical exercise is unnecessarily avoided.

Fig. 25-6. A clay figure created by a congenitally totally
blind 8-year-old. The synthetic approach is used in his
modeling, since the different parts are separately created
and then put together. (Courtesy of Professor J.A.S. Mac-
Donald.)

ART

Even totally blind children can produce impressive works of art.
Since they cannot imitate someone else's style, each child reveals his
own individuality in simple, sometimes naïve, but unpretentious form.
The sculptures of blind children tell us a great deal about their concept
formation, their body image, the way they perceive objects through
touch, and their understanding of space (Figs. 25-6 to 25-9). Like the
sighted, they can express emotions through art but must be taught to
do so.

Sculpting by the congenitally blind reveals that they create the various
pieces separately and then put them together (synthetic approach). This
is an example of how they learn in life. They gather information piece
by piece and then put it together like an incomplete puzzle. For example,

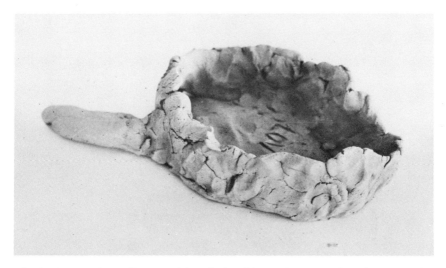

Fig. 25-7. "Ashtray." Artwork by blind children. (Courtesy of Professor J.A.S. MacDonald.)

many visually impaired children are afraid to touch a dog and, therefore, have an incomplete concept of how it really looks. When they try to mold the image of a dog from clay, it may appear to be a human figure with a tail sticking out of the middle of the back. In contrast, sculpting done by sighted children shows that they usually first mold the body out of one piece and only then start working on the various smaller parts of that particular figure. They view the entire object first and then analyze the details. Hence, they are using the analytic approach. Vision unifies information and, thus, the sighted do not have the sometimes enormous gaps in their concepts that are found in the blind. Children who lost their sight but still have visual imagery use the analytic approach in their art work.

The quality of sculpting improves as the visually impaired child grows. First, actual objects are composed of balls, flat surfaces, and sticks (Figs. 25-7 to 25-9). They can easily produce smooth or rough surfaces, indentations, and projections because through touch they perceive these differences well while using their tactile memory. Probably because young blind children know their arms, fingers, and face well, these parts are generally represented in exaggerated proportions in their art work. A young sighted child can easily reproduce a model of his house. The blind person without visual imagery can make the walls, windows, and doors, but not the ceiling or the roof, since he has not touched them, and visual descriptions from the sighted are of relatively

Fig. 25-8. "Hamburger." Artwork by blind children. (Courtesy of Professor J.A.S. MacDonald.)

Fig. 25-9. "Man in a Canoe." Artwork by blind children. (Courtesy of Professor J.A.S. MacDonald.)

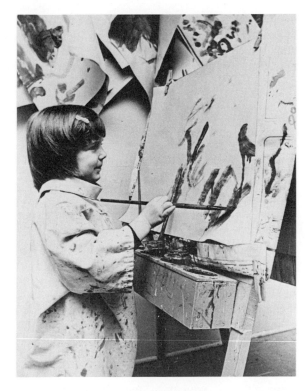

Fig. 25-10. "What are you painting?" "I am painting a
fine day." (Courtesy of the Vancouver *Province*.)

little help. Their concept of space is based mostly on tactile experience.
As the blind child develops, he is able to recreate finer details in more
exact proportions and, in fact, he may be taught the use of the analytic
approach to sculpting.

Art done by the blind has been studied.[18-21] A valuable book was
written by Fukurai, an art teacher for the blind in Japan, who proved
to the world that the artistic ability of the blind is comparable to that
of the sighted.[19] His students won many distinguished prizes, even in
competition with sighted children.

Visually impaired children, even the totally blind, are able to draw,[19]
but the less vision they have, the more disorganized their drawings
(Fig. 25-10). Some with limited partial vision, in order to be able to
see, must lean over the paper so close that they can only draw small
parts of the total picture at one time and have to join the lines together
later. They have to scan the picture up and down to complete it. They
have difficulties reproducing even simple geometric shapes, such as a

circle, triangle, square, or diamond, because only small segments of the total design are visible to them. The inexperienced psychologist who is looking for visuo-motor perceptual problems may incorrectly view these inaccuracies and distortions as evidence of organic brain dysfunction. Great caution needs to be exercised in any such interpretations.

CONCLUSIONS

1. Masturbation is reported much more frequently in both blind and partially sighted children than in the sighted; this difference may be real or apparent.
2. Parents of the visually impaired in our study were more concerned about their child's masturbation.
3. Menstrual difficulties were reported more frequently in visually impaired than in sighted girls.
4. Sexual incidents must be handled with great caution and tact; assumptions about the nature of the incident must be accepted with some scepticism, as there are often distortions involved.
5. Visually impaired children are likely to receive and absorb less information about sexuality, and this can sometimes become a major problem. Consideration of family- and school-based educational programs would seem essential.
6. Appropriate physical education may be therapeutic for visually impaired children as it tends to improve their muscle tone, coordination, balance, posture, gait, orientation, reduces stereotyped mannerisms, and helps to develop better self image, among many other benefits.
7. Even totally blind children can produce impressive works of art.

REFERENCES

1. Johnson WR: Sex Education and Counseling of Special Groups: The Mentally and Physically Handicapped and the Elderly. Springfield, Ill, Charles C Thomas, 1975
2. Elonen AS, Zwarensteyn SB: Sexual trauma in young blind children. New Outlook for the Blind 69:440–442, 1975
3. Foulke E, Uhde T: Do blind children need sex education? New Outlook for the Blind 68:193–200, 1974
4. Scholl GT: The psychosocial effects of blindness: Implications for program planning in sex education. New Outlook for the Blind 68:201–209, 1974
5. Torbett DS: A humanistic and futuristic approach to sex education for blind children. New Outlook for the Blind 68:210–215, 1974

6. Van't Hooft F, Heslinga K: Sex education of blind-born children. New Outlook for the Blind 62:15-21, 1968
7. Bidgood FE: A study of sex education programs for visually handicapped persons. New Outlook for the Blind 65:318-323, 1971
8. Dickman IR (ed): Sex Education and Family Life for Visually Handicapped Children and Youth: A Resource Guide. New York, Sex Information and Education Council of the United States and American Foundation for the Blind, 1975
9. Roth M: The physical education of the blind. Presented at a conference in York, July 25, 1883. Obtained from the Index Catalogue of the National Library of Medicine, Canada
10. Resnick R: Creative movement classes for visually handicapped children in a public school setting. New Outlook for the Blind 67:442-447, 1973
11. Buell CE: Physical Education for Blind Children. Springfield, Ill, Charles C Thomas, 1966
12. Buell CE: Motor performance of visually handicapped children. Except Child 17:69-72, 1950
13. Buell CE: Physical education and recreation for the visually handicapped. Washington, DC, American Association for Health, Physical Education, and Education, 1973
14. Kratz LE: Movement Without Sight. Palo Alto, California, Peek Publications, 1973
15. Bishop VE: Teaching the Visually Limited Child. Springfield, Ill, Charles C Thomas, 1971
16. Morgan RW, Speakman JS, Grimshaw SE: Inuit myopia: An environmentally induced "epidemic"? Can Med Assoc J 112:575-577, 1975
17. Tsvetkov VL: The conference on prevention, pathogenesis and treatment of eye disease in children. Journal of Pediatric Ophthalmology 9:121-123, 1972
18. MacDonald JAS: A report on art therapy classes offered at Jericho Hill School for the Blind. Vancouver, 1974 (unpublished data)
19. Fukurai S: How Can I Make What I Cannot See? New York, Van Nostrand Reinhold Co, 1974
20. Kewell J: Sculpture by Blind Children. New York, American Foundation for the Blind, 1955
21. Lowenfeld V: Creative and Mental Growth, ed 3. New York, Macmillan, 1957

26
Dentistry

Good oral health, which is essential to every person, is especially important to the well being of the visually impaired.

Blind children tend to have more dental problems than their sighted peers. There are several reasons for this. Prenatal abnormalities, syndromes, infections such as rubella or toxoplasmosis and other diseases that cause the ocular disorder may also affect the teeth. Satisfactory oral hygiene is more difficult to achieve in those individuals who have cerebral palsy, mental retardation, seizures treated with medications, etc., and visually impaired children are frequently multihandicapped. Solid foods are introduced later to blind infants than to the sighted (see chapter 15). Prolonged bottle feeding of milk and juices causes dental decay and as a result the "milk-bottle syndrome" is commonly seen among the young blind population. The management of major associated handicaps may overshadow dental problems, which then tend to be neglected. Many dentists, like other health professionals, feel insecure when asked to treat visually impaired children, many of whom have unrealistic fears because of previous hospitalization. The anxieties of the child may influence his parents to delay or even neglect visits to the dentist.

The literature on the dental management of blind children is meagre. However, the reading of one review article[1] on this subject is highly recommended to dentists.

OFFICE VISITS

It is essential that office visits (especially the first one) are carefully planned by the parents and the dentist, who should know beforehand the cause of the ocular disorder, the onset, the degree of visual loss,

Fig. 26-1.   Father introduces his deaf-blind daughter to the dentist after some
conversation in the reception area.

other handicaps, and the child's behavior, among other facts. For example,
the lighting beam (which can be easily adjusted) may make the photophobic
patient extremely uncomfortable. A youngster who lost his sight in later
life may already have visual memories of visits to the dentist's office.
A child with useful sight could be shown the instruments, whereas the
totally blind must rely on verbal descriptions and on touch. The office
visit should be relaxed and free from anxiety as much as possible. The
dentist and his staff must be patient while every procedure is carefully
planned and explained. The presence of the parents, a sib, or a favored
toy can be extremely beneficial in relieving tension. There is no need
to give a general anaesthetic for a minor procedure, as too often happens.

The following figures (Figs. 26-1 to 26-9) demonstrate in sequence
several aspects of management. The patient is a 10½-year-old girl, deaf
and blind due to congenital rubella syndrome. The dentist is Dr. Richard
R. Rolla, DDS,* who demonstrates that an office visit is a pleasant
experience for this child.

---

*Child Development and Mental Retardation Center, University of Washington, Seattle,
Washington 98105.

Fig. 26-2. Child is introduced to dental chair by directing her exploration by touch.

Fig. 26-3. Father provides support and encouragement for child's accomplishment. Parents remain nearby to provide security for the child in a new environment.

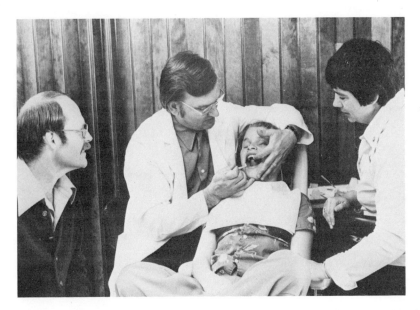

Fig. 26-4. Father provides suggestions to the dentist for effective methods of eliciting child's cooperation during oral inspection.

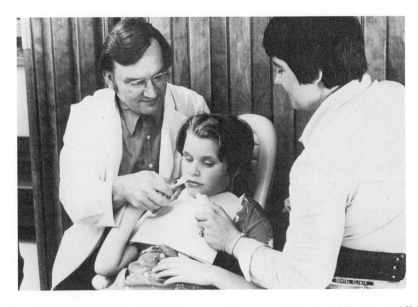

Fig. 26-5. The child is given the opportunity to smell the dentrifice to establish familiarity with a known object, toothbrush, and a known procedure, toothbrushing.

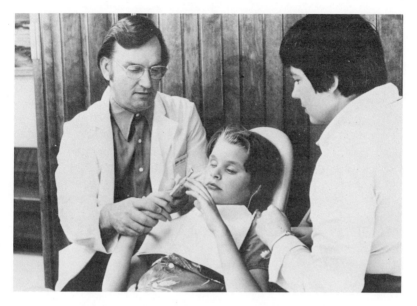

Fig. 26-6. The child uses touch to establish the similarity between a regular toothbrush and the dentist's special toothbrush.

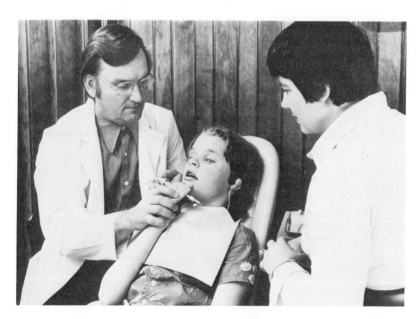

Fig. 26-7. The child feels the vibration of the rotating handpiece before it is placed to the mouth.

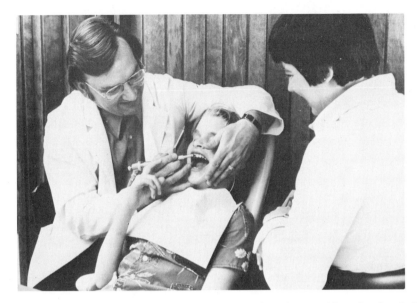

Fig. 26-8. The child participates in the procedure by touching the dentist's hand. The child receives verbal praise and physical contact for appropriate behavior.

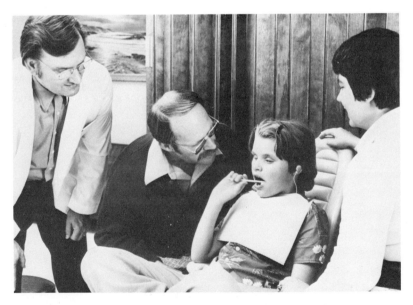

Fig. 26-9. The parent is included in the dental office procedure to encourage follow-up with oral hygiene at home.

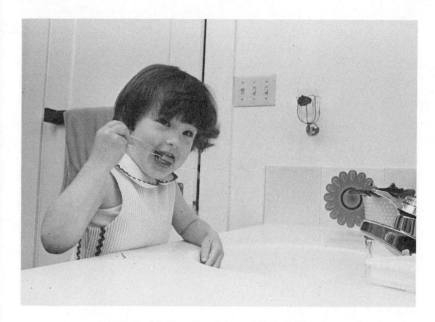

Fig. 26–10.   Brushing teeth is fun!

DENTAL HEALTH EDUCATION

Toothbrushing (Fig. 26–10) and other oral hygiene procedures can be taught to blind children just as well as to the sighted, although it may take more effort. Parents should explain how teeth grow, why they decay, the need for proper nutrition, the benefits of good oral hygiene, and other facts.

CONCLUSIONS

1. Blind children tend to have more dental problems than their sighted peers.
2. It is essential that office visits are carefully planned by the parents and the dentist.
3. Effective, preventive dental-health measures should include the teaching of home-care techniques and satisfactory dental-health education.

REFERENCE

1. Lebowitz EJ: An introduction to dentistry for the blind. Dent Clin North Am 18:651–669, 1974

27
The Parents' Role

The content of this chapter is extracted from the book we wrote for parents of blind children. Professionals who work with the visually impaired will find this work useful because it contains many practical suggestions.

Scott, E. P., Jan, J. E., and Freeman, R. D. *Can't Your Child See? A Guide for Parents and Professionals.* Baltimore: University Park Press, 1977.

Since medical treatment can seldom restore loss of vision, professionals are just beginning to realize that blindness becomes much more of a parent problem than a child problem. Parents nowadays expect their doctor to understand that, because of the heavy physical and emotional demands on them, there is a realistic basis for their anxiety and that they require a good deal of support in the first few years. The entire family needs to have a clear understanding of the cause, nature, and extent of the handicap, but they also must come to terms with their own feelings before they can effectively meet the needs of the child. Even experienced parents will be filled with doubts about their ability to raise a handicapped child.

The parents will need information about how lack of sight can affect normal development, and what can be done to lessen the impact. They should also be helped by practical suggestions about the daily care of the child and what they can expect of him. It is too frequently assumed by professionals and parents that blindness by itself inevitably limits development. This is not so, but it may result in inadequate expectations, deprivation of emotional satisfactions, and a paucity of meaningful experiences for the visually impaired child. Informed and loving parents can do more than anyone else to provide their child with a positive climate for healthy growth and development.[1]

BONDING

One of the more subtle effects of blindness, and one that can profoundly affect the whole future relationship between the mother and the child, is the impairment of communication between the mother and her visually impaired baby. Since early communication is primarily visual, the mother may feel rejected if her baby does not smile or respond to her approach. Both father and mother must learn to show their love by cuddling, stroking, talking, singing, and playing with their baby. If they understand that it is more difficult for a blind baby to recognize them by their voice, touch, or smell, they will persist until they are rewarded by his smiles and obvious recognition.

Parents should be encouraged to maintain a good deal of bodily contact with their infants, e.g., holding while feeding, using a back or front pack to carry, having the child beside them while reading or watching television, as well as playing and talking to him frequently. In this way he will identify his mother's and father's presence by their voices and will be aware of them even when they are not touching him. The mother should try to keep him in the same room with her whenever he is awake, so that he learns to like being with people. A visually impaired infant tends to be undemanding and may be quite content to spend long hours unattended in his crib. The busy mother may inadvertently leave him there unless she knows it is detrimental to his development.

MOTOR DEVELOPMENT

Vision plays a vital role in the motor development of normal infants, especially in the first few months of life. It provides both stimulus and reward for learning such diverse motor skills as head control, reaching and grasping, sitting, rolling over, pulling self erect, creeping and walking. The infant with a severe visual loss will be content to lie on his back indefinitely, since there is no motivation for him to learn to move his body purposefully. However, he can acquire all these motor skills in the same sequence and roughly in the same time frame as the sighted child (with some modifications) if his parents know how to teach him. They must make each activity pleasurable for him to practice until he can do it well. The parents should be encouraged to improvise and by trial and error find reward or rewards that will induce the child to learn whatever skill they want to teach him. For instance, to help him hold his head up, they might hold him erect with his cheek against theirs and talk to him, stroke his skin or hair, or balance him on their laps so he will associate head control with pleasurable sensations.

Mothers should place the baby on a blanket on the floor several times each day from 2 or 3 months of age, so that he can learn to hold his head up when lying on his stomach. It is also easier for him to roll over on a firm surface, but he may need to be shown how and helped until he can do it alone. Lying on the floor will give him the freedom to roll and move around more easily than in his crib. The moving will be accidental rather than purposeful at first, but parents can encourage him to wiggle and squirm his way toward them by calling and touching him. In this way, he will discover that he can move from place to place on his own. The child may need to be shown how to raise himself up on his elbows, then knees, and later on both so that he is eventually able to get into a creeping position. These activities in themselves will not be particularly satisfying to him and, therefore, should be well spiced with parental enthusiasm and admiration.

The child with little or no useful vision will not be interested in learning to sit unsupported unless his parents convince him that it is worthwhile, i.e., by making it fun or by feeding him.

The child with sight is motivated to pull himself erect so he can see a wider area. Because he is unaware of anything beyond arm's reach, the blind child will not stand unless taught how to get up and get down. When he is ready to creep or crawl, it will be necessary for his parents to provide sufficiently tempting reasons for him to want to move. This can be done in a variety of ways. Some children will move toward the parent's voice, respond to the offer of a favorite toy or a cookie, and others out of a desire to be in the midst of whatever is going on with the rest of the family if it sounds intriguing.

After he can move from place to place by creeping on all fours and has had time to make a mental map of the house, the parents will gently have to show him that he can also move around by walking. At first he will be fearful of standing unsupported and will need to reassure himself by touching the walls and furniture, but with encouragement will be brave enough to strike out on his own. Parents can help the child with his orientation by identifying the furniture, doors, steps, etc., as the child encounters them in his prowling. He will gradually learn that the television is by the window and that food is in the kitchen where the floor feels different and where he can hear the humming of the refrigerator.

He will avoid obstacles by learning to listen to the echo of his breathing and clothing sounds as they bounce back from obstacles in his path and will move cautiously until he knows that his way is clear. Since walking without sight is more difficult, it may take him a few weeks longer if he is totally blind than if he has good partial sight. The use of walkers seems to impede the development of vertical balance and will delay independent walking.

The visually impaired child should be encouraged to use his hands as soon as possible. This can be done by hanging small, noisy toys over his crib where his hands will touch them as he waves them about, and by providing small toys that are easily held and showing him how to grasp them, shake them, locate and pick them up when he drops them. There should always be a variety of playthings (toys and otherwise) within easy reach so that whenever the child is awake he will be encouraged to explore his immediate environment to find out what is there.

Visually impaired toddlers are often poor feeders. Since they are unaware of the variety of meals the family enjoys, they are particularly reluctant to try strange foods. The introduction of different flavors and textures during the first year of life will encourage their acceptance of a broader diet later on. A teaspoon of boiled rice added to pureed vegetables will provide a different texture and get the tongue used to manipulating small lumps. Hand feeding should be introduced just as soon as the baby has learned to put his hand to his mouth. Foods that have a strong smell and flavor seem to be better accepted for sucking and licking by the child who cannot see, e.g., soft bacon, ginger snaps, dry celery sticks, garlic sausage. He will not be able to bite off pieces, but they are much more interesting than the usual tasteless teething biscuits.

Finger feeding of small, bite-sized pieces of vegetables, fruit, and other foods should be introduced before the use of the spoon, so that the child can understand how to locate the food and how to get it from the plate into his mouth. Loading a spoon is a complicated procedure and, if it is introduced too early, he may become so frustrated that feeding will become a problem. Standing behind him will make it simpler to guide the spoon in his hand to his mouth. He may also need help in loading it (Fig. 27-1). A heavy dish with straight sides makes it a little easier to load the spoon, as do sticky foods like potatoes and gravy or chocolate pudding. It is discouraging to the child if he keeps finding his spoon empty when it gets to his mouth, particularly if he is hungry. A small plastic drinking cup should be introduced for juice and water at around 6 months. He should be taught from the beginning how to locate a glass on the table, pick it up, drink, and put it back (Fig. 27-2).

BODY AWARENESS AND DAILY LIVING SKILLS

The visually impaired child is unable to learn by observation and imitation how other children use their bodies and interact with their environment. The parents must literally teach him everything he needs to know about his body parts and how they work, e.g., feet are for standing, walking, kicking, jumping; hands are for picking up, shaking,

Fig. 27-1. The loading of a spoon may be difficult.

Fig. 27-2. A visually impaired child checks the rising level of fluid with her finger.

rattling, banging, eating; bottoms are for sitting. He will have to be taught such simple tasks as dressing, turning on taps, opening doors, climbing onto a chair—all the skills of daily living. But he must also be taught in ways that make sense to him, and this will involve patience and ingenuity on the part of his parents.

Each skill should be broken down into component parts and taught step by step over a period of time. For example, to wash hands: Find the plug (that round thing), pick it up, find the hole, put the plug in the hole; find the tap, put your hand on the top of the tap (the part that has bumps on it), turn it this way, feel the water come out here, now turn the tap the other way like this, and feel the water stop. Now find the soap, pick it up, put it in the water, hold it in your two hands, squeeze it, and put it back; rub your hands together like this, do the backs like this, put both hands in the water and wiggle them; find the towel, dry your hands like this, then the backs, and now put the towel back where you found it on the towel rack. While this seems complicated, it is the way a blind child finds out how to wash his hands, admittedly not in one day or even one week. Then he will never reply as one blind child did when asked how he washed his hands, "Mum does it with a wet rag."

SPEECH AND LANGUAGE

There are three prerequisites for any child if he is to learn to communicate successfully. There should be exposure and interaction with talking people, so that he finds that they do communicate with each other by words. He needs help in developing a meaningful vocabulary, and he must have an opportunity to talk.

The visually impaired youngster may be exposed to "talking people," but he may miss out on the interaction. It is essential that he knows that his mother is talking to him, so she should hold and play with him while she talks.

His parents will have to teach him the words of familiar objects and actions as he encounters them. They should name each garment as he is dressed and each body part, e.g., put your left arm in the sweater, now the right (Fig. 27-3). He needs to hear the name of an object more often than a sighted child. He will seldom ask, "What's that?" The parents must bring to his attention the hundreds of objects in the home and neighborhood so he will know what people are talking about. If he is suddenly put into a tub of water without any warning, it will frighten him. But if he knows the word *bath*, he can anticipate it.

It is not unusual to find that a visually impaired child has no need

Fig. 27-3. "Put your left arm in the sweater, now the right."

to talk. The mother may be in the habit of responding to his whining
or gestures, or she may anticipate his needs. When he has some
vocabulary, the parents should consciously seek opportunities to encourage him to talk. The child must be confident that his parents are listening
to him and they should answer him verbally, not with nods or smiles.
The development of good language skills is essential if the visually
impaired child is to live a normal life.

PLAY

Play skills range from holding and shaking a small rattle to climbing
a ladder to a slide or riding a tricycle (Fig. 27-4). These will not come
automatically to the blind child, but have to be taught in such a way
that the pleasurable side of the activity is apparent. Parents tend to
be so earnest and anxious about the child learning how to play with
a toy properly that the fun element tends to be lost. Play skills are
more readily learned from other children, if the parents can engage
their interest and cooperation.

The world of the child with little or no useful vision is very different
from that of his parents, and his understanding of the environment will
be curtailed by his lack of sight and limited mobility. For this reason
the parents should provide both encouragement and opportunity for him

Fig. 27-4. Let him take risks.

to explore and learn about the objects in his home, yard, neighborhood, parks, farms, and even in supermarkets. Walking through puddles, feeling the rain and wind on his face, touching trees, leaves, fences, animals, smelling and handling fruit and vegetables at the store and putting them away at home should all be part of his life. Descriptions and discussions should be meaningful to him, e.g., not "snow is white and sparkling," rather "snow is cold and turns to water in your hand." He should be encouraged to touch, listen, taste, and smell to gather as much information as he can about his environment.

SLEEPING

The sleeping patterns of totally blind and partially sighted infants are much the same as those of their sighted siblings. However, during the second year, the child often reverses night and day, napping off

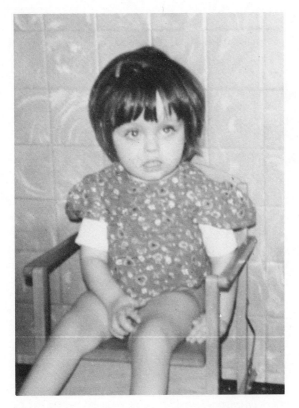

Fig. 27-5. The use of a small training chair is less frightening.

and on during the day and sleeping only 2 or 3 hours at night. The parents, who are reluctant to let him lie awake unattended, quickly become exhausted from lack of sleep. The child soon learns that he gets more attention if he refuses to sleep at night. If the parents are unable to change this habit, it may then be necessary for the physician to prescribe a sedative for 5 or 6 nights until a new sleep pattern is established. Night prowling throughout the house can be controlled by a lock on the child's bedroom door. Many parents are reluctant to do this because they feel cruel (or fear being called so). It is relatively common for visually impaired children to require less sleep than their siblings. In this instance the parents should insist that the small child play quietly in his crib with the toys provided or in his own room as he becomes older, so the rest of the family is not disturbed.

TOILET TRAINING

Toilet training is often difficult for the simple reason that the visually impaired child does not understand what is expected of him. The use of a small training chair will be less frightening for the child who cannot see how high he is from the floor (Fig. 27-5). Family bathroom parades may help. Anxiety or pressure on the part of the mother will make him less willing to cooperate as he will become anxious and confused about expectations.

MUSIC

The fallacy that all blind children will be gifted musicians leads some parents to excessive use of the radio or stereo as a means of keeping them amused. Continuous music tends to mask the normal household sounds, which the blind child should be using to determine where the other members of the family are and what they are doing. In other words, he should be tuned in to living rather than to the radio. If he is preoccupied with listening to music, he will have less incentive to move about, to seek out other people, and to learn to entertain himself by active play.

CONCLUSIONS

There is no question that the visually impaired child needs a great deal of maternal attention in his first few years of life, with the inherent danger of smothering from too much care. His parents need to be convinced that he is much more like other children than he is different, and the same old rules of "love him; set limits; let him grow up" still apply. They should know that there is no one, special, universally used method to teach a blind child. Whatever technique is comfortable for that family will probably be the best one for him. When the parents develop confidence in themselves to innovate and experiment with methods and, above all, are able to convince their child that they expect him to grow and learn, then they will feel pride in their parenthood.

REFERENCE

1. Mac Keith R: The restoration of the parents as the keystone of the therapeutic arch. Devel Med Child Neurol 18:285-286, 1976

Author Index

Subject Index

D

3